William Codville

A Concordance to the Hymnal of the Methodist Episcopal Church

To which are Added Several Important Indexes

William Codville

A Concordance to the Hymnal of the Methodist Episcopal Church
To which are Added Several Important Indexes

ISBN/EAN: 9783337081737

Printed in Europe, USA, Canada, Australia, Japan

Cover: Foto ©Lupo / pixelio.de

More available books at **www.hansebooks.com**

A CONCORDANCE

TO THE

HYMNAL

OF THE

METHODIST EPISCOPAL CHURCH,

TO WHICH ARE ADDED SEVERAL IMPORTANT INDEXES.

BY

WILLIAM ÇODVILLÊ,

Member of the Faculty of the M'Keesport (Pa.) Academy.

NEW YORK:
PHILLIPS & HUNT.
CINCINNATI:
HITCHCOCK & WALDEN.
1880.

PREFACE.

NEXT in importance to the sacred Scriptures is the Hymn Book; we read it, we sing from it, we memorize it, we apply it to our several states of experience, and are largely, though perhaps unconsciously, molded by its teachings. Nor is this to be regretted. "From the early days of the Christian Church down to our own time," says Mr. Stephen C. Drew, "men have put their highest thoughts and their best feelings into the form of hymns and anthems. Thus we have in them an embodiment of the love and faith, the aspiration and hope of those who have in times past and present set their faces heavenward, walking in the same path of temptation and difficulty which we are now treading. . . . We also read in Acts that Paul and Silas 'praised and sang praises to God' in the jail at Philippi. Paul, also, exhorts the brethren to sing 'psalms and hymns and spiritual songs;' and, again, in his Epistle to the Colossians, he says, 'teaching and admonishing one another in psalms and hymns and spiritual songs.'"

Our literature is exceedingly rich in holy song; indeed, so much so, as to render a complete collection, even of the best hymns, impracticable for general use. The Hymnal of the Methodist Episcopal Church certainly does not contain *all* the best hymns in our language, and yet we are free in saying we have not met any collection of hymns for public use equal to it.

Of all Christian bodies Methodism is especially indebted to sacred song; she had her birth in hymn singing, and lives only while she sings. Charles Wesley struck the key-note, not only of Methodism, but also of modern revivalism, in his famous lines:

> To that Jerusalem above
> With SINGING I repair,

which is being responded to by the Church universal in the words of an eminent contemporary of Wesley:

> O tell of His might, and *sing* of his grace.

It is believed by some that in the great revival meetings of Messrs. Moody and Sankey the singing of the latter did more to arouse popular sympathy and earnestness than even the preaching of the former.

Nor has the use of hymns been confined alone to singing; they have also proved a powerful auxiliary in preaching. A single stanza from the lips of Whitefield filled the chapels of America and England with a blaze of enthusiasm, never to be forgotten; Benson's richest sermons were those in which poetic quotations chiefly abounded. In his celebrated sermon on the death of Mrs. Foster no fewer than eleven of those are found. The writer was present at a meeting some years ago which became a Pentecost at the recitation by a lady of that familiar verse:

> And if our fellowship below
> In Jesus be so sweet,
> What height of rapture shall we know
> When round his throne we meet!

Of course there were reasons for this; it was uttered with power, it was highly appropriate, and was offered just at the proper moment.

Cruden has done more than any other to familiarize the student with the *whole* of Scripture; no work of analysis, or list of subjects, or index of chapters and verses, can supply the place of his admirable Concordance, for by it every line of Holy Writ stands out boldly before us. That work is universally regarded as indispensable in the study of the Bible.

How is it the Church has never had a Concordance to her hymns? A work that will open the treasures of the Hymn Book in the way that Cruden has opened the Scriptures? A work that will bring every line, yes, every important thought to our service? Indexes are valuable as far as they go, but who has not, over and again, found them totally inadequate and unsatisfactory? The truth is we have long needed a Concordance.

A minister of some note several years ago, in the preparation of one of his best sermons upon the redemptive work of Christ, desired to complete one of his finest sentences with an appropriate stanza. Reflecting a moment he exclaimed with delight, as Archimedes was accustomed to do upon solving a problem—"I've found it, I've found it!" Unlike Archimedes, however, he was doomed to disappointment, for being unable to recall any but the last line of the verse, his index, of course, was utterly unserviceable. That line was

> The iron fetters yield.

In vain he strove to remember the first words of this stanza, in vain he searched and researched his Hymn Book for its hidden treasure; all was to no purpose, and, what was most to be regretted, his patience and inspiration had well-nigh departed. "That unfortunate occurrence," he afterward said, "almost cost me a Sabbath's usefulness." Has not this been the experience of thousands of others? Has it not been the experience of every minister in the Church? And now, in view of nearly four hundred hymns being added to the collection, will it not probably continue to be the experience of the future?

This will serve to show, at least in part, the utility of the Concordance we now offer the public. With this work no such difficulty need again occur. Let the reader try the facility with which this lost line is now recovered by simply turning to the word "fetters;" he will also find that that word, in its singular and plural form, occurs about eight times in the Hymnal, and that possibly some other stanza there referred to may be even more appropriate than the one he has selected.

But this Concordance is of still further use in the wise and judicious selection of hymns to be sung. It is true, we have an excellent "Index of Subjects," and yet there are hundreds of subjects preached upon not found in that Index. We have also a prudently arranged "Index of Scripture Texts," but there are thousands upon thousands of texts preached upon not found in that Index, and hence the usefulness of these Indexes is, of necessity, limited and unsatisfactory. This, however, is not the case with a Concordance which is limited only by the Hymnal itself.

A few examples will make this plain. Take 2 Tim. i, 12: "For the which cause I also suffer these things: nevertheless I am not ashamed; for I know whom I have believed, and am persuaded that he is able to keep that which I have committed unto him against that day." We search in vain the "Index of Scripture Texts" for any reference whatever to this important text, and justly conclude that no hymn in the collection exactly suits it; but in this we are mistaken. Let us now try the Concordance upon either "ashamed" or "committed," and we are directed to number 595, to which we turn and find the following appropriate hymn:

> 1 I'm not *ashamed* to own my Lord,
> Or to defend his cause;
> Maintain the honor of his word,
> The glory of his cross.
>
> 2 Jesus, my God! I know his name;
> His name is all my trust;
> Nor will he put my soul to shame,
> Nor let my hope be lost.
>
> 3 Firm as his throne his promise stands,
> And he can well secure
> What I've *committed* to his hands,
> Till the decisive hour.

Another example, Isa. xxxv, 4: "Say to them that are of a fearful heart, Be strong, fear not: behold, your God will come with vengeance, even God with a recompense; he will come and save you." This text is not found in the Index, nevertheless a hymn may be found to suit.

Turn to "fearful" or "strong" in the Concordance, and we are referred to hymn 479. Here it is:

> 1 Prisoners of hope, lift up your heads,
>   The day of liberty draws near!
> Jesus, who on the serpent treads,
>   Shall soon in your behalf appear;
> The Lord will to his temple come;
> Prepare your hearts to make him room.
>
> 2 Ye all shall find, whom in his word
>   Himself hath caused to put your trust,
> The Father of our dying Lord
>   Is ever to his promise just;
> Faithful, if we our sins confess,
> To cleanse from all unrighteousness.
>
> 3 O ye of *fearful* hearts, be *strong!*
>   Your downcast eyes and hands lift up!
> Ye shall not be forgotten long;
>   Hope to the end, in Jesus hope!
> Tell him ye wait his grace to prove;
> And cannot fail, if God is love.

Again, no hymn is given in the Index to Matt. x, 16: "Behold, I send you forth as sheep in the midst of wolves: be ye therefore wise as serpents, and harmless as doves." The words "serpents" and "dove," however, point in the Concordance to hymn 810, verse 3, which is based upon this very text:

> Be wise as *serpents* where you go,
>   But harmless as the peaceful *dove;*
> And let your heaven-taught conduct show
>   Ye are commissioned from above.

The same is true of Gen. vi, 3: "And the Lord said, My Spirit shall not always strive with man." "Strive," in the Concordance, points to hymn 353, verse 4:

> God's Spirit will not always *strive*
>   With hardened, self-destroying man;
> Ye, who persist his love to grieve,
>   May never hear his voice again.

We might employ examples almost without number, but one more will suffice, Luke xiv, 16-18: "Then said he unto him, A certain man made a great supper, and bade many; and sent his servant at supper time to say to them that were bidden, Come; for all things are now ready. And they all with one consent began to make excuse," etc. Now, should a hymn be desired suitable to the invitation we are, very properly, pointed in the Index to number 364: "Come, sinners, to the gospel feast;" but should our subject be the *excuses* of sinners, also found in the above text, we are left in the dark for an appropriate hymn. But here, again, the Concordance comes to our assistance, and, under the word "excuses," refers us to one of the finest hymns in the entire collection, 834. What congregation can sing the following hymn after an appropriate sermon and not be influenced by it?

> 1 The King of heaven his table spreads,
> And blessings crown the board;
> Not paradise, with all its joys,
> Could such delight afford.
>
> 2 Pardon and peace to dying men,
> And endless life are given,
> Through the rich blood that Jesus shed
> To raise our souls to heaven.
>
> 3 Millions of souls, in glory now,
> Were fed and feasted here;
> And millions more, still on the way,
> Around the board appear.
>
> 4 All things are ready, come away,
> *Nor weak* EXCUSES *frame;*
> Crowd to your places at the feast,
> And bless the Founder's name.

Every minister of the gospel owes it to both his Lord and congregation to have his discourse followed, not only by an appropriate hymn, but by the *most* appropriate one in the collection. This is, indeed, indispensable to complete unity, strength, and success in preaching. We are led to hope that, to some extent at least, this desired end may be assisted by the work we now offer the Church.

At the end of this work will be found several Indexes, to the importance of which we will now call attention.

First in order, and immediately associated with the Concordance, is the "Consecutive Index," arranged according to number. The utility of this index may be best explained as follows:

The preacher, having chosen his text, desires the most appropriate hymn to follow his sermon; the hymn in which occurs "The iron fetters yield" is the one desired. He turns to "fetters" and finds that hymn to be 185. Three inquiries may now arise in his mind. Hymns, like individuals, are best known by their faces—the face of a hymn is its first line—hence he asks, 1. What *hymn* is it? 2. Of what *meter* is it? and, as the old Hymn Book will, in all probability, be in use for some years to come in many of the churches, 3. Where is it found in the old book? All these inquiries are immediately answered in the "Consecutive Index" by simply running the eye down the page to number 185. Here it is:

> 185 C. Hark, the glad sound! the Saviour comes, 118.

Here he at once recognizes this as an old and familiar hymn; its meter is "common," and, as indicated by the figures on the right, its number is 118 in the old book. In this way the face of the hymn, the meter, and position in the old book (if found there) of every reference in the Concordance can be immediately known.

The second is the "Alphabetical Index," the use of which will abridge the reader's labor if he is already in possession of the first line of the hymn, but not its number, meter, and position in the old book.

The "Metrical Index" will prove of great service when the *meter* of the hymn is a matter of importance—and there are no fewer than seventy-four varieties of meter in the Hymnal.

How often is the preacher requested to select a hymn within a certain meter, to which some newly-learned or old familiar tune may be sung, and how great is sometimes his embarrassment in finding one that will at once suit both tune and discourse. This embarrassment is entirely obviated by the use of the "Metrical Index," in which any meter is found at a glance, with all hymns thereto belonging arranged in alphabetical order. This Index will be especially appreciated by choirs and by all persons having charge of public singing. When it is also more generally understood that some well-known tune is suited to a number of excellent hymns not generally used, it will extend the influence of the collection as a whole, as well as to greatly add to the freshness of the services.

Our last is an "Index of Hymns found in the Hymnal, not in the Hymn Book, and of hymns in the Hymn Book not used in the Hymnal." In this Index will be seen about 375 hymns, now in use, not found in the old book, and also a few more than this number dropped from service. Among the "dropped" hymns will be recognized some of the "good old hymns our fathers sang;" these hymns, however, were not dropped because they had fallen from grace, but because—like our fathers themselves—having nobly served their day they were honorably laid to rest.

One word more. With the Bible in her right hand and the Hymnal in her left, Methodism has nothing to fear in her grand march to battle and victory. Cried the illustrious hero of her ecclesiastical existence, "The best of all is, God is with us!" and the unbroken history of one hundred and fifty years but sustains this claim. "Lo, I am with you alway, even unto the end of the world." Let, then, the battle-cry of Martin Luther—the sequel of that of his campaign against Worms—ever be sung "in Spirit and in truth," and all will be well unto the end of time.

> And though this world, with devils filled,
> Should threaten to undo us;
> We will not fear, for God hath willed
> His truth to triumph through us.

M'KEESPORT, PA., *Sept. 15, 1879.* WM. CODVILLE.

CONTENTS.

	PAGE
Concordance to the Hymnal	11
Doxologies	189
Consecutive Index of First Lines of Hymns	191
Index of Hymns adopted from the old Hymn Book without Change; of Hymns adopted with Change; of Hymns added; and of Hymns dropped	199
Summary	205

CONCORDANCE TO THE HYMNAL

OF THE

METHODIST EPISCOPAL CHURCH.

ABB   ABU

ABBA, FATHER.
429 And, *a., F.*, humbly cry
438 And, Father, *a., F.*, cry
439 And boldly, *a., F.*, cry
440 *A., F.*, hear thy child
477 Ceaseless may, *a., F.*, cry
643 I have called thee, *a., F.*

ABHOR, ABHORRED.
482 like thine, *A.* the thing unclean
525 I would be by myself *abhorred*

ABIDE.
14 My heart to thee: here, Lord, *a.*
93 *A.* with me! Fast falls the
102 *A.* with me from morn till
338 There, safe thou shalt *a.*
648 Come and with us, e'en us, *a.*
702 *A.* with us, and let thy light
742 Saviour, with me *a.*
748 'Tis there I would always *a.*
760 Come quickly and *a.*, Or life
804 Let us thus in God *a.*
862 *A.* with us, O Lord, we pray

ABIDETH, ABIDING.
166 No thanks to them—*a.*
648 We've no *abiding* city here

ABODE.
65 Make this a place of thine *a.*
89 to them That love the dear *a.*
241 To heaven, the place of his *a.*
264 Makes with mortals his *a.*
501 Their soul is his *a.*
556 Be thou my sure *a.*
581 parting breath, To his divine *a.*
657 The saints' secure *a.*
713 And grace her mean *a.*
980 To bear him to their bright *a.*
998 yon heaven, that blissful *a.*
1034 shining dust Of my divine *a.*
1035 Removes his blest *a.*
1042 O glorious hour! O blest *a.*
1052 In this divine *a.* Change
1063 And mount to our native *a.*
1064 Where Jesus has fixed his *a.*

ABODES.
777 Fair *a.* I build for you

ABOUND.
52 In our hearts and lives *a.*
70 those who in thy grace *a.*
288 day to day, Be in us and *a.*
317 To every soul *a.*
809 O let our love and faith *a.*

ABOUNDING.
371 live, Through his *a.* grace
865 Rejoice in thy *a.* grace
903 *A.* grace repay.

ABOVE.
12 the blest hour, when from *a.*
41 heavenly powers, To carry us *a.*
484 I lift my heart to things *a.*
530 Is the full heaven enjoyed *a.*
600 And seek the glorious things *a.*
780 that binds The happy souls *a.*
786 Lift up your hearts to things *a.*
880 I shall see him and hear him *a.*
1009 There is a world *a.*
1078 And seek the things *a.*

ABRAHAM.
274 In *A.'s* breast, and sealed
451 And raised us into *A.'s* sons
471 *A.*, when severely tried
523 word, thy oath, to *A.'s* race
614 If called, like *A.'s* child
1075 The God of *A.* praise
1077 Hail, *A.'s* God, and mine

ABSENT.
534 While thou art *a.* from the
553 *A.* from thee, my Light
1050 *A.* from him I roam

ABSOLVED.
238 Fully *a.* through these

ABSTINENCE.
107 May *a.* the flesh restrain

ABUNDANCE.
50 And then in rich *a.* The
901 From our *a.* to impart

ABUNDANTLY.
557 spirit cries, *A.* forgive

ABUSE, ABUSED.
336 delay not, why longer a.
580 Oft *abused* thee to thy face

ABYSS.
97 Whose throne is in the vast a.
126 O God, thou bottomless a.
430 O Love, thou bottomless a.
492 Thou, a. of love and goodness
681 Still out of the deepest a.

ACCENTS.
528 O still in a. sweet and strong
621 In soothing a. Jesus said
692 With what glad a. shall I rise
711 No a. flow, no words ascend
889 O shall not warmer a. tell

ACCEPTED.
79 Thou hast a. those alone
286 Holy Ghost! In this a. hour
353 Thy last a. time may be
361 Now is the a. time
405 relieve, In this a. hour
454 praise to the Lamb! a. I am
449 Come in this a. hour
610 A. at thy throne of grace
869 In Christ a. stand
1057 In this the a. day

ACCEPTANCE.
32 And let them now a. have
36 To heaven, and find a. there

ACCORD.
19 And sweetly join with one a.
25 When they meet with one a.
41 Join in a song with sweet a.
79 both heaven and earth a.
275 Assembled here with one a.
280 We meet with one a.
485 Tuned by thee in sweet a.
845 Give we all with one a.
876 Your voices with one a.
915 And all, with one a.
1012 sing with one heart and a.

ACCOUNT.
365 How stands that dark a.
574 A strict a. to give
1021 Who such a strict a. must give
1023 Ere the dread a. be past

ACHING.
401 My a. breast inspire
898 Whose a. heart or burning

ACT, ACTS.
476 My every a., word, thought, be
841 All thy wondrous acts proclaim
987 All his mighty a. record

ACTIONS.
107 Through all the a. of the day
573 By a., words, and tempers
630 By a. show your sins forgiven
732 please Through all their a. run
863 Hence may all our a. flow

ACTUATE.
440 A., and fill the whole
806 Move, and a., and guide

ADAM.
154 Let all the sons of A. rise
155 sleep, as A. in his bower
207 A second A. to the fight
207 Which did in A. fall
320 For A.'s lost race Christ hath
422 And bled for A.'s helpless race
519 more I have. As the old A. dies
792 Tame the old A. in our soul
863 The perfect world by A. trod

ADAMANT.
396 O Lord, an a. would melt
588 Armed with that a. and
771 Till hearts of a. shall break

ADORE.
5 The Lord your God a.
6 And to eternity Love and a.
10 The Son and Spirit we a.
27 All that breathe, your Lord a.
37 Thou whom all thy saints a.
39 We would a. our Maker too
48 The true and only Son a.
54 All thy people shall a.
56 Thus unite we to a. him
64 Our hearts a. thy name
67 Thy saints a. thy holy name
68 glorious name let all a.
111 And nature's God a.
136 holy! all the saints a. thee
143 This God is the God we a.
182 Him whom heaven and earth a.
186 Angels a. him in slumber
188 Hasten, mortals, to a. him
244 Your Lord and King a.
246 All the heavenly hosts a. thee
247 There forever to a. him
298 bid the admiring world a.
332 To a. the all-atoning Lamb
480 With joy unspeakable a.
552 Yet I love thee and a.
554 Blest Saviour I a.
616 That mercy I a.
631 all heaven's host a. their King
634 faithful grace I know and I a.
649 We joyfully a. thee
701 Thy wondrous love a.
819 We thee unseen a.
878 May we praise thee and a.
965 Thee we a., eternal Name
1013 Yea, Amen! let all a. thee
1063 Then in hymns of praise a.
1075 I shall his power a.
1085 And with your lives a. him
1096 Come let our souls a. the Lord
1109 Him with quiet joy a.
1112 Thy wisdom here we learn to a.

ADORED.
10 Thou God of hosts by all a.
20 Be thy glorious name a.
120 Father. .By all the earth a.
137 Forever be thy name a., Thy

144 By the heavens and earth a.
170 Forever be thy name a.; I
177 Forever be his name a.
181 Prince of peace, For evermore a.
190 Christ by highest heaven a.
245 By angel hosts a.
290 Forever be thy name a. For
494 As in heaven be here a.
896 So let the Saviour be a.
908 Be thou O Christ a.
1006 Be thy holy name a.
1097 Who thy great name a.

ADORATION.
52 Thanks we give and a.
186 Richer by far is the heart's a.

ADORING.
223 There a. at his feet

ADORNED, ADORNING.
14 A. with prayer and love
878 Which a. the Saviour-child
1035 New Jerusalem ... A. with
647 Thus the Christian life *adorning*

ADVENT.
850 With the last a. we unite
1016 Let the mighty a. chorus

ADVOCATE.
110 And be my A. with God
230 Jesus my A. above
239 Almighty A., to thine
251 Our A. with God He
252 The glorious A. on high
258 Still our A. in heaven
378 My Friend and A. with God
440 Hear my A. divine
720 Christ our A. is made

AFFECTIONS.
496 Nail my a. to the cross
519 My vile a. crucify
647 Let my best a. center
602 Thither the warm a. move
852 O let our warm a. move
1048 His freed a. rise.

AFFLICTED.
1002 Though a. not alone

AFFLICTION.
179 In the midst of a. my table is
335 To soothe your a. or banish
640 Where such a light a.
661 With this beneath a.'s load
759 On whom in a. I call
761 A.'s deepest gloom
1011 The mortal a. is past
1072 A.'s waves may round
1073 The storms of a. beneath

AFFLICTIONS.
177 A. came at thy command
628 But these a. of the dust
758 'Midst outward a. shall
1054 In all my a. to thee

AFRAID.
630 Lo! it is I; be not a.
647 Never need we be a.
1027 Who sometimes am a. to die

AFRIC.
879 I, from A.'s barren sand
930 Where A.'s sunny fountains

AGE.
373 Our eyes have seen the steps of a.
658 And now in a. and grief thy name
788 through one bright eternal a.
875 wintry hour Of man's maturer a.
876 promise ... Fulfilled to latest a.
959 Mine a. is naught with thee
1011 The a. that in heaven they spend

AGES.
132 A thousand a. in their flight
139 Through endless a. still the same
233 To thee the endless a. through
580 That through the a. it be given
953 The God of a., praise
964 A thousand a. in thy sight
991 Long as eternal a. roll
1055 While endless a. waste away

AGED.
1116 Be to thine a. servant given

AGONY.
207 The double a. in man
209 Bespeaks thy soul's deep a.
219 Saviour ... is stretched in a.
221 Thee by thy painful a.
236 Through earth's most bitter a.
665 the fainting heart, The a.
670 Behold thy mother's a.
723 By thine a. of prayer
836 Thine a. and bloody sweat
850 His fearful drops of a.

AGONIES.
399 The a. I feel
423 on the tree, In a. and blood
487 A. of strong desire

AGONIZING.
246 Hail thou a. Saviour
340 A. in the garden
383 By thine a. pain

AGREE.
37 We now with all thy saints a.
101 Lord let us in our homes a.
785 Let all our hearts a.
789 And cordially a.
790 The souls that here a.
793 We all shall then in one a.
804 Let us in thy name a.
806 Sweetly may we all a.
811 all their heart and strength a.

AID.
168 In trouble our unfailing a.
178 Thou very present A.
266 Thy celestial a. possessing

AIM 14 ANC

399 Jesus thine *a*. afford
430 A sure and present *a*.
462 O Love thy sovereign *a*. impart A
477 O Love thy sovereign *a*. impart T
496 Jesus, thy timely *a*. impart
511 Haste to mine *a*., thine ear
615 I thy timely *a*. implore
651 I ask in faith his promised *a*.
679 thy God, I will still give thee *a*.
681 Ah! whither shall we flee for *a*.
707 When mortal *a*. is vain
712 Thy gracious *a*. I seek
773 Behold him present with his *a*.
791 And swift our hands to *a*.
868 Hast power to *a*. or bless
895 With *a*. and peace for him
1031 No more demands thine *a*.

AIM, AIMS.

506 A single, steady *a*.
602 The only end and *a*. of man
718 Its restless *aims* and fears.

ALARM, ALARMS.

555 *A*. me in this hour
823 watchmen take the *a*. they
75 No rude *alarms* of raging foes
970 Or shake at death's *a*.

ALIEN.

729 I wander an *a*. from thee.

ALL.

31 They find their *a*. in thee
127 And *a*. we have and all we are
212 Let *a*. I have and all I am
214 I give myself away,—'Tis *a*. that
332 For *a*., for all, my Saviour died
335 That I shall find my *a*. in thee
451 Thou art my Life, my God, my *A*.
469 Our *a*., no longer ours but thine
470 *A*. I have and all I am
635 thee in *a*., Having all in thee
643 Thou from hence my *a*. shalt be
856 And so give *a*. to him

ALL IN ALL.

67 But thou to us art *a*. in *a*.
121 Our God is *a*. in *a*.
283 Thou art *a*. in *a*. to me
357 Find in Christ your *a*. in *a*.
434 Our God our *a*. in *a*.
468 Let Christ be *a*. in *a*.
446 Let my Lord be *a*. in *a*.
525 And feel that Christ is *a*. in *a*.
736 Jesus my *a*. in *a*. thou art
746 My life in death, my *a*. in *a*.
751 For thou art *a*. in *a*.
866 Thou, O Christ, art *a*. in *a*.
925 God in Christ is *a*. in *a*.

ALLEGHANY.

923 On *A*.'s mountains

ALLOY.

182 Pure and free from sin's *a*.
704 O 'tis delight without *a*.
1054 A country of joy without any *a*.

ALMIGHTY.

6 Thou who *a*. art, Now rule
128 The work of an *a*. hand
170 I rest beneath the *A*.'s shade
481 God of *a*. love
766 'Tis thine own work, *A*. God
772 And safe in his *a*. hands
926 Hisown *a*. hand shall
1101 A word of thine *a*. breath

ALMS.

896 Then for his sake thine *a*. impart

ALONE.

87 But thou art not *a*. In courts
125 In glory all *a*.
125 O God, yet not *a*.
327 'Tis thee I love, for thee *a*.
735 God cries out, Let me *a*.
737 And I am left *a*. with thee
951 Let me *a*.! his mercy cried
953 Cried, Let it still *a*.
975 I shall not die *a*.

ALPHA.

491 *A*. and Omega be

ALTAR.

5 flame From his own *a*. brought
99 Now from the *a*. of our hearts
189 Saints before the *a*. bending
467 all I am, Upon his *a*. lay
471 Dies on the *a*. of thy cross
488 Never shall the *a*. fire
562 On the mean *a*. of my heart
808 Beside thy sacred *a*., Be
868 Where the heart is the *a*. whence
921 And souls beneath the *a*. groan
1085 Heap on his sacred *a*. The gifts
1107 Before thine *a*.-throne

ALTARS.

135 Till all thy living *a*. claim
920 And cast their *a*. to the ground

ALWAY.

908 I would not live *a*.; no

AMAZING.

41 The thought of such *a*. bliss
211 Love so *a*., so divine
896 *A*. thought —unmoved I
422 *A*. love! how can it be

AMBITION.

643 Perish every fond *a*.
962 Vain his *a*., noise, and

AMEN.

569 *A*., Lord Jesus, grant our
1050 *A*., so let it be!

AMETHYST.

1050 With *a*. unpriced

ANCHOR.

420 Sure my soul's *a*. may remain
421 My *a*. holds within the veil

ANC 15 ANT

526 Thou art the a. of my hope
649 This a. shall my soul sustain
1004 Weigh thine a., spread thy
1110 An a. to steady the soul

ANCIENT.
6 reign over us, A. of days
36 Thou to whom in a. time
132 Before the birth of a. time
140 and Defender, the A. of days
148 A. of eternal days
166 For still our a. foe
274 Remember, Lord, the a. days
310 mountains...a. seats forsake
805 Sing as in the a. days
924 take thine a. people home
953 A. of endless days
1075 A. of everlasting days
1197 And in more a. years

ANEW.
18 He forms their ruined souls a.
285 And form me all a.
309 To form the heart a.
453 my Saviour shall make me a.
497 Till thou a. my soul create
536 And form my soul a.
923 By sovereign grace be formed a.

ANGEL.
42 Let all the a. throng Give
134 And a. bands are waiting
192 The a. of the Lord came down
257 No a. in the sky, Can fully
433 What a. tongue can tell
614 Some a. may be there in time
646 Till, by a.-hands attended
705 theme demands an a.'s tongue
707 That ear is filled with a. songs
823 what might fill an a.'s heart
886 the story which a. voices tell
973 Till the last a. rise and break
1008 No, a.! seek thy place
1095 And let thine a. stand between

ANGELS.
56 Earth takes up the a.' cry
57 Praise him, a., in the height
97 Thy a. shall around their beds
106 And with the a. bear thy part
108 While well-appointed a. keep
119 A. with both wings veil
120 To thee all a. cry aloud
144 Eyes of a. are too dim
148 Mighty God! while a. bless thee
170 me, whom watchful a. keep
193 And a. flew with eager joy
194 From a. bending near the earth
194 And hear the a. sing
233 The shining a. as they speed
235 Lord is risen indeed; Attending a.
237 And a. chant the solemn lay
325 While a. view with wondering
342 O ye a. hovering round us
350 Ready for you the a. wait
356 A. our servants are
442 And the a. could do nothing
443 Where the a. praise their

517 As a. who behold thy face
694 Among the a. pure and bright
710 While a. in their songs
759 ten thousand of a. rejoice
787 Behold...innumerable hosts of a.
804 On the wings of a. fly
860 Nor a.' claims restrain his
886 To sing among his a.
980 And a. are attending near
984 While a. watch the soft
1004 A., joyful to attend
1035 Attending a. shout for joy
1070 A. of Jesus, a. of light
1083 Give his a. charge at last
1088 And joyous a. o'er me

ANGELIC.
58 See! the a. hosts have crowned
125 A. spirits, countless souls
188 Lo! the a. host rejoices
246 Help ye bright a. spirits
259 Hark! a. voices cry

ANGER.
172 Whose a. is so slow to rise
390 Nor in thy righteous a. swear
455 Lord, and is thine a. gone
481 Be a. to my soul unknown
804 Free from a. and from pride
818 To stand, or how thine a. bear?
1103 Whose a. smites them, and

ANGUISH.
157 A. and sin and dread
217 Yet he that hath in a. knelt
320 And tears of a. flow
344 Ye by fiercer a. torn
618 O by the a. of that night
683 here tell your a.: Earth has no
839 While yet in a. he surveyed
1007 And no sigh of a. sore
1043 The a. and distracting care

ANOINTED.
181 Hail to the Lord's A.
188 Christ is born the great A.
246 By almighty love a.
438 His dear A. One

ANSWER.
124 Unless in a. to our Lord
216 A. thou Man of grief and love
282 And a. when thy children
383 Send the a. from above
425 A. if mine thou art
498 And waits to a. prayer
607 Who will a., gladly saying
607 A. quickly when he calleth
735 And send a peaceful a.
793 And send a peaceful a. down
945 The peaceful a. give
1021 And a. in that day

ANTS.
547 Go to the a. for one poor grain

ANTEPAST.
439 That a. of heaven

ANTHEM.
- 56 Bid we thus our *a.* flow
- 122 To thee an *a.* raise
- 145 O catch the *a.* that from heaven
- 257 Hark, how the heavenly *a.* drowns
- 8,1 Loud will swell the pealing *a.*
- 917 O let that glorious *a.* swell
- 922 The *a.* of thy praise to roll
- 1093 Swell the *a.*, raise the song

ANTHEMS.
- 195 Loud with their *a.* ring
- 201 Let pealing *a.* rend the
- 227 Glory to God in full *a.* of
- 233 heavens resounding with *a.*
- 447 Let cheerful *a.* fill his house
- 563 Loud your *a.* raise
- 611 And faultless *a.* raise
- 820 Till with their *a.* ours shall
- 916 We all with vows and *a.*
- 988 While the *a.* of rapture
- 1036 Their endless *a.* raise

ANXIOUS.
- 171 Bid my *a.* fears subside
- 176 Why should this *a.* load
- 632 When *a.* cares would break
- 994 Rest for the *a.* brow
- 1078 free from every *a.* thought
- 1115 Every *a.* thought repress

APOSTLE, APOSTLES.
- 900 When doomed to death the *a.* lay
- 10 Apostles join the glorious throng
- 120 The *a.'* glorious company
- 144 Thee *a.*, prophets thee
- 585 The *a.* of my Lord
- 812 sprang the *a.* honored name
- 1041 *A.*, martyrs, prophets, there

APOSTOLIC.
- 275 The *a.* promise given
- 815 Make good their *a.* boast
- 831 Make good our *a.* boast

APPEAR.
- 30 Son of the living God *a.*
- 65 our God in majesty *a.*
- 210 Or God *a.* to me
- 216 Till in glory we *a.*
- 412 O how shall I *a.*
- 479 Shall soon in your behalf *a.*
- 487 When his glory shall *a.*
- 489 Son of God *a.*, *a.*
- 493 And wait till Christ *a.*
- 512 And he will soon *a.*
- 515 Christ shall in me *a.*
- 524 *A.*, our glorious God, *a.*
- 545 And duly shall *a.*, in verdure
- 742 O when will thou, my life, *a.*
- 646 My saviour doth not yet *a.*
- 680 Til thou *a.* thy members
- 751 And when Jesus doth *a.*
- 755 *A.*, and bid me turn again
- 916 Before our God *a.*
- 951 To see our Lord *a.*
- 1014 Lord of lords shall soon *a.*
- 1065 And see thee in glory *a.*

APPEARING.
- 617 Bid us look for his *a.*
- 943 Still we wait for thine *a.*
- 1029 You who long for his *a.*
- 1065 We long thy *a.* to see.

APPETITES.
- 326 And bids your longing *a.*

APPLE.
- 455 As the *a.* of thine eye.
- 497 Quick as the *a.* of an eye, the
- 511 Quick as the *a.* of an eye, O God
- 770 Dear as the *a.* of thine eye

APPOINTS, APPOINTED.
- 782 Where he *a.* we go
- 21 In thine own *appointed* way
- 181 Hail in the time *a.*
- 188 O receive whom God *a.*
- 1020 The *a.* hour make haste

APPROACH.
- 511 I want the first *a.* to feel
- 827 Permit them to *a.*, he cries
- 835 We now *a.* to God

APPROVE, APPROVES, APPROVED.
- 313 None else will Heaven *a.*
- 389 Who would himself to thee *a.*
- 877 And God will well *a.*
- 391 Thy righteous law *approves* it
- 791 and show yourselves *approved*

ARABIA.
- 163 By night, *A.'s* crimsoned sands

ARCH, ARCHES.
- 87 Thy temple is the *a.*
- 185 And heaven's eternal *arches* ring
- 226 though heaven's high *a.* ring

ARCHANGEL, ARCHANGELS.
- 38 Thee while the first *a.* sings
- 241 soon shall hear the *a.'s* voice
- 1019 The great *a.'s* trump shall
- 1023 Shall the *a.'s* trumpet tone
- 1027 Whene'er the *a.'s* trump shall
- 18 Whose praise *archangels* sing
- 111 Angels and *a.* sing
- 1065 Not all the *a.* can tell
- 1077 The great *a.* sing

ARDENT.
- 78 With *a.* hope and strong desire
- 380 Hear, O hear, my *a.* cry.
- 1051 fire Our hearts with *a.* love

ARK.
- 266 Pointing to an *a.* of rest
- 588 Behold the *a.* of God
- 1111 O hide them safe in Jesus' ark

ARM.
- 33 thine *a.* of power hath saved
- 96 And *a.* my soul with grace
- 112 Strong is his *a.* and shall fulfill
- 160 Thine *a.* unseen conveyed me
- 395 When from the *a.* of flesh set free

451 And bared thine *a.* in all our
451 Thy single *a.*, almighty Lord
548 Thine *a.* that upward stayed
567 The *a.* of flesh will fail you
587 But take *a.* yon for the fight
587 But *a.* yourselves with all the
677 *A.* me in this fiery hour
707 There is an *a.* that never tires
707 That *a.* upholds the sky
778 Strong were thy foes; but the *a.*
790 And gather with thine *a.*
821 The Lord makes bare his *a.*
876 Who with his own right *a.*
891 His *a.* the strength imparts
920 *A.* of the Lord awake, awake, Pu
931 Who holdest in thine *a.* the
951 often when his *a.* was bared
964 Sufficient is thine *a.* alone
997 Whose *a.* alone can save
1043 *A.* of the Lord awake, awake, Th
1097 thy right hand, thy powerful *a.*
1099 Thine *a.*, O Lord, in days of old
1105 O God, whose *a.* sustained
1105 And lean on thy sustaining *a.*

ARMS.

123 Within thy circling *a.* I lie
155 And lodge us in the *a.* divine
169 Secure within thine *a.* to lie
170 Thine everlasting *a.* of love
359 Now to thine *a.* of mercy fly
392 Open thine *a.* and take me in
420 Thine *a.* of love still open are
577 When we shall cast our *a.* away
582 Stand to your *a.* the foe is nigh
651 Still be thy *a.* my sure defense
653 When his loving *a.* receive us
698 Let others stretch their *a.* like
746 are spread, The everlasting *a.*
822 The *a.* of love that compass me
827 lambs, And folds them in his *a.*
880 That his *a.* had been thrown
887 In thine *a.* and at thy breast
889 Gathered with thine *a.* and
967 Within the *a.* of God
970 To call them to his *a.*
999 But the wide *a.* of mercy are

ARMOR.

418 Arm me with thy whole *a.*, Lord
543 My soul with thy whole *a.* arm
556 Seize your *a.*, gird it on
566 Gird ye on the *a.* bright
567 Put on the gospel *a.*
568 To lay thine *a.* by
581 Nor lay thine *a.* down
584 Thine *a.* is divine
587 And put your *a.* on
599 In all the *a.* of his God
690 keeps the Christian's *a.* bright

ARMY, ARMIES.

563 Like a mighty *a.* Moves the
564 fiery pillar At our *a.'s* head
567 unto victory His *a.* shall he lead
1033 One *a.* of the living God
324 While all the *armies* of the skies
593 And all thy *a.* shine

1035 And the bright *a.* sing.
1062 The *a.* of the ransomed saints

ARRAY, ARRAYED.

909 thy strength, Thy beautiful *a.*
966 Before me place in dread *a.*
238 flaming worlds, in these *arrayed*
1064 I long to behold him *a.*

ARROW, ARROWS.

955 The *a.* is flown,—the moment
956 As the wingéd *a.* flies
116 Though the *arrows* past us fly
1073 And outfly all the *a.* of death

ART.

490 As thou *a.*, so let us be
515 With me, I know, I feel, thou *a.*
586 O may I learn the *a.*
609 O that all the *a.* might know

ASCEND.

443 Who shall *a.* on high
623 *A.* into a purer clime
657 And you and I *a.* at last
816 heart and mind may evermore *a.*
970 Ye saints *a.* the skies
981 Shall then *a.* to meet the Lord
991 Ah! when shall we *a.*
1055 Then let me, gracious Lord, *a.*
1073 Come let us *a.*, my companion

ASCENDS, ASCENDING.

322 through the clouds *a.* to God
1048 Thither his soul *a.*
932 A thousand hearts *ascending*

ASHAMED.

595 I'm not *a.* to own my Lord
604 A mortal man, *a.* of thee

ASHES.

38 what shall earth and *a.* do
490 Dust and *a.* though we be
973 These *a.*, too, this little dust
979 Securely shall my *a.* lie
1012 While *a.* to *a.*, and dust

ASK.

103 Will furnish all we ought to *a.*
164 *A.* and receive in Jesus' name
179 O what shall I *a.* of thy providence
295 Naught we can *a.* to make us
467 And humbly *a.* for more
498 My soul *a.* what thou wilt
508 requires, Is that we *a.* for more
508 For more we *a.*; we open then
537 I have the things I *a.* of thee
675 And if some things I do not *a.*
689 *A.* but in faith, it shall be done
700 To those who *a.* how kind thou
719 Bids thee *a.* him, waits to hear
735 Father see *a.* in Jesus' name
856 What they *a.* of thee to gain
952 We *a.* in faith for every soul

ASLEEP.

979 *A.* in Jesus! blessed sleep

2

ASPIRE, ASPIRES, ASPIRING, ASPIRINGS.

37 To thee our trembling hearts *a.*
78 To that our laboring souls *a.*
445 To thee our humble hearts *a.*
481 To thee with my whole heart *a.*
640 To him continually *a.*
661 my heart *A.* in vain to thee
15 To thine abode my heart *aspires*
488 All my heart to thee *a.*
608 Heavenward our every wish *a.*
618 *Aspiring* to the plains of light
105 There our last *aspirings* end

ASSAIL, ASSAILS.

333 *A.* my peace on every side
420 Hither, when hell *assails*, I flee

ASSAULT, ASSAULTS.

555 For each *a.* prepared
69 From all *assaults* of hell and sin

ASSEMBLED, ASSEMBLING.

7 midst....*A.* in thy name
30 With us thou art *a.* here
71 *A.* in thy sacred name
798 fears...Since we *a.* last
922 *A.* at thy great command
54 In thy name, O Lord, *assembling*

ASSEMBLY.

37 Still let it on the *a.* stay
787 Behold the blest *a.* there

ASSIST.

1 *A.* me to proclaim, To spread

ASSURANCE.

212 What joy the blest *a.* gives! He
212 What joy the blest *a.* gives, I
657 In peace and full *a.* go
1011 Where all is *a.* and peace

ASTONISHED, ASTONISHMENT.

161 By day along the *a.* lands
405 Be thou *a.*, O my soul
525 Lost in *astonishment* and love

ASTRAY.

872 Seek us when we go *a.*
877 show the mind which went *a.*
889 From thy fold to go *a.*

ASUNDER.

797 When we *a.* part
1020 'Twould tear my soul *a.*, Lord

ATOM.

1000 Every *a.* of thy trust Rests

ATONE, ATONED, ATONING.

305 Hath power sufficient to *a.*
311 nor prayers Can e'er for sin *a.*
415 These for sin could not *a.*
651 His blood for me did once *a.*
857 And for sinners to *a.*
458 His blood *atoned* for all our race
854 All partake the grace *atoning*

ATONEMENT.

26 Hear the world's *a.* thou
210 The grand and full *a.* made
228 For all a full *a.* made
246 Thou hast full *a.* made
331 High-priest hath full *a.*
378 For all my sins *a.* made
533 The *a.* of thy blood apply

ATTEND, ATTENDANT.

155 Angels where'er we go *a.*
610 My life and death *a.*
236 *Attendant* in thy train

ATTRIBUTES.

16 sing his *a.* and name
125 New *a.* sublime
126 Thy countless *a.* to show
139 Confess thine *a.* divine
449 To bless his *a.* divine

AUSPICIOUS.

73 On this *a.* morn
193 To hail the *a.* day

AUTHOR.

231 Thou of life the *a.*, death
851 *A.* of our salvation, thee
851 *A.* of this great mystery
933 Great *A.* of salvation

AUTUMN.

644 And the *a.* winds have come
1080 Our hope when *a.* winds
1082 Thy hand in *a.* richly pours
1084 All that liberal *a.* pours

AVENGE, AVENGER.

569 To him who can *a.* your
1092 the Omnipotent! mighty *Avenger*

AWAKE.

555 Say to me now, *A.*, awake
889 *A.*, awake, my tuneful powers
954 With all the dead, *a.*
970 *A.*, ye nations under ground
994 In the dust, *A.*, come forth

AWE.

47 Serve him with *a.*, with
112 Keep the wide world in *a.*
296 All my spirit sinks with *a.*
511 The filial *a.*, the fleshly heart
531 And rapturous *a.* and silent
860 With *a.* like theirs, on earth
929 To *a.* the bold, to stay the weak

AWFUL.

9 Before Jehovah's *a.* throne
41 This *a.* God is ours
152 Give glory to his *a.* name
151 And speak his *a.* hand
444 Trembling before thine *a.* throne
1020 That *a.* day will surely come

AZURE.

261 High above yon *a.* height
863 The broad expanse of *a.* sky

B.

BABE.
192 The heavenly b. you there shall

BABEL.
194 And ever o'er its B. sounds

BACK.
381 And bring me b. to God
402 What is it keeps me b.
893 Than hold it b. from thee

BACKSLIDING, BACKSLIDINGS.
559 A poor b. soul restore
557 And freely my *backslidings* heal

BAITS.
505 cast behind The b. of pleasing

BALL.
248 Who fixed this earthly b.
248 On this terrestrial b.
698 Or on this earthly b.

BALM.
72 O b. of care and sadness
94 Our b. in sorrow, and our
208 The b. of life, the cure of woe
306 But can no sovereign b. be found
306 A b. for all thy grief and woe
311 The b. of pardoning love
324 A sovereign b. for every wound
327 Jesus, thy b. will make it whole
344 B. that flows for every wound
380 B. to heal my every wound
386 B. of all my grief and pain
449 Poured b. into my bleeding
671 From lips divine like healing b.
752 for warfare, b. for grief
802 To find a b. for woe
986 There's b. in their assuaging
1089 A b. for every wounded breast

BALMY.
538 Till mercy with its b. aid

BAND, BANDS.
1044 Will join the glorious b.
1052 Amid the shining b.
434 He bound me with the *bands* of
583 Ye blood-besprinkled b.
767 God himself shall loose thy b.
987 Death may the b. of life unloose
1033 And greet the blood-besprinkled b.

BANISH, BANISHED.
409 And b. all my sin
358 Lest we be *banished* from thy
419 If I were b. from thee
557 Call home thy b. one
720 O ye b. seed, be glad
937 Then be b. grief and pain
1020 What! to be b. from my Lord

BANISHMENT.
450 The road that leads from b.
696 I pass my years of b.

BANKS.
774 Close by its b. in order fair

BANNER.
219 The royal b. is unfurled
228 O let thy conquering b. wave
567 Lift high the royal b.
568 Beneath his b. true
577 The foe before his b. flies
804 Come and spread thy b. here
838 Under his b. thus we sing
853 Jesus spreads his b. o'er us
883 We'll flock around his b.
921 Now all abroad thy b. fling
938 See Jehovah's b. furled
939 Wave the b.-cross on high
1014 Shall the saints his b. see

BANNERS.
563 See, his b. go
1104 Our troops shall lift their b.

BANQUET.
851 And b. with our Lord
853 He the b. spreads before us
853 Precious b.; bread of heaven
1054 To find at the b. of mercy
1073 To a taste of the b. above

BAPTISMAL.
800 One sole b. sign
832 Once shared the blest b.

BAPTIZE.
276 B. the nations; far and
785 B. into thy name
830 B. this soul with blood
831 Sent to b. into thy name

BAPTIZED.
671 B. into the sanctities
826 I am b. into thy name
826 B. in Christ, I fear not
829 B. into the Father's name
829 B. in thine, we own thy
829 B. into the Holy Ghost

BAPTIZING, BAPTIZER.
831 The inward, pure, b. grace
831 *baptizer* of our spirits thou

BAR, BARS.
349 Before his b. your spirits
954 to call The nations to his b.
1021 I at thy b. appear
1024 Before whose b. severe
90 When its *bars* their weakness
237 Loose all your b. of massy

BARDS.
36 The lyre of Hebrew b. was strung
194 By prophet-b. foretold

BARK.
187 wind that tossed my foundering b.
613 My little b. is confident
634 With thee within my b.
1110 Though heaves our b. far from

BARREN.
678 water-spring To a dry, b. place
769 The dry and b. ground
953 B. and withered trees
1305 brought them to this b. shore

BARRIER.
393 Hath broken every b. down

BATHE.
659 There I shall b. my weary
730 With my tears his feet I'll b.

BATTLE.
526 Now the b. will be won
567 This day the noise of b.
581 The b. ne'er give o'er
582 The day of b. is at hand
584 The b. soon will yield
587 To b. all proceed
591 And in the darkest b.-field
596 Upon this b.-field of earth
921 Set time's great b. in array
991 The b.'s fought, the race is won
1017 Gird thee for the b.
1017 Peace shall follow b.

BATTLEMENTS.
763 We mark her goodly b.

BEAM.
293 In each a heavenly b. I see
283 And every b. conducts to thee
411 By thy all-perceiving b.
540 O may one b. of thy blest light
555 Work till the last b. fadeth
623 Eternal B. of light divine
644 Of the day's last b. is flown
708 But when the keener, purer b.
950 A b. from heaven is sent to
982 How mildly b. the closing eyes

BEAMS.
17 His b. are majesty and light
34 Their common b. unite
67 With b. of everlasting day
72 With pure and radiant b.
111 O let thy rising b. The night
153 Whose b. create our days
284 Send forth thy b. divine
250 The gathered b. of ages shine
290 With b. of heavenly day
416 Till thy mercy's beams I see
428 Display thy b. divine
448 That thy bright b. on me
553 With b. of mercy shine
620 He sheds the b. of light divine
661 Where thy full b. impart
665 And glory b. around thy head
701 With b. of sacred bliss
868 Which b. on the soul and
897 And send its glorious b. afar
911 Arise, and with the morning b.
913 Like the b. of morning fly
914 Life and joy thy b. impart
1014 B. the Saviour, shines the
1034 Shall there his b. display
1065 Enjoying the b. of his love

BEAMING.
61 love B. from every page
464 Sweetly b. in my face
730 compassion B. in his gracious eye

BEAR.
317 Thou dost with sinners b.
335 To b. up your spirit when
487 Thee he in his arms shall b.
644 But he will b. us through

BEARS.
147 B. and forbears, as thou hast done
251 What every member b.
724 In his hands he gently b. us
754 He b. them all, and frees us
772 Their souls forever b.

BEATIFIC.
657 face shall see; The b. sight
1065 The sight b. they prove

BEAUTY.
206 Full of b., truth, and grace
238 My b. are, my glorious dress
702 O Jesus, thou the b. art
775 Thy b. and thy strength put on
870 And here thy b. see
959 the bloom of earthly b. flies
1058 True vision of true b.
1064 His b. of holiest love

BEAUTIES.
17 His b., how divinely bright
31 Thy uncreated b. shine
299 And still new b. may we see
545 On all thy glorious b. gaze
662 My Saviour, let thy b. be
977 The short-lived b. die away
1054 I long, dearest Lord, in thy b.
1063 Where Jesus' b. display

BEAUTIFUL.
147 how b., The sight of thee
769 How b. the sweet accord
871 temples...How b. they stand
880 In that b. place he has gone
971 How b. on all the hills

BECKON, BECKONS, BECKONED.
796 Where none shall b. us away
1078 And angels b. me away
591 And beckons thee his road
1004 Lo! he b. from on high
165 He beckoned, and the winds were

BED.
108 watchful stations round my b.
167 When on the b. of death we lie
170 He smooth's my b., and gives me
186 Low lies his b. with the beasts
208 And gilds the b. of death with
412 When rising from the b. of death
612 Angels shall hover round my b.
633 When I remember on my b.
970 graves...And softened every b.
971 To mourners round his b.
1007 In its narrow b. 'tis sleeping

BEDS.
97 Thy angels shall around their *b*.
113 Upon our *b*. to rest; So death
197 dress is by our *b*. of pain

BEFRIEND.
167 'Tis yours the spirit to *b*.
872 We are thine, do thou *b*. us

BEG.
893 O rather let me *b*. my bread

BEGUILE.
530 Shall aught *b*. me on the

BEHALF.
438 Sacrifice in my *b*. appears
927 To thee in their *b*. we cry
953 Thou didst in our *b*. appear

BEHAVIOR.
1021 account...For my *b*. here

BEHEST.
151 Without his high *b*.

BEHIND.
254 Look not *b*., make no delay
362 Leave all you have and are *b*.
364 Ye need not one be left *b*.
564 before us, Not a look *b*.
758 live in glory and leave me *b*.
945 forsake, Or cast his words *b*.

BEING, BEINGS.
347 God who did your *b*. give
605 What is my *b*. but for thee
774 Great source of *b*. and of
508 B. of *beings*, God of love

BELIEVE.
28 Come, let us who in Christ *b*.
220 B., believe the record true
275 Lord, we *b*. to us and ours
302 I would *b*. thy promise, Lord
307 Lord, if thou wilt, I do *b*.
311 O that I could *b*.
367 B., believe in Jesus' name
386 hear, And help me to *b*.
406 O Jesus, could I this *b*.
432 Self-desperate, I *b*.
503 Father, I dare *b*. Thee merciful
512 I steadfastly *b*. Thou wilt
517 the Way, In whom I now *b*.
535 Power to *b*., and go in peace
535 Thou canst, thou wilt, I dare *b*.
583 B., and conquer all
620 Only *b*., in living faith
688 B. his word, and trust his grace
835 And sensibly *b*.
1012 To those who *b*. in the Lord

BELIEVERS.
573 And show them how *b*. true
664 To bring *b*. home
719 Only to *b*. shown, Glorious
804 Show how true *b*. live
804 Show how true *b*. die

BELLS.
1070 Far, far away, like *b*. at evening

BELOVED.
255 our Lord...B., obeyed, adored
471 And less *b*. than God alone
759 Say, if in your tents my *B*.

BELOW.
256 The joy of all *b*.
592 Servant...While dwelling here *b*.
956 They have done with all *b*.
995 O may we bless thy grace *b*.
1067 Once they knew, like us *b*.

BEND, BENDS, BENDING.
35 Before thy throne we sinners *b*.
60 Lord, when we *b*. before thy
64 Low at thy feet we *b*.
182 There to *b*. the knee before thee
723 Low we *b*. the adoring knee
1091 In thy holy place we *b*.
1048 There his adoring spirit bends
31 Sinners...Come *bending* at thy

BENEDICTION.
271 On us thy *b*. shower
856 And thy fullest *b*. shed
1060 His land and *b*. Thy

BENEFITS.
364 His offered *b*. embrace
1087 be not God's *b*. forgot

BENIGHTED.
270 To our *b*. minds reveal
285 on this poor *b*. soul...shine
553 On this *b*. heart...shine
664 sheds...light...O'er this *b*. soul
805 Lights in a *b*. land
815 The lights of a *b*. land
929 B. in this land of light
920 Shall we to men *b*...lamp
943 Every poor, *b*. heart

BEQUEST.
833 And gave his own their last *b*.

BESET.
123 I lie, B. on every side
854 death...B. thy path, nor

BEST.
88 Day of all the week the *b*.
500 live or die, I know not which is *b*.
637 dark or bright, As *b*. may seem
655 joy or sorrow...As *b*. to thee may
672 knows What *b*. for each will

BETHEL.
724 Out of...griefs B. I'll raise

BETHLEHEM.
187 It is the Star of *B*.
187 The Star, the Star of *B*.
190 Christ is born in *B*.
195 More bright on *B*.'s...plains
907 Yet doth the star of *B*.

BET 22 BLE

BETHANY.
203 Gracious One of *B.*

BETRAY, BETRAYAL, BETRAYED.
574 Assured if I my trust *b.*
850 And thus that dark *betrayal*
853 When Jesus was for us *betrayed*

BETTER.
488 Choose thee as the *b.* part
952 We choose the *b.* part at last

BEWILDERED.
200 That bids *b.* souls rejoice

BIDDING.
363 How sweet the *b.,* Come

BILLOW, BILLOWS.
1111 tossed on the breast of the *b.*
266 When the *billows* fill with
1031 And as thy *b.* flow
1054 Though now my temptation like *b.*
1110 sound Of *b.* that never can sleep

BIND.
67 O *b.* us to each other, Lord
726 *B.* my wandering heart to thee
960 slender...ties That *b.* us to a

BIRD, BIRDS.
305 Nor bleeding *b.,* nor bleeding
122 The *birds* that rise on quivering
141 The *b.,* without barn or store
1086 By him the *b.* are fed

BIRTH.
139 Let all who owe to thee their *b.*
155 Encircled from our second *b.*
417 By thy *b.* and by thy tears
530 Born by a new, celestial *b.*
561 purpose Spring to glorious *b.*
597 Then let us prove our heavenly *b.*
853 When the angels sang thy *b.*
881 orbs...Sprang to *b.* beneath thy
1074 Of heavenly *b.,* though wandering
1081 goodness marked its secret *b.*

BIRTHRIGHT.
227 If tears were our *b.,* and

BITTER, BITTERLY, BITTERNESS.
161 The bud may have a *b.* taste
167 To earth in *b.* sorrow weighed
349 No God regard your *b.* prayer
623 I take the cup...Though *b.* to
628 *B.* the cup of woe
272 It grieves me *bitterly*
997 The *bitterness* of death

BLADE.
575 The tender *b.,* the stalk, the ear
1083 First the *b.,* and then the ear

BLAST.
172 If one sharp *b.* sweep o'er the
807 Safe from each *b.* that blows
1071 The fiercer the *b.,* the sooner
1084 *B.* each opening bud of joy

BLAZE.
97 Than the full *b.* of day
119 Before the insufferable *b.*
395 Amid the *b.* of gospel day
562 With inextinguishable *b.*
657 And wide diffuse the golden *b.*
915 and *b.* abroad Thy name
936 Sets the kingdoms on a *b.*

BLAZING.
130 Who can behold the *b.* light
135 Before the ever-*b.* throne

BLEED, BLEEDS.
211 Alas! and did my Saviour *b.*
215 vast the love...To *b.* and die
294 There I behold the Saviour *b.*
250 The Lord, who *bleeds* and dies

BLEEDING.
230 The *b.* Prince of life and
320 The stricken soul Lies *b.*
350 spreads for you his *b.* hands
1002 Jesus, while our hearts are *b.*

BLED.
66 sinned, he *b.,* To save us from
90 Who had, sinless, *b.* for sin
422 And *b.* for Adam's helpless

BLEND, BLENDED.
115 Where our spirits only *b.*
602 The near and future *b.* in
793 *Blended* and gathered into one

BLESS.
6 Come, and thy people *b.*
50 And *b.* us in thy grace
50 The Lord our God shall *b.* us
142 where his love resolves to *b.*
212 To *b.* me thou a curse wast
212 He lives to *b.* me with his love
234 Come, all thy faithful *b.*
688 Engage the waiting soul to *b.*
711 Jesus alone can *b.*...Jesus is mine
746 Christ shall *b.* thy going out
760 O *b.* me now, my Saviour
855 As we from thy table go, *B.* us
887 *B.,* and make them like to thee
980 God's own Spirit deigns to *b.*
1099 now, O Lord, be near to *b.*

BLESSING.
21 Till a *b.* thou bestow
29 Once more his *b.* ask
30 Thy promised *b.* give
32 Thy *b.* we implore
50 God shall his *b.* send
55 O may all enjoy the *b.*
88 Let us now a *b.* seek
89 Lord, send thy *b.* down to
121 Thyself the *b.* give
173 They cannot keep a *b.* back
216 Worship, honor, power, and *b.*
282 share Thy *b.* from on high
313 The long-sought *b.* give
377 The *b.* seek and find
386 Thy *b.* to receive

BLE 23 BLO

407 O that I could the *b.* prove
440 Till the *b.* thou bestow
458 The *b.* of thy love bestow
491 Thee we would be always *b.*
501 May ours this *b.* be
506 This *b.*, above all, Always
616 Each *b.* to my soul more
638 The word of *b.* give
672 Thy every act pure *b.* is
690 Brings every *b.* from above
730 Sweet the moments, rich in *b.*
757 What a *b.* to know that my Jesus
811 And sends the promised *b.* down
831 We now thy promised *b.*
884 Redeemer, grant thy *b.*
887 Holy Father, send thy *b.*
947 *B.*, and thanks, and love
967 And death the *b.* shall restore
1084 And when every *b.*'s flown
1107 And bring a *b.* from above

BLESSINGS.

2 And *b.* more than we can
29 To each thy *b.* suit
65 And shed thy *b.* here
77 Which scatters *b.* from its
102 With *b.* from thy boundless
159 O may the *b.* of each hour
159 And all the *b.* we receive
161 and shall break In *b.* on
179 With *b.* unmeasured my cup
183 He comes to make his *b.* flow
224 Heavenly *b.*, without measure
228 The *b.* thou hast died to give
261 *B.* on his Church below
287 These *b.* of thy grace
458 While marked with *b.* every
689 The *b.* God designs to give
758 my neighbors may share These *b.*
761 His boundless *b.* prove
795 Jesus, from whom all *b.* flow
802 God, from whom all *b.* flow
806 Christ, from whom all *b.* flow
834 And *b.* crown the board
855 Bless us with eternal *b.*
878 Thou hast heavenly *b.* shed
919 Their early *b.* on his name
1008 mild, With *b.* on thy head
1084 Source whence all our *b.* flow
1100 And heavenly *b.* round us
1101 peace, with her what *b.* fled

BLESSEST.

892 And gladly as thou *b.* us

BLEST.

173 Engage to make us *b.*
328 Obey, and be forever *b.*
337 *B.* in Christ this moment be
345 Hasten, sinner, to be *b.*
382 The good wherewith I would be *b.*
419 all engaged to make me *b.*
442 I was perfectly *b.*
454 In him I am *b.*, I lean on his
487 Jesus hath pronounced thee *b.*
510 Thou knowest that I am not *b.*
550 And none more *b.* than I
591 Thrice *b.* is he to whom is

602 And, early called, how *b.* are
627 Deem not that they are *b.* alone
633 *B.* is the man, O God
755 My heart is light and *b.*
787 where Jesus is, Must be forever *b.*
809 wrought, They shall be *b.* indeed
816 We shall with them be *b.*
933 In him are fully *b.*
987 Protection...In me be ever *b.*
996 Or numbered with the *b.*
1001 *B.*, unutterably blest
1024 A lot among the *b.*
1038 happy place, And be forever *b.*

BLIGHTING.

1008 Haste from this *b.* land

BLIND.

1 Ye *b.*, behold your Saviour
40 When *b.*, and deaf, and dumb
65 Here let the *b.* their sight obtain
201 When the *b.* suppliant in the way
364 Ye poor...and halt and *b.*
384 Thou canst make the *b.* to see
395 A poor *b.* child I wander
427 Was *b.*, but now I see
564 *B.* they grope for day
740 Lord pours eyesight on the *b.*
1099 To thee they went, the *b.*, the

BLINDLY.

617 We *b.* shun the latent good

BLISS.

31 From thee they all their *b.*
85 sing...away To everlasting *b.*
132 Where life and *b.* shall never
222 What *b.*, till now was thine
356 Unto that heavenly *b.* They all
358 The *b.* for which we sigh
401 To seek and taste no other *b.*
453 I shall see the *b.* of thine own
499 Make it my highest *b.* Thy
502 then translate To my eternal *b.*
512 I taste the unutterable *b.*
520 The perfect *b.* to prove
530 Is heavenly *b.* begun below
605 Such *b.* as crowns me at thy
624 I feel the *b.* thy wounds
667 taste, e'en here, the hallowed *b.*
770 And brighter *b.* of heaven
788 saints above Their *b.* and glory
791 And heaven's unutterable *b.*
807 When *b.* each heart shall fill
823 Lord Did heavenly *b.* forego
936 All partake the glorious *b.*
966 Eternal *b.* to insure
1031 But O, the *b.* to which I tend
1032 That only *b.* for which it pants
1034 And each the *b.* of all shall
1068 Welcomed to partake the *b.*
1076 With streams of sacred *b.*

BLOOD.

234 A thousand drops of richer *b.*
260 Lo! he sets in *b.* no more
306 in the Saviour's dying *b.*
310 But through the Saviour's *b.*

320 One only stream, a stream of b.
338 Sprinkled now with b. the
339 Covered with his flowing b.
356 For he whose b. is all our boast
422 An interest in the Saviour's b.
442 Which I felt in the life-giving b.
446 That b. which doth for sinners
446 The faith in thy all-cleansing b.
495 Since his own b. for thee was
534 And wait till his redeeming b.
582 All stained with hallowed b.
583 Through b. ye must the
735 Whose b. proclaims our sins
803 Feels the cleansing b. applied
811 My life, my b., I here present
823 This is my b., which seals
833 My b., so freely shed for you
834 Through the rich b. that
841 The Son, his flesh and b.
847 Christ, whose b. was shed
920 No more let creature b. be
953 Jesus, thy speaking b.

Atoning BLOOD.
210 I plead the atoning b.
253 through whose atoning b., Each
281 Through Christ's atoning b.
451 Sprinkled with the atoning b.

His BLOOD.
1 His b. can make the foulest
229 feel with me his b. applied
243 Has shed his b. and died
320 His b. flows most freely in
340 Pleads the merit of his b.
348 Could he more than shed his b.
397 For you the Saviour spilt his b.
435 Our interest in his b.
436 ground Of Jesus and his b.
437 And feel his b. applied
452 When Jesus doth his b. apply
454 In him I confide, his b. is applied
612 Sweet to remember that his b.
757 Redeemer to know, to feel his b.
828 The cup in token of his b.

Jesus' BLOOD.
111 Or Jesus' b., like evening dew
330 'Tis Jesus' b. that washes white
420 While Jesus' b., through earth
421 Than Jesus' b. and righteousness.
1075 save me . Through Jesus' b.

Precious BLOOD.
238 Lord, I believe thy precious b.
243 His precious b. did once atone
314 In Jesus' precious b.: 'Tis this
725 Interposed his precious b.
743 I'd sing the precious b, he spilt
770 With his own precious b.
817 O precious b.! For us so freely
841 His precious b. was shed
957 O wash me in thy precious b.

Sprinkled BLOOD.
460 the sprinkled b. to apply
772 And feel his sprinkled b.
854 All the sprinkled b. receive

The BLOOD.
32 Ready thou art the b. to apply
258 Father, bear the b. of Jesus
371 now he waits the b. to apply
435 'Tis thine the b. to apply
442 received through the b. of the
456 The b. by faith alone applied
511 And drive me to the b. again
843 Thine was the b. of sacrifice
851 We see the b. that seals
920 The b. that flowed from
1066 In the b. of yonder Lamb

Thy BLOOD.
228 Jesus, thy b. and righteousness
246 Through the virtue of thy b.
305 Jesus, thy b., thy blood alone
383 Let thy b. by faith applied
389 Thy b. is always nigh
393 But that thy b. was shed for me
401 Till sprinkled with thy b.
407 But let me feel thy b. applied
503 And waiting for thy b. to
514 Thy b., we steadfastly believe
521 A heart that always feels thy b.
527 Sprinkle me, saviour, with thy b.
533 Sprinkle me ever with thy b.
668 Still let me live thy b. to show
708 Which made thy b. to flow
718 There thy b.-bought right
721 Firmly trusting in thy b.
829 As ransomed by thy b.
835 Let it thy b. impart
848 Drink thy b. for sinners shed

BLOOM, BLOOMS.
644 For the b. of life is withered
652 B. the fair flowers the earth too
959 At thy rebuke the b. of earthly
966 But thou shalt yet in beauty b.
977 So blooms the human face divine
1055 Where naught that b. shall die

BLOSSOM, BLOSSOMS.
232 The first bright b. may be found
950 though earth's fairest blossoms

BLOT.
249 approaching night shall b. out
353 To rid my soul of one dark b.
1022 And b. it with thy bleeding hand

BLUSH, BLUSHED.
170 I b. in all things to abound
598 Or b. to speak his name
604 Let evening b. to own a star
604 No; when I b., be this my shame
357 To shame our sins he blushed in

BOARD.
834 millions Around the b. appear
841 Approach his royal b.
845 Call us round his heavenly b.
852 Yet while around his b. we meet

BOAST.
453 For thou art their b., their glory
531 I cannot of my goodness b.
604 Till then I b. a Saviour slain

BODY.
166 The b. they may kill : God's truth
488 B., soul, and spirit joined
833 Take, eat, this is my b., given
836 Thy b. broken for my sake
841 His b. bruised, for sin
844 Those his b. who discern
844 Here, one b., we unite
847 Gives his b. for the feast
851 Thy b. and thy blood it shows
961 My b. with my charge lay down
906 born to die? To lay this b. down
1012 His b., which came from the earth
1032 And let this feeble b. fail
1050 Here in the b. pent, Absent
1054 I sigh from this b. of sin to be free
1064 And then from the b. set free
1116 Must shortly lay my b. down

BODIES.
66 His sovereign power our b. made
782 Our b. may far off remove
782 And b. part no more
816 And let our b. part, To
963 And all who now in b. dwell
989 Those b. that corrupted fell
990 Their b. in the ground
995 Shall these vile b. shine

BOLD.
238 B. shall I stand in thy great
422 B. I approach the eternal
499 Thou canst not be too b.
505 B. to take up, firm to sustain

BOLT.
951 And turned the vengeful b. aside

BOND, BONDS.
67 By one great b.,—the love of thee
240 Breaks the firm b. and frees
447 O happy b., that seals my vows
447 And bless in death a b. so dear
243 In willing bonds beneath thy feet
383 Burst our b., and set us free
1000 Thus the b. of life he breaks
1054 Sweet b. that unite all the

BONDAGE.
163 from the land of b. came
352 No heed, but still in b. live
382 From this b., Lord, release
758 In b., O why, and death
895 In b., heart and soul
912 Hail to the millions from b.

BONES.
30 And these dry b. shall live

BOOK.
291 Thy b. be my companion still
295 Naught.. is in this b. denied
297 How precious is the b. divine
612 my name in life's fair b. set
1022 In God's recording b., Our sins

BORE.
4 For those whose sins he b.
18 He b. the curse to sinners due

118 Left his throne and b. our load
220 B. all my sins upon the tree
259 He who b. all pain and loss
582 He b. the cross for all

BORN.
192 Is b., of David's line, The Saviour
305 And b. unholy and unclean
424 witness…That I am b. of God
438 And tells me I am b. of God
741 B. but for one brief day
783 None who are truly b. of God
867 That crowds were b. to glory
1001 Angels sing, A child is b.
1001 B. into the world above

BORNE.
52 B. on angels' wings to heaven
226 He has b. our sins away
648 who all our sins hast b., Freely
676 What must be b. in thee
676 B. onward, sin and death behind
679 still in my bosom be b.

BOSOM.
60 And not a thought our b. share
113 O may we in thy b. rest
212 And ever in thy b. rest
238 Who from the Father's b. came
244 Let every b. swell With pure
291 While on the b. of my Lord
307 And save me from my b. sin
395 I shall upon thy b. fall
548 Within that b. which hath
600 Deep in the Father's b. lies
638 Where, on the b. of their God
656 Let me to thy b. fly
658 O yet this b. feels the fire
679 Like lambs…in my b. be borne
748 Are fed, on his b. reclining
780 Through every b. flow
861 In every b. fix thy throne
889 In thy b. may we be
988 Calm on the b. of thy God
1006 From my b. to his own
1007 Heaves that little b. more
1012 Returns to the b. of God
1038 Father's face, And in his b. rest
1064 But when, on thy b. reclined

BOSOMS.
284 Our inmost b. fill
872 With thy love our b. fill
1103 Our b. tremble and rejoice

BOUGHT.
32 What thou hast b. so dear
220 Ye all are b. with Jesus' blood
229 For thou hast b. with tears
333 If grace were b. I could not
346 B. by love and life the price
456 Who b. me with his blood
460 That b. my guilty soul for
463 Thou hast b. me with thy
872 Thou hast b. us, thine we are
941 Souls that Jesus b. by dying
1030 Who b. the sight for me
1032 O what hath Jesus b. for me

BOUNDLESS.
53 And the Father's *b.* love
294 All nature sings thy *b.* love
325 Of bliss a *b.* store
335 that his mercy is *b.* and free
476 Jesus, thy *b.* love to me
492 God, whose *b.* love Makes
510 things Thy *b.* love can give
913 *B.* as ocean's tide Rolling

BOUNTY.
119 Yet free as air thy *b.* streams
180 Thy *b.* shall my pains beguile
241 Since from his *b.* I receive
338 See with richest *b.* stored
340 God's free *b.* glorify
414 share The *b.* of his hand
713 And seen by thy sweet *b.* made
777 All his *b.* shall bestow

BOUNTIES.
612 And still his royal *b.* flow
892 May we thy *b.* thus As
893 Thy *b.* how complete
1081 How rich thy *b.* are
1103 Thy first and noblest *b.*

BOW (*Rainbow.*)
403 His *b.* is in the cloud
620 His *b.* of love and peace

BOW.
3 Come, *b.* before the Lord
9 Ye nations *b.* with sacred joy
21 At thy feet we humbly *b.*
26 *B.* thine ear, in mercy bow
33 Ne'er may we *b.* the knee
48 And *b.* our souls before thy
63 And *b.* before his throne
109 God, our light! to thee we *b.*
238 *B.* the knee, embrace the Son
372 We *b.* before thy gracious throne
389 And *b.* myself before thy face
447 Till in life's latest hour I *b.*
485 At thy word my will shall *b.*
819 Father of mercies, *b.* thine ear
837 Jesus, we *b.* our souls to thee
883 We'll *b.* before his throne
915 To *b.* them low before the Lord
954 When thou dost the heavens *b.*
1027 Before thy feet with them we *b.*
1075 I *b.* and bless the sacred name

BOWS, BOWED, BOWING.
119 Which *b.* thee down to me
215 See where he *b.* his sacred head
152 And *bowed* the heavens most high
381 And *b.* that sacred head
1005 By him who *b.* to take
653 At the name of Jesus *bowing*

BOWELS.
254 His *b.* melt with love
738 To me, to all, thy *b.* move

BOWL.
890 Lost by the fiery, maddening *b.*
895 Are maddened by the *b.*
901 Dash to earth the poisoned *b.*

BRAIN.
86 On weary *b.* and troubled breast
991 Rest for the fevered *b.*

BRANCH.
441 As the *b.* is to the vine

BRASS.
185 The gates of *b.* before him burst
504 Would be but sounding *b.*

BRAVE, BRAVED, BRAVELY.
208 It makes the coward spirit *b.*
677 Who *braved* a tyrant's ire
263 *Bravely* bear and nobly strive

BREAD.
39 And satisfies with living *b.*
141 let us learn to trust for our *b.*
171 *B.* of heaven, Feed me till
568 with *b.* of heaven, Thy fainting
641 Will give his children *b.*
683 Here see the *b.* of life; see
691 taste thee, O thou Living *B.*
716 Give us this day our daily *b.*
732 *B.* of life! on thee we feed
759 Or cry in the desert for *b.*
833 and blest, and brake the *b.*
835 The *b.* thy mystic body be
835 The living *b.* sent down from
836 My *b.* from heaven shall be
838 By faith we take the *b.* of life
840 We eat the *b.* and drink the wine
841 Remember this in eating *b.*
844 our Saviour broke the *b.*, And
848 Taste thee in the broken *b.*
849 O *B.* to pilgrims given
850 Is here, in this memorial *b.*
851 The *b.* doth visibly express
851 And eat the *b.* so freely given
858 fed With thy word, the heavenly *b.*
1086 He gives our daily *b.*

BREAK, BREAKING.
215 But soon he'll *b.* death's envious
104 And *b.* this heart of stone
414 His heart begins to *b.*
689 By thee we shall *b.* through
581 And let the *breaking* day prolong

BREAST.
102 Forever on my Saviour's *b.*
170 I lean upon my Saviour's *b.*
178 reclined On the Redeemer's *b.*
283 flee To my Saviour's *b.*
369 humble sinner, in whose *b.*
370 To clasp thee to his *b.*
382 And take me to thy *b.*
400 And force me to thy *b.*
420 I look into my Saviour's *b.*
426 Thy head upon my *b.*
456 From the haven of his *b.*
491 Breathe... Into every troubled *b.*
510 upon The dear Redeemer's *b.*
613 I climb E'en to thy tender *b.*
635 Safe in thy *b.* my head I hide
643 'Twill but drive me to thy *b.*
681 And lull me to sleep on thy *b.*

703 When love inspires my *h*.
718 Take possession of my *h*.
745 Lean on thy Redeemer's *h*.
748 Or rise to be hid in thy *h*.
976 While on his *h*. I lean my
987 lambs…lay them in my *h*.
996 That tears my anxious *h*.
997 Leaning on Jesus' *h*., May I
1031 extends…To take me to his *h*.
1078 Receive me to thy *h*.
1109 understand, In a believer's *h*.

BREASTS.
986 torn From our fond *h*. away

BREAST-PLATE.
599 With righteousness a *b*.

BREATHE.
30 *B*. on us, Lord, in this our day
79 Let all that *b*. call Jesus
116 Saviour, *b*. an evening
122 *B*. forth thy holy name
262 *B*. thyself into my breast
265 *B*. thy life, and spread thy
286 One soul, one feeling *h*.
347 Dead to God while here you *h*.
435 And *b*. the living word
491 *B*., O breathe thy loving Spirit
519 The Holy Spirit *b*.; my vile
904 In whom we *b*., and move
974 When loved ones *b*. their
976 And *b*. my life out sweetly
1089 Let all that *b*. partake

BREATHES, BREATHED, BREATHINGS.
140 It *b*. in the air, it shines
445 Whose Spirit *b*. the active
280 blest Redeemer, e'er he *breathed*
671 *B*. through the lips which
487 Restless *breathings*, earnest
661 Lord, shall the *b*. of my heart

BREEZE, BREEZES.
373 Death rides on every passing *b*.
779 Every *b*. shall whisper peace
932 Each *b*. that sweeps the ocean
930 What though the spicy *breezes*
1055 And healthful *b*. sigh
1086 The *b*. and the sunshine
1111 O let thy heavenly *b*. blow

BRETHREN.
196 In us, thy *b*., see
720 Fear not, *b*., joyful stand
893 But thou hast *b*. here below
1078 For me my elder *b*. stay

BRIDAL.
719 For our *b*. day prepare

BRIDE.
355 The *b*., the Church of Christ
784 Receive thy ready *b*.
924 Come, Lord, the *b*. on earth
1076 white and pure His spotless *b*.
1107 And happy was the *b*.

BRIDEGROOM.
346 Hark, it is the *B*.'s voice
373 the *B*. will relent. Too
375 *B*. is so sweet! O let us in
540 To hear the *B*.'s voice
603 hear the *B*.'s voice
952 shout to find the *B*. nigh
954 Behold the…*B*. nigh
1107 And glad the *B*.'s heart
1107 The *B*. and the bride

BRIEF.
132 But our *h*. life's a shadowy
959 My days, how *b*. their date
1059 *B*. life is here our portion

BRIGHT.
128 How *b*. thy beaming glories
137 *B*. in thy deeds and in thy
147 Thy majesty how *b*.
236 With all thy *b*. ones of the sky
418 Their souls are over *b*. as
426 And all thy day be *b*.
624 I know that all is *b*. above
638 *B*. is their glory now
768 to bring thee forth more *b*.
907 Grow every year more *b*.
940 Bring the *b*., the glorious day
1041 So *b*., that all which spreads
1052 Come to the *b*. and blest
1061 And *b*. with many an angel
1086 For all things *b*. and good

BRIGHTER.
67 With *b*. still and brighter ray
199 Where *b*. than the sun he
296 In *b*. worlds above
300 But lo! a *b*., clearer light
565 Work, when the day grows *b*.
647 Points to *b*. worlds above
709 Of *b*. scenes in heaven
960 There is a *b*. world on high

BRIGHTEST.
662 The *b*. things below the sky
704 The glory of my *b*. days

BRIGHTNESS.
50 The *b*. of thy face
148 *B*. of the Father's glory
231 Show thy face in *b*.
270 The *b*. of his face
290 But makes its *b*. more
912 Hail to the *b*. of Zion's glad

BRINK.
543 And, starting, cry from ruin's *b*.
997 When on the *b*. of death
1053 Are slipping over the *b*.

BROADCAST.
575 *B*. it o'er the land

BROKEN.
185 He comes, the *b*. heart to
305 And make these *b*. hearts
320 One only heart, a *b*. heart
339 Saviour, take my *b*. heart

BRO   28   CAL

518 O Saviour, in this *b.* heart
775 Look up, thy *b.* heart prepare
776 He, whose word cannot be *b.*
810 With care bind up the *b.* heart
850 His body *b.* in our stead
901 Nor leave the *b.* heart unbound
929 bind and heal the *b.* heart

BROOD.
279 *B.* o'er our nature's night
1108 O Holy Spirit! who didst *b.*

BROOK.
305 Nor running *b.,* nor flood

BROTHER.
719 Christ, our *B.* and our
720 *B.* to our soul becomes
780 *b.'s* failings...show a brother's
901 His weaker *b.* in the dust
906 Turn thee, *b.*; God can save
1001 They our happy *b.* greet

BROTHERHOOD.
993 And, 'mid the *b.* on high

BRUISED.
310 *B.* and mangled by the fall
892 O, hearts are *b.* and dead

BUBBLE.
813 To sin! a *b.* on the wave

BUD.
913 Shall *b.* and blossom then

BUILD.
483 And *b.* me up in love
781 Help us to *b.* each other up
789 He bids us *b.* each other up
802 *B.* we each other up
856 His hands *b.* not for one

BUILDER, BUILDERS.
795 Great *B.* of thy Church
1063 And brightly her *B.* displays
76 The Stone the *builders* set at
766 The foolish *b.,* scribe and
857 By wise master-*b.* squared

BUILDING.
766 Yet must this *b.* rise

BUILT.
164 The Lord, who *b.* the earth
168 *B.* by the word of his command
773 *B.* on his truth, and armed
869 *B.* over earth and sea

BULWARK, BULWARKS.
123 And like a *b.* prove
168 A *b.* never failing
168 Firm as his throne the *bulwarks*
761 With stately towers and *b.*
772 round Jerusalem The hilly *b.*
871 And *b.* of our land
1014 The *b.* with salvation strong
1050 With jasper glow thy *b.*

BURDEN.
109 Lay down the *b.* and the
146 I'll drop my *b.* at his feet
212 For me the *b.* to sustain
323 Your every *b.* bring
335 If sin is your *b.,* why
391 Here on my heart the *b.* lies
495 Thy light and easy *b.* prove
681 This *b.* of body and pain
727 Feel the *b.* o' our sin
801 Each the other's *b.* bear
808 Content to bear the *b.*
825 The welcome *b.* of thy cross
1001 Here they laid their *b.* down
1065 Resigned to the *b.* we bear

BURDENS.
176 Come, cast your *b.* on the Lord
338 Why beneath thy *b.* groan
408 Our *b.* and our fears
577 It makes our *b.* light
751 My *b.* and my cares
801 Each other's *b.* learn to bear
1053 Where we lay our *b.* down

BURDENED.
196 For, ever on thy *b.* heart
262 Set the *b.* sinner free
316 Pilgrim, *b.* with thy sin
362 Ye laboring, *b.,* sin-sick souls
402 *B.,* and sick, and faint

BURN, BURNS, BURNING.
66 *B.* every breast with Jesus' love
291 And *b.* with everlasting love
488 *Burns* with love to thee, my Lord
117 In depths of *burning* light
163 A *b.* and a shining light
518 Spirit of *b.,* come
1019 And smile to see a *b.* world

BURST.
78 He *b.* the bars of death
96 And *b.* the heavy chain that
226 He has *b.* his bands asunder
260 Christ has *b.* the gates of death

BURY, BURIED.
519 *B.* me, Saviour, in thy grave
62 Though *buried* deep, or thinly
826 *B.* with Christ, and dead to
973 Yet not thus *b.,* or extinct

BUSINESS.
597 Of *b.,* toil, and care
822 'Tis all my *b.* here below
906 Be this my one great *b.* here

BUY.
362 Mercy and free salvation *b.*
362 *B.* wine, and milk, and
386 No good...Bring I to *b.* thy grace

C.

CALIFORNIA.
933 waves. On C.'s shore

CALL.

340 Sinners Jesus came to c.
353 It was the Spirit's gracious c.
359 Answer the Saviour's c.
360 C. while he may be found
362 Sinners, obey your Maker's c.
364 Sent by my Lord, on you I c.
384 Whilst thou'rt calling, O c. me
477 My heart, that lowly waits thy c.
494 For thee, O Christ, I c.
555 Give me on thee to c.
625 God of my life, to thee I c.
751 my Love, To thee, to thee I c.
856 To this temple, where we c. thee
878 Still on thee we c.

CALLS, CALLED.

352 He c. me still; can I delay
379 Would not hearken to his c.
400 It c. me still to seek thy face
758 My soul, don't delay; be c. thee
914 And c. aloud for thee
427 But God, who *called* me here
1102 None ever c. on thee in vain

CALLING.

46 Help us to make our c. sure
574 My c. to fulfil
789 To our high c.'s glorious hope

CALLING. (*verb*.)

352 God c. yet! shall I not hear
607 Hark, the voice of Jesus c.
1088 friends...Are c. from on high

CALM.

80 Feels the sweet c., and melts
82 This heavenly c. within the
109 Give deeper c. than night
164 Be c., and sink into his will
195 There comes a holier c.
274 C. in distress, in danger bold
418 And c. as summer evenings
495 Where all is c., and joy, and
549 A c. and heavenly frame
684 There is a c., a sure retreat
691 Make all our moments c. and
709 Be c. as this impressive hour
982 A c. which life nor death
1041 Across that c., serene abode
1109 Who the c. can understand

CALMS, CALMLY.

41 And c. the roaring seas
173 hope, That c. my troubled breast
630 God c. the tumult and the
275 *Calmly* we wait the promised

CALVARY.

206 When on C. I rest
206 Lovely, mournful C.
209 From C. a cry was heard
223 C.'s mournful mountain climb
224 voice...Sounds aloud from C.
341 Come to C.'s holy mountain
378 Jesus, remember C.
381 The man transfixed on C.
333 O remember C.

438 wounds...Received on C.
762 Thou Lamb of C.
836 I rest on C.
860 From C., in brightest rays
884 The tale of C.

CANA.

1107 When Jesus deigned in C.'s hall

CANAAN.

37 To C.'s bounds point out
171 Land me safe on C.'s side
528 The C. of thy perfect love
1036 On C.'s peaceful shore
1037 So to the Jews old C. stood
1038 To C.'s fair and happy
1062 On C.'s happy shore
1076 To C.'s bounds I urge

CANDLESTICK.

815 And let our c. be gold

CANOPY.

140 robe is the light, whose c.

CAPTAIN.

564 shrinking, By our C. led
568 Trust only Christ, thy C.
569 Great C., now thine arm
582 Your C.'s footsteps see
589 Your C. gives the word
825 C. of our salvation, take
825 In all their C.'s steps
1033 And shout to see our C.'s sign
1036 His C. at our head

CAPTIVE.

21 Heal the sick, the c. free
174 Our c. souls surround
181 To set the c. free
237 The powers of hell are c. led
302 And Satan binds our c. souls
311 And let the c. go
387 C., beaten, bound, reviled
485 C., yet divinely free
767 Mourning c., God himself
775 God shall set the c. free
892 The c. to release
895 Led c. at the tyrant's will
900 And lead the c. forth to light
923 The exiled c. to receive
1000 And the ransomed c. flies

CAPTIVES, CAPTIVITY.

148 Came to ransom guilty c.
24 Captive led *captively*
264 Captive leads c.

CARE.

45 Amid the hours of worldly c.
100 O let the same almighty c.
105 The bliss of thy paternal c.
128 To thy sure love, thy tender c.
176 And trust his constant c.
352 And basely his kind c. repay
359 On thee would cast our c.
394 One only c. my soul shall
449 Who with a Father's tender c.

477 save me from low-thoughted c.
510 My only c., delight, and bliss
511 My soul to thy continual c.
609 Careful, without c. I am
629 We cast our earthborn c.
663 Each c., each ill of mortal birth
674 strife be o'er of sublunary c.
672 By self-consuming c.
709 away From every cumbering c.
712 All time, and toil, and c.
722 Kindly for thy people c.
784 And feel a brother's c.
800 His constant, latest c.
801 And join with mutual c.
804 Let us for each other c.
872 Much we need thy tenderest c.
878 Still thy constant c. bestow
916 Thy still continued c.
973 Our Father's c. shall keep
1055 Where not a c. shall stir
1081 Proclaim thy constant c.

Every CARE.
661 This can my every c. control
673 And every c. be gone
686 On whom I cast my every c.
688 I'll cast on him my every c.

From CARE.
117 Free from c., from labor free
540 From c., and sin, and sorrow
696 be calm and free from c.
1051 And then from c. released

My CARE.
175 I cast my c. on thee
436 My c. and sadness he dispels
476 be all my c. To guard the
505 On thee I cast my c.
669 Lord, it belongs not to my c.

Of CARE.
287 Make every cloud of c.
688 calls me from a world of c.
728 Cumbered with a load of c.
960 Beyond the reach of c. and pain
1007 In this world of c. and pain

Thy CARE.
465 Safe alone beneath thy c.
546 O make my soul thy c.
635 My spirit, on thy c., Blest
637 I leave entirely to thy c.
1004 Venture all thy c. on him
1113 Supported by thy c.

CARES.
78 No c. to break the long repose
81 No mortal c. shall seize
82 The end of c., the end of pains
84 From our worldly c. set free
301 Let not this life's deceit'll c.
366 When life and all its c. shall end
408 To thee our inmost c. impart
592 Careless through, c. I go
620 And worldly c. and worldly
655 Choose thou my c. for me
689 If c. distract, or fears dismay

692 When anxious c. would break
709 And all my c. and sorrows
770 To her my c. and toils be
927 For no man c. their souls to
960 Dispel our c., and chase
962 Vain are the c. which rack
964 With all their c. and fears

CAREFUL.
675 More c. not to serve thee
1021 How c., then, ought I to live

CARELESS.
547 How c. to secure that crown
977 As c. of the noontide heats
1049 C. sinner, what will

CAREER.
423 And stopped my wild c.

CARMEL.
198 With C.'s hoary prophet

CARNAL.
83 And drive each c. thought
719 Bliss to c. minds unknown

CARPENTER.
592 Son of the c., receive

CAST, CASTING.
43 Nor from thy presence c. away
390 Nor c. the sinner quite away
696 Could I be c. where thou art
136 Casting down their golden

CATHOLIC.
800 The c., the true, On all

CAVE.
228 Now welcome from the c.

CELESTIAL.
34 The Father of c. powers
41 C. fruit on earthly ground
185 To pour c. day
170 As by the c. host
628 No sorrows dim c. love
640 Of right c. worth
865 And spread c. joys around
940 Cheered by no c. ray
915 Press nt with the c. host
968 C. joys, or hellish pains
1008 In yon c. sphere
1033 To joys c. rise
1052 bright, c. air The Spirit

CELL.
109 But in the Spirit's secret c.

CENTER.
135 C. and soul of every sphere
117 Fixed on this blissful c., rest
751 And c. of my soul
958 From the c. to the skies

CENTRAL.
337 From the c. point of bliss

CENTURIES.
290 More glorious still, as c. roll
844 Many c. have fled

CEYLON.
930 Blow soft o'er C.'s isle

CHAFF.
778 They fled like the c. from

CHAIN.
215 soon he'll break death's envious c.
259 Christ hath broken every c.
363 Sinking beneath the heavy c.
413 though I cannot break my c.
780 Love is the golden c. that binds
788 Sun, moon...In one mysterious c.
895 And break the galling c.
899 Fast bound in passion's c.
900 To break his c. and bid him
900 Who struggle with that fatal c.
930 Their land from error's c.
1102 O bind us in that heavenly c.

CHAINS.
151 And c. you to the shore
189 Mercy calls you...break your c.
302 Satan bind...Fast in his slavish c.
394 My wants I mourn, my c. I
422 My c. fell off, my heart was free
843 'Till from self's c. released
900 C. yet more strong and cruel
901 To live by forging c. to bind
937 Bound in c., shall hurt no
1000 Spirit, cast thy c. away
1042 Then burst the c., with sweet

CHAINED.
692 And I am c. to earth no more

CHALLENGE.
34 we meet, And c. them to sing

CHAMPIONS.
805 Dying c. for their God

CHANGE, CHANGES.
111 With joy we view the pleasing c.
130 From c. to change the creatures
150 Chance and c. are busy ever
309 O c. these hearts of ours
396 And melt and c. this heart
440 C. my nature into thine
475 O'er rule or c., as seems thee
529 Accomplished in the c. of mine
612 That, when my c. shall come
642 No c. my heart shall fear
747 Would make any c. in my mind
1052 C. leaves no saddening trace
1057 O what a mighty c.
642 For nothing *changes* here
675 And the c. that are sure to
747 No c. of season or place
768 But no c. Can attend Jehovah's

CHANGED.
491 C. from glory into glory

CHANGELESS.
150 Will his c. goodness prove
308 Faith in thy c. name I
727 C. rings the immortal

CHANT, CHANTING.
188 Which they c. in hymns of joy
193 And c. the solemn lay
744 With all who c. thy name on
884 To c. thy love divine
144 *Chanting* everlastingly To the

CHAOS.
913 whose almighty word C. and
1108 Upon the c., dark and rude

CHARGE.
228 For who aught to my c. shall
423 It seemed to c. me with his death
574 A c. to keep I have
823 Their solemn c. receive

CHARIOT, CHARIOTS.
237 There his triumphal c. waits
703 'Tis love that drives my c.
1073 Come up into the c. of love
140 His *chariots* of wrath the deep
778 were their steeds and their c.
1104 And some of c. make their boast

CHARITY.
381 Reveal the c. divine
563 One in hope, doctrine, One in c.
586 With perfect c.

CHARM, CHARMS.
211 All the vain things that c. me
643 O 'twere not in joy to c. me
708 It loses all its power to c.
1 Jesus! the name that *charms*
325 Saviour! O what endless c.
327 Ah! who against thy c. is proof
332 Jesus! harmonious name, It c.
516 world...It has no c. for me
714 Thine image...c. my ravished
827 Shepherd...with all-engaging c.
975 When, though their c. I own
987 Methinks I see a thousand c.
1051 Fair land!...But half its c.

CHARMING.
321 Grace! 'tis a c. sound
821 How c. is their voice

CHASTENED, CHASTENING.
177 gentle rod That c. us for sin
618 O to the c., let thy might
676 Yet may the c. child
986 Who shall forbid our c. woe
1094 bow Beneath thy *chastening* hand

CHEEK, CHEEKS.
373 rosy...Of youth's soft c. decay
405 And shall our *cheeks* be dry!

CHEER.
129 O c. us with thy sacred beams
284 when deep griefs o'erflow C. us

398 Their sorrows c., their wants
425 And c. my drooping heart
450 Every mourn of sinner c.
456 raise my head, and c. my heart
640 And O, to c. their heedless gloom
7.8 Let thy love my soul c.
731 Words of c. and words of love
752 Then most thou c. my soul to be
760 With joy and gladness c.
845 The bread. To c. each round
164 No matter what c. we meet

CHEERS, CHEERED, CHEERFUL.
111 Yet c. both earth and sky
2.7 But Jesus hath *cheered* the dark
852 C. by each promise thou hast
11 Sing...with *cheerful* voice
111 With c. heart I close mine
285 C. to thee will I devote
852 A c. song of sacred praise

CHEERLESS.
416 Dark and c. is the morn

CHERUB, CHERUBS.
1088 seek thy place Amid yon c. train
1045 And c. and seraph adore
48 *Cherubs* proclaim thy praise
727 C. and seraphic legions

CHERUBIC.
175 Myriads of bright, c. bands
193 Hark! the c. araches shout
229 C. legions swell The radiant
231 C. legions guard him home

CHERUBIM.
56 C. and seraphim Filled
130 Both c. and seraphim, Continually
136 C. and seraphim falling
141 C. and seraphim Veil their
152 On c. and seraphim Full
861 O Thou, who o'er the c.

CHIDE, CHIDINGS.
155 Dost thou no longer c.
731 Slow to c. and swift to
467 dost not, Lord, my sorrow c.
1058 unto heaven, And c. at my delay
911 Let no brother's bitter *chidings*

CHIEF, CHIEFLY.
359 Me, the c. of sinners spare
385 I the c. of sinners am
620 Yet, O, the c. of sinners spare
441 C. of sinners though I be
421 But *chiefly*, Lord, the thanks

CHILD.
131 The Lord is King! c. of the dust
181 To us a C. of hope is born
191 For to us a C. is born
631 Form a c. and yet a king
3* Thou shalt be a c. confessed
128 happy c. Beneath, without a
431 The Father sought his c.
428 He owns me for his c.; I can
430 And know myself thy c.

477 Make me thy beauteous c., that
481 O may I... a little c.
552 Gentle toward the c. she bare
613 C. of heaven, shouldst thou
675 I would be treated as a c.
677 rage Against a c. of thine
771 Like Jesus, The Father's holy c.
832 This c. we dedicate to thee
857 Let thy holy C., who came
875 Lo! such the c. whose early
886 Saviour Was once a c. like me
887 Didst vouchsafe a c. to be
889 This lovely c. thus early torn
1006 Now the darling c. is dead
10.6 Take the c. no longer mine
1020 How happy every c. of grace

CHILDHOOD.
157 prayers... Our lips of c. frame
675 In c., manhood, age, and

CHILDREN.
16 Old men and c. praise
101 Where c. early lisp his
172 And c.'s children ever find
252 Their c. when they cry
282 We c. of thy grace
424 Why should the c. of a King
469 Among the c. of thy grace
729 C. of the heavenly King
871 C., loud hosannas singing
876 Come, Christian c., come
877 C. our kind protection claim
880 And many dear c. are
882 Let all the c. sing
882 To Christ, the c.'s King
883 The c. all stood singing
883 His love to c. still
884 C., thy favors sharing
885 Hither our c. bring To
892 How blest the c. of the Lord
1058 Where they shall dwell as c.
1103 Their c.'s children long

His CHILDREN.
134 Then may *his* c. cease to sing
981 Unfold, to make *his* c. way
1046 Much more to us *his* c.

Little CHILDREN.
828 To *little* c. he extends
878 Which the *little* c. raise
880 How he called *little* c. as

Thy CHILDREN.
67 Still may *thy* c. in thy
545 That, with *thy* c., I may
830 With grateful joy, *thy* c. rear
885 On *thy* c. gathered here
889 Which on earth *thy* c. sing
1105 Thy c.'s cry to thee, Father

CHOICE.
3 Come, like the people of his c.
5 Ye people of his c.
25 As the people of his c.
351 bade thee make the better c.
413 happy day that fixed my c.

CHO   33   CHU

540 Master's feet...this my happy c.
635 And count thy c. the best
695 world my c. deride, Yet
742 Thou art my only c.; O bid
801 Ready thy c. to approve
891 Lord, may it be our c.

CHOOSE, CHOOSING.
609 I still would c. the better
615 O who so wise to c. our lot
655 I dare not c. my lot
655 C. out the path for me
655 C. thou my good and ill
673 Leave to his sovereign sway To c.'
166 The man of God's own *choosing*

CHOSEN.
13 Thou to thy c. dost afford
329 blessing of God's c. race
665 Thy c. ones obtain
766 C. of God, to sinners dear
856 C. of the Lord, and precious
868 Which filled...courts where thy c.

CHOIR.
13 That I the joyful c. may join
19 sing, with all the heavenly c.
34 By faith the upper c. we meet
48 Thee all the c. of angels sing
58 Come, assist the c. of heaven
480 Till, added to that heavenly c.
485 Love, the leader of the c.
694 singing with the angels' c.
991 Lodged by the ministerial c.
1000 Thus the c. of angels sing
1014 Come to join us with his c.

CHOIRS.
42 Ye heavenly c. proclaim
47 United c. of angels sing
153 Praise...Lord, ye immortal c.
195 Celestial c. from courts above
235 Join, all ye bright celestial c.
414 But I amid your c. shall shine
733 While the angel c. are crying
1073 Join all the glad c.

CHORAL.
151 And bid the c. song ascend
414 Is shaken with the c. strain
1093 Let us join the c. song

CHORUS.
187 hark! to God the c. breaks
193 With joy the c. we repeat
218 And swell the c. of the skies
227 Loud was the c. of angels
245 In one great c. join
569 A joyful c. to thy praise
934 Shall send the c. round
1051 join The c. of the sky
1067 'Mid the c. of the skies

CHRIST.
214 When C., the mighty Maker
220 Our C. hath brought us over
376 entreating C. to let thee in
441 C. is all in all to me

477 No more, but C. in me, may live
486 None but C. to me be given
518 While C. is all the world to me
521 Where only C. is heard to speak
607 And C. shall be my song
721 May I prove it C. to live
808 Send us, O C., to be Content
885 Jesus, thou C. of God, By thy

In CHRIST.
232 *In* C. we live, in Christ we
270 That we *in* C. may live
432 I shall *in* C., at that glad
437 We who *in* C. believe
452 *In* C. to endless ages mine
587 That was *in* C., your Head

To CHRIST.
71 *To* C., Creator, Saviour, King
364 Ye all may come *to* C. and live
469 Christian lives *to* C. alone; To
525 All glory be *to* C., my Lord
733 Love and praise *to* C. belong

With CHRIST.
492 Ever one *with* C. may be
508 And be *with* C. in God
582 Go up *with* C. your Head
1048 *With* C. before the throne

CHRISTIAN, CHRISTIANS.
832 We still may act the C.'s part
974 'Tis like the peace the C. gives
1000 While the faithful C. dies
1058 Arise, arise, good C.
573 how...real *Christians* live
783 See how true C. love
795 How C. lived in days of
800 When C. love and live as one
865 Here C. join the song
974 So calmly C. sink away

CHRISTMAS.
195 Breaks the first C. morn

CHURCH.
37 And join the general C. above
56 With his holy C. below
72 The C. her voice upraises
76 Now raised in glory, o'er his C.
82 Which for the C. of God remains
88 Till we join the C. above
120 The holy C. throughout the
144 Thee, the C. in every land
199 glory that the C. shall share
291 And join me to the C. above
319 Till all the ransomed C. of God
467 Till gathered to the C. above
563 mighty army Moves the C. of
563 Gates...'Gainst that C. prevail
563 But the C. of Jesus, Constant
648 The C. of the first-born to
680 Head of the C. triumphant
763 not like kingdoms...Thy holy C.
764 clime and age This glorious C.
765 The C. triumphant in thy
770 The C. our blest Redeemer saved
809 Build up thy rising C.

3

CHU 34 CLI

816 The C. of the first-born, We
841 feast...Ever by his C. retained
850 Binding all the C. in one
923 Head of the C., whose Spirit
1033 One C. above, beneath

Thy CHURCH.

74 O deign to dwell within thy C.
569 Thy C. with strength defend
727 Thus thy C., whate'er her
763 But, Lord, thy C. is praying
770 I love thy C., O God
779 On thy C., O Power divine
815 Still in thy C. do thou appear
815 The angels of thy C. below
818 send forth...into thy C. abroad
843 feast Spread for thy C. by the
857 Let thy c. rise, strong and
885 Infants...Who to thy C. belong
921 O fill thy C. with faith and
928 Jesus, thy C. with longing

CIRCLE, CIRCLES, CIRCLED, CIRCLING.

751 The c. where my passions
952 Through all yon radiant circles
261 Circled round with angel powers
100 goodness...fills the circling hours

CITY.

89 Pray for Jerusalem, The c. of
108 The c. of our God remains
648 We've no abiding c. here
648 But seek a c. out of sight
758 Lo, onward I move to a c. above
764 God's holy c. shone
773 stream Supplies the c. of our God
787 Zion's hill, The c. of our God
889 Church...The c. on the hill
1036 And the bright c.'s cleansing
1044 O when, thou c. of my God
1063 The c. of saints shall appear
1064 Secure in the c. above
1064 And then to the c. receive
1095 That c. of God, the great King

CITIES.

1098 Our c. with prosperity

CLAIM, CLAIMS.

210 And in thy right I c. my heaven
419 Indulge my humble c.
429 Allow my humble c.
446 And ascertains our c. to heaven
522 I c. the blessing now
526 And will not quit my c.
469 He justly claims us for his own

CLARION, CLARIONS.

1092 Who ordainest Thunder thy c.
215 The clarions of the sky Proclaim

CLAY.

9 Made us of c., and formed us
223 Where they laid his breathless c.
475 Mold us thou wilt thy passive c.
612 This trembling house of c.
608 Jesus, support the tottering c.

704 My soul would leave this heavy c.
711 Perishing things of c., Born but
968 And props the house of c.
982 labor done, as sinks the c.
986 borne To its lone bed of c.
995 limbs...Lie moldering in the c.
1000 Spirit, leave thy house of c.
1000 Soul, rebuild thy house of c.
1046 treasure...In a vile house of c.
1056 We know, If this vile house of c.

CLEAN.

307 turn my heart and make it c.
391 make my guilty conscience c.
486 Speak the second time, Be clean
490 Gladly would I now be c.
496 Be c., as thou, my Lord, art clean
503 And bid my heart be c.
514 Thy blood...make us thoroughly c.
531 O when shall I be c.
539 I wait till he shall touch me c.
808 Clothe us...in linen c. and white

CLEANSE.

110 Jesus, c. me with thy blood
267 C. this guilty heart of mine
292 Lord, c. my sins, my soul
307 I know thou canst this moment c.
393 Whose blood can c. each spot
479 To c. from all unrighteousness
490 C. me now from every sin
493 To c. us all, both you and me
533 And c. and keep me clean
531 Shall c. me from all sin
546 Blood Applied to c. my soul
843 C. from all unrighteousness
857 To c. our sin-polluted souls
872 Grace to c., and power to
1091 Jesus' blood can c. from all

CLEANSED, CLEANSING.

71 But chiefest in our c. breast
336 To wash and c. in his
983 C. from all sin, and pure
283 Tell me much of cleansing blood
339 Unseal that c. tide
503 Now thy all-c. blood apply

CLEAVE, CLEAVING.

528 And let my spirit c. to thee
535 That I to sin may never c.
674 And still my soul would c. to
685 Still shall my spirit c. to thee
782 Closer and closer let us c.
1115 Bid them to each other c.
724 on joyful wing Cleaving the sky

CLEFT.

415 Rock of ages, c. for me
748 Concealed in the c. of thy side

CLIME, CLIMES.

36 To thee at last in every c.
908 Redeemer's name Thro' every c.
1059 There surely is some blessed c.
1058 all mankind, we pray, Of every c.
204 Let distant climes thy name
816 To different c. repair
1113 Through burning c. they pass

CLING, CLINGS.
384 Let me live and *c.* to thee
436 I *c.* to God, who yet shall save
628 forgive the heart that *clings*

CLOSE, CLOSED, CLOSER.
549 So shall my walk be *c.* with God
461 heart.. Forever *closed* to all but
558 thy languid eye Was *c.* that we
549 O for a *closer* walk with God
782 *C.* and closer let us cleave

CLOTHE, CLOTHES, CLOTHED.
198 And *c.* us with the Spirit's
641 Will *c.* his people too
749 He *clothes* us with his love
893 thou mayest be *clothed* and fed

CLOUD.
54 Till thy glory Without *c.* in
93 Through *c.* and sunshine
102 O may no earth-born *c.* arise
198 From the low-bending *c.* above
408 Dispel the gloomy *c.* of grief
428 Behold, without a *c.* between
454 Not a *c.* doth arise
620 By many a *c.* o'ercast
690 Prayer makes the darkened *c.*
697 When I appear in yonder *c.*
732 In the land of *c.* and shadow
776 See the *c.* and fire appear
868 Father, come in! but not in the *c.*
936 Saw ye not the *c.* arise
960 The evening *c.*, the morning
1051 No *c.* those regions know
1067 There no *c.* can intervene

CLOUDS.
110 O chase the *c.* of guilt away
135 All, save the *c.* of sin, are
161 The *c.* ye so much dread
182 Where no *c.* thy glory hide
225 All around the *c.* are breaking
229 The *c.* are backward rolled
270 bring us where no *c.* conceal
328 Dark *c.* of gloomy night be
445 The *c.* disperse, the shadows
623 As *c.* before the midday sun
628 Though *c.* and darkness shroud
628 While *c.* and darkness brood
642 Where deepest *c.* have been
672 Who points the *c.* their course
747 O drive these dark *c.* from
826 When darkest *c.* around I
946 Till Jesus in the *c.* appear
966 When thou with *c.* shalt come
978 Though *c.* may darken
1013 Lo! He comes, with *c.* descending
1028 Judge...On *c.* of glory seated
1057 No *c.* or tempests rise
1085 By him the *c.* drop fatness

CLOUDLESS.
721 To the land of *c.* sky
1070 life shadows break in *c.* love

COAST.
1033 And long to see that happy *c.*

COLD.
195 And Christian hearts be *c.*
200 Though love wax *c.*, and faith
277 Kindle a flame...In these *c.* hearts
378 love...In this *c.* heart of mine
575 *C.*, heat, and moist, and dry
1071 Paradise...where love is never *c.*

COLUMN.
163 Returned the fiery *c.*'s glow

COME.
4 Ye blessed children, *c.*
335 invites you, the Spirit says, C.
344 *C.*, said Jesus' sacred voice
348 No, ye will not *c.* to me
355 Spirit...Is whispering, Sinner, *c.*
363 A heavenly whisper, *C.* to me
364 *C.*, all the world! come, sinner
377 *C.* unto me and rest from sin
393 O Lamb of God, I *c.*! I come
402 My Saviour bids me *c.*; Ah! why
427 many dangers...have already *c.*
450 Lo! glad I *c.*; and thou blest
539 And lo, he saith, I quickly *c.*
539 *C.* in, my Lord, come in
603 The midnight peal, Behold I *c.*
609 Lo! I *c.* with joy to do
703 I *c.*, O Lord! I come
845 Till he *c.*: O let the words
850 show the death...Until he *c.*
879 Each the welcome Come awaits
924 *C.*, Lord, the bride on earth
949 To thee we *c.*, O gracious Lord
1016 *C.*, Lord Jesus, quickly come
1029 He will say, *C.* near, ye blessed
1052 *C.*, trusting spirit, to thy God
1070 *C.*, weary souls, for Jesus
1078 I *c.*, thy servant, Lord, replies
1083 *C.*, with all thine angels, come
1083 Even so, Lord, quickly *c.*
1107 *C.* thou again to-day

COMES.
954 He *c.*, he comes to call
1018 He *c.*! he comes! the Judge
1053 solemn thought *C.* to me

COMING.
386 *C.*, as at first I came
494 I wait thy *c.* from above
551 His *c.* like the morn shall
791 We wait thy *c.* from above
928 For thine expected *c.* waits
953 each in the day of his *c.* may
1016 Christ is *c.*! Come, thou

COMFORT.
7 The mighty *c.* feel
21 *C.* those who weep and
88 Conquer sinners, *c.* saints
156 thy rod And staff me *c.* still
273 Is *c.*, life, and fire of love
314 law...We find no *c.* there
442 The sweet *c.* and peace
442 That sweet *c.* was mine
455 *C.*, and confirm, and heal
510 The *c.* of thy strengthening

622 O words with heavenly c.
632 And find our sweetest c.
649 Though every c. be withdrawn
652 Seeking for c. from your
674 The springs of c. seem to fail
701 And c. of my nights
706 Yields c. to the mourners
736 mighty name....C. it brings
757 I am thine; what a c. divine
759 My c. by day, and my song
802 Solid c., settled hope
825 Thou Holy Ghost will c.
892 To c. and to bless
898 Go thou and c. him
926 C., ye...Comfort the people

COMFORTS.
82 let the day, In holy c. pass
118 Who upholds and c. us
165 morning broke, Thy c. rose
178 thy face....It sweetly c. me
641 When c. are declining
660 And earthly c. flee
664 Where endless c. flow
717 When our earthly c. fail
797 Our c. and our cares

COMFORTED.
671 that mourn...shall be c.

COMFORTER.
6 Come, holy C., Thy sacred
48 The saints' eternal C.
179 No harm...with the C. near
236 Lord, send thy promised C.
261 Send the gracious C.
266 C. of minds distressed
275 Now, Lord, the C. bestow
280 A Guide, a C. bequeathed
287 Blest C. divine, Let rays
287 Great C., to us impart
411 Blest C., with peace and
424 Great C., descend and
487 C. of all that mourn
683 Here speaks the C.
729 And the C. forever
855 Gracious C., be with us

COMFORTABLE.
398 With c. words and

COMFORTLESS.
777 C., afflicted, broken
781 Leave us not c.

COMMAND.
9 Wide as the world is thy c.
459 O Thou, who hast at thy c.
471 Abraham...with the harsh c.
588 I see the exceeding broad c.
696 And labor on at thy c.
817 Lord, if at thy c. The
835 Jesus, at whose supreme c.
997 Waiting to...Great God, at thy c.
1033 To his c. we bow
1075 At whose supreme c.
1086 Attends thy dread c.
1113 sea,...At thy c. is still

COMMANDS.
141 And, when thy c. are done
176 How gentle God's c.
394 Father, all thy c. to do
485 Waiting for thine high c.
609 Faithful to my Lord's c.
992 now we wait thine own c.

COMMANDING.
145 Who, by his c. might
850 with the great c. word

COMMEND.
511 My soul to...I faithfully c.
556 My soul...Now therefore I c.
672 To him c. thy cause

COMMERCE.
1101 Reviving c. lifts her

COMMISSION, COMMISSIONED.
815 Their high c. let them prove
820 make your great c. known
810 Ye are *commissioned* from above

COMMIT, COMMITTED.
672 C. thou all thy griefs
595 What I've *committed* to his hands

COMMON.
19 let us praise our c. Lord
28 Our c. Saviour praise
719 Jesus is our c. Lord
789 The c. peace we feel
792 shall praise our c. Lord
805 Glory to our c. Lord

COMMUNE.
117 Lord, we would c. with thee
713 Does she c. with God

COMMUNING.
830 By the c. Spirit poured

COMMUNION.
45 To hold c. with his God
53 And possess, in sweet c.
92 Seeks c. with the skies
266 Symbol of divine c.
748 For closer c. I pine
770 Her sweet c., solemn
787 saints...But one c. make
799 songs...Make their c. sweet
816 enjoy C. with our Lord
1054 sweet to the soul is c.
1054 hinders my joy and c.

COMPANY.
272 lost But for thy c.
737 My c. before is gone
1040 O what a glorious c.
1069 What a countless c.
1073 The whole heavenly c.

COMPANIONS.
89 My old c. say, Come
1011 And left his c. behind
1033 Our old c. in distress

COMPASSION, COMPASSIONS.
21 In c. now descend
336 The love and c. of Jesus
491 Jesus, thou art all c.
730 I see divine c. Beaming
733 Moved by thy divine c.
894 He felt c. rise
943 Save us in thy great c.
172 But thy *compassions*, Lord

COMPEL.
608 C. the wanderer to come

COMPLAIN, COMPLAINS.
157 When we did c., Didst all
531 I cannot of my cross c.
661 My heart no more *complains*

COMPLAINT, COMPLAINTS.
402 And pour out my c.
403 Give ear to my c.
552 Lord, it is my chief c.
625 Where...lodge my deep c.
64 with our praises and *complaints*
88 Bring relief for all c.
98 Our songs and our c.
160 To all my weak c.
421 When wilt thou banish my c.
669 Then I shall end my sad c.
773 Ere we can offer our c.
1054 'Mid scenes...and creature c.

COMPLETE.
193 Good-will and peace now c.
241 And makes my joy c.
475 Thy work is all c.
809 deeds C. in Jesus' name

COMPREHEND.
711 God himself doth c.
959 That I may timely c.

CONCEAL, CONCEALED.
751 Or but c. his face
813 C. the word of God most
407 A life *concealed* in him
600 real life, with Christ c.
1030 Our life in Christ c.

CONCEIVE.
54 Than they could c. before
124 One holy thought c.

CONCERN, CONCERNS.
175 Henceforth my great c.
506 A jealous, just c.; For
833 And full of kind c., looked
968 My sole c., my single
366 O think what vast *concerns*

CONCERT.
27 In the c. bear your parts
75 In c. with the blest
1073 What a c. of praise

CONDEMNED.
181 Whose souls, c. and
391 I am c., but thou art

CONDEMNATION.
422 No c. now I dread, Jesus
448 No c. now I dread, I taste

CONDESCEND, CONDESCENDING.
142 King Of glory c.
68 And yet with *condescending*
400 Thy c. grace To
828 Behold what c. love
991 In c. love Thy

CONDITION.
643 Yet how rich is my c.

CONDUCT.
810 let your heaven-taught c.

CONFESS.
17 Then shall the race of men c.
120 O God, we praise thee, and c.
284 Let all who Christ c.
369 And there my guilt c.
398 To thee, O Jesus, I c.
480 So shall we thankfully c.
493 If we our sins c., Faithful
559 But I now my sins c.
605 And my last hour of life c.
701 Jesus, may all c. thy name
729 I will in my life c. thee
805 We our dying Lord c.
829 O Lord, while we c. the worth
893 And wilt c. their humble
1019 we, who now our Lord c.

CONFESSED.
14 Where Christ, the ruler, is c.
1029 But to those who have c.
1075 By earth and heaven c.

CONFESSING.
116 Sin and want we come c.
403 I wait, C. all my sin
887 Let them all, thy name c.
932 While sinners, now c.

CONFESSION, CONFESSIONS.
1094 And pouring forth c.
60 And our *confessions* pour

CONFIDE.
454 In him I c., his blood
617 Our cheerful hopes c.
745 And still in God c.
772 Who in the Lord c.
1073 Who in Jesus c.

CONFIDING.
641 For while in him c., I
642 And safe in such c.

CONFIDENCE.
437 felt and seen With c.
438 With c. I now draw nigh
505 With humble c. look up
517 I ask in c. the grace
522 In all my c. of hope
541 My c. is all in thee
785 With c. we seek thy face

856 Zion... And her c. alone
979 With holy c. to sing

CONFIDENT.
738 But c. in self-despair

CONFIRM, CONFIRMS.
518 C. the trembling will
661 C. my hope, that where
142 His truth *confirms* and seals

CONFLICT.
91 thy voice shall bid our c. cease
393 With many a c., many
417 By thy c. in the hour
417 By the fearful c. there
567 Forth to the mighty c.
583 Through many a c. here
682 when that last c.'s o'er
836 Gethsemane...thy c. see
1054 here in the valley of c. I stay

CONFLICTS.
110 My c. o'er, my labors
587 And all your c. passed
657 Our c. here shall soon
767 All thy c. End in
798 What c. have we passed

CONFLICTING.
982 Farewell, c. hopes

CONFORM, CONFORMED, CONFORMITY.
498 C. our wills to thine
519 C. me to thy death
46 *Conformed* in all things to
202 Still more and more c.
529 That full divine *conformity*

CONFOUND, CONFOUNDS, CONFOUNDING.
171 Our wondering thoughts c.
525 C. o'erpower me by
721 Nothing shall my heart c.
142 *Confounds* the powers of hell
1091 our sins, our hearts *confounding*

CONFUSION.
276 C., order in thy path
288 It bids c. cease
511 Expires, in sweet c. lost
1054 'Mid scenes of c. and

CONGREGATION, CONGREGATIONS.
51 The great c. his
265 Rest upon this c.
889 name... praised in the great c.
1011 Where *congregations* ne'er break

CONQUER.
21 Songs of praise shall c. death
212 He lives, and I shall c. death
583 Shall c., though they die
631 O may I c. through thy blood
867 To c. foes, and cheer his

940 Win and c., never cease
983 Like thee they c. in the strife

CONQUERED.
272 love...At last it c. me
597 For Christ hath c. there
566 Jesus c. when he fell
847 Thou hast c. in the fight
1061 Leader, Have c. in the fight

CONQUERING.
318 Proclaims thy c. arm
928 The triumphs of thy c. power

CONQUEROR.
229 Rise, glorious C., rise
237 And Jesus is the C.'s name
240 Great C., never more to die
243 Our C. and King, Thy
251 Jesus, the C., reigns
261 C. over death and sin
491 I yield...And own thee c.
515 C. through him, I soon
519 C. of hell, and earth
583 withstand its ancient C.
587 Who in... Is more than c.
701 Thou C. renowned
704 Would bear me c. through
908 Ride forth, victorious C.
921 Shall o'er the world a c.

CONQUERORS.
437 And, c. of the world, we
589 And take the c. home
879 C. over death and sin
985 Who makes us c.
1066 More than c. at last

CONQUEST, CONQUESTS.
1015 Ascribe their c. to the
816 To further *conquests* go

CONSCIENCE.
107 May we, O Lord, with c.
263 King within my c. reign
291 gives my laboring c. peace
310 Let not c. make you
372 And bid my guilty c.
423 My c. felt and owned
459 And let my sprinkled c.
511 The tender c. give
511 O God, my c. make
740 He sends the laboring c.
826 My c. tells of sin, yet
930 But to each c. be applied.

CONSECRATE.
101 To thee I c. my days
158 I c. my lengthened days
460 And c. to thee my all
170 C. to thee alone
472 I c. to thee; Me to H line
173 rest me of days, I c. to theo

CONSECRATED.
457 Divide this c. soul
616 And may this c. hour
665 Is this the c. dower

666 The c. cross I'll bear
826 Among thy c. hosts
946 And all my c. powers

CONSOLATION, CONSOLATIONS.
59 Fill each breast with c.
342 And, with news of c.
671 The heavenly c. fell
688 May I thy c. share
534 The *consolations* of thy word

CONSTANT, CONSTANCY.
430 On thee alone my c. mind
497 O that to thee my c. mind
524 Thy c. mind in us be shown
615 Father's love, So c. and so
730 C. still in faith abiding
317 promises declare Thy *constancy*

CONSTRAIN, CONSTRAINS.
221 O let thy love my heart c.
364 O let his love your hearts c.
400 When shall thy love c.
455 Let thy love my heart c.
814 The love of Christ doth me c.
811 of Christ their hearts *constrains*

CONSUME.
228 Nor change can e'er c.
269 C. our sins, and calm
488 Love shall all my sins c.
518 might fall...And all my sins c.

CONTEMPLATION.
443 Borne on c.'s wing
641 In holy c., We
1061 Beneath thy c.

CONTEND, CONTENDING.
310 Ah, how shall guilty man C.
623 who shall c. with God
737 And murmur to c. so long
1046 Then let us lawfully c.
600 *Contending* for your native place
648 C. for our native heaven

CONTENT, CONTENTED, CONTENTMENT.
561 The sacred joy...sweet c.
622 C., whatever lot I see
675 C. to fill a little space
696 My Lord, how full of sweet c.
739 *Contented* now, upon my thigh
664 Whence...contentment springs

CONTEST.
934 Proclaim the c. ended

CONTRITE.
60 Our c. spirits pitying see
281 Our c. hearts inspire
404 A humble, c. heart
412 O may my broken, c. heart
521 O for a lowly, c. heart
551 With c. hearts return
794 And make the c. heart
837 we, with thankful, c. hearts
838 Where every humble, c. heart

862 Cast not our c. prayer
870 Wherever sighs a c. heart
1095 With c. hearts, to thee

CONTRITION.
553 mercy hears C.'s humble
1091 Lo, with deep c. turning

CONTROL, CONTROLLED.
106 direct. c., suggest this day
209 If e'er I lose its strong c.
459 Our wishes, our desires c.
463 Prince of Peace, c. my will
500 O Thou who all things canst c.
586 C. my every thought
633 fears subside at his c.
636 All yield at thy c.
761 His Spirit shall, with sweet c.
434 I would not be *controlled*
434 I love to be c., I love

CONVERSE, CONVERSING.
199 The Lord holds c. high
291 Subject of all my c. be
1048 Henceforth our c. be
712 With thee *conversing*, we forget

CONVERT, CONVERTS, CONVERTING.
818 C. and send forth more
966 O God, my inmost soul c.
298 *Converts* the sorrows of the mind
817 And let the soul-*converting*

CONVICTION.
543 The keen c. dart

CORD, CORDS.
785 A band of love, a threefold c.
49 draw them with the *cords* of love

CORDIAL.
324 A c. for our fears

CORN.
542 A land of c. and wine
575 And the full c. at length
1082 To raise the c., and cheer
1083 Then the full c. shall appear

CORNERS.
402 Into its darkest c. shine

CORNER-STONE.
856 Christ, the Head and C.-s.
857 Where we lay this c.-s.
857 Bless, with thee, this c.-s.
857 Jesus Christ its C.-s.
859 Built on the precious C.-s.
863 His fiat laid the c.-s.
1060 And the c.-s. is Christ

CORRUPTS, CORRUPTION.
305 C. his race, and taints
239 My fullness of *corruption* show

COTTAGES.
1106 And c., possessing

COUCH.
116 And our c. becomes our tomb
1099 In crowded street, by restless c.

COUNSEL, COUNSELS.
173 Still let them c. take
513 The c. of his grace in me
673 His c. shall appear
814 Fulfill thy sovereign c.
966 Thine utmost c. to fulfill
295 The *counsels* of redeeming grace
922 Our c. aid; to each impart

COUNSELOR.
184 The Wonderful, the C.
483 my Guide, My C. thou

COUNTENANCE.
428 Lift up thy c. serene

COUNTRY.
648 Swift to our heavenly c.
696 My c. is in every clime
758 A c. I've found where
933 Our c.'s vo'ce is pleading
1030 A c. far from mortal
1058, 1059, 1060, 1061, O sweet and blessed c., The home of
1069 For thee, O dear, dear c.
1074 No longing we find for the c.
1074 A c. of joy without any
1089 My c., 'tis of thee
1089 My native c., thee
1090 Do thou our c. save
1094 Beset our c. round
1097 That did their c. save
1098 Our c. we commend

COURAGE.
161 Ye fearful saints, fresh c.
567 Your c. rise with danger
583 C.! your Captain cries
584 Satan's...To beat thy c. down
593 Increase my c., Lord
596 And we lose c. then
639 My soul with c. wait
797 hope revives Our c. by the
922 hopes revive; our c. raise
1097 'Twas not their c., nor

COURSE, COURSES.
92 When the Christian's c. is run
145 All the day his c. to run
299 Our onward c. must be
935 Peace and truth its c. portends
1068 Rivers... Nor stay in all their c.
1101 And marks their c. and
812 Through all the *courses* of the

COURT, COURTS.
98 I will frequent thy holy c.
1078 Confined to neither c. nor cell
25 Meet.. In his courts on holy days
63 When in his earthly c. we
79 Millions within thy c. have
83 Then to thy c. when I
87 Within thy c. we bend
680 Approach his c., besiege

657 Shall fill the heavenly c.
660 Grant me within thy c.
868 Which filled the bright c.
869 Within these c. to bide
1044 when.. Shall I thy c. ascend
1051 Prepared...For thy bright c. on

COVENANT.
23 Who the c. sealed with
181 time shall never His c.
311 he will never break his c.
403 Jehovah's c. is sure
531 'Stablish with me the c.
771 Their c. again renew
853 Eternal c. of my grace
857 O c. of life and peace
945 In a perpetual c. join
945 The c. we this moment make
945 To each the c. blood apply

COVET.
489 We will c. nothing less
748 There only I c. to rest

CRADLE.
186 Cold on his c. the dew
1008 Because thy c.-care

CRAFT.
166 His c. and power are great

CREATE.
9 He can c., and he destroy
145 God, Who by wisdom did c.
240 Thou didst c. the stars of
482 Thy creature, Lord, again c.
505 On thee, almighty to c.

CREATED.
125 Ere...C. light had shone
664 aloof From all c. things
1028 The end of things c.

CREATION.
2 The whole c. join in one
57 Heaven and earth, and all c.
72 On thee, at the c., The light
91 Who, c.'s Lord and Spring
107 And wake c. with its ray
265 Author of the new c.
453 My soul's new c., a life
910 nations ...Are by c. thine
916 The new c. shall ascribe
938 All c.'s harmonies; See
1062 O day, for which c. And

CREATOR.
8 Let the C.'s praise arise
131 Attempt thy great C.'s praise
198 Both his C.'s power display
211 Him, their true C., all his
257 C. of the rolling spheres

CREATURE.
247 Loved, adored, by every c.
411 Thy new-made c. crown
456 adieu, With all of c. good
172 In Christ a c. new

630 No c. is by him forgot
662 The fondness of a c.'s love
952 The c. is their sole delight
1078 From every c.-love

CREATURES.
146 name...On all thy c. writ
271 All c. live and move
516 C. no more divide my
859 Endue the c. with thy grace

CRESCENT.
939 Wave it till the c. set

CRIME, CRIMES.
111 O may no gloomy c. Pollute
1022 The c., the wrath, the wandering
214 Was it for *crimes* that I have
302 wash...From c. of deepest dye
367 Your basest c. he bore
381 And by reiterated c.
391 My c. are great, but don't

CRIMSON.
754 To wash my c. stains
830 There gushed a c. flood
974 How beautiful...c. light is shed

CROOKED.
371 Why will you in the c. ways
926 C. be straight, and rugged

CROSS.
118 By whose c. and death we are
148 To the c. of deepest woe
178 It hallows every c.
204 In the c. of Christ I glory
204 Never shall the c. forsake me
204 From the c. the radiance
204 By the c. are sanctified
205 Sin, which laid the c. on thee
208 Of him who died upon the c.
208 The c.! it takes our guilt away
211 When I survey the wondrous c.
213 And gaze upon thy holy c.
214 While his dear c. appears
219 The c. is reared on high
219 Hail, holy c.! from thee we
240 In thy dear c. a grace is
241 For me he bore the shameful c.
256 To them the c., with all its shame
259 Comfortless upon the c.
260 Ours the c., the grave, the skies
276 The triumphs of the c. record
314 High lifted on the c.
338 From the c. uplifted high
400 Here at that c., where flows
464 Die with Jesus on the c.
468 Before the c. of him who died
495 The c. all stained with
505 sustain, The consecrated c.
563 With the c. of Jesus going
582 Let all to Jesus' c. draw nigh
590 Lord, as to thy dear c. we flee
590 Our daily c. to bear
601 Take up thy c., nor heed
632 Each needful c. thou shalt
638 When we have borne the c.

640 The c. that Jesus carried
643 Jesus, I my c. have taken
664 Courage, my soul, thy bitter c.
666 Must Jesus bear the c. alone
666 No, there's a c. for every one
666 And there's a c. for me
670 The shameful c. beneath
695 Thy poverty and shameful c.
715 Long as the c. we bear
723 By the c., the nail, the thorn
724 E'en though it be a c.
720 Which before the c. I spend
730 While upon the c. I gaze
742 For thee the c. I'll bear
784 help...Each other's c. to bear
786 And joyfully sustain the c.
798 Let us take up the c., Till
813 The c., endured, my Lord, by thee
814 No c. I shun, I fear no shame
836 When to the c. I turn mine
843 Still at the c., as at the feast
846 The c. on which he bows his head
914 Thine was the c., with all
921 The C.! the C.! the battle-call
939 High the bleeding c. display
939 Preach the c. of Christ to all
1016 story Of thy bitter c. and pain
1022 And by the c., and by the grave
1032 I now the c. sustain
1040 They bore the c., despised the
1047 that cometh By the holy c.
1053 Nearer leaving the c.
1066 These are they that bore the c.

His CROSS.
220 let us sit beneath *his* c.
315 They tell the triumphs of *his* c.
370 Come to *his* c., and, grateful
423 eyes on me, As near *his* c. I stood
566 swell the The triumphs of *his* c.
595 Maintain...The glory of *his* c.
730 Low before *his* c. I lie
933 Till all *his* c. beholding
1028 Beneath *his* c. I view the

Thy CROSS.
93 Hold thou *thy* c. before my
205 Never further than *Thy* c.
205 Through *thy* c. made pure and
209 Lord, on *thy* c. I fix mine eye
221 *Thy* c. and passion on the tree
222 O show *thy* c. to me
325 Beneath *thy* c. I fall
374 Open their eyes *thy* c. to see
415 Simply to *thy* c. I cling
417 By *thy* c. and dying cries
483 And hang upon *thy* c.
450 To *thy* c. my spirit bind
492 Draw us by *thy* c. to thee
503 While at *thy* c. I lie
524 O let us by *thy* c. abide
601 Take up *thy* c., the Saviour said
694 *Thy* c., the staff whereon I lean

CROWN.
14 Until the glorious c. be won
157 Thy mercies c. our fleeting
253 The kingly c. is on his brow

422 And claim the c. through
461 Decked with a never-fading c.
476 My joy, my treasure, and my c.
478 Thee will I love, my joy, my c.
485 At thy feet her golden c.
487 Thine the cross, and thine the c.
493 Ye soon the c. shall wear
567 overcometh, A c. of life
568 And wear...The c. of victory
581 Till thou obtain the c.
543 See there the starry c.
584 Against thy heavenly c.
594 And an immortal c.
599 Through mercy, an immortal c.
601 hope to wear the glorious c.
603 Is near,—a kingdom and a c.
638 Bright shall the c. of glory be
640 The c. that Jesus weareth
657 The cross, shall wear the c.
666 For there's a c. for me
732 Thou the c. of life wilt give
786 Till we receive the c.
790 And each a starry c. receive
798 Till we the c. obtain
801 Till all receive the starry c.
914 Be thine the c. of glory now
971 world...For an immortal c.
1004 Reaches out the c. of love
1010 The c. of life he weareth
1032 In hope of that immortal c.
1040 And win, like them, a c. of
1053 Nearer gaining the c.
1059 But then shall wear the c.

Thy CROWN.
12 wear our praises as *thy c.*
229 triumphant go And take *thy c.*
236 To pass unto *thy c.*
1001 Enter and receive *thy c.*

CROWN, (Verb.)
69 And c. that grace with glory too
162 C. him, ye nations, in your song
248 And c. him Lord of all
249 C. him, c. him; Crowns
249 C. the Saviour, angels, crown
249 C. the Saviour King of kings
257 C. him with many crowns
865 And with thy favor c. This
896 To c. his head, or grace his
920 And c. the saviour, Lord of all

CROWNS.
136 Casting down their golden c.
205 Cast our c. before thy feet
247 There to cast our c. before him
257 Crown him with many c.
315 cast their c.,—Those crowns
491 Till we cast our c. before thee
563 C. and thrones may perish
595 C. of glory you shall gain
757 Sing and cast their c. before
879 Gives the c. his followers win
917 With c. of joy upon our
919 And c. of life to gain
983 They cast their c. before
1046 And c. upon our head
1069 C. of glory on their head

CROWNED.
58 See! the angelic hosts have c. him
63 Behold your Lord, your Master, c.
256 c. with thorns...with glory now
816 And c. with endless joy
991 And thou art c. at last
1018 See the almighty Jesus c.
1022 O Son of God, in glory c.
1053 Like theirs with glory c.

CRUCIFY.
317 C. your Lord again
477 My vile affections c.

CRUCIFIED.
134 The Man of love, the C.
137 O Jesus, Lamb once c.
229, 461 My Lord, my Love, is c.
230 Is c. for me and you
332 For all my Lord was c.
333 For guilty sinners c.
337 Turn to Jesus c.; Fly
339 C. the eternal Son
374 have trod, And c. afresh
456 Only Jesus...And Jesus c.
468 Let every sin be c., Let
481 With Christ may I be c.
600 Your creature-love is c.
637 in thy hand, Jesus, the c.
722 Nothing know...Jesus, and him c.
782 Nothing desire...But Jesus c.
792 Our Jesus, and him c.
818 Show thyself the C.
1009 The C. thy praise

CRUSHED.
671 Until the hopes by sorrow c.

CRY.
154 Thou hear'st thy children's c.
165 Thus to the Lord I raised my c.
229 A bitter and heart-rending c.
346 Knock—He knows the sinner's c.
403 depths...To thee, O Lord, I c.
649 And c. aloud, and give to God
681 abyss of trouble, I mournfully c.
683 Early to thee my soul shall c.
723 Listen to our humble c.
818 hear Thy needy servants' cry
952 Now let us hear the mighty c.
1077 Hail, Father...They ever c.
1080 To thee aloud we c.
1091 And humbly, with united c.
1104 Attend his people's humble c.
1108 O hear us when we c. to thee

CRIES.
254 Poured out strong c. and tears
374 Open...Their ears, to hear thy c.
702 To thee our inmost spirit c.
811 With c., entreaties, tears, to save
865 attend our interceding c.
145 And poured out c. and tears

CRYSTAL.
153 Shine to his praise, ye c.
1053 Nearer the c. sea
1063 As c. her buildings are clear

CUMBERED.
953 We c. long the ground

CUP.
156 And my c. overflows
173 My Father's hand prepares the c.
179 With blessings...my c. runneth
623 Thankful I take the c. from
628 To drink the bitter c. I go
655 Take thou my c., and it
675 In my c. of blessing be
833 He took into his hands the c.
835 The c. of blessing, blest by thee
836 Thy testamental c. I take
891 To sweeten many a c. of woe
898 neighbor? He who drinks the c.
901 Bondage and death the c.
1005 bowed to take The death-c. for

CURB.
107 C. thou for us the unruly tongue
413 And c. my headstrong will

CURE.
306 Where shall sinner find a c.
397 gracious Lord, my sickness c.
415 Be of sin the double c.
538 Hath wrought a perfect c.
683 no sorrow that Heaven cannot c.

CURRENTS.
631 Howe'er life's various c. flow

CURSE.
183 Far as the c. is found
235 Whose c. and shame he bore

D.

DAMNED.
820 He shall be d. who wont
996 Shall I be with the d. cast out

DANCE, DANCES.
952 every heart shall d. for joy
332 And *dances* his glad heart for joy

DANGER.
100 From every d., every snare
543 And show the d. near
601 And calmly every d. brave
662 We should suspect some d.
667 That when in it, knows no fear
726 He, to rescue me from d.
1092 in mercy, O save us from d.

DANGERS.
141 troubles assail, and d. affright
160 Through hidden d., toils, and
403 And d. threaten loud
427 Through many d., toils, and
553 Through dangers, fears, and
634 Where thickest d. be
965 D. stand thick through
1094 When d., like a stormy
1113 In midst of d., fears

DANGEROUS.
888 Keep them in all life's d.
965 To walk this d. road

DARK.
94 For d. and light are both
111 How d. and sad before
140 And d. is his path on the
240 The world grew d. as shades
284 On our d. souls to shine
375 No light! so late! and d.
392 D., till in me thine image
395 O d.! dark! dark! I still
611 How d. this world would be
618 When the d. hour came on
627 For every d. and troubled night
655 Thy way...However d. it be
670 This d. and dreadful way
731 O'er our pathway, d. and drear
741 D. is the wilderness. Earth
950 A d. and cloudy day
1015 Life is d., and earth is dreary
1070 And through the d., its echoes
1112 Which d. to human eyes appear

DARKEST.
150 E'en the hour that d. seemeth
402 Into its d. corners shine
843 That d. and that brightest
902 illume The d. hours of life
913 And in earth's d. place

DARKNESS.
93 The d. deepens—Lord with me
107 And in their train the d.
110 And turn my d. into day
116 D. cannot hide from thee
136 holy! though the d. hide thee
152 he cast The d. of the sky
181 Their d. turn to light
206 D. rushes o'er my sight
227 He burst from the fetters of d.
231 Tread the path of d.
234 A solemn d. veils the
267 Turn my d. into day
271 D. and doubt dispel
276 Be d., at thy coming, light
386 And leave thee in d. to
403 D. surrounds me, but I
408 And make our d. bright
421 When d. seems to veil
451 The people that in d. lay
507 In whom no d. is
507 Thy d. passed away
564 Forward through the d.
611 As d. shows us worlds
633 When we in d. walk
639 In d. and temptation
644 from out the gathered d.
702 Dispel the d. of our night
724 D. be over me. My
732 Light to those who sit in d.
762 bid d. turn to day
912 Joy to the lands that in d.
925 The d. of o'erspreading
931 That man may sit in d.
932 The d. disappears
940 O'er the gloomy hills of d.

940 Kingdoms wide that sit in d.
943 In our deepest d. rise
947 Who turns our d. into light
981 Christ, our Lord, from d. sprang
997 Dispel the d. that surrounds
1031 Nor's all one moment's d. mix
1017 How the powers of d. Rage

DART, DARTS.
380 Justly might thy vengeful d.
588 Repelled his every fiery d.
457 The pointless darts of death
646 When temptation's d. assail
659 And fiery d. be hurled
956 As the lightning... D., and leaves

DAVID.
81 Like D.'s harp of solemn sound
181 Great D.'s greater Son
192 To you, in D.'s town...of David's
274 And breathed in D.'s hallowed
883 Hosanna To D.'s royal Son
1023 D.'s harp, and sibyl's page
1061 There is the throne of D.

DAWN.
70 With morning's earliest d. arise
78 D. on these realms of woe and sin
83 The d. of this returning day
87 D. on thy servan's' sight
263 D. upon this soul of mine
284 We know no d. but thine
929 Till faith shall d., and
935 For the morning seems to d.
998 lurid mornings that d. on us here
1015 Comes the reddening d. of day
1070 The day must d., and

DAY.
74 With joy we hail the sacred d.
75 On this glad d. a brighter
76 This is the d. the Lord hath made
78 On this thy d., in this thy house
85 Welcome, sweet d. of rest
909 dawns...The Lord's appointed d.
913 Pouring d. upon our eyes
948 Ye bring eternal d.
1009 To pure and perfect d.
1026 Lo, the d., the day of life
1057 Infinite d. excludes the night

DAYS.
113 And when our d. are past
871 Saviour We behold In latter d.
878 Thou who art, from endless d.
965 Shorter still,...As d. and

DAYLIGHT.
92 O'er the earth as d. fades
201 Then, in clear d., shall
231 Bring again our d.; day
595 Work, for d. flies
1061 The d. is serene

DAYSPRING.
86 O D., rise upon our night
195 The D. from on high
416 D. from on high, be near

DAZZLED, DAZZLING.
200 When d. with excess of light
130 thou form'st thy dazzling robe
1013 Still his d. body bears
1024 With all thy Father's d. train

DEAD.
1 New life the d. receive
23 Now nmy He who from the d.
231 Lo, the d. is living, God for
232 in Christ are no more d.
304 And dwelt among the d.
336 The d., small and great, in the
317 D., already dead within
350 The d.'s alive! the lost is found
373 Beneath us lie the countless d.
443 Sink with Christ among the d.
600 D. to the world and sin ye
657 It brings to life the d.
668 him who raised thee from the d.
822 And life into the d.
814 We too with him are d.
828 May the d. be laid to rest
870 In many a heart now d. in sin
895 To raise the d. to life
899 Life from the d.! For those
909 He calls thee from the d.
958 Of all the pious d. May
996 The dreary regions of the d.
1001 Happy are the faithful d.
1004 Mortals cry, A man is d.
1028 graves restore The d. which
1029 At his call the d. awaken

DEAF.
1 Hear him, ye d.; his praise

DEATH.
7 The d. of sin remove
90 There revealing d. dethroned
116 Should swift d. this night
141 life sinks apace, and d. is in view
160 And after d., in distant worlds
187 D.-struck, I ceased the tide to
202 And d., that sets the prisoner
211 Boast, Save in the d. of Christ
218 life to us was d. to thee
221 Thy precious d. and life I pray
227 The being he gave us d. cannot
234 And led the monster D. in chains
247 When we pass o'er d.'s dark
260 D. in vain forbids his rise
347 Pant ye after second d.
358 Around the second d.
365 D., at the farthest, can't be far
372 The d. that never dies
376 D. comes down with reckless
423 Thus, while his d. my sin
456 He tasted d. for me
468 And d. the gate of heaven
501 Whenever d. shall come
544 D., only death, can cut the knot
552 Free and faithful, s rong as d.
601 Nor think t ll d. to lay it down
622 E'en d.'s cold wave I will not
623 O D.! where is thy st ng
634 I'll dare d.'s threatening tide
640 That d. alone can cure

DEA 45 DEE

645 By thy dreadful *d.*, I pray
666 cross I'll bear, Till *d.* shall
721 D.'s dark stream shall never
755 I know no *d.*, O Jesus, Because
837 O wondrous *d.!* O precious
846 And still we by his *d.* are
847 Now no more can *d.* appall
850 And show the *d.* of our dear Lord
967 If *d.* my friend and me
968 What after *d.* for me remains
969 O *D.*, where is thy sting
971 Is not e'en *d.* a gain to those
985 To triumph o'er approaching *D.*
989 And *D.* yields up his ancient
990 O for the *d.* of those Who
993 It is not *d.* to die
993 It is not *d.* to close The eye
993 It is not *d.* to bear The wrench
993 It is not *d.* to fling Aside this
1010 Ah! *d.* but safely lands him
1020 And *d.* forever fly
1035 And *d.* itself shall die
1043 By *d.* and hell pursued in
1043 And pass through *d.* triumphant
1049 There is no *d.* in heaven
1095 Bestrews the land with *d.*
1113 And *d.*, when death shall be

From DEATH.

106 Lord, when I *from d.* shall wake
239 Save me *from d.*, from hell
271 *From d.* to life our spirits raise

In DEATH.

316 Refresh my soul *in d.*
670 eye, Ere yet it closed *in d.*
988 They that have seen thy look *in d.*

Of DEATH.

108 when the night *of d.* shall come
113 The night *of d.* draws near
179 the valley and shadow *of d.*
358 Nor all *of d.* to die
544 Thy love...burst the shades *of d.*
619 When, in the solemn hour *of d.*
961 Shrinking from...cold hand *of d.*
965 unconcerned...the brink *of d.*
1088 'Mid scenes *of d.* and sin

Thy DEATH.

385 I shall feel *thy d.* applied
526 Surely *thy d.* shall raise me up
755 *Thy d.* it is which frees us

To DEATH.

339 Still *to d.* pursue our God
434 He found me nigh *to d.*
900 When, doomed *to d.*, the apostle

When DEATH.

646 In the hour *when d.* draws
692 *When d.* o'er nature shall
705 *When d.* shall close mine
714 *When d.* these mortal eyes
782 *When d.* shall all be done

DEATHS.

169 Through varied *d.* my soul

DEATHLESS.

225 Join, O man, the *d.* voices
307 Devote its *d.* powers to thee
644 Holy, *d.* stars shall rise
692 Long as a *d.* soul can live
1004 *D.* spirit, now arise

DEBT, DEBTOR.

212 How pay the mighty *d.* I owe
214 ne'er repay The *d.* of love I owe
322 The *d.* that sinners owed, Upon
559 From my *d.* of sin set clear
612 his blood My *d.* of suffering paid
893 How pay the mighty *d.*
726 O to grace how great a *debtor*

DECAY, DECAYS.

93 Change and *d.* in all around
134 His might *d.*, his love forsake
287 rejoice, Though earthly joys *d.*
478 though my flesh and heart *d.*
658 Till sinking slow, with calm *d.*
697 I'll sing...When all things else *d.*
868 soon shall our frailer erection *d.*
902 wealth...Which cannot know *d.*
948 Ye mortal powers *d.*
973 And all our powers *d.*
995 This well-wrought frame *d.*
1056 tabernacle...In ruinous *d.*
1088 leaves...Are preaching of *d.*
150 Man *decays*, and ages move

DECEASED.

1001 Of a saint in Christ *d.*
1011 Weep not for a brother *d.*

DECEITFUL, DECEITFULNESS.

877 rising race From the *d.* paths
559 Sin's *deceitfulness* hath spread

DECEIVE.

204 Hopes *d.*, and fears annoy
439 I would not, Lord, my soul *d.*
643 Human hearts and looks *d.* me

DECEMBER.

747 *D.'s* as pleasant as May

DECLINE.

468 No more from thee *d.*
1088 Say I must, too, *d.*

DECREE, DECREES.

173 To frustrate his *d.*
619 in death, I wait thy just *d.*
921 Fulfill the Father's high *d.*
968 comply With nature's stern *d.*
1025 Stand the omnipotent *d.*
1080 We wait on thy *d.*
126 Whate'er thy will *decrees* is done
142 His great *d.* and sovereign will

DEDICATE.

685 chief desire...To *d.* myself to

DEED, DEEDS.

212 I, I alone have done the *d.*
13 Who can his mighty *deeds*

809 O let our d. begin and end
891 sweeten... By d. of holy love
919 From evil d. that stain the past

DEEP, DEEPS.
443 Who to the d. shall stoop
506 Out of the d. on thee to call
651 passing through the watery d.
676 D. unto deep may call, but I
773 Down to the d., and buried there
939 isle In the bosom of the d.
1108 Who walkedst on the foaming d.
1110 We ride on the d. without fear
1111 While o'er the d. thy servants
3 He formed the *deeps* unknown
197 In vain we search the lowest d.

DEFEND.
100 My heedless steps d.
158 A hand almighty to d.
240 Us by thy mighty power d.
255 To lead, console, d.
595 Or to d. his cause
767 God thy Saviour will d. thee
1091 Hear us, spare us, and d.
1104 D. them in the needful hour

DEFENSE.
162 He's your d., your joy, your
365 Death enters, and there's no d.
453 my Lord is now my d.
617 O let thy power be our d.
651 Still be thy arms my sure d.
715 He is Israel's sure d.
764 Thy God is thy d.
964 And our d. is sure
1113 How sure is their d.

DEFENSELESS.
656 Cover my d. head

DEFILED.
305 But we're d. in every part

DEITY.
42 Incarnate D., Let all the
146 Here the whole D. is known
657 That great mysterious D.

DELAY.
336 D. not, delay not, O sinner
361 Now, sinners, come without d.
361 Then why should you d.
401 And can I yet d.
402 Ah! why do I d.? He calls
440 Holy Ghost, no more d.
660 Seek ye my face! Without d.
758 My soul, don't d.; he calls
1035 Shall this bright hour d.

DELIGHT.
128 With whom dost thou d. to
128 All thy d. in us fulfill
175 Lord, I d. in thee, And on
299 pages be Our ever dear d.
325 And spreads d. around
318 If your death were his d.
418 Heaven prepares for their d.

429 Not all notes... Could so d. my
442 height Of that holy d.
605 And call it my supreme d.
616 My heart shall find d. in praise
662 danger... Where we possess d.
759 whose presence my soul takes d.
791 D. in what thyself hast given
834 Not paradise... Could such d.
842 O What d. is this, Which
1031 view With infinite d.
1037 There is a land of pure d.
1038 And rivers of d.
1038 Filled with d. my raptured
1066 God doth in his saints d.

DELIGHTS, DELIGHTFUL.
849 Till, earth's d. resigning
959 All that d. our eyes
713 Well, the *delightful* day will come
871 churches... His most d. seat

DELIVER, DELIVERED, DELIVERING.
331 Born thy people to d.
491 Come, almighty to d.
930 They call us to d. Their
552 I *delivered* thee when bound
254 We shall obtain *delivering* grace

DELIVERANCE.
611 angel... D. shall arise
664 D. soon will come
767 Great d. Zion's King
871 grace, And seek d. there
895 D. to the captive bring
1091 Now for their d. rise
1097 To us d. bring
1104 And send d. from on high

DELIVERER.
118 Strong D. In our need
171 Strong D., Be thou still my
231 high your great D. reigns
544 My great D. thou! Haste
650 And shouted our D.'s name
1032 Till my D. come, And wipe
1099 Be thou our great D. still

DELUDED.
890 And the d. throng

DENY.
103 Room to d. ourselves, a road
318 Why will ye your Lord d.
318 Me, who life to none d.
601 D. thyself, the world forsake
617 The lil we ask, d.

DENIED, DENIES, DENIEST.
111 what is fitting shall ne'er be d.
501 Grant... Whatever be d.
675 To none that ask d.
610 Thy sovereign will *denies*
615 Good... Nor less when he d.
1051 Whate'er thou *deniest*, O give

DEPART.
6 And ne'er from us d.
28 Nor force him to d.

61 narrow way We never may *d.*
167 O Christian soul, in peace *d.*
264 Never will he thence *d.*
283 Come to me, but ne'er *d.*
447 Nor ever from thy Lord *d.*
456 breast Shall never more *d.*
466 Nor from his cause will we *d.*
738 Nor wilt thou with the night *d.*
748 abide, And never a moment *d.*
906 Or else—*d.* to hell
1020 Pronounce the word, *D.*

DEPEND, DEPENDS.
21 Lord, on thee our souls *d.*
175 And on thy care *d.*
430 On thee will I *d.*
456 my happiness, On Jesus to *d.*
460 And on that grace I dare *d.*
686 On whom for all things I *d.*
689 *D.* on him; thou canst not fall
722 Who on thee alone *d.*
742 my prayer, On thee *d.*
1115 All who on thy love *d.*
124 My soul on thee *depends*

DEPENDENCE.
322 Our firm *d.* place

DEPTH, DEPTHS.
207 And in the *d.* be praise
813 From that dark *d.* of woes
25 Praise him from the *depths*
325 How rich the *d.* of love divine
403 Out of the *d.* of woe. To thee
422 To sound the *d.* of love divine
540 Desire in vain its *d.* to see
552 Deeper than the *d.* beneath
665 Out of the *d.* to thee I cry
804 All the *d.* of love express

DESCEND, DESCENDS.
18 And here in saving power *d.*
278 *D.* with all thy gracious power
282 Spirit now *d.* and fill the place
378 O might he now *d.*, and rest
589 Till Christ the Lord *d.* from high
650 Our Jesus shall from heaven *d.*
678 O *d.* on me, and bring thy
124 gift From thee alone *descends*

DESCENDED, DESCENDING.
152 The Lord *d.* from above
221 Jesus *d.* from above
934 Him...slain, Again to earth *d.*
189 Suddenly the Lord, *descending*
867 And thou, *d.*, fill the place

DESERT.
255 To make the *d.* bloom and sing
564 Forward through the *d.*
613 release From this dark *d.*, and
759 Or cry in the *d.* for bread
887 Through life's *d.* dark and dreary
912 Lo, in the *d.* rich flowers are
918 Speak, and the *d.* shall rejoice
927 See where o'er *d.* wastes they
1036 Our *d.* path we tread
1036 Soon, when the *d.* shall be crossed
1105 Their footsteps in this *d.* land

DESERTS.
434 O'er *d.* waste and wild
821 And *d.* learn the joy
1085 The *d.* bloom and spring

DESERT, DESERTS, (verb.)
679 I will not *d.* to his foes; That
596 Or be *deserts* us in the hour The

DESIGN, DESIGNS.
106 All I *d.*, or do, or say
146 But when we view thy strange *d.*
216 explain Thy wonderful *d.*
475 My every weak, though good *d.*
801 Enter into thy wise *d.*
877 To aid this blest *d.*
1078 Already saved from low *d.*
130 And all thy vast *designs* are one
142 And all their dark *d.*
161 He treasures up his bright *d.*

DESIRE.
64 Come, thou *D.* of all thy saints
189 Seek the great *D.* of nations
239 Jesus, my heart's *d.* obtain
334 Dear *D.* of every nation
401 My one *d.* be this, Thy only
457 Nothing on earth do I *d.*
469 Fulfill my heart's *d.*
477 Nothing *d.* or seek, but thee
481 Be thou alone my one *d.*
489 Be thou all my heart's *d.*
497 And mark the risings of *d.*
506 A pure *d.* that all may learn
520 My soul breaks out in strong *d.*
523 And tell my infinite *d.*
535 Thou seest my heart's *d.*
545 That sacred, infinite *d.*
562 Jesus, confirm my heart's *d.*
694 Ah, then I have my heart's *d.*
809 Our souls with this intense *d.*
991 Of all thy heart's *d.* Triumphantly
1014 Lo! 'tis he! our heart's *d.*

DESIRES.
15 With warm *d.* to see my God
44 To teach our faint *d.* to rise
45 send to Heaven his warm *d.*
370 Those new *d.* which in thee burn
411 From low *d.* set free
484 My faint *d.* receive

DESOLATE.
551 nor will leave The *d.* to mourn
553 How *d.* my way
639 When faint and *d.*
850 Let not our hearts be *d.*
897 We...Would seek the *d.*

DESPAIR, DESPAIRING.
33 Hath saved us from *d.*
308 To save me from *d.*
314 Speaks nothing but *d.*
349 In that lone land of deep *d.*
371 Shut up in black *d.*
412 For never shall my soul *d.*
621 O let my heart no more *d.*
635 Thou wilt not leave me to *d.*

DES 48 DIE

775 Shake off the bands of sad d.
939 Chase away his dark d.
1030 O wretched state of deep d.
1096 But let us not d.
1111 Aroused by the shriek of d.
302 Ho! ye *despairing* sinners, come

DESPERATE.

572 His d. state explain
830 To meet our d. want

DESPISE, DESPISED.

352 Can I his living voice d.
356 The men whom ye d.
643 Let the world d. and leave me
222 Yet, though *despised* and gory
216 Hail, thou once d. Jesus
625 Poor I may be, d., forgot

DESTRUCTION.

116 Though d. walk around us
365 But, ah! d. stops not there

DEVILS.

69 And d. at thy presence flee
166 though this world, with d. filled
822 Jesus...name...d. fear and fly

DEVIOUS.

180 Through d., lonely wilds I
646 When in d. paths we stray
885 Shepherd...Through d. ways

DEVOTE, DEVOTED.

112 My life I would anew d., O
952 D. our every hour to thee
474 *Devoted* solely to thy will
904 To thee our all d. be

DEVOTION.

64 songs...With warm d. rise
74 Church...With pure d. glow
133 Raised on d.'s lofty wing
186 We yield him, in costly d.
277 And our d. dies
711 D. dwells upon the theme
869 And pure d. rise
1092 thy people, with thankful d.

DEVOUR.

790 The sheep he never can d.

DEW, DEWS.

86 Shed thou thy freshening d.
301 O let the d. of heaven descend
551 As d. upon the tender herb
565 Work, while the d. is sparkling
578 The d. of promise from the skies
799 Where joy like morning d. distills
878 Like the d., upon each head
1081 And the refreshing d.
974 And now above the *dews* of night
1085 His blessed d. and sunshine

DIADEM.

187 I'll sing, first in night's d.
218 Bring forth the royal d.
253 Each wears his d.

256 A royal d. adorns The
584 The d. of God

DIE.

105 Teach me to d., that so I may
203 Lord, when I am called to d.
223 Learn of Jesus Christ to d.
228 We d. with thee: O let us live
255 died, That we might never d.
319 my theme, And shall be till I d.
347 Sinners, turn; why will ye d.
348 Why will ye resolve to d.
365 O think before thou d.
369 stay away...I must forever d.
377 thee, who wouldst not have me d.
378 Didst thou not d. the death for me
406 Surely thou canst not let me d.
422 thou, my Lord, shouldst d. for me
435 That he who did for sinners d.
441 Died that I might never d.
500 Jesus, I d. to thee...To d....is life
576 For thou so soon must d.
669 Whether I d. or live; To love
718 Let me d. thy people's death
885 So now, and till we d., Sound
927 Why should they d., when thou
968 And aim I only born to d.
975 For I must d. alone
975 To d. is now my wish, my choice
980 Who would not wish to d. like
988 No more may fear to d.
993 Thy chosen cannot d.
1001 In the Lord who sweetly d.
1003 D., to live a life of glory
1020 banished...And yet forbid to d.
1033 margin come...we expect to d.

DIES.

215 He bows his head and d.
234 He d.! the Friend of sinners
234 The Lord of glory d. for man
312 To save a world he d.
339 For a sinful world he d.
371 For thee he weeps and d.
968 death That never, never d.

DIED.

32 Thou who for all hast d.
208 We sing the praise of Him who d.
209 He d. that we might never d.
210 Christ for a guilty world hath d.
218 meekly bowed his head and d.
220 The Son of God for me hath d.
232 Christ d. and rose for me
234 Who d. for me, e'en me to atone
255 Jesus, the Lord of glory, d.
257 sing of him who d. for thee
257 For thou hast d. for me
270 Once he d., our souls to save
312 In him who d. for all
333 Therefore I know he d. for me
333 I know the Saviour d. for me
341 tide, Opened when our Saviour d.
347 D. himself, that ye might live
357 For Christ, his Son, has d.
377 know That thou hast d. for all
385 chief...But Jesus d. for me
385 Jesus, thou for me hast d.

422 *D.* be for me, who caused his
435 Hath surely *d.* for me
437 believe That he for us hath *d.*
411 *D.* that I might live on high
526 For thou hast *d.* that I might
583 Jesus hath *d.* for you and me
588 Jesus hath *d.* for you ! What
694 Since thou hast *d.*, the pure
706 Who once for sinners *d.*
742 Saviour, who *d.* for me
762 As thou hast *d.* for me, O
803 Daily feel that Christ hath *d.*
840 repeat, For me he *d.*, for me
876 And *d.* that you might live
927 Hast *d.* to bear their sins away

DIGNITY.
48 The same in *d.* and power

DIM, DIMLY, DIMMED.
654 star of hope Grow *d.* and
669 The eye of faith is *d.*
216 Whom angels *dimly* see
217 The star has *dimmed* that lately
444 Ye angels, never *d.* your
628 Though these frail eyes are *d.*

DIRECT, DIRECTS, DIRECTED, DIRECTLY.
169 And still *d.* my paths to thee
672 He shall *d.* thy wandering feet
889 Thus *d.* us, and protect us
295 light... *Directs* our doubtful feet
889 By thy look of love *directed*
612 draw their bliss *Directly*, Lord

DISCIPLE, DISCIPLES.
217 E'en that *d.* whom he loved
601 If thou wouldst my *d.* be
831 Sent to *d.* all mankind
30 See, Jesus, thy *disciples* see
199 How with the three *d.* there

DISDAIN, DISDAINS.
157 O Saviour, do not now *d.*
429 *D.* a Father's name
885 Help thou dost not *d.*
1078 His soul *disdains* on earth to

DISEASE, DISEASES, DISEASED.
373 Each season has its own *d.*
308 All my *d.*, my every sin
502 The seed of sin's *d.*
1095 The fell *d.* on every side
1099 It triumphed o'er *d.* and death
754 He healeth my *diseases*
965 And fierce *d.* wait around
977 Safe from *d.* and decline
411 To my *diseased*, my fainting soul

DISEMBODIED.
1032 Shall join the *d.* saints

DISMAY, DISMAYED.
1005 From whom the last *d.*
642 about me, And can I be *dismayed*
679 I am with thee, O be not *d.*
684 When tempted, desolate, *d.*

DISORDERED.
279 On our *d.* spirits move

DISPLAY, DISPLAYS, DISPLAYED.
296 For such a bright *d.*
416 More and more thyself *d.*
793 And every soul *displays* thy love
828 love Jesus on earth *d.*
75 scene Of glory was *displayed*
128 In Jesus, God with us, *d.*
839 What love his latest words *d.*
926 The glory of the Lord *d.*

DISROBE.
113 So death will soon *d.* us all

DISSOLVE, DISSOLVED.
336 The earth shall *d.*, and
427 The earth shall soon *d.*
987 Death...can't *d.* my love
1019 *D.*, by raging flames
1025 Let this earth *d.* and blend
520 heart...fire To be *dissolved* in
1000 Dust, be thou *d.* in death

DISTILL, DISTILLS.
104 Gently *d.* like early dew
870 May grace divine *d.*
799 joy, like morning dew, *distills*

DISTRACTION.
592 From all *d.* free

DISTRESS.
177 smiling God where deep *d.* had
241 He saw me plunged in deep *d.*
410 give The sensible *d.*
583 Through much *d.* and pain
678 In the time of my *d.*
679 sanctify to thee thy deepest *d.*
681 Away from a world of *d.*
688 In seasons of *d.* and grief
723 By thy days of sore *d.*
871 In every new *d.* We'll
893 And in their accents of *d.*
894 sons of grief In deep *d.* are
897 through scenes of deep *d.*
905 Bore every form of life's *d.*
1066 Out of great *d.* they came
1067 They shall feel *d.* no more

DISTRESSED.
621 The Lord beheld me sore *d.*
896 And help for all *d.*
1039 There is a joy for souls *d.*
1058 Sweet cure of all *d.*

DIVIDE, DIVIDED.
481 Let earth no more my heart *d.*
662 partners...How they *d.* our
790 can devour...Unless he first *d.*
563 We are not *divided*, All one body
755 I know no life *d.*, O Lord
1033 Though now *d.* by the stream

DIVINE.
378 my breast, And make it all *d.*
480 To make us share the life *d.*

4

591 Blest too is he who can *d.*
875 Whose years...Were all alike *d.*

DOCTRINE, DOCTRINES.
322 We confess The *d.* most divine
563 One in hope and *d.*
810 Then shall your *doctrines* be

DOLEFUL.
810 That *d.* night before his
1014 Hark, on earth the *d.* cry
1050 And fix my *d.* station

DOMINION.
227 And short the *d.* of death and
267 Long hath sin...Held *d.*
949 May thy lasting, wide *d.*

DOOM, DOOMED.
125 I see thee when the *d.* is o'er
166 For lo! his *d.* is sure
308 I dread impending *d.*
366 This hour may fix our final *d.*
735 It cannot seal the sinner's *d.*
766 To meet a joyful *d.*
972 Great God! is this our certain *d.*
189 *Doomed* for guilt to endless
825 And *d.* to endless woe

DOOR, DOORS.
28 He now stands knocking at the *d.*
115 Gather round my lowly *d.*
357 The *d.* is open wide
376 List.—thy bosom *d.!* How it
376 waiteth; But thy *d.* is fast
377 Open the *d.* of faith and love
388 Behold the open *d.*
625 whose open *d.* invites the
669 Must enter by his *d.*
857 Open wide, O God, thy *d.*
898 O enter thou his humble *d.*
936 He the *d.* hath opened wide
1021 If now thou standest at the *d.*
954 The everlasting *doors* Shall
981 Faith sees the bright, eternal *d.*

DOUBT.
157 And never *d.* thy aid
173 Here then I *d.* no more
333 I am pressed by *d.* and fear
382 No, my God, I cannot *d.*
420 Away, sad *d.* and anxious
528 From *d.*, and fear, and sorrow
575 To *d.* and fear give thou no
615 Why should we *d.* a Father's love
637 Why should I *d.* or fear
667 In darkness feels no *d.*
752 Hushed is each *d.*, gone every
819 We take, and *d.* no more
861 No anxious *d.*, no guilty
996 Who can resolve the *d.*

DOUBTS.
173 And *d.* no longer mine
596 And *d.* will come If God
628 There shall no *d.* disturb
633 Soon shall our *d.* and fears
636 Soon shall our *d.* and fears All

671 But, O, when *d.* prevail
1067 Gloomy *d.*, distressing fears

DOUBTING, DOUBTINGS.
335 If still you are *d.*, make
463 Chase these *doubtings* from my

DOVE.
266 In the olive-bearing *d.*
277 Come, Holy Spirit, heavenly *D.*
279 Expand thy wings, celestial *D.*
283 Brood not o'er me like a *d.*
388 Like Noah's weary *d.*
403 For, lo! the swift-returning *d.*
424 May thy blest wings, celestial *D.*
547 Come, holy *D.*, from the heavenly
549 Return, O holy *D.*, return
793 Send down thy mild, pacific *D.*
810 harmless as the peaceful *d.*
913 Life-giving holy *D.*, Speed forth
1052 Breathe...The spirit of the *d.*

DOWER.
902 precious wealth shall be their *d.*
1060 And thine the golden *d.*

DOWNWARD.
356 And throng the *d.* road
1008 The dark and *d.* way

DRAW, DRAWS, DRAWINGS.
49 And *d.* them with the cords of
54 We, thy people, now *d.* near
213 *D.* us and all men after thee
397 To *d.*, redeem, and seal, are thine
429 Nor while, unworthy, I *d.* nigh
477 Each moment *d.* from earth
581 To *d.* thee from the skies
45 when God himself *draws* nigh
87 And earth *d.* near to heaven
87 When man *d.* near to God
509 And *d.* the heart from earth
348 All his *drawings* from above
439 Thy *d.* from above

DREAD.
165 Teach me to live, that I may *d.*
147 How *d.* are thine eternal
975 But O, I will not view with *d.*

DREADFUL.
37 And O how *d.* is this place
47 And own how *d.* is this place
153 Appear in all your *d.* forms
410 Wilt from the *d.* day remove
1017 How...meet that *d.* day?

DREAM, DREAMS.
366 The past, alas! is all a *d.*
632 Than waking *d.*, and
714 Like some bright *d.* that comes
762 When once life's transient *d.*
855 Our life is a *d.*; our time
956 All below is but a *d.*
964 They fly, forgotten, as a *d.*
1026 None can *d.*, and none can tell
1042 This life's a *d.*, an empty
291 I sink in blissful *dreams* away

873 And d. of days to come
724 Yet in my d. I'd be Nearer
741 Farewell, ye d. of night; Jesus
756 Of all our golden d.

DREAMLESS.
1008 child! Go to thy d. bed

DREARY.
943 Light of those whose d. dwelling
1070 though life be long and d.

DRESS, DRESSED.
238 my beauty are, my glorious d.
743 In which all-perfect, heavenly d.
1079 Dressed in beauty not my own

DRINK, DRINKS, DRUNK.
323 And d., for Jesus' sake
323 And d., adore, and bless
327 I d.. and yet am ever dry
355 And freely d. the stream of life
426 Stoop down, and d., and live
785 Make us into one spirit d.
794 And bid us freely d. and eat
833 And, D. ye all of this, he said
851 Our spirits d. a fresh supply
341 He that drinks need thirst no
125 spirits...Of thee have drunk

DROOP, DROOPING.
652 Come...all ye who d. in sadness
297 It sweetly cheers our drooping
398 My d. soul exults to hear
541 It lifts my d. spirits up
557 Say to my d. soul
577 'Twill serve our d. hearts

DROP, DROPS.
131 A d. of that unbounded sea
670 word...D. on them from above
234 He shed a thousand drops for
384 Let some d. now fall on me
936 shower D. already from above

DROSS.
205 earth's precious things seem d.
396 Thy Spirit can from d. refine
496 Wash out its stains, refine its d.
518 Burn up the d. of base desire
647 Mixed with d. the purest gold
679 Thy d. to consume, and thy
695 And deem its treasures only d.

DROWSY.
96 Unfold thy d. eyes
104 And quickens all my d. powers
547 My d. powers, why sleep
965 Waken, O Lord, our d. sense

DULL, DULLNESS.
547 Yet nothing's half so d.
273 The dullness of our blinded sight

DUMB.
1 his praise, ye d., Your loosened
209 Let the d. world its silence
836 when these failing lips grow d.

DUNGEON.
422 I woke, the d. flamed
608 In spite of d., fire, and
751 cheer This d. where I dwell
993 From d. chain, to breathe

DUST.
212 Covered with d., and sweat
365 Thy flesh...Shall into d. consume
452 When. d., he turns to d. again
458 Can sinful d. and ashes do
510 Till humbled in the d.
531 My mouth as in the d. I hide
723 Saviour, when, in d., to thee
959 man Is d. and vanity
973 Unheeded, o'er our silent d.
988 D., to its narrow house beneath
993 fling Aside this sinful d.
1012 and d. We give unto dust, in

DUTY, DUTIES.
29 O may not d. seem a load
98 Make every path of d. straight
106 Thy daily stage of d. run
507 Where d. calls, or danger, Be
573 Their d. by my life explain
602 Yet where our d.'s task is
803 In the bonds of d. joined
82 In holy duties, let the day

DWELL.
20 Till we come to d. with thee
44 Dost d. with those of humble
61 D. richly in each heart
91 D. within my heart alone
117 Take us, Lord, to d. with thee
264 He vouchsafes to d. in man
207 D. within this heart of mine
271 In us forever d.
284 D. in each breast
331 And safe in Jesus d.
378 And d. forever in my breast
443 And ever d. in me
502 O come, and d. in me
507 God, by grace, shall d. in thee
696 Where'er I d., I dwell with thee
865 How God can d. with men
956 May we d. with him above

DWELLING, DWELLINGS.
17 His d.-place, how fair
156 God's house...My d.-place shall
280 make our hearts thy d.-place
491 Fix in us thy humble d.
731 From his d.-place above
859 That shall adorn thy d.-place
873 To the d. of our Father
15 how fair The dwellings of thy love
64 And fill thy d. here
769 How lovely are thy d., Lord

DYE.
374 Turn, and your sins of deepest d.

DYING.
4 Sing of his d. love
110 cheer and bless my d. bed
222 For this, thy d. sorrow

EAG   52   EAR

222 Be near me when I'm *d*.
224 Saints the *d*. words record
258 Let us by his *d*. live
277 live At this poor *d*. rate
311 Come, ye *d*., live forever
347 O ye *d*. sinners, why
383 Lamb of God, whose *d*. love
383 By thy *d*. love to man
495 The labor of thy *d*. love
558 Give me, through thy *d*. love
605 His *d*. love, his saving power
667 ray Illumes a *d*. bed
732 Dead to sin, and daily *d*.
755 O blessed thought! in *d*.
835 The tokens of thy *d*. love
836 This will I do, my *d*. Lord
840 Did, almost with his *d*. breath
891 So Jesus looked on *d*. man
928 And grace revive a *d*. world
969 O the pain, the bliss of *d*.
970 *d*. members rest...with...dying
972 Then, when we drop this *d*. flesh
976 Jesus can make a *d*. bed
985 faith, To cheer my *d*. hours
995 hopes we owe, Lord, to thy *d*. love
1004 Him, whose *d*. love and power
1009 And faith beholds the *d*. here

E.

EAGLE, EAGLES.

657 On faith's strong *e*. pinions rise
684 There, there on *e*. wings we soar
749 And like the *e*. he renews The
851 Till, borne on *e*. wings, we fly
952 By thee on *e*. wings upborne
1033 And on the *e*. wings of love
1075 I shall, on *e*. wings upborne
512 It bears on *eagles*' wings

EAR.

138 In reason's *e*. they all rejoice
158 An *e*. for every call
320 Let every mortal *e*. attend
360 His *e*. will hear thy cry
564 Glories...*E*. hath never heard
621 I love the Lord! he bowed his *e*.
707 There is an *e*. that never shuts
771 Now lend thy gracious *e*.
815 Give them an *e*. to hear thy word
953 The Father mild inclines his *e*.

EARS.

821 How happy are our *e*.
865 Here may thine *e*. attend
1057 fathers...told, In our attentive *e*.

EARS.

1083 fruitful *e*. to store In his garner

EARNEST.

262 *E*. of immortal rest
408 We sinners, Lord, with *e*. heart
424 Thou art the *e*. of his love
842 An *e*. of our glorious bliss
891 *E*. of joy above
1056 Who hast the *e*. given

EARTH.

10 The *e*. and heavens are full of
38 *E*. from afar hath heard thy
76 O *e*., rejoice and sing
93 *E*.'s joys grow dim, its glories
129 *E*., air, and sea, before thy sight
289 gospel...Through *e*. extended
321 echo...And all the *e*. shall hear
363 *E*. is a resting-place for thee
659 Should *e*. against my soul
711 *E*. has no resting-place, Jesus
753 to rove O'er all the *e*. abroad
779 *E*. shall yield her rich increase
796 What else has *e*. for us in store
821 bare his arm Through all the *e*.
845 Seems the *e*. so poor and vast
845 Some from *e*., from glory some
908 Till *e*., subdued, its tribute brings
917 That all the *e*. is now the Lord's
951 Attend, O *e*., his sovereign
1063 From *e*. we shall quickly
1072 Then fail the *e*., let stars
1076 And *e*. and hell withstand

On EARTH.

20 While on *e*. ordained to stay
131 Let all on *e*. bow down to thee
470 Let thy will on *e*. be done
857 On *e*. establish his abode
878 And when life on *e*. is o'er
886 King...Came down on *e*. to dwell
959 And seen on *e*. no more
1051 And dwell on *e*. no more.

Spacious EARTH.

321 echo fly The *spacious e*. around
908 It fly The *spacious e*. around
910 spread The *spacious e*. around
922 To spread the *spacious e*.

This EARTH.

530 Or can I love *this e*. so well
648 *This e*., we know, is not our place
905 *This e*. were but a weary place
1030 *This e*., he cries, is not my place
1068 Time shall soon *this e*. remove

To EARTH.

367 To *e*. the great Redeemer came
387 Soon to come to *e*. again
911 Wide to *e*.'s remotest strand
971 Gladly to *e*. their eyes they

EARTHLY.

91 peace throughout our *e*. life
182 And when *e*. things are past
457 Empty my heart of *e*. love
610 Father, whate'er of *e*. bliss
647 *E*. joys no longer please us
786 On *e*. good look down
994 That which was sown an *e*. seed

EARTHLINESS.

590 Our *e*. refine

EARTHQUAKE.

330 whisper higher Than *e*.
763 Though *e*. shocks are

EASE.
344 Seek for *e*., but seek in vain
371 stings...Deprive your souls of *e*.
576 Fling *e*. and self away
593 carried...On flowery beds of *e*.
598 In selfish *e*. we lie
706 It gives the burdened spirit *e*.

EAST, EASTERN, EASTWARD.
172 *e*. is from the west...our guilt
633 Speed on from *e*. to west
939 gates...Open on the palmy *E*.
940 And, from the *eastern* coast to
564 Forward, marching *eastward*

EAT, EATING.
833 Take, *e*., this is my body, given
840 We *e*. the bread, and drink
849 Manna...To *e*. till richly filled
851 And *e*. the bread so freely given
841 Remember this in *eating* bread

EBENEZER.
726 Here I'll raise mine *E*.

ECHO, ECHOES.
153 *E*. the glories of your King
193 And loud the *e*. rolled
321 Heaven with the *e*. shall
324 Salvation! let the *e*. fly
340 Sweetly *e*. with his name
692 strains Which *e*. o'er the
712 My...heart shall...*e*. to thy voice
713 Shall *e*. through the realms
867 Loud may they *e*. with thy
934 fountains Shall *e*. the reply
444 And dying *echoes*, floating
874 *E*. now the songs we raise
912 from the mountain-tops *e*. are

ECLIPSE.
260 Lo! the sun's *e*. is o'er
844 Through the Church's long *e*.

ECSTASY, ECSTASIES.
137 Thou source of *e*. and love
206 When, in *e*. sublime, Tabor's
991 In *ecstasies* of praise, Long as

EDEN.
125 I see thee walk in *E*.'s shade
221 Our loss of *E*. to retrieve
623 where *E*.'s bowers bloom, By
652 There, like an *E*. blossoming
786 raised...With God in *E*. live
860 It beamed on *E*.'s guilty days
916 And earth again, like *E*. crowned
1011 And lodged in the *E*. of love
1044 happier bowers than *E*.'s bloom

EFFECTUAL.
32 The great, *e*. door
438 They pour *e*. prayers
818 Answer our faith's *e*. prayer

EFFULGENT, EFFULGENCE.
290 Becomes *e*. more and more
1063 And bright in *effulgence* divine

ELDERS.
25 Let the *e*. praise the Lord

ELECT, ELECTION.
1058 The home of God's *e*.
968 How make mine own *election*

ELIJAH.
274 As when *E*. felt its power
785 As Moses or *E*. prays

ELOQUENCE.
13 What mortal *e*. can raise
711 inspires The *e*. divine

EMBLEM, EMBLEMS.
88 Day...*E*. of eternal rest
90 *E*., earnest, of the rest
844 Come, the blessed *emblems* share
960 Of earthly hopes are *e*. true

EMBRACE, EMBRACES, EMBRACING.
347 Wooed you to *e*. his love
448 with the arms of faith *e*.
508 open...Our hearts to *e*. thy
520 wait with arms of faith to *e*.
703 I leap to meet thy kind *e*.
751 heaven to rest in thine *e*.
782 Closer...To his beloved *e*.
1008 Shall love, with weak *e*.
1068 To rest in his *e*.
754 His right hand me *embraces*
907 And in his kind *e*. lose
213 *Embracing* in thy wondrous love

EMERALD.
1060 Thy streets with *e*. blaze

EMPIRE, EMPIRES.
148 Through thine *e*.'s wide domain
417 By the *e*. all thine own
763 O where are kings and *empires*
919 While western *e*. own their

EMPLOY, EMPLOYED.
19 O let us all our lives *e*.
606 For thee delightfully *e*.
458 Be all my adored life *employed*
811 For Jesus day and n'ght *e*.

EMPRESS.
1034 moon, Pale *e*. of the night

EMPTY, EMPTIED.
303 *E*. of him who all things
326 vainly strive...To fill an *e*. mind
457 *E*. my heart of earthly love
608 What *e*. things are all the
422 *Emptied* himself of all but love

EMULATE, EMULATION.
600 And *e*. the angel choir
692 And *e*., with joy unknown
58 Filled with holy *emulation*

ENCOMPASSED.
157 Our souls *e*. round
216 With glorious clouds *e*.

END.
401 E. of faith, as its beginning
556 And love me to the e.
575 Then, when the glorious e.
650 O keep us faithful to the e.
657 And all that to the e. endure
959 Lord, let me know mine e.
966 And to the e. endure

ENDED, ENDING, ENDLESS.
1003 Happy soul, thy days are e.
1059 The life that knows no ending
73 Through endless years to live and
294 Through e. years thy praise
394 And feel what e. years
812 The long round of e. years
834 And e. life are given

ENDURE, ENDURES.
406 What did thine only Son e.
418 My joy to e. and do thy will
614 O teach us to e. The sorrow
825 Accustomed daily to e.
829 And by thy strength e.
1056 mansion...Shall evermore e.
427 As long as life endures

ENEMY, ENEMIES.
228 Our e. is put to shame
938 Man's last e. shall fall
566 Soon, your enemies all slain
772 protects...From all their e.
950 A host of e. without

ENERGY.
39 With sovereign power and e.
268 His richest e. declare
285 Come, Holy Spirit...With e.
289 Its e. exert in the believing

ENGINES.
912 Fallen are the e. of war

ENGRAVE.
494 E. thy name on high

ENJOYMENT, ENJOYMENTS.
54 Full e., Full and pure
513 A rest where pure e.
1074 forego...our enjoyments below

ENLARGE.
46 E. and fill us all with
458 E. my heart to compass
598 E. my heart to understand

ENLIVENED, ENLIVENING.
483 That I may now e. be
478 whose enlivening voice bids

ENMITY.
789 None...Can live in e.

ENOUGH.
317 E. for all, enough for each
325 There's mercy in Jesus, e. and to
638 E., if thou at last The word
998 Are e. for life's woes, full enough

ENRICH.
162 His honors shall e. your verse
185 grace To e. the poor
295 gales, That so e. the mind

ENSHRINED.
507 dwells in cloudless light e.

ENSNARE.
664 This anxious breast e.

ENTANGLEMENTS.
753 From all e. beneath

ENTER.
11 So come, my Sovereign! e. in
28 rejoice, That thou wilt e. in
210 And all mankind may e. in
264 E. our devoted breast
375 too late! ye cannot e. now
401 E., and keep my heart
443 Christ would quickly e. there
513 rest...Believe and e. in
519 E. my soul, and work within
527 E. thyself, and cast out sin
664 But shall not e. there
791 E., and find that God is here
955 E. into my joy, and sit down
976 And yet we dread to e. there
1051 woe, can never e. there

ENTERTAIN, ENTERTAINMENTS.
794 Our hearts to e. our Lord
81 How sweet thine entertainments

ENTHRONE, ENTHRONED.
249 In the seat of power e. him
47 To him, enthroned above all
65 Jesus...e. in every breast
119 I, with thee E., may reign
133 E. amid the radiant spheres
139 In heaven thou reign'st e.
241 Majestic sweetness sits e.
246 Jesus hail! e. in glory
253 E. is Jesus now
953 Who reigns e. on high
991 With saints e. on high

ENTIRE.
587 And stand e. at last

ENTRANCE.
721 Thus, O thus an e. give
926 waits to make his e. there

ENTRANCED.
900 E., enwrapt, alone with thee

ENTREATED, ENTREATING.
573 Easy to be e., mild
876 'tis thine to stand entreating

ENVY.
288 And changes e., hatred, strife
780 When, free from e., scorn, and

EQUIP.
586 E. me for the war

EQUITY.
181 And rule in *e*.

ERRING.
544 One only way the *e*. mind
632 mysterious now thy ways To *e*.
869 May *e*. minds that worship

ERROR.
564 Forward, out of *e*., Leave
761 In *e*.'s maze my soul
857 Man from *e*. to reclaim

ESCAPE, ESCAPES.
310 none can meet him, and *e*.
330 E. to the mountain; For
968 But how I may *e*. the death
1050 By death I shall *e*. from death
117 Naught *escapes*, without, within

ESPOUSALS.
12 Like our *e*., Lord, to thee

ESPOUSED.
1014 Come for his *e*. below

ESTATE.
675 In whatsoe'er *e*.

ETERNAL.
149 And the heart of the *E*.
225 Life *e*.! heaven rejoices
297 clearer light Of an *e*. day
381 The one *e*. God and true
445 *E*. life with thee is given
520 In him *e*. life receive
966 *E*. things impress
993 To spend *e*. years

ETERNITY.
6 And to *e*. Love and adore
25 From *e*. the same
25 Like his own *e*.
31 tongues employ Through all *e*.
87 stupendous march Of vast *e*.
112 in service...spend A long *e*.
160 Through all *e*. to thee A
164 person be, In time and in *e*.
168 Where, in *e*. of light, The city
337 in Christ....Blest to all *e*.
431 we glide To our *e*.
441 Jesus' love ..Lasting as *e*.
460 Be thine through all *e*.
483 die to prove An *e*. of love
530 and see The glories of *e*.
656 Rise to all *e*.
705 And to *e*. prolong Thy vast
739 Through all *e*. to prove
741 Welcome *e*., Jesus is mine
743 A blest *e*. I'll spend
750 He speaks! and *e*., filled
955 millennial year...*e*.'s here
956 Teach us to live With *e*. in view
1000 And *e*. thy day
1009 A whole *e*. of love
1063 The day of *e*. come
1110 *E*. comes in the sound
1117 one smile...And drops into *e*.

ETHER.
195 strain The realm of *e*. fills
217 'Tis midnight; and from *e*.-plains

ETHEREAL.
138 With all the blue *e*. sky
237 And wide unfold the *e*. scene

EUCHARISTIC.
846 This *e*. feast Our

EVE.
575 At *e*. hold not thy hand
620 At *e*. it shall be light
752 And blest that solemn hour of *e*.

EVENING.
108 And every *e*. shall make
109 Again as *e*.'s shadow falls
345 Ere this *e*.'s stage be run
346 And when the *e*. shades
961 ages....Are like an *e*. gone
974 Behold the western *e*. light
1058 To light that hath no *e*.

EVENT, EVENTS.
616 In each *e*. of life how clear
685 Whate'er *events* betide, Thy will

EVENTIDE.
98 Fast falls the *e*.

EVIDENCE.
250 Sure *e*. of things unseen
445 With strong, commanding *e*.

EVIL.
155 And *e*. turn aside
317 Delights our *e*. to remove
410 Before the *e*. come
423 In *e*. long I took delight
532 What! never speak one *e*. word
543 stand by Throughout the *e*. day
555 warn My soul of *e*. near
686 *E*. and danger turn away
715 wants relieve In this our *e*. day
716 From *e*. set us free
830 Rites cannot...Undo the *e*. done
1058 The world is very *e*.
1058 To terminate the *e*., To diadem

EVILS.
1031 Its *e*. in a moment end.

EXALTED.
2 Worthy the Lamb...To be *e*. thus
70 *E*. be thy glorious name
255 Through earth and heaven *e*. be
337 Rise *e*. by his fall
852 To Jesus, our *e*. Lord, The

EXAMPLE.
471 The bright *e*. may pursue
573 I must the fair *e*. set
592 Thy bright *e*. I pursue
878 Thine *e*. kept in view
894 Thy bright *e*. trace
992 Thy bright *e*. be

EXCEEDING.
225 O what glory, far e.

EXCELLENCE, EXCELLENCES.
31 Infinite e. is th'ne
16 name alone All excellences meet

EXCHANGE.
362 Nothing ye in e. shall
719 Misery we e. for bliss

EXCLAMATION.
1014 With what different e.

EXCLUDE.
390 anger swear To e. me from

EXCUSE, EXCUSES.
310 for...faults A just e. devise
834 Nor weak excuses frame

EXHAUSTLESS.
31 live On thy e. store
255 from his love's e. spring

EXILE, EXILES, EXILED.
603 For toil comes rest, for e. home
1032 And take his e. home
1054 No more as an e. in sorrow
1088 An e., to his home
1016 Long thy exiles have been pining
1058 Who here as e. mourn
909 Thine exiled bands, Where'er

EXPANSE.
139 Nature's e. before thee spread
145 Heaven's e. and all its state
193 Swift through the vast e. it dew

EXPECT, EXPECTED, EXPECTING.
30 Thee, we e., our faithful
331 Come, thou long-expected Jesus
1015 O thou long-e., weary
1026 By the just e. long
30 we look to thee, Expecting to
517 in faith I pray, e. to receive

EXPECTATION, EXPECTATIONS.
530 The glorious e. now
615 Full of trembling e.
797 While each in e. lives
1104 Our surest expectations are From

EXPIRE, EXPIRES, EXPIRING.
407 And in his arms e.
469 And in thy cause e.
488 altar-fire, Kindled on my heart, e.
212 Sinks and expires the Son of God
221 What means that strange expiring
982 Gently heaves the e. breast

EXPLORE.
422 Who can e. his strange design

EXULT, EXULTS.
923 Our hearts e. in songs of
437 Exults our rising soul

EXULTING.
271 E. then we feel and own
824 giants...E. in their might
1076 They all e. stand

EXULTATION.
1013 Cause of endless e.

EYE.
98 To thee lift up mine e.
117 Thou, whose all-pervading e.
121 Thine e. doth all things see
136 Though the e. of sinful man
257 downward bends his burning e.
303 Regard me with a gracious e.
386 To thee I lift mine e.
401 And to thy gracious e. present A
481 Jesus, my single e. Be fixed
505 A quick discerning e.
525 Open my faith's interior e.
558 love Drop from thy gracious e.
561 And kept our e. on him alone
591 E. hath not beheld them
616 My lifted e., without a tear
651 To him mine e. of faith I turn
670 Thou whose filmed and failing e.
685 Thy glorious e. pervadeth space
707 There is an e. that never sleeps
707 That e. that arm, that love
710 The upward aiming of an e.
732 Where no human e. can see
815 Us with thy flaming e. behold
873 We may turn our tearless e.
898 Whose e. with want is dim
922 The single e., the faithful heart
992 To thee we lift our e.
1013 Every e. shall now behold him
1046 Him e. to eye we there shall see
1048 Ere long we e. to eye shall see
1101 Thy sovereign e. looks calmly
1103 beneath whose piercing e. The

EYES.
32 Come, then, and in thy people's e.
97 and deed his piercing e. With
107 And close our e. against the throng
185 And on the e. oppressed with night
201 On e. oppressed by mortal night
212 O'erflow my e., and heave my
309 error...From reason's darkened e.
327 He closed his e. to show us God
361 See him set forth before your e.
377 Open mine e. to see thy face
381 O give us e. of faith to see
408 Our e. thy face would see
415 When my e. shall close in death
435 And give us e. to see
483 I lift mine e. to thee
524 O let our e. behold thee near
632 O God, to thee we raise our e.
711 Jesus, these e. have never seen
720 Lift your e., ye sons of light
745 steal On his all-seeing e.
821 How blessed are our e., That
918 revealed To our admiring e.
1031 grief shall swell into mine e.
1035 appears To our believing e.
1057 tears wiped Forever from our e.

1069 Lift your *e.* of faith and see
1105 To thee, O God, we lift our *e.*

EYELIDS.
97 Our *e.* with the morn unclose
102 My wearied *e.* gently steep
974 And *e.* that are sealed in death

F.
FABRIC.
1056 firm...That heavenly *f.* stands
1060 Thy saints build up its *f.*

FACE.
233 Their Lord's beloved *f.* to see
669 made me meet Thy blessed *f.* to see
714 Thy blessed *f.* and mine
1042 I shall behold thy blissful *f.*

FACE TO FACE.
199 To see thy glory *f. to f.*
738 I see thee *f. to f.*, and live
738 Through faith I see thee *f. to f.*
1026 Jesus *f. to f.* shall see
1040 They see the Saviour *f. to f.*

Glorious FACE.
526 I wait to see thy *glorious f.*
543 appear Before thy *glorious f.*
609 And see thy *glorious f.*
779 Cause thy *glorious f.* to shine
849 Thy *glorious f.* to see

Heavenly FACE.
1065 The light of his *heavenly f.*

His FACE.
41 There we shall see *his f.*
233 *His f.* with love's own radiance
360 If thou wilt seek *his f.*, His
451 Called us to stand before *his f.*
515 I, even I, shall see *his f.*
566 You soon shall see *his f.*
572 Christ in all, Before *his f.* I fall
657 We shall before *his f.* appear
743 And I shall see *his f.*
747 Content with beholding *his f.*
789 Together seek *his f.*
961 And glory in *his f.* appears
1075 I shall behold *his f.*, I shall

Lord's FACE.
758 till admitted to see my *Lord's f.*

Lovely FACE.
295 And here the Saviour's *lovely f.*
451 In Jesus' *lovely f.* displayed
987 charms Spread o'er thy *lovely f.*

Open FACE.
481 Beholding thee with *open f.*
545 I soon may view thy *open f.*
657 We soon with *open f.* shall see
715 Behold thy *open f.*, Where faith

Other's FACE.
798 alive, And see each *other's f.*
801 To see each *other's f.*; To join

802 See with joy each *other's f.*
816 There we shall see each *other's f.*

Thy FACE.
47 Still may we stand before *thy f.*
110 To see *thy f.* and sing thy praise
130 And see but shadows of *thy f.*
178 gone, Whene'er *thy f.* appears
303 Behold *thy f.*, and live
305 Behold, we fall before *thy f.*
399 I long to see *thy f.*
406 Could I but see *thy f.*
448 heaven and earth flee from *thy f.*
453 joy is to walk in the light of *thy f.*
484 And humbly seek *thy f.*
488 Ever since I saw *thy f.*
536 burn, And always see *thy f.*
537 In confidence to see *thy f.*
550 O when shall I behold *thy f.*
557 Let me again behold *thy f.*
605 'Tis my delight to see *thy f.*
625 none shall seek *thy f.* in vain
634 What shall it be to see *thy f.*
643 Show *thy f.*, and all is bright
648 And restless to behold *thy f.*
660 Forever to behold *thy f.*
660 *Thy f.*, Lord, will I seek
681 The heaven of seeing *thy f.*
694 Forever I behold *thy f.*
700 But sweeter far *thy f.* to see
708 pale before The beauty of *thy f.*
712 Thou callest me to seek *thy f.*
831 In these, for whom we seek *thy f.*
865 Till all who humbly seek *thy f.*
893 *Thy f.* with reverence and with
922 Before *thy f.*, dread King, we
946 we go To seek *thy f.* above
958 We dwell before *thy f.*
961 Expect with joy *thy f.* to see
1022 And ere before *thy f.*, we stand
1056 And rise prepared *thy f.* to see
1064 *Thy f.* I am strengthened to see

FACES.
115 before me *F.* I shall see no more

FACULTIES.
19 And all our *f.* shall feel
96 Thine active *f.*

FADE, FADES.
336 dissolve, and the heavens shall *f.*
711 *F.*, fade, each earthly joy
875 The rose...Must shortly *f.* away
1008 Where flowers so quickly *f.*
117 light of day *Fades* upon our
132 A passing thought...That *f.* with
982 So *f.* a summer cloud away

FAIL, FAILINGS.
141 Though friends should all *f.*
363 Come, for all else must *f.* and die
427 when this flesh and heart shall *f.*
440 suit...Joined to his, it cannot *f.*
479 And cannot *f.*, if God is love
968 And, when I *f.* on earth, secure
780 Each can his brother's *failings*

FAINT, FAINTS.

44 To teach our *f.* desires to rise
180 When in the sultry globe I *f.*
277 Our love so *f.*, so cold to
403 Thou comfortest the *f.*
506 And never, never *f.*
603 Toil on, *f.* not; keep watch
665 *F.* not, O faltering feet
776 Who can *f.* while such a
777 O my people, *f.* and few
1082 body fail, And let it *f.* and die
569 though courage sometimes *faints*

FAINTING.

208 cross...holds the *f.* spirit up
222 And should I *f.* be, Lord
283 Help my *f.* soul to flee
306 Look up, O *f.* soul, and live
313 And cheer the *f.* heart
323 Poor, sinful, thirsty, *f.* souls
406 How would my *f.* soul rejoice
645 By thy *f.* In the garden
657 It lifts the *f.* spirits up
674 My *f.* hope relies

FAIR, FAIRER, FAIREST.

80 All *f.* with evening's setting
1047 How they speak thee *f.*
41 marching...To *fairer* worlds on
241 *F.* is he than all the fair
764 Yet *f.*, and in strength complete
695 The *fairest* of the fair is he

FAITH.

39 And *f.* be mixed with what we
39 And may we, in thy *f.* and fear
80 *F.* sees the smiling heaven above
205 Here we gather *f.* to die
213 Give us an ever-living *f.*
222 These eyes, new *f.* receiving
225 O what wonders Crowd on *f.*
232 With *f.* to call thee mine
254 Then let our humble *f.* address
268 That *f.* and love may make all
329 The *f.* that sweetly works by love
397 With simple *f.*, on thee I call
411 On thee, all *f.*, all hope be
432 *F.*, mighty faith, the promises
439 And should I not with *f.* draw
445 *F.*, like its finisher and Lord
446 A *f.* thou must thyself impart
446 This is the *f.* we humbly seek
448 From *f.* to faith, from grace to
471 O for a *f.* like his, that we
486 Give me *f.* to make me whole
501 Had I such *f.* in God As
523 That mighty *f.* on me bestow
523 On me the *f.* divine bestow
539 Give me the *f.* that casts out sin
578 Be *f.*, which looks above
585 I have the *f.* maintained
588 If *f.* surround your heart
604 *F.* of our fathers! living still
609 Joyful thus my *f.* to show
648 Like them in *f.* to bear
610 The *f.* by which we see him
665 Let *f.* transcend the passing
667 O for a *f.* that will not shrink
667 Lord, give us such a *f.* as this
671 A noble *f.* succeeds
677 Breathe their *f.* into my breast
711 *F.* grasps the blessings he desires
714 Must rest in *f.* alone
781 Whose *f.* the victory won
800 One *f.*, one hope divine
854 Now the living *f.* impart
869 May *f.* grow firm, and love
974 So *f.* springs in the heart of
980 When *f.* endued from heaven
989 Let *F.* exalt her joyful voice

By FAITH.

178 The soul *by f.* reclined
445 Whate'er we hope, *by f.* we have
498 Teach us to live *by f.*
593 *By f.* they bring it nigh
600 For who *by f.* your Lord
620 *By f.* and not by sight
636 To live *by f.* alone
643 Armed *by f.*, and winged by
709 I love *by f.* to take a view
1030 A country... Yet O, *by f.*
1073 *By f.* we are come To our
1115 Bid them come *by f.* to thee

My FAITH.

570 My *f.* hath fixed its eye
609 Joyful thus *my f.* to show
762 *My f.* looks up to thee
1053 Strengthen the might of *my f.*

Of FAITH.

46 The work *of f.* in us fulfill
377 The gift *of f.* is all divine
415 In us the work *of f.* fulfill
481 Called the full power *of f.* to
517 With hands *of f.* and wings
552 When the work *of f.* is done
562 My acts *of f.* and love repeat
581 The work *of f.* will not be done
718 Let me live a life *of f.*

Our FAITH.

12 Nor let *our f.* forsake its hold
250 O that *our f.* may never move
583 Before *our f.* they fall
773 *Our f.* shall never yield to fear
802 Pray we for *our f.*'s increase
803 Still, O Lord, *our f.* increase
846 Who thus *our f.* employ
885 Make *our f.* strong
892 Though dim *our f.* may be

FAITHFUL.

33 Thy *f.* people bless
115 Ever *f.*, ever sure
199 And *f.* hearts are raised
270 Fulfill in us thy *f.* word
302 And trust a *f.* Lord
311 God is *f.*; he will never
479 *F.*, If we our sins confess
650 O keep us *f.* to the end
677 God of Israel's *f.* three
764 The *f.* of each clime and
792 Accomplish now thy *f.* word
794 And own thee *f.* to thy word

826 Still keep me in thy *f*.
924 Spirit...flows through every *f*.
1001 Good and *f*. servant thou
1019 And *f*. to the end endure
1046 Bear in our *f*. minds the
1115 Jesus, let our *f*. mind

FAITHFULNESS.
322 And on thy *f*. and power
432 power And *f*. I give
541 O God, thy *f*. I plead
688 Him, whose truth and *f*.

FALL.
51 *F*. down on their faces, and
153 While thousands *f*. on every side
222 Lo, here I *f*., my Saviour
231 beholding human nature's *f*.
244 And *f*. beneath his feet
248 We at his feet may *f*.
302 Into thine arms I *f*.
341 Sinners ruined by the *f*.
400 Lord, at thy feet I fall
412 Thou to *f*. at his feet, And the
448 Into thy gracious hands I *f*.
518 that it now from heaven might *f*.
543 Before I wholly *f*. away
625 Afflicted, at thy feet I *f*.
905 stay, and strengthen those who *f*.
1027 Nor let me *f*., I pray

FALLEN.
221 That every *f*. son of man
231 All that now is *f*. raise to
310 Ah, how shall *f*. man Be just
362 'Tis God invites the *f*. race
656 Raise the *f*., cheer the faint

FALLOW.
953 Break up our *f*. ground

FALSE.
656 *F*. and full of sin I am
662 How *f*., and yet how fair

FALTER.
596 To *f*. would be sin
603 Yet *f*. not; the prize you

FAME.
38 Earth...hath heard thy *f*.
133 O what tongue can speak his *f*.
154 And spread thy *f*. abroad
398 Jesus, thy far-extended *f*.
643 Go, then, earthly *f*. and treasure
1076 And swell the growing *f*.

FAMILY.
467 Born in thy *f*. below
573 And lead my faithful *f*.
804 remove To the *f*. above
987 infant...compose The *f*. above
1033 One *f*. we dwell in him

FAMINE.
414 prodigal...The *f*. in this land
844 'Mid the *f*. of the word
906 Is a mighty *f*. now In thy

FAST, FASTING.
1047 Watch, and pray, and *f*.
853 In thy *fasting* and temptation
1091 Hear us, *f*., praying, mourning

FATE, FATAL.
373 And *f*. descend in sudden night
608 sweet would be their children's *f*.
628 I will not fear The *f*. provided
347 He the *fatal* cause demands
968 prepare Against that *f*. day

FATHER.
414 Far off the *F*. saw him move
458 Thou, with thy promised *F*., come
660 When *f*., mother, kindred fail

My FATHER.
142 *My F*. and my Friend
419 Thou art *my F*. and my God
429 *My F*., God! that precious word
434 I did not love *my F*.'s voice
436 Thou, God, *my F*. art
637 *My F*.'s hand will never
688 bids me, at *my F*.'s throne
1038 When shall I see *my F*.'s face

Our FATHER.
22 Join, and to *our F*. raise
41 *Our F*. and our Love
356 And God himself *our F*. is
590 Like thee, to do *our F*.'s will
614 trust...to thee, *Our F*. and our
716 *Our F*., God, who art in
1110 *Our F*., we look up to thee

Thy FATHER.
81 In thee *thy F*.'s glories shine
338 To *thy F*.'s bosom pressed
475 pleasing in *thy F*.'s sight
717 To *thy F*. come and wait
793 To us *thy F*.'s name declare
893 Before *thy F*.'s face

FATHERS.
163 Her *f*. God before her
608 Faith of our *f*.! holy faith
720 In the way our *f*. trod
734 To our *f*. in distress
958 Our *f*.. where are they
958 God of our *f*., hear
1089 Land where my *f*. died
1094 Our *f*.' sins were manifold
1097 O Lord, our *f*. oft have told
1097 As thee their God our *f*. owned
1100 Here thou our *f*.' steps didst
1102 The wonders that our *f*. told
1103 Thy kindness to our *f*. shown
1105 Our *f*. led across the sea
1105 Our *f*.' God, incline thine ear

FATHERLESS.
891 God of the *f*., be near
892 To tend the lone and *f*.

FATIGUE.
78 No more *f*., no more distress

FAVOR, FAVORS.

13 Extend to me thy *f.*, Lord
53 With the Holy Spirit's *f.*
186 Vainly with gifts would his *f.*
222 Look on me with thy *f.*
258 O receive us to thy *f.*
351 The *f.* and the peace of God
442 When the *f.* divine I received
453 Since I have found *f.*, he
734 Praise him for his grace and *f.*
872 Early let us seek thy *f.*
878 And in *f.* while below, With
99 New time, new *favors*, and new

FEAR.

5 Who would not *f.* his holy name
11 Him serve with *f.*, his praise
17 All nations *f.* his name
50 And people all shall *f.* him
54 Hear thy word with godly *f.*
147 O how I *f.* thee, living God
154 love is joined with holy *f.*
165 I will not *f.*, though armed
166 We will not *f.*, for God hath
172 Lord's pity... To those that *f.* his
178 Sorrow and *f.* are gone
192 *F.* not, he said,—for mighty
316 And drives away his *f.*
316 *F.*, the hope of heaven shall
351 The godly *f.*, the pleasing smart
427 grace that taught my heart to *f.*
438 I can no longer *f.*
449 If I have only known thy *f.*
496 No foes, no violence I *f.*
497 Lord, fill me with a humble *f.*
499 Be it my greatest *f.* Thy
505 I want a godly *f.*
511 principle... Of jealous, godly *f*
513 Where *f.*, and sin, and grief
570 Nor sin nor Satan can I *f.*
583 Yet, O disdain to *f.*
626 Away, my unbelieving *f.*
629 trembling faith is changed to *f.*
646 Suffer not our souls to *f.*
651 Who formed me...forbids my *f.*
659 I bid farewell to every *f.*
673 That caused thy needless *f.*
675 I do not *f.* to see
677 My soul disdains to *f.*
680 Nor will we *f.*, while thou
731 Stilling every anxious *f.*
746 And banishes thy *f.*
813 Shall I, for *f.* of feeble man
884 That each thy *f.* possessing
915 We never will throw off his *f.*
979 No *f.*, no woe, shall dim that
1020 With most tormenting *f.*
1052 *F.* hath no dwelling here
1101 save us, Lord, from slavish *f.*

FEARS.

113 Secure from all our *f.*
118 In the midst of *f.* and woes
144 And fills us with *f.*, we
173 Away, my needless *f.*
262 All my guilty *f.* remove
427 And grace my *f.* relieved
403 Bid my *f.* and doubtings cease

553 Shall guilty *f.* prevail
604 No *f.* to quell, no soul to save
634 Shine through my stormy *f.*
673 Give to the winds thy *f.*
730 Here will love my *f.* away
797 Our *f.*, our hopes, our aims
819 To him who died our *f.* to quell
913 Chasing all our *f.*, and cheering
950 Distressing *f.* within
959 Have pity on my *f.*
981 cease, ye vain, desponding *f.*

FEARFUL.

161 Ye *f.* saints, fresh courage take
479 O ye of *f.* hearts, be strong

FEARING.

141 Not *f.* or doubting, with Christ
645 Feeling much, and *f.* more

FEARLESS.

651 *F.*, their violence I dare
977 As *f.* as the evening cold

FEAST, FEASTS.

88 taste Of our everlasting *f.*
329 prepared A soul-reviving *f.*
357 O *f.* upon the love of God
361 Come, sinners, to the gospel *f.*
457 But night and day to *f.* on thee
512 makes me for some moments *f.*
683 Come to the *f.* of love; come ever
691 And long to *f.* upon thee still.
757 I haste to the heavenly *f.*
805 Celebrate the *f.* of love
838 We keep the sacred *f.*
838 The heavenly *f.* above
840 This solemn *f.* ordain
840 To keep the *f.*, Lord, we have
843 No gospel like this *f.*
844 And this sacred *f.* ordained
845 See, the *f.* of love is spread
847 At the Lamb's high *f.* we sing
849 Jesus, this *f.* receiving
885 Thou hast prepared the *f.*
85 And *feasts* his saints to-day

FED.

164 Who *f.* thee last, will feed thee
357 Come, and be richly *f.*
641 No creature but is *f.*
834 Millions... Were *f* and feasted
838 With which our souls are *f.*
850 And so our feeble love is *f.*
858 Let the living here be *f.*

FEED, FEEDS.

145 All his creatures God doth *f.*
180 And *f.* me with a shepherd's
326 souls, That *f.* upon the wind
568 Thy fainting spirit *f.*
761 His power defend; his bounty *f.*
819 Teach them thy chosen flock to *f.*
841 Come, on truth immortal *f.*
862 Thyself to *f.* the flock
1066 Them the Lamb shall always *f.*
153 And *feeds* you with his love

FEEBLE, FEEBLEST, FEEBLENESS.
140 children of dust, and *f.* as frail
172 He knows our *f.* frame
455 heal my *f.*, sin-sick soul
619 This *f.* body see
888 All the *f.* gently leading
965 How *f.* is our mortal frame
158 The least and *feeblest* there may
556 Thou seest my *feebleness*
1117 In age and *f.* extreme

FEEL, FEELS, FEELING.
61 And, as we read, O may we *f.*
203 Surely, none can *f.* like thee
285 And may I daily, hourly, *f.*
397 I see my sin, but cannot *f.*
435 Then, only then, we *f.* our
470 All I know, and all I *f.*
520 And all thy love to *f.*
1047 Christian, dost thou *f.* them
82 none but he who *feels* it knows
254 And in his measure *f.* afresh
372 Nor *f.* his need of thee
396 Of *feeling*, all things show some

FEET.
15 thither bring our willing *f.*
64 Low at thy *f.* we bend
130 Beneath thy *f.* we lie afar
182 So may we with willing *f.*
241 He brings my weary *f.*
257 And round his pierced *f.*
455 Help me at thy *f.* to lie
463 Saviour, at thy *f.* I fall
495 To lay my soul at Jesus' *f.*
533 Wash me, but not my *f.* alone
554 O keep me at thy sacred *f.*
730 With my tears his *f.* I'll bathe
752 that which calls me to thy *f.*
879 Who are they whose little *f.*
961 I soon shall gather up my *f.*
1008 Before thy *f.* could turn
1053 Feel as I would when my *f.*
1085 When at his *f.* ye fall
1094 While at thy *f.* we fall

FELICITY.
1033 And full *f.*

FELLOWSHIP.
507 That *f.* of love
561 In *f.* with him we loved
589 In *f.* alone To God
675 I have a *f.* with hearts
684 Where friend holds *f.*
781 The band of *f.*, the
788 One *f.* of mind
789 And if our *f.* below
791 hand Of *f.* to you we
791 Truly our *f.* below
796 And none our *f.* destroy
803 prove, *F.* in Jesus' love
803 Dearest *f.* we prove

FERVENT.
36 grateful song, the *f.* prayer
65 And *f.* prayer arise
74 breathe the humble, *f.* prayer
91 O that *f.* love to-day May

FESTAL.
338 Spread for thee the *f.* board
796 To sing the song of *f.* joy
1107 And sweet the *f.* lay

FESTIVAL.
796 Nor bid our *f.* be done

FETTER, FETTERS.
726 Let thy goodness, like a *f.*
185 The iron *fetters* yield
227 He burst from the *f.* of darkness
580 Break sin's strong *f.*, lead us
727 Feel the *f.* which have bound us
822 Jesus the prisoner's *f.* breaks
899 That from their iron *f.* freed
900 And from his limbs the *f.* fell

FEW.
744 Too *f.* we find the happy hours

FIELD.
591 That God is on the *f.*, when he
599 Undaunted to the *f.* he goes
1683 All the world is God's own *f.*
1083 From his *f.* shall in that day
1084 For the blessings of the *f.*
1087 From *f.* to garner throng

FIELDS.
183 While *f.* and floods, rocks, hills
330 We'll range the blest *f.* on the
602 Better the toil of *f.* like these
626 The *f.* elude the tiller's toil
747 The *f.* strive in vain to look
903 In the fair, fertile *f.* above
933 Wide *f.*, for harvest whitening
1037 Sweet *f.* beyond the swelling
1038 Sweet *f.* arrayed in living
1055 Are there bright, happy *f.*
1070 O'er earth's green *f.* and ocean's
1098 bless...Our *f.* with plenteousness

FIEND, FIENDS.
901 Whose power the giant *f.* obeys
968 With *fiends*, or angels spend

FIGHT.
566 Now the *f.* of faith begin
581 F. on, my soul, till death
584 Hold on the fearful *f.*
585 I the good *f.* have fought
586 And teach my hands to *f.*
593 Sure I must *f.*, if I would
596 deserts...The *f.* is all but lost
631 Thou, Lord, the dreadful *f.* hast
639 Firm in the *f.* I stand
801 To *f.* our passage through
1046 And *f.* our passage through
1059 And now we *f.* the battle
1062 Their *f.* with death and sin

FIG-TREE, FIG-TREES.
953 To cut the *f.-t.* down
626 The withering *fig-trees* droop

FIG 62 FLA

FIGHTS, FIGHTINGS.
599 *F.* the good fight, and wins
383 *Fightings* within, and fears
708 *F.* without, and fears within

FILIAL.
429 Father's grace I share a *f.*
468 Give to my soul, with *f.* fears
511 The *f.* awe, the fleshly heart
541 To serve the Lord with *f.* fear
701 And walk in *f.* fear

FILL, FILLED, FILLEST.
263 *F.* and nerve this will of mine
539 I quickly come, To *f.* and rule
815 And *filled* with faith and hope
924 *F.* with the glory of the Lord
806 Thou who *fillest* all in all

FIND.
21 Grant that all may seek and *f.*
295 search...Assured that we shall *f.*
383 Yea, all I need, in thee to *f.*
395 Thee, only thee, I fain would *f.*
443 Surely I shall *f.* him there
479 Ye all shall *f.*, whom in his
540 Give me, O Lord, to *f.* in thee
656 More than all in thee I *f.*

FINGER.
1088 Point on, with faithful *f.*

FINISH, FINISHED.
486 *F.* thy great work of grace
210 'Tis *finished!* all the debt is paid
218 'Tis *f.!* yes, the race is run
223 It is *f.!* hear him cry
224 It is *f.!* hear the dying Saviour
340 It is *f.!* Sinners, will not
592 'Tis *f.*, Lord, and die
955 I have *f.* the work thou didst
1062 'Tis *f.*, all is finished

FIRE.
40 touch thy servants' lips with *f.*
129 And fill us with thy holy *f.*
220 And clap his wings of *f.*
268 and crown us now with *f.*
269 Thou *F.* of love, and Fount of life
278 Come as the *f.*, and purge our
281 Kindle...The pure celestial *f.*
286 give us hearts and tongues of *f.*
380 ingot...Send me to eternal *f.*
415 Increase in us the kindled *f.*
481 Holy Ghost, all-quickening *f.*
487 Love's suppressed, unconscious *f.*
518 O that in me the sacred *f.*
550 My longing heart is all on *f.*
560 my...breast with heavenly *f.*
562 The pure celestial *f.* to impart
650 We have through *f.* and water
651 And through the *f.* pursue my
654 The *f.* forgets its power to burn
657 three...walked, unhurt, in *f.*
710 The motion of a hidden *f.*
936 To bring *f.* on earth he came
1009 Nor life's affection transient *f.*
1068 *F.* ascending seeks the sun

FIRES, FIRED.
509 To shun the eternal *f.*
936 Jesus' love the nations *f.*
488 Love has filled and *fired* my

FIRMAMENT.
138 The spacious *f.* on high
201 That lit the glorious *f.*
225 See that glowing *f.*
293 The starry *f.* on high

FIT, FITNESS, FITTING.
392 cannot be That I should *f.*
972 grace To *f.* our souls to fly
340 Nor of *fitness*...All the fitness he
141 His saints what is *fitting* shall

FIX, FIXED.
18 And *f.* thy blest abode
39 And *f.* our hearts and hopes
187 One star alone...Can *f.* the
490 *F.*, O fix my wavering mind
1048 To *f.* on things above
70 My heart is *fixed* on thee, my
293 But *f.* for everlasting years
184 eye Be *f.* on thee alone
513 soul's desire is *f.* on things above
516 Have *f.* my roving heart
649 *F.* on this ground will I remain
685 That all my hopes are *f.* on thee
811 'Tis *f.*; I can do all through thee
956 *F.* in an eternal state

FLAGS.
1104 Our navies spread their *f.* abroad

FLAME.
5 O for the living *f.* From his
64 love raise In us the heavenly *f.*
135 One holy light, one heavenly *f.*
251 flax, But raise it to a *f.*
274 O for that *f.* of living fire
278 purge...Like sacred nal *f.*
282 That all may feel the heavenly *f.*
476 Be thou alone my constant *f.*
476 This holy *f.*, this heavenly fire
488 Glowing still with quenchless *f.*
497 Might with an even *f.* aspire
562 Kindle a *f.* of sacred love
634 Nor feel the heavenly *f.*
679 The *f.* shall not hurt thee
703 I feel the sacred *f.*
791 We want to catch the spreading *f.*
805 Let the purer *f.* revive
881 Shed that love's undying *f.*
896 O that all might catch the *f.*
936 See how great a *f.* aspires
914 Love's pure *f.* and wisdom's

FLAMES, FLAMING.
185 Thy glory *f.* from sea and
476 Strange *f.* far from my heart
654 The lambent *f.* around me
1014 orbs...In brighter *f.*, a revel
1042 home below, with *f.* devour
928 'Midst *flaming* worlds, in these
342 Thou Son of God, whose *f.* eyes
1017 The *f.* heavens together roll

FLA   63   FOE

FLATTER, FLATTERING.
613 World may...*f.* and allure
662 Give but a *flattering* light

FLAX.
254 never quench the smoking *f.*

FLEE, FLED.
175 To thee in every trouble *f.*
318 From sin and death we *f.*
354 F. for thy life, the mountain
363 It tells me where my soul may *f.*
526 earth, and hell, and sin shall *f.*
674 Yet, Lord, where shall I *f.*
713 Far from the world, O Lord, I *f.*
949 From evil.. .We now desire to *f.*
126 When earth and heaven are *fled*
679 who for refuge to Jesus have *f.*

FLEETING.
132 With thee are as a *f.* day
358 pang Outlasts the *f.* breath
415 While I draw this *f.* breath
705 bless God...Through all my *f.*
956 Swiftly thus our *f.* days
967 Pass a few *f.* moments more

FLESH.
34 But God made *f.* is wholly ours
108 My *f.* shall rest beneath the
190 Veiled in *f.* the Godhead see
206 God, in *f.* made manifest
212 'Tis I thy sacred *f.* have torn
216 Didst thou not in our *f.* appear
254 He, in the days of feeble *f.*
505 Nor *f.* nor soul hath rest or
322 Saviour...feeble *f.* as 'unes
365 Thy *f.*, perhaps thy greatest care
374 And turn the stone to *f.*
397 'Tis thine a heart of *f.* to give
440 I no longer...Living in the *f.*
474 Thou hast my *f.*, thy hallowed
478 My soul and *f.*, O Lord of
537 perfect will. Shall in my *f.* be
649 my heart fail, and *f.* decay
668 If in this feeble *f.* I may
688 This robe of *f.* I'll drop and
694 Renew this wasted *f.* of mine
720 Us to save our *f.* assumes
737 What though my shrinking *f.*
742 But, Lord, the *f.* is weak
782 day Which shall our *f.* restore
835 Thy *f.* for all the world is given
844 For his *f.* is meat indeed
970 There once the *f.* of Jesus lay
1001 When from *f.* the spirit freed
1031 While in the *f.* my hope, my love
1042 And *f.* and sin no more control
1042 My *f.* shall slumber in the

FLIGHT.
189 Angels...Wing your *f.* o'er all
336 resisted, may take his sad *f.*
390 Nor take thine everlasting *f.*
448 Nor take thy *f.* from me away
452 Which take their everlasting *f.*
688 I view my home, and take my *f.*

913 and darkness...took their *f.*
1011 With songs let us follow his *f.*

FLOCK, FLOCKS.
11 We are his *f.*, he doth us feed
71 Thy *f.*, redeemed from sinful
564 Forward! *f.* of Jesus
569 Fear not, O little *f.*, the foe
572 Where Christ's *f.* enter in
790 Thy little *f.* in safety keep
872 Keep thy *f.*, from sin defend us
888 Saviour, who thy *f.* art feeding
929 A scattered, homeless *f.*, till all
189 Watching o'er your *flocks* by
641 Nor *f.*, nor herds be there
759 where with his *f.* he is gone

FLOOD, FLOODS.
219 And shed that sacred *f.*
341 'Tis a soul-reviving *f.*
431 Of joy, the swelling *f.*
593 Must I not stem the *f.*
721 Safely I shall pass the *f.*
964 Are carried downward by the *f.*
997 Waiting to pass that awful *f.*
1033 Part of his host have crossed the *f.*
1036 The *f.* of death passed o'er
152 He sat serene upon the *floods*
290 Pours out its *f.* of light and
406 When rising *f.* my soul
650 But saw thee on the *f.* appear

FLOWER, FLOWERS.
122 A tongue in every *f.*
172 Or like the morning *f.*
915 Truth from the earth, like to a *f.*
986 Bright *f.* of heavenly dye
994 Shall rise a heavenly *f.*
1086 He paints the wayside *f.*
181 And love and joy, like *flowers*
565 Work 'mid springing *f.*
652 Bloom the fair *f.* the earth
708 And *f.* and fruits abound
912 Lo, in the desert rich *f.* are
977 The morning *f.* display
1037 And never-withering *f.*
1039 There fragrant *f.* immortal
1058 Of *f.* that fear no thorn

FLY.
178 Jesus, to whom I *f.*, Doth all
395 Jesus, my soul shall *f.* to thee
430 Jesus, to thee I now can *f.*
611 If...We could not *f.* to thee
612 And long to *f.* away
678 thy breast, O Son of man, I *f.*
686 F. back to Christ, for sin is near

FOE.
93 I fear no *f.*, with thee at hand
168 What *f.* can make my soul afraid
207 Should strive afresh against the *f.*
228 We fear our *f.* no more
301 Let not the *f.* of Christ and man
508 Fear not the secret *f.*
585 And, dying, find my latest *f.*
597 For thee, and not thy *f.*
613 The world may call itself my *f.*

639 What *f.* have I to fear
704 I'd break through every *f.*
778 Shout, for the *f.* is destroyed that
927 Why should the *f.* thy purchase
981 Death, the last *f.*, was captive led

FOES.

69 From *f.* without, and foes within
196 Thy *f.* might hate, despise, revile
226 Thus he fills his *f.* with shame
237 The Lord, that all our *f.* o'ercame
244 sits...Till all his *f.* submit
245 His *f.* beneath his feet shall
264 While his *f.* from him receive
273 Keep far our *f.*, give peace at
369 The *f.* that interrupt my rest
567 Against unnumbered *f.*
568 thy Leader, Shall all thy *f.*
581 Ten thousand *f.* arise
593 Are there no *f.* for me to face
643 *F.* may hate...friends may shun
717 When the *f.* of life prevail
727 Here on earth, where *f.* surround
759 Thy *f.* will rejoice when my
767 Have thy *f.* been proud and
767 All thy *f.* shall flee before thee
768 All her *f.* shall be confounded
778 Awake, for thy *f.* shall oppress
778 Strong were thy *f.*; but the arm
795 Mighty their envious *f.* to move
908 ride, Till all thy *f.* submit
979 sleep...Unbroken by the last of *f.*
1043 And cast thy *f.* with fury down
1033 Kept by him, no *f.* annoy
1105 And *f.* beset on every hand

FOLD, FOLDS, FOLDED.

9 He brought us to his *f.* again
229 And where in many a *f.* The
434 I did not love the *f.*
434 he that brought me to the *f.*
434 Love the peaceful *f.*
726 Wandering from the *f.* of God
790 Unless the *f.* we first forsake
888 Then within thy *f.* eternal
927 Nor *f.*, nor place of refuge near
929 Be gathered to thy peaceful *f.*
872 For our use thy *folds* prepare
179 in green pastures, safe-*folded*

FOLLOW.

300 Who meekly *f.* Christ on earth
496 Dauntless, untired, I *f.* thee
557 We *f.* thee through grace
601 And humbly *f.* after me
602 Take up thy cross and *f.* Christ
631 And *f.* thee where'er thou go
643 All to leave and *f.* thee
713 beauty...For those who *f.* thee
730 And we still will *f.* thee
742 Joy to me To *f.* only thee
744 Divinely drawn to *f.* thee
761 While I live...Still *f.* me
886 And if I try to *f.* His footsteps

FOLLOWED.

201 He *f.* where his Master went
422 I rose, went forth, and *f.* thee
434 He *f.* me o'er vale and hill

FOLLOWER.

201 So will the Lord his *f.* join
385 Meanest *f.* of the Lamb, His
573 A *f.* of my God
593 A *f.* of the Lamb
622 His faithful *f.* I would be

FOLLOWERS.

328 To heaven he led his *f.*' way
614 And we his *f.* here
650 Thy feeble, tempted *f.* here
786 Lift...hearts...Ye *f.* of the Lamb
802 *F.* of the bleeding Lamb
848 Come, and meet thy *f.* here
867 And that thy *f.* may be tried
973 We, *f.* of our suffering Lord
1066 *F.* of the dying God

FOLLY, FOLLIES.

255 Bears with our *f.*, soothes our
356 Why will ye *f.* love
371 ways of sin and *f.* go
108 But be forgiven my *follies* past

FOOD.

39 With *f.* divine may we be fed
602 beauties be My soul's eternal *f.*
849 O *F.* that angels eat
853 Cheers our famished souls with *f.*
927 And neither *f.* nor feeder have
1007 That its heavenly *f.* are giving
1086 Our life, our health, our *f.*

FOOLISH, FOOLISHNESS.

169 *F.*, and impotent, and blind, Lead
356 So *f.*, impotent, and poor
544 thousand ways To *f.* man
368 begin Our *foolishness* to mourn

FOOT.

276 Where'er the *f.* of man hath trod
373 danger...Where'er thy *f.* can

FOOTSTEPS.

61 while thy words our *f.* guide
159 Thy hand will there our *f.*
161 He plants his *f.* in the sea
157 which my Saviour's *f.* shine
582 Your Captain's *f.* see
586 In all thy *f.* tread
665 Whose fainting *f.* trod
782 And still in Jesus' *f.* tread
886 follow His *f.* here below
915 His *f.* cannot err
958 pious dead...we the *f.* trace
988 E'en while with us thy *f.* trod
1045 They marked the *f.* that he
1112 Throughout the deep thy *f.* shine

FOOTSTOOL.

118 Leave thy *f.*, take thy throne
880 Yet still to his *f.* in prayer

FOREIGN.

633 Though in a *f.* land
1113 In *f.* realms and lands remote

FOREFATHERS.

179 the path which my *f.* trod
828 promise...To our *f.* given

FORERUNNER, FORERUNNERS.
308 *F*. of the sun, It marks
640 What are they but *forerunners*

FORESTS.
1087 *F*. and mountains ring

FORETASTE, FORETASTES.
1054 even now, a sweet *f*. of home
45 *Foretastes* of future bliss are

FORGET, FORGETS, FORGETFUL.
886 He never will *f*. me
625 Yet God, my God, *forgets* me not
552 Yes, she may *forgetful* be
554 thoughts depart, *F*. of his word

FORGOT, FORGOTTEN.
376 virgin, Hast thou then *f*.
398 Hast thou *f*. thy gracious skill
996 dead, Where all things are *f*.
479 Ye shall not be *forgotten* long

FORGIVE.
105 *F*. me, Lord, for thy dear Son
157 How ready to *f*.
221 *F*. them, Father, O forgive
258 blood cries out, *F*. them
307 Thou canst this instant now *f*.
312 He will your sins *f*.
370 learn How freely he'll *f*.
371 His mercy will the guilt *f*.
423 I freely all *f*.
438 *F*. him, O forgive, they cry
503 Thou wilt my guilty soul *f*.
557 *F*., my stricken spirit cries
558 My Saviour prayed, forgive
716 And as we those *f*. Who
861 when thou hearest, Lord, *f*.
949 *F*. this nation's many sins

FORGIVES.
108 But he *f*. my follies past
749 The Lord *f*. thy sins

FORGIVEN.
219 And look, and be *f*.
243 The joyful news of sins *f*.
246 All thy people are *f*.
258 Father, show their sins *f*.
259 How the penitent *f*.
283 Show me sin, but sin *f*.
360 perish...And never be *f*.
367 And all your sin 's *f*.
407 And live and die *f*.
424 And show my sins *f*.
428 On me, through grace *f*.
433 Through Christ abundantly *f*.
437 know His sins on earth *f*.
439 The sense of sin *f*.
444 The newborn peace of sins *f*.
446 faith that shows our sins *f*.
455 much. For I have much *f*.
465 All our sins by thee *f*.
467 Who hath my sins *f*.
472 Most graciously *f*.
545 know My sins on earth *f*.
590 And pray to be *f*.

648 Freely and graciously *f*.
650 Retain our sense of sin *f*.
730 Love I much ? I've much *f*.
752 Then are my sins by thee *f*.
787 Their vilest sins *f*.
841 came...That we might be *f*.
939 Bid him hope to be *f*.
1001 they knew their sins *f*.
1030 Who knows his sins *f*.

FORGIVENESS.
342 Free *f*. in his name
1023 Grant *f*., Lord, at last
1064 *F*. and holiness give

FORGIVING.
172 And his *f*. love, Far as the
439 Thy sweet *f*. love
449 The joy of his *f*. love
590 *F*. and forgiven, O may
716 may we *F*. grace receive

FORM, FORMS, FORMED.
714 That radiant *f*. of thine
305 No outward *forms* can make us
989 And mortal *f*. shall spring
3 He *formed* us by his word
123 thoughts lie open...Before...*f*.
153 Praise him who *f*. you of his
651 Who *f*. me man forbids my fear
776 *F*. thee for his own abode

FORSAKE.
216 Will he *f*. his throne above
352 I wait, but he does not *f*.
401 Though late, I all *f*.
679 I'll never...no never *f*.
728 Do thy friends despise, *f*. thee
945 We will no more our God *f*.
1052 *F*. the world, no longer roam
1075 I all on earth *f*.

FORSAKEN.
217 Is not *f*. by his God
1002 cast down, we're not *f*.
1092 earth hath *f*. Thy ways

FORSAKING, FORSAKEST.
492 Well for him who all *f*.
613 I know thou ne'er *forsakest* him

FORTRESS.
166 A mighty *f*. is our God
556 My *f*. and my tower
623 Thy power...my *f*. is

FORWARD.
563 *F*. into battle, See, his
564 *F*.! be our watchword
564 *F*.! flock of Jesus, Salt
568 Go *f*., Christian soldier
612 Sweet to look *f*., and behold

FOUGHT.
260 *F*. the fight, the battle won
593 While others *f*. to win the prize
955 I have *f*. my way through

FOUND.

41 Where'er...seek thee, thou art *f*.
349 While yet a pardoning God is *f*.
399 And wilt thou yet be *f*.
414 The long-lost son is *f*.
422 For, O my God, It *f*. out me
436 It is through him that I have *f*.
721 Still in thee may I be *f*.
781 Be lost and *f*. in him
821 And sought, but never *f*.
954 Be *f*.—as, Lord, thou find'st
1024 O may we all be *f*. Obedient

FOUNDATION.

76 The sure *f*. and the strength
672 How firm a *f*., ye saints
766 Behold the sure *F*.-stone
773 Nor can her firm *f*. move
856 Christ is made the sure *F*.
859 Rejoicing this *f*. lay

FOUNDED, FOUNDER.

809 Deep *f*. in the truth of grace
1063 Immovably *f*. in grace
648 Whose *founder* is the living God
834 And bless the *F*.'s name

FOUNT, FOUNTS.

266 Holy Spirit, *F*. of blessing
691 Thou *F*. of life! thou Light of
701 Thou *F*. of living fire
726 Come, thou *F*. of every blessing
849 A *f*. of love thou art
986 These flowing *founts* supply

FOUNTAIN.

13 The *f*. of eternal love
171 Open now the crystal *f*.
178 I have the *f*. still
279 *F*. of life and love
302 To the blest *f*. of thy blood
319 There is a *f*. filled with blood
319 thief...That *f*. in his day
330 Adam's...Christ hath opened a *f*.
336 A *f*. is open, how canst
341 Here a pure and healing *f*.
341 Health this *f*. will restore
355 To Christ, the *f*.. come
431 *F*. of life, to all below
533 *F*. for guilt and sin
602 The *f*., and the noonday shade
612 What must the *f*. be
623 *F*. of unexhausted love
656 Thou of life the *f*. art
694 drink of thee, the *F*. head
724 *F*. of o'erflowing grace
774 From thine exhaustless *f*.
849 A *f*. purely flowing
1060 Dear *f*. of refreshment
1081 *F*. of mercy, God of love

FOUNTAINS.

1012 But never thy *f*. of love
1066 To the living *f*. lead

FRAGRANCE.

47 courts with grateful *f*. till
257 Their *f*. ever sweet

551 herb, Diffusing *f*. round
611 plants that throw Their *f*.
754 Like *f*. on the breezes
868 till the air with the *f*. of heaven

FRAIL.

685 And fix my *f*., inconstant
959 How *f*. my best estate
962 Teach me to know how *f*. I am
962 How *f*., at best, is dying man
1009 Were this *f*. world our only rest

FRAME.

85 would stay in such a *f*. as
139 voice Called forth this universal *f*.
254 He knows our feeble *f*.
421 I dare not trust the sweetest *f*.
700 No voice can sing, no heart can *f*.
734 Well our feeble *f*. he knows
915 and all shall *f*. To bow

FRATERNAL.

788 In one *f*. bond of love

FREE.

13 When thou return'st to set them *f*.
58 Sweet the theme, a *f*. salvation
117 Then, from sin and sorrow *f*.
221 Thy love, for every sinner *f*.
222 Come, Lord, and set me *f*.
224 O'er hearts thou makest *f*.
283 Sin hath ruled me, set me *f*.
332 hears, And is from sin set *f*.
334 Born to set thy people *f*.
446 Thy grace, O Lord, is *f*. indeed
453 the man whose heart is set *f*.
457 And set my longing spirit *f*.
473 With a glad heart and *f*.
477 shall my heart from earth be *f*.
493 We shall from all our sins be *f*.
495 And fully set my spirit *f*.
496 burst these bonds, and set It *f*.
514 Since thou wouldst have us *f*.
516 But grace hath set me *f*.
520 From every wish set *f*.
521 A heart from sin set *f*.
580 Set us, believing, *f*.
580 kindness...As *f*. and true as
626 And all the world go *f*.? No
742 Thy love, so full, so *f*.
758 assures you *f*. grace is so nigh
784 Till thou hast made us *f*. indeed
797 From...sin we shall be *f*.
900 And lo! the saint, as *f*. as air
992 Soul of the just, set *f*.
1054 sigh from this body of sin to be *f*.
1089 Land of the noble, *f*.

FREES, FREED.

735 Thy death it is that *f*. us
478 Bids my *freed* heart in thee
535 Impatient to be *f*.
561 That *f*. us from the fear of men
1011 And *f*. from its bodily chain

FREEDOM.

470 *F*., friends...Consecrate
580 And singing, *f*. found

FRIEND (continued from FRE)

909 The day of f. dawns at
921 Of life and f., light and peace
923 The f. Jesus has to give
1089 mountain side Let f. ring
1089 Sweet f.'s song
1089 With f.'s holy light
1093 Peace and f. we enjoy
1100 Here f. spreads her banner

FRENZY.
1099 And youth renewed and f.

FRIEND.
34 The F. of earth-born man
87 Our Father and our F.
143 Our faithful, unchangeable f.
175 My best, my only F.
178 Stripped of each earthly f.
239 My F. before the throne of love
255 Our all-sufficient F.
284 Come, tenderest F., and best
593 Is this vile world a f. to grace
605 serve the cause of such a F.
613 To this tried F. and sure
728 What a F. we have in Jesus
730 From the sinner's dying F.
738 Jesus, the feeble sinner's F.
767 He himself appears thy F.
768 F. to friend unfaithful prove
786 The King is now our f.
839 burn To feel a f. is nigh
958 hear, Thou everlasting F.
967 I soon shall find my f. again
967 give me back my parted f.
1009 F. after friend departs
1098 Her everlasting f.

FRIENDS.
89 For f. and brethren dear
141 Though f. should all fail, and foes
611 The f. who in our sunshine
643 Foes may hate, and f. may shun
650 His f. and witnesses to own
655 Choose thou for me my f.
698 what's my...Or all my f. to me
794 Call us thy f., and love
816 joined in heart The f. of Jesus
1032 Take life or f. away
1033 Come, let us join our f. above
1044 And soon my f. in Christ
1088 The f. gone there before me

FRIENDSHIP, FRIENDSHIPS.
797 And perfect love and f. reign
799 Where zeal and f. meet
807 When shall sweet f.
1062 knitting severed *friendships*

FROWN.
380 F. not, lest I faint and die
478 will I love, beneath thy f. Or
543 let me see thy gathering f.
667 unmoved, the world's dread f.
813 Awed by a mortal's f., shall I
967 Or f. my tears to see

FROWNING.
119 Astonished at thy f. brow
659 And face a f. world

FROZE, FROZEN.
187 Deep horror then my vitals f.
285 O melt this *frozen* heart
396 thaw...this f. heart of mine
547 And warm our f. hearts

FRUIT.
29 Produce abundant f.
50 The earth her f. shall bring
58 F. of everlasting love
641 Their wonted f. should bear
671 The f. of loving deeds
774 And on their f. the nations
826 The f. of all thy sorrows share
953 No f. of holiness
953 And let our gracious f.
953 And f. unto perfection bear
1083 F. unto his praise to yield

FRUITS.
52 May the f. of thy salvation
88 Make the f. of grace abound
288 And all its f., from day to day
499 Thy blessed f. to know
892 To thee our first-f. give
1084 For the f. in full supply

FRUITFUL.
181 showers Upon the f. earth
769 As through a f., watery dale
1085 seasons In f. order move

FUGITIVE.
681 To take a poor f. in
955 And the f. moment refuses

FULLNESS.
56 Earth is with its f. stored
175 Thy f. is the same
265 Rest...With the f. of thy grace
325 Thy f. I implore
431 Into thy f. fall
442 As if...with the f. of God
492 In whom all our f. lies
508 With all thy f. fill
510 The f. which thy own redeemed
535 Thy f. I require
545 My soul for all thy f. cries
754 All f. dwells in him
757 That indeed is the f., but
782 Expect his f. to receive
801 With all thy f. fill
860 And may the f. of thy grace
1059 In f. of his grace
1085 He filleth with his f. All things

FUNERAL.
1025 Like flames o'er nature's f. pyre

FURNACE.
768 In the f. God may prove thee

FURROWS.
62 The hope in earthly f. sown

FUTURE.
366 The f. is unknown
605 Nor f. days nor powers

G.

GABRIEL.
743 And vie with G. while he sings

GAIN.
49 How boundless our eternal g.
115 heaven We may hope to g. at last
211 My richest g. I count but loss
422 that I should g. An interest
451 Counting g. and glory loss
471 And loss shall be eternal g.
643 With thy favor, loss is g.
721 Let me know it G. to die
736 my peace; in loss, my g.
856 What they g. from thee forever
1007 Then the g. of death we prove
1010 And death to him is g.
1047 Counting g. but loss
1050 And life eternal g.

GALE, GALES.
122 There seems a voice in every g.
421 In every high and stormy g.
636 We'll own the favoring g.
982 So sinks the g. when storms
1004 Trust to that propitious g.
1111 Send thou...the prosperous g.
931 Arise, ye gales, and waft them

GALILEE.
195 O'er the blue depths of G.
197 faith...Olivet, And love its G.
233 Eager they haste to G.

GALILEAN.
246 Hail, thou G. King

GARDEN, GARDENS.
207 And in the g. secretly
217 'Tis midnight; in the g. now
645 By thy fainting in the g.
777 like streams that feed the g.
1084 For the stores the gardens yield

GARMENT, GARMENTS.
133 He glory like a g. wears
143 We lay our garments by, Upon
142 The g. he assumes Are
430 I wash my g. in the blood
811 In his rich g. clad
1049 Arrayed in g. washed
1076 Arrays in g. white and pure

GARNER, GARNERS.
1083 fruitful ears...In his g. evermore
575 mature the grain For garners in

GATE.
246 Opened is the g. of heaven
246 Now within the g. rejoice
353 And yet the g. of mercy find
376 At the g. of heaven l eating
453 Opened wide the g. to God
820 house of God, the g. of heaven
976 Death is the g. to endless joy
976 fearless through death's iron g.

GATES.
9 We'll crowd thy g. with thankful
11 O enter then his g. with praise
185 The g. of brass before him burst
225 Christ has passed the eternal g.
237 Lift up your heads, ye heavenly g.
261 Lift your heads, eternal g.
289 And shake the g. of hell
326 The happy g. of gospel grace
563 G. of hell can never 'Gainst
570 Close by the g. of death and hell
634 The g. of heaven, Lord, open
765 What though the g. of hell
777 And your g. shall all be praise
879 Lift your heads, ye golden g.
936 Shakes the trembling g. of hell
1044 And pearly g. behold
1062 Fling open wide the golden g.

GATHER, GATHERED.
109 We g. in these hallowed walls
644 Quickly, reapers, g. quickly
848 Where angels soon shall g.
1083 G. thou the people in
25 ransomed...Gathered out of every
1052 G. from every land
1083 All is safely g. in.

GAVE.
999 He g. thee, he took thee, and
1012 He g., and he taketh away

GEM, GEMS.
187 From every host, from every g.
890 Mourn for the tarnished g.
185 Gems of the mountain, and pearls
884 No g. from earth's deep mine

GENERATIONS.
907 Earth's g. pass

GENNESARETH.
1099 As by G.'s shore

GENTILES.
300 star...led...G. to the lowly bed
912 G. and Jews the blest vision
924 The fullness of the G. call
924 Thine heritage the G. take
941 Draw the G. unto thee

GENTLE, GENTLENESS.
176 How g. God's commands
1008 G., and meek, and mild
196 That gentleness and grace that
328 From lips of g. and grace
480 Thy joy, and peace, and g.
527 And all thy g. is mine

GERM.
575 Grace keeps the precious g. alive

GETHSEMANE.
223 Go to dark G.
836 G., can I forget

GIANTS.
824 As g. may they run their race

GIFT.

124 Convinced that every perfect g.
264 Thou the G. and Giver too
269 Most blessed g. which God can
337 God's great g. to all mankind
377 The g. unspeakable impart
377 g. of faith...gracious g. bestow
406 O let me now receive that g.
433 Prove the g. unspeakable
445 And ask the g. unspeakable
452 One only g. can justify
480 The g. unspeakable sent down
485 Hourly some new g. to bring
520 the grace The g. unspeakable
562 And still stir up thy g. in me
650 With thanks for thy continued g.
789 The g. which he on one bestows
831 sign The g. unspeakable impart
843 Ours is the free g., given
866 receive this g. Thy willing
884 The dearest g. of heaven
892 Whate'er the g. may be
896 No g. too rare she thought
903 Grace shall the humble g. receive
934 Pour out the promised g. on all
1006 Take the g. awhile bestowed

GIFTS.

33 So shall thy choicest g., O Lord
46 Thy g. abundantly increase
91 With his g. of living flame
104 Thy g. are every evening new
182 As they offered g. most rare
186 Vainly with g. would his favor
231 All good g. returned with her
266 Greater than all g. below
273 Who dost thy sevenfold g. impart
284 Thy sacred g. impart
389 Will g. delight the Lord most
397 Thy g. I only can receive
467 I'll take the g. he hath bestowed
520 Thy g., alas! cannot suffice
627 Though life its common g. deny
794 On thy own g. and graces feast
806 Divers g. to each divide
812 Scattered his g. on man below
812 From Christ...all their g. receive
837 All the rich g. of gospel grace
930 The g. of God are strown
949 For countless g. received
1085 Heap on...altar The g. his
1086 Accept the g. we offer

GIVE.

128 Lo, all we are to thee we g.
214 Here, Lord, I g. myself away
400 And g. up all to thee
457 And freely g. up all the rest
471 May gladly g. up all to thee
508 To thee ourselves we g.
892 We g. thee but thine own
904 Freely may we rejoice to g.

GLAD.

89 G. was my heart to hear
168 Whose streams make g. the
185 Hark, the glad sound! the Saviour
192 G. tidings of great joy I bring

251 And bids the earth be g.
426 And he hath made me g.
841 And every heart be g.
952 Thy praise shall our g. tongues
1058 vision Shall g. the saints

GLADNESS.

12 The g. of that happy day
50 Their songs of g. raise
77 Let g. dwell in every heart
182 As with g. men of old
280 The passover of g.
453 And share in the g. of all
616 When g. wings my favored
652 like an Eden blossoming in g.
684 The oil of g. on our heads
796 Where none shall bid our g. cease
853 Wine of g. flowing free
1015 When, O when, shall I the g.
1043 With everlasting g. crowned
1058 To heavenly g. lead

GLASS.

174 As through a g. we see

GLIDE. GLIDES.

950 years. How swift they g. away
418 The day glides sweetly o'er their
955 time...G. swiftly away

GLOBE.

17 He framed the g.; he built the sky
130 glance of thine runs through the g.
153 Thou restless g. of golden light

GLOOM. GLOOMY.

77 A guilty world in g.
86 And chase its g. away
110 And from death's g. my spirit
150 From the g. his brightness
228 If thou art there to break the g.
286 And chase our g. away
287 Amid our g. and darkness shine
336 To sink in the g. of eternity's night
363 Yet 'midst the g. I hear a sound
507 Glory shall chase away its g.
622 'mid scenes of deepest g.
682 Lead...amid the encircling g.
723 By the g. that veiled the skies
777 Change to-day the g. of night
824 The g. of hellish night
973 Amid the deepening g.
974 It melts the deepening g.
998 tomb...I dread not its g.
1023 Through the deep and silent g.
1041 To dissipate the g. of night
940 O'er the gloomy hills of darkness
1028 No g. fears their souls

GLORY.

18 Whose g. fills the realms above
22 Be eternal g. given
34 Whose g. fills the sky
37 And all the house with g. fill
41 G. begun below
106 In thy sole g. may unite
120 The world is with the g. filled
131 Thine only g. we declare

199 What g. shall be theirs above
215 And in full g. shine
296 Till g. breaks upon my view
320 Now g. to God in the highest
448 And g. end what grace begun
459 And while we to thy g. live
461 That thou shouldst us to g.
478 In thy sole g. may unite
546 And saw his g. shine
552 Thou shalt see my g. soon
572 To show the g., where Christ's
604 And O, may this my g. be
643 Haste thee on from grace to g.
680 By faith we see the g.
700 In thee be all our g. now
869 Lord, from thine inmost g. send
1033 With those to g. gone
1040 In God's eternal g. blest
1088 O rise to g., hither, And find

His GLORY.

150 Every-where *his* g. shineth
546 And saw *his* g. shine
980 They tell us of *his* g. nigh

In GLORY.

6 May we *in* g. see, And to
56 Round the Lord, *in* g. seated
259 Lives *in* g. now on high
874 Still *in* g. Thou wilt hear

Thy GLORY.

19 *Thy* g. be our whole design
20 Till we *thy* g. see
48 *Thy* g. fil's both earth and
56 Lord, *thy* g. fills the heaven
88 May *thy* g. meet our eyes
146 Father, how wide *thy* g. shines
469 And let us to *thy* g. live
475 And to *thy* g. live and die
484 And to *thy* g. live
484 *Thy* g. be my aim
536 I only for *thy* g. burn
562 There let it for *thy* g. burn
600 And here *thy* g. see
689 What will *thy* g. be
712 Till I *thy* g. see
810 *Thy* g. if we now intend
817 Who to *thy* g. live
826 And hereafter in *thy* g.
861 *Thy* g. never hence depart
925 Shall come *thy* g., Lord, to see
941 Let them see thee in *thy* g.
1016 She shall yet behold *thy* g.
1016 Soon they shall *thy* g. see
1060 The mention of *thy* g.

To GLORY.

461 That thou shouldst us *to* g. bring
643 Haste thee on from grace *to* g.
851 And take *to* g. all who
1033 With these *to* g. gone
1088 O rise *to* g., hither

GLORIES.

31 Thy g. will their tongues employ
60 Then on thy g. while we dwell
63 Crowned With g. all divine

93 Earth's joys grow dim, its g. pass
127 Thy never-ceasing g. shine
137 Thy g. let the world proclaim
142 His g. shine with beams so
241 Shows me the g. of my God
266 May our lips thy g. show
298 adore The g. of thy grace
428 And cause the g. of thy face
561 G. upon glories Hath our
653 In whom the Father's g. shine
743 O could I sound the g. forth
743 Make all his g. known
770 The brightest g. earth can
860 Whose g. through creation shine
910 Thy radiant g. shine
918 Ere all its g. stand revealed
1045 How bright their g. be

GLORIFY.

258 Father, g. thy Son
276 The name of Jesus g.
464 G. thyself in me
506 And g. thy grace
571 To g. my God below
574 A charge to keep...God to g.
786 And g. his name
915 And g. thy name
945 His name to g.

GLORIFIED.

271 Our Saviour g.
675 If thou be g.
936 Jesus' word is g.
983 Yet g. by grace alone
1045 With g. millions to praise

GLORIOUS.

57 Praise the Lord, for he is g.
81 Then I shall share a g. part
489 Fill us with thy g. power
519 O make me g. all within
567 In th's his g. day
608 And hasten to thy g. day
714 All ...g. as thou art
719 believers shown, G. and
981 Canst thou forget thy g. work

GLOW.

49 Our love shall never cease to g.
263 G. within this heart of mine
271 And g. with energy divine
518 Me Might now begin to g.
780 In every action g.
783 With love to man will g.

GLOWS, GLOWETH, GLOWING.

160 That g. will in my ravished
204 Lo! it g. with peace and joy
711 And warm and warmer g.
492 heart who rein it *glow*ing Calm
417 Well may this *glow*ing heart
561 O where is now that g.

GO.

110 Lord, I will not let thee g.
536 And will not let thee g.
626 But shall I therefore let him g.
715 I will not let thee g.

GOD 71 GOS

715 I will not let thee *g.*, unless
758 What light... *g.* after him, *g.*
1006 I shall *g.* to him, but he Never

GOD.

68 Who is like *G.!* so great, so high
118 We all believe in one true *G.*
481 And know that I am one with *G.*
596 As though there were no *G.*
642 But *G.* is round about me
945 For *G.* to live and die
1029 Then shall say, Th:s *G.* is mine
1089 Our fathers' *G.!* to thee

GOD-MAN.

737 I shall with the *G.-m.* prevail

My GOD.

425 *My G.*, my *G.*, to thee I cry
435 Thou art my Lord, *my G.*
693 O God, thou art *my G.* alone
698 There's nothing like *my G.*
1042 I shall be near, and like *my G.*
1075 He calls himself *my G.*

GODS.

145 For of *g.* he is the God
908 And heathen *g.*, forsaken, fall

GODHEAD.

10 One *G.*, blest for evermore
35 Mysterious *G.!* Three in One
121 Thy *G.* we adore
144 *G.* One, and Persons Three
231 Of the Father's *G.* true and
428 The *G.* reconciled
435 And make to us the *G.* known
480 To make the depths of *G.* known
527 Jesus, in whom the *G.*'s rays

GOLD.

186 Myrrh from the forest, and *g.*
194 Comes round the age of *g.*
249 Pass through the gates of *g.*
329 And *g.* is dross compared to her
564 Shine the gates with *g.*
679 Thy dross to consume, and thy *g.*
859 The *g.* and silver, make them

GOLDEN.

903 Treasures... Brighter than *g.* ore
906 Squandered life's most *g.* hours
933 More rich than *g.* ore
959 Where the *g.* gates of day
1058 The light so new and *g.*

GOOD.

11 the Lord our God is *g.*, His
49 Source of all *g.*, thou gracious
69 w.tholds No real *g.* from
141 The *g.* that we seek we ne'er
157 How *g.* thou art! how large
284 Divinely *g.* thou art
386 No *g.* word, or work, or thought
401 To seek... No other *g.* below
427 The Lord has promised *g.* to me
436 My soul's eternal *g.*
447 With him of every *g.* possessed

504 No faith could work effectual *g.*
571 And walking in the *g.*
615 *G.*, when he gives—supremely
635 I know thee *g.*, I know thee just
635 It must be *g.* for me
643 All must work for *g.* to me
744 Our day is spent in doing *g.*
1006 Let him do as seems him *g.*

GOODNESS.

19 Thy *g.* to proclaim
68 Through all the earth his *g.*
100 Whose *g.* lengthens out our
121 Thy *g.* we rehearse
151 Let every tongue thy *g.*
159 Thy *g.* never dies
160 Thy *g.* I'll pursue
176 His *g.* stands approved
179 Let *g.* and mercy my
250 Thy *g.* is unchanged
317 That, saved, we may thy *g.* feel
317 His *g.* must endure
390 Ten thousand times thy *g.* seen
465 Let us all thy *g.* share
480 Thy *g.* and thy truth we
484 And let me in thy *g.* trust
536 And all thy *g.* know
619 O thou from whom all *g.* flows
646 Let thy *g.* never fail us
658 Thy *g.*, tried so long
699 Thy *g.* I adore
761 Thy *g.* ever nigh
801 Till all thy utmost *g.* prove
809 Thy *g.* to proclaim
951 And makes me see his *g.*
1094 Thy *g.* hath been shown
1101 Confess thy *g.*, and adore
1113 Thy *g.* we'll adore

GOODS.

470 All my *g.*, and all my hours

GOOD-WILL.

192 *G.-w.* henceforth from heaven
193 *G.-w.* and peace are heard
194 Peace on earth, *g.-w.* to men

GOSPEL.

55 From the *g.* Now supply thy
72 Where *g.* light is glowing
289 Thy *g.* then shall greatly grow
292 Nor shall thy spreading *g.* rest
292 Thy *g.* makes the simple wise
322 majesty... Through all the *g.*
323 amazing words... in the *g.* found
350 Sinners, obey the *g.* word
361 The *g.* bids you come
361 Come, sinners, to the *g.* feast
451 Have seen a glorious *g.-*day
515 O joyful sound of *g.* grace
526 Me from the *g.* hope can move
599 His feet are with the *g.* shod
817 shower Of *g.* blessings send
820 Go, preach my *g.*, saith the
830 And ye shall prove my *g.*
825 Thy *g.* through the world to
861 The blessed *g.* of thy Son
910 has sent Thy *g.* to mankind

913 And where the *g.* day Sheds
923 The joy the *g.* will bestow
924 Let all obey the *g.* word
926 And cheer them by the *g.* word
932 The *g.* call obey, And seek
933 Christ's precious *g.* taking
937 every clime, shall the *g.* call obey
940 Send the *g.* To the earth's
940 Fly abroad, thou mighty *G.*
943 Come, and bring the *g.* grace

GOSPEL'S.

52 Thanks...For thy *g.*'s joyful
65 And let thy *g.*'s joyful sound
88 May thy *g.*'s joyful sound
288 The *g.*'s glorious sound
290 Upon the *g.*'s sacred page
328 sweetly flowed the *g.*'s sound
349 How sweet the *g.*'s charming
578 And the blest *g.*'s saving health
910 To spread the *g.*'s rays
918 Far let the *g.*'s sound be known
939 Spread the *g.*'s richest feast
1100 We praise thee for the *g.*'s light

GRACE.

7 We meet the *g.* to take
19 Vouchsafe the *g.* we humbly
49 Thy never-failing *g.* to prove
69 All needful *g.* will God bestow
200 Till we too change from *g.* to
210 All *g.* is now to s.nners given
275 Great *g.* be now upon us all
329 Happy the man who finds the *g.*
340 Every *g.* that brings you nigh
382 Let me then obtain the *g.*
421 I rest on his unchanging *g.*
427 How precious did that *g.* appear
427 'Tis *g.* hath brought me safe
461 O wondrous *g.!* O boundless
503 Jesus, the *g.* bestow
514 O that the perfect *g.* were given
537 I thank thee for the present *g.*
545 Saviour, on me the *g.* bestow
545 Jesus, the crowning *g.* impart
552 O for *g.* to love thee more
609 By thee, to exercise their *g.*
612 Sweet to reflect how *g.* divine
638 Lord, may that *g.* be ours
656 Plenteous *g.* with thee is found
662 And *g.* command my heart away
679 My *g.,* all-sufficient, shall be
685 O Lord, thy heavenly *g.* impart
708 shine in glory and in *g.*
732 Thou the *g.* of life supplying
738 the *g.* Unspeakable I now receive
782 And *g.* to answer grace
818 Thy universal *g.* proclaim
913 Moved...By thine almighty *g.*
919 And pray for *g.* to keep the faith
953 From God obtained the *g.*
1024 With all thy glorious *g.*
1048 Where sin abounded, *g.* May
1105 Surround us with thy heavenly *g.*

By GRACE.

333 By *g.* alone I draw my breath
385 Am freely saved by *g.*

446 We only can be saved by *g.*
446 Save us by *g.* through faith

His GRACE.

28 The glory of *his g.*
47 Who know his power, *his g.,* who
111 The word of *his g.* shall comfort
161 But trust him for *his g.*
327 Ask but *his g.,* and lo, 'tis given
333 Yet, since I know *his g.* is free
347 Will ye not *his g.* receive
360 *His g.* forever nigh
362 And find *his g.* is free for all
422 So free, so infinite *his g.*
456 Daily in *his g.* to grow
466 But on *his g.* rely
493 And glory in *his g.*
633 *His g.* will to the end stronger
749 *His g.* to thee proclaim
787 And of *his g.* partake
1075 And sing the wonders of *his g.*

Of GRACE.

41 The men *of g.* have found
316 With boundless stores *of g.*
343 Soon the day *of g.* is over
557 O Jesus, full *of g.*
1028 The day *of g.* is past and gone

Rich GRACE.

21 Fill our hearts with thy *rich g.*
646 Thy *rich g.* in all our fears
762 May thy *rich g.* impart

Saving GRACE.

17 His *saving g.* proclaim
35 To us thy *saving g.* extend
307 Thou canst the *saving g.* impart
346 Watch, for the *saving g.* is nigh
351 O'erwhelming power of *saving g.*
377 Work in my heart the *saving g.*
532 The fullness of thy *saving g.*
851 Figure and means of *saving g.*

Thy GRACE.

93 What but *thy g.* can foil the
123 So let *thy g.* surround me still
151 *Thy g.* is ever nigh
269 Come with *thy g.* and heavenly
273 With the abundance of *thy g.*
274 Is not *thy g.* as mighty now
317 And all *thy g.* declare
377 Thou bidd'st us ask *thy g.*
389 What shall I bring to gain *thy g.*
610 The blessings of *thy g.* impart
669 And this *thy g.* must give
668 Grant me the visits of *thy g.*
699 Send down *thy g.,* O blessed Lord
765 We in the kingdom of *thy g.*
875 We seek *thy g.* alone

GRACES.

72 New *g.* ever raining
149 And more *g.* for the good
165 On our so.s thy *g.* shower
446 Hear, and all the *g.* shower
698 Without thy *g.* and thyself
771 And let our dying *g.* live

GRA 73 GRI

812 fed by Christ, their *g.* live
807 With all the *g.* of his train

GRACIOUS.
43 And lend a *g.* ear
102 Now, Lord, thy *g.* work begin
317 Thou waitest to be *g.* still
868 In this our *g.* day

GRAIN.
575 Shall foster and mature the *g.*
602 life, though falling like our *g.*
1080 The green ear, and the golden *g.*
1081 Matured the swelling *g.*
1083 Wholesome *g.* and pure may be
1086 The warmth to swell the *g.*

GRANDEUR.
38 Becomes the *g.* of a God
148 For the *g.* of thy nature

GRASS.
172 Our days are as the *g.*
907 shadows...Flit o'er summer *g.*
944 As the new-mown *g.* for rain
960 The withering *g.*, the fading
977 Perish the *g.*, and fade the flower

GRATEFUL.
22 *G.* for thy love divine
33 song With *g.* hearts we raise
204 He lifts my *g.* thoughts on
839 And owns the *g.* tie
852 In glad returns of *g.* love

GRATITUDE.
160 The *g.* declare
459 Of love, and *g.*, and praise
571 With loving *g.*
839 The *g.* we owe
932 ascending In *g.* above
1100 Our hymn of *g.* we raise

GRAVE.
90 At thy dawn the *g.* gave way
93 Where is death's sting? where, *g.*
105 The *g.* as little as my bed
227 dominion of death and the *g.*
228 Around thine empty *g.*
228 point the path that from the *g.*
232 Go to his *g..* and with thee
232 The *g.* hath no more prey
234, 260 Where's thy victory...*G.*
241 He saves me from the *g.*
304 Entered the *g.* in mortal
319 tongue Lies silent in the *g.*
349 death command you to the *g.*
417 By thy triumph o'er the *g.*
541 show thyself beyond the *g.*
601 And leads to victory o'er the *g.*
623 Thy boasted victory, O *G.*
681 And then in the *g.* to lay down
694 My couch, the *g.* where thou
847 Now no more the *g.* enthrall
905 We're traveling to the *g.*
969 O. *G.*, where is thy victory
981 Forever molder in the *g.*
984 Passed through the *g.*, and

985 Where is thy boasted victory, *G.*
989 O *G.*, where is thy victory
996 I from my *g.* shall rise
997 The entrance to the *g.*
999 Thou art gone to the *g.*; but
1000 *G.*, the guardian...treasury of
1012 No terror has death or the *g.*
1099 O'er darkness and the *g.*

GRAVES.
850 Until the ancient *g.* be stirred
895 To fill dishonored *g.*
970 The *g.* of all his saints
989 When opening *g.* shall yield
1019 Tear up the *g.* and cleave

GRAVEN.
770 And *g.* on thy hand
839 name So deeply *g.* there

GREAT.
675 Seeking for some *g.* thing to do
722 Save us from the *g.* and wise

GREEK.
923 And slave and freeman, *G.* and

GREENLAND.
879 I from *G.'s* frozen land
930 From *G.'s* icy mountains

GRIEF.
75 With *g.* and pain extreme
214 But drops of *g.* can ne'er repay
220 And say, was ever *g.* like his
303 Who seest and know'st my *g.*
304 Beheld our helpless *g.*
320 And feeleth for our *g.*
368 Fill every soul with sacred *g.*
372 And fill his heart with sacred *g.*
404 A heart with *g.* oppressed
450 My *g.* a burden long has been
558 A portion of thy *g.* unknown
590 And *g.'s* dark day come on
618 Hallow this whelming *g.*
621 And chased my *g.* away
623 And *g.*, and fear, and care
627 And *g.* may bide an evening
629 drooping pleasure turns to *g.*
631 When *g.* my wounded soul
643 O 'tis not in *g.* to harm me
667 But in the hour of *g.* and pain
670 The sword of *g.* is driven
674 To thee I tell my *g.*
730 Love and *g.* my heart dividing
773 Our *g.* allays, our fear
954 Far from a world of *g.* and
986 With silent *g.* is gently borne
1034 No more the drops of piercing *g.*
1043 There sighing *g.* shall weep
1049 There is no *g.* in heaven
1095 In *g.* and fear to thee, O
1107 Bade *g.* and ill depart

GRIEFS.
157 Didst all our *g.* remove
170 My *g.* expire, my troubles
236 And girt with *g.* and tears
295 Our numerous *g.* are here

GRI 74 GUE

383 Let all our g. and troubles
417 By thy human g. and fears
634 My g. are like a tossing sea
645 By thy sorer g. to cheer me
657 Awhile forget your g. and fears
682 And g. would tear my
723 By the sacred g. that wept
724 Out of my stony g. Bethel
754 I lay my g. on Jesus
762 And g. around me spread
777 But, your g. forever ending
839 The g. which thou didst bear
914 Chase all our g. away
986 And often shall our g. renewed

GRIEVE.
196 Like thee, O Lord, to g.
317 Will ye g. your God, and die
352 And shall I dare his Spirit g.
353 Ye, who persist his love to g.
353 O shouldst thou g. him now
407 And never g. thee more
499 Thy holiness to g.
511 No more thy goodness g.
535 And never g. Thee more
1010 Have there no power to g.

GRIEVED.
272 I g. thee long, alas! thou
336 Spirit of grace Long g. and
376 G., away thy Saviour goeth
379 G. him by a thousand fails
390 thousand times thy goodness g.
401 For having g. my God
511 For having g. thy love

GROAN.
337 Life by his expiring g.
400 I g. to be set free
412 And hear my Saviour's dying g.
560 I g., I strive, I watch, I pray
706 To him there's music in a g.
723 By thy deep, expiring g.
854 Let us g. thy inward groaning
961 O that without a lingering g.
1025 Nature's...bear her final g.

GROANS.
167 Blest Jesus, thou whose g.
215 Hark! how he g., while nature
264 Deepens our imperfect g.
312 In g., and tears, and blood
344 Not all our g. and tears
487 Deep, unutterable g.
914 Jesus, thy fair creation g.
957 Remember, Lord, thy dying g.
1016 Bid her g. and travail cease

GROANED, GROANING.
214 He g. upon the tree
231 For him who g. beneath your
359 Groaning beneath your load

GROUND.
430 Now I have found the g. wherein
436 I rest upon the g. Of
649 Fixed on this g. will I remain
738 determined on that happy g.

GROVES.
418 Where g. of living pleasure
1076 Where g. of living joy

GROVEL.
217 Look, how we g. here below
530 Why should I g. here on earth

GROW, GROWN, GROWTH.
301 seed...and g. in faith and love
781 Let us in all things g.
1083 Unto joy or sorrow grown
806 Let us daily growth receive
1080 The wondrous g. unseen

GUARD.
94 G. thou the lips from sin
97 Whom thou dost g., O King
106 G. my first springs of thought
110 G. me, my Saviour, while I rest
113 May angels g. us while we sleep
123 To g. my soul from every ill
155 Can boast a g. like ours
167 An angel g. to us supply
170 he himself becomes my g.
176 Shall g. his children well
180 And g. me with a watchful
462 And g. the gift thyself hast
476 To g. the sacred treasure there
517 We, for whose g. the angel
555 Forever standing on my g.
562 Still let me g. the holy fire
580 Let us keep steadfast g.
581 My soul, be on thy g.
637 Is now my g. and guide
651 And g. in fierce temptation's
1105 And g. us with thy constant

GUARDS.
116 Angel g. from thee surround
165 His presence g. his people's
746 G. from all impending harm
1003 Go, by angel g. attended
1076 He g. them by his side

GUARDIAN.
96 God's g. shield was round
104 Great G. of my sleeping
112 me down. Beneath his g. care
139 Since thou art my g.
360 Its g. hand by day
693 Thy g. wings are round
713 Author and G. of my
772 In Jesus' g. love
872 Be the g. of our way
1000 Grave, the g. of our dust
1100 In danger still our g. be
1103 Great God, our G., Guide

GUEST.
28 quickly in, thou heavenly G.
83 Nor would receive another g.
251 Come, divine and peaceful G.
275 And fix in us the G. divine
280 A gracious, willing G.
284 Our most delightful G.
329 Thrice happy, who his g. retains
504 Let every soul be Jesus' g.

GUI   75   GUL

578 With prayer, your constant g.
694 On earth I'm but a passing g.
794 Come in, thou heavenly G.
838 Is made a welcome g.
861 Here to abide, no transient g.

GUIDE.

163 An awful g., in smoke and
266 Heavenly G. from paths of
273 Where thou art g., no ill
648 Leader of faithful souls, and G.
999 lamp of his love is thy g. through

My GUIDE.

93 Who, like thyself, my g. and
187 It was my g., my light, my
448 Still let thy wisdom be my g.
476 In death as life be thou my g.
483 My Wisdom and my G.
655 Be thou my g., my strength
718 As my g., my guard, my
761 Led onward by my g.
762 Be thou my g.
968 Be thou my g., be thou my

Our GUIDE.

465 Thine forever! thou our G.
577 We follow thee, our G.
687 Be thou our g., be thou our
885 Ever be thou our g.
964 Be thou our g. while life
1038 O that we now might grasp our G.

GUIDE. (verb.)

297 This lamp...shall g. our way
344 I will g. you to your home
413 Thou my impetuous spirit g.
483 Which thou wilt g. aright
504 And all my actions g.
506 Till thou my patient spirit g.
691 'Twill g. thee to a better home
617 Thy love our footsteps g.
624 In all my acts may wisdom g.
643 God's own hand shall g. thee
687 G., and lead, and go before them
941 G. them from their darkness
943 G. into thy perfect peace

GUIDE me.

171 G. me, O thou great Jehovah
180 And g. me through the dreadful
642 Wherever he may g. me
1075 Shall g. me all my happy

GUIDE my.

96 And g. my dark, bewildered
98 O may thy Spirit g. my feet
119 And g. my steps, that I
586 And g. my words aright

GUIDE our.

20 G. our footsteps in thy way
466 Lord, g. our doubtful feet
784 But g. our feet into the way

GUIDE us.

14 Thy Holy Spirit g. us on
89 And g. us to the realms of
143 Whose Spirit shall g. us safe
465 G. us to the realms of day
873 G. us, Saviour, in the

To GUIDE.

182 Where they need no star to g.
255 And now he reigns supreme, to g.
269 not, with thee to g., Turn from
297 To g. our souls to heaven
300 To g. us to our God
696 But with a God to g. our
880 It glowed to g. benighted

GUIDES, GUIDED, GUIDING, GUIDANCE.

167 Ye heavenly g., speed not
570 Guided by thee, through all I
675 And g. where I go
475 I wait thy guiding hand to
878 Lead...By thy g. hand
881 Shed that wisdom's g. light
1105 To thee, O God, whose g. hand
57 Laws...For their guidance
61 The g. of thy hand

GUILE.

212 No g. hath in thy lips been

GUILT.

172 Doth all our g. remove
212 No g. thy spotless heart
217 'Tis midnight; and for others' g.
281 With g. and fear oppressed
205 While g. disturbs and breaks
314 Convinced of g., with grief
350 Come, all by g. oppressed
359 O take our g. away
389 Full of g., alas! I am
412 O'erwhelmed with g. and fear
420 Nor spot of g. remains on
534 From g., and fear, and pain
604 When I've no g. to wash
689 If g. deject, if sin distress
735 Our g. and punishment
754 I bring my g. to Jesus
762 Take all my g. away
837 From every stain of g.
1091 Let that blood our g. efface
1094 The g. is ours, but grace
1096 Great is our g., our fears

GUILTLESS.

531 But, sunk in g. shame

GUILTY.

243 The g. conscience need's
310 Ah, how shall g. man
327 Arise, ye g.,—he'll forgive
389 G. I stand before thy face
1019 Sinners shall lift their g. head
1024 With holy joy or g. dread
1096 And save a g. land

GULF.

304 Plunged in a g. of dark
544 And bear me from the g.
722 Fix a mighty g. between

H.

HABITATION.
265 Make our hearts thy *h.*

HALLELUJAH, HALLELUJAHS.
10 And spread the *h.* round
10 Loud *hallelujahs* to thy name
21 Heaven with *h.* rang
188 Heavenly *h.* rise
434 All *h.* swelling
100 While with *h.* ring
1062 What rush of *h.*
1085 Your *h.* raise

HALLOW, HALLOWED, HALLOWING.
496 *H.* each thought; let all
44 every place is *hallowed* ground
46 Cause us thy *h.* name to
478 Give to my heart chaste, *h.*
551 That *h.* morn shall
716 All *h.* be thy name
1001 *H.* and made meet for
439 And by thy *hallowing* Spirit
538 Till bold to say, My *h.*

HALO.
902 A *h.* round the tomb

HAMMER.
311 Strike with the *h.* of thy word
368 Strike with the *h.* of thy word

HAND.
37 take our seats at thy right *h.*
98 Nor dwell at thy right *h.*
159 Thy *h.*, O God, we see
169 In all my ways thy *h.*, I
176 That *h.* which bears all
177 A Father's *h.* we felt
236 At thy right *h.* on high
320 One only *h.*, a pierced hand
320 Lift up thy bleeding *h.*, O Lord
347 At God's right *h.* in heaven
548 It is thy *h.* which on my
555 Lay to thy mighty *h.*
606 Thee will I set at my right *h.*
622 Still 'tis God's *h.* that leadeth
622 Lord, I would clasp thy *h.*
631 Shall I be found at thy right *h.*
637 My times are in thy *h.*
639 With God at my right *h.*
643 God's own *h.* shall guide thee
654 Into thy *h.* of love
680 see thee stand at God's right *h.*
712 I lay my *h.* in thine
789 We *h.* in hand go on
796 There, *h.* in hand, firm
835 Stretch forth thy *h.*, O
915 And *h.* in hand are set
1027 Be found at thy right *h.*

HANDS.
219 See! through his holy *h.* and feet
223 His pierced *h.* to them
257 Behold his *h.* and side
261 See, he lifts his *h.* above
329 Her *h.* are filled with
348 All day long he spreads his *h.*
406 Father, I stretch my *h.* to
419 I'll lift my *h.*, I'll raise
483 Out of thy *h.* my cause
522 Wash... My *h.*, my head
543 my careless *h.* hang down
573 Into thy *h.* receive
735 God's *h.* or bound or
737 Look on thy *h.*, and read
805 *H.*, and hearts, and voices raise
880 I wish that his *h.* had been
1056 Not made with mortal *h.*

HANG, HANGS, HANGING.
240 When thou didst *h.* upon
512 Jesus, I *h.* upon thy word
221 Why *hangs* he then on yonder
423 I saw one *hanging* on a tree

HAPPY.
164 May I that *h.* person be
337 Ye may now be *h.* too
348 Cries, I will not *h.* be
407 Live *h.* in my Saviour's
720 They are *h.* now, and we
741 How *h.*, gracious Lord, are
747 But when I am *h.* in him
717 No mortal so *h.* as I
1026 O how past all utterance *h.*

HAPPINESS.
33 And heaven its *h.*
515 The *h.* of heaven
696 The soul this is *h.*
720 Soon their *h.* shall
989 Then wake to perfect *h.*
994 Eternal *h.* or woe
1031 Nor can its *h.* or woe
1078 This *h.* in part is mine

HARBINGER.
915 His royal *h.*

HARDENED.
353 With *h.*, self-destroying

HARDNESS.
32 The *h.* of our hearts remove
513 Remove this *h.* from my
559 A *h.* o'er my heart

HARDSHIP.
505 To *h.*, grief, and loss

HARM.
91 From *h.* and danger keep
179 No *h.* can befall, with my
318 Nor death nor hell shall *h.*
651 They cannot *h.*, for God is
873 Naught can *h.* us

HARMONY.
89 peace And *h.* be found
789 United... in perfect *h.*
783 Where all is love and *h.*
898 Where saints of all ages in *h.*
1073 In the spirit of *h.* join

HARP.

36 The holy prophet's *h.* was
81 Like David's *h.* of solemn
319 A golden *h.* for me
778 Extolled with the *h.* and the
1016 Let no *h.* remain unstrung
1079 Sweet as *h.*'s melodious

HARPS.

20 Then, with angel-*h.* again
188 Loud our golden *h.* shall
194 To touch their *h.* of gold
217 Strike their *h.*, and loudly
304 Strike all your *h.* of gold
330 With our *h.* in our hands
350 Tuning their *h.*, they long to
414 The angels tuned their *h.* anew
444 Ye on your *h.* must lean to
633 Your *h.*, ye trembling saints
652 Sweet are the *h.* in holy
751 Not all the *h.* above
916 What strains will angel-*h.*
1062 What ringing of a thousand *h.*

HART.

550 As pants the *h.* for cooling
739 And as a bounding *h.* fly

HARVEST.

62 By whom the *h.* blest
575 And heaven shout, *H.*-home
579 The *h.* dawn is near
602 wait in heaven, their *h.* day
808 Lord of the living *h.*
818 Lord of the *h.*, hear
818 The *h.*, truly, Lord, is great
941 Lo! the hills for *h.* whiten
1080 Thine is the *h.*, thine the seed
1081 A kindly *h.* crowns thy love
1081 Seed-time nor *h.*, night
1083 Raise the song of *h.*-home
1083 Lord of *h.*, grant that
1083 And shall take his *h.* home
1083 To thy final *h.*-home
1083 Raise the glorious *h.*-home
1085 Sing to the Lord of *h.*! Sing
1085 Sing to the Lord of *h.* A song
1087 The God of *h.* praise
1087 And in your *h.* song

HARVESTS.

607 Fields are white, and *h.* waiting
731 Golden *h.* shall be won
903 To ample *h.* grow

HASTE.

349 Come, sinners, *h.*, O haste
576 Make *h.*, O man, to live
757 Yet onward I *h.* to the heavenly
933 *H.*, haste the glorious day

HASTEN.

345 *H.*, sinner, to be wise
388 *H.* to gain that dear abode
782 Then let us *h.* to the day
937 *H.*, Lord, the glorious time
1074 come to our rescue, and *h.*

HATE.

60 And *h.* what we deplore
213 Make us to *h.* the load of sin
481 *H.*, envy, jealousy, be gone
482 The thing my God doth *h.*
549 I *h.* the sins that made thee

HAVEN.

656 Safe into the *h.* guide
678 To the *h.* of thy breast
816 That *h.* of repose to find
1004 See the *h.* full in view
1011 Our brother the *h.* hath gained
1110 As on toward the *h.* we roll

HEAD.

46 Conformed in all things to our *H.*
170 He had not where to lay his *h.*
203 I will lay my *h.* on Jesus
214 Would he devote that sacred *h.*
225 Child of God, lift up thy *h.*
238 With joy shall I lift up my *h.*
242 He lives, my everlasting *H.*
260 Follow our exalted *H.*
422 Alive in him my living *H.*
448 Alive in thee, my living *H.*
512 I find him lifting up my *h.*
600 And glorious as your *H.*
673 God shall lift up thy *h.*
782 Joined in one spirit to our *H.*
784 Up into thee, our living *H.*
787 All join in Christ, their living *H.*
800 *H.* of thy Church beneath
816 following our triumphant *H.*
841 Members of one common *H.*
954 Your *H.* to glorify, With
970 rest, But with their dying *H.*
985 Through Christ, our living *H.*
992 Thou art thy Church's *H.*
997 hand Beneath my sinking *h.*
1001 Where their *H.* is gone before

HEADS.

14 Lift up your *h.*, ye mighty
859 The *h.* that guide endue with
952 With joy upon our *h.* return
1014 Lift up your *h.*, ye friends

HEAL.

21 *H.* the sick, the captive free
212 To *h.* me, thou hast borne
320 Can *h.* the sinner's wound
382 *H.* me of my grief and pain
397 Lord, I despair myself to *h.*
398 *H.* the diseased, and cure
611 But thou wilt *h.* that broken
623 Powerful the wounded soul to *h.*
656 *H.* the sick, and lead the blind
670 Its touch shall *h.* with love
674 For thou alone canst *h.*
683 no sorrow that Heaven cannot *h.*
986 To *h.* the wounded heart
1099 Was strong to *h.* and save

HEALS, HEALED, HEALETH.

314 'Tis this that *h.* the mortal wound
478 and *healed* my wounded mind
552 when bleeding, *h.* thy wound

НЕА 78 НЕА

719 He *healeth* thine infirmities
754 He *h.* my diseases

HEALING.

60 And let a *h.* ray from thee
149 There is *h.* in his blood
171 Whence the *h.* waters flow
190 Risen with *h.* in his wings
220 And gladly catch the *h.* stream
298 The *h.* beams of light
362 For you in *h.* streams it
411 With *h.* in thy wing
641 With *h.* on his wings
656 Let the *h.* stream abound
739 Hath risen with *h.* in his
821 Their *h.* wings display
913 On thy redeeming wing, *H.*
916 that *h.* sound shall quell

HEALTH.

1 'Tis life, and health, and peace
50 Thy saving *h.* be shown
231 Maker and Redeemer, life and *h.*
307 And let my soul, to *h.* restored
502 Spirit of *h.*, remove
532 To perfect *h.* restore my soul
698 And *h.*, and safe abode
913 *H.* to the sick in mind

HEAR.

20 Deign our humble songs to *h.*
157 And *h.* us when we prayed
448 O King of glory, *h.* my call
465 *H.* us from thy throne above
861 *H.* thou in heaven, thy dwelling
862 But *h.* from heaven thy
872 *H.*, O hear us, when we pray
913 *H.* us, we humbly pray
1064 But *h.* us from thy lofty throne
1096 Lord, *h.* thy servants, hear thy

HEARETH, HEARD.

355 Let him that *h.* say
465 He *heard* me from his holy hill
621 I love the Lord: he *h.* my cries

HEARKEN, HEARKENING.

28 Through grace we *h.* to thy
403 O *h.* to my voice
555 O may I *h.* and obey
959 *H.* to my request
33 If meekly *hearkening* to thy

HEART.

28 door Of every sinner's *h.*
83 I yield my *h.* to thee alone
119 Who would not give his *h.* to
117 ask... The love of my poor *h.*
183 Let every *h.* prepare him room
270 Thy Spirit in our *h.*
287 O fill thou every *h.*
325 And every *h.* rejoice
402 O take my *h.*, And fill it
419 With *h.*, and eyes, and lifted
429 Impress On my expanding *h.*
435 And speak to every *h.*
496 His work within my *h.*
491 Take my poor *h.*, and let
491 Enter every trembling *h.*
507 Thy *h.* made truly his
509 Down in your *h.* of hearts
510 I know no place in all my *h.*
518 love Shed in my *h.* abroad
528 Give me a new, a perfect *h.*
532 The abundance of a loving *h.*
550 When every *h.* was tuned to
572 shine In this poor *h.* of mine
592 My *h.* is still with thee
596 And not sometimes lose *h.*
624 I find thee, Saviour, in my *h.*
649 Though my *h.* fail, and flesh
718 Eternally held in thy *h.*
780 And joy from *h.* to heart
782 We still are one in *h.*
792 And make us of one *h.* and
796 And *h.* to heart enfolded all
816 O that our *h.* and mind

HEARTS.

22 May our *h.* be ever thine
49 lift our *h.* above, And draw
111 We lift our *h.* to thee
121 The *h.* of all mankind
220 And give up all our *h.* to him
241 Had I a thousand *h.* to give
244 Lift up your *h.*, lift up your
261 Grant our *h.* may thither
269 To fill the *h.* which thou hast
269 And make our *h.* o'erflow with
274 And while to thee our *h.* we
377 And cause our *h.* to feel and
514 O that our *h.* were all a heaven
551 Our *h.*, If God we seek to know
561 Our *h.* were fixed on things
608 O how our *h.* beat high with
650 to thee our *h.* we lift.—Our hearts
799 Whose *h.* and hopes are one
852 Fain would our *h.* and voices
883 No; while our *h.* are tender
926 Open your *h.* to make him
936 Kindled in some *h.* it is
951 *h.* to pay...hearts shall beat
1048 There let our *h.* be found
1071 Our *h.* and our treasure
1106 God bless these *h.* made one
1111 And on their *h.*, where'er they

HEAT.

62 The sultry sun's intenser *h.*
296 The gracious light and *h.*
750 In weary *h.* of day

HEATHEN, HEATHENS.

17 His glory let the *h.* know
908 And *h.* gods, forsaken, fall
918 O point the *h.* to the skies
918 Dispel the gloom of *h.* night
930 Say to the *h.*, from thy throne
923 Behold the *h.* waits to know
930 The *h.* in his blindness
932 See *h.* nations bending
937 *H.* tribes his name adore
941 Souls in *h.* darkness lying
942 Can the *h.* world proclaim
942 *Heathens* will be still the same

HEAVEN.

64 A h. on earth appear
105 'Tis h. on earth, 'tis heaven
158 And h. to crown it all
193 'Twas more than h. could
206 Thou art h. on earth to me
259 How we, too, may enter h.
373 Above us is the h.
373 Shall live for hell or h.
377 And take me into h.
385 Who their h. in Christ have
395 Of all thou hast in earth or h.
407 Of all in earth or h.
420 When h. and earth are
442 'Twas a h. below My Redeemer
450 Jesus, my all, to h. is gone
500 Makes h. forever mine
520 And where thou art is h.
524 Hasten to make our h.
547 Yet we, who have a h. to
564 Where the h. is bright
568 And h. is all possessed
590 And form our souls for h.
609 Find their h. begun below
643 H.'s eternal day 's before thee
650 wait for all our inward h.
664 Shall bear thee to thy h. above
684 And h. comes down our souls to
712 And find my h. in thee
730 Here it is I find my h.
750 With h. then close the day
751 'Tis h. to rest in thine embrace
765 Their h. on earth begun
768 H. and earth at last remove
786 And wait his h. to share
828 Of such will h. consist
842 Our h. begun below
845 Let us think how h. and
952 And gain the highest h. of love
969 H. opens on my eyes; my
1017 When h. and earth shall pass
1024 Thou shalt from h. come down
1028 When h. and earth shall
1035 From the third h., where God
1039 And all is drear; 'tis h.

HEAVEN OF HEAVENS.

613 The h. of h. is won
757 To the h. of h. in Jesus's love
1064 My h. of h. in thee
1073 For the h. of h. is love

In HEAVEN.

7 That we may meet in h.
15 Till each in h. appears
38 God is in h., and men below
45 Then may I spend in h. at
188 Till in h. ye sing before him
405 In h. alone no sin is found
491 Till in h. we take our place
693 For whom have I in h. above
696 In h., in earth, or on the
716 will be done In h. and
752 My spirit seems in h. to stay
971 eyes...To open them in h.
988 home...In h. is now thine
1030 I seek my place in h.
1033 And land us all in h.

1039 'Tis found above, in h.
1057 No sin in h. is found

Of HEAVEN.

337 Find on earth the life of h.
342 Haste ye to the court of h.
467 We sing the songs of h.
1030 O would he more of h. bestow
1039 Appears the dawn of h.

To HEAVEN.

274 bade their souls to h. aspire
283 Help me home to h.
327 he turns your hell to h.
365 To h., or down to hell
367 That you might come to h.
450 Jesus, my all, to h. is gone
571 And find my way to h.
588 Believe yourselves to h.
590 And follow thee to h.
640 ladder, set up to h. on earth
680 To take us up to h.
822 It turns their hell to h.
834 To raise our souls to h.
929 And lift to h. the voice of
947 Who turns our hell to h.
1056 And take our souls to h.
1075 upborne, To h. ascend

HEAVENS.

9 High as the h. our voices
57 Praise the Lord! ye h., adore
95 Wide as the h. on which he
292 The h. declare thy glory
441 Higher than the h. above
641 Beneath the spreading h.
788 The h. with all their train
1023 And the h. together roll

HEAVENLY.

4 Sing on your h. way
396 O for a glance of h. day
418 oft they look to the h. hills
445 Their h. origin display
647 Seek we, then, for h. treasures
703 Swift I ascend the h. place
744 haste to join those h. powers
751 Can make a h. place
780 How sweet, how h. is the sight
966 Removes me to that h. place
995 every face, Be h. and
1007 To the sunny h. plain
1111 guide them to the h. shore

HEAVENWARD.

228 Leads h. up to thee
363 H. direct thy weeping
508 H. our every wish
1008 Thy h. flight detain

HEAVY, HEAVILY.

213 That lay so h. on our God
560 Yet h. is my soul, and faint
673 Still h. is thy heart
277 Our souls, how heavily they go

HEED, HEEDS, HEEDLESS.

352 and shall I give No h., but still
603 Men h. thee, love thee, praise

1021 So shall I to my ways take *h*.
217 *Heeds* not his Master's grief and
160 With *heedless* steps I ran

HEIR, HEIRS.
158 A child of God, O glory's *h*.
789 And he 's an *h*. of heaven who
826 Proclaim me as thy child and *h*.
966 An *h*. of endless bliss or pain
18 And make them *heirs* of heaven
158 Reserved for all the *h*. of grace
407 Number me with salvation's *h*.
424 And seal the *h*. of heaven
783 *H*. of the same immortal bliss
825 These *h*. of immortality
828 And call them *h*. of heaven

HELL.
78 Nor sin, nor *h*. shall reach the
139 And *h*.'s deep gloom are open
231 *H*. to-day is vanquished, heaven is
237 sin, death, and *h*. o'erthrew
371 Your way is dark and leads to *h*.
391 And if my soul were sent to *h*.
394 God will destroy the power of *h*.
563 *H*.'s foundations quiver
566 Though all earth and *h*. appear
569 Not earth nor *h*. with all their
679 That soul, though all *h*. should
684 Or how the hosts of *h*. defeat
739 *H*., earth, and sin, with ease
751 If thou depart, 'tis *h*.
822 over all, In *h*., or earth, or sky
847 *H*.'s fierce powers beneath thee
908 And all the powers of *h*. resign
924 the might of *h*. o'erthrown
966 Or shuts me up in *h*.
1019 And shrink to see a yawning *h*.
1043 terror clothed, *h*.'s kingdom sLake

HELMET.
599 Salvation's *h*. on his head

HELP.
103 And *h*. us this and every day
124 plea Obtained the *h*. for all
165 There is no *h*. in God for thee
181 To *h*. the poor and needy
197 A present *h*. is he
212 He lives to *h*. in time of need
253 Thy blessed *h*. supply
332 No other *h*. is found, No other
406 No other *h*. I know
417 Saviour, *h*. me or I die
513 *H*., Lord, to whom for *h*. I fly
541 My present *h*. in time of need
581 And *h*. divine implore
632 Thy needful *h*., O God, afford
656 Ad my *h*. from thee I bring
726 Hither by thy *h*. I 'm come
732 Wanting *h*. in time of need
739 My *h*. is all laid up above
745 *H*., while yet I ask, is given
784 *H*. us to help each other, Lord
790 To thee for *h*. we fly
798 And still he doth his *h*. afford
801 And kindly *h*. each other on
820 And may they by thy *h*. abide

961 O God, our *h*. in ages past
1091 And *h*. us when we pray
1094 And *h*. in thee was found

HELPER, HELPERS.
14 The Lord is just, a *h*. tried
166 Our *H*. he, amid the flood
541 Thou canst, thou wilt, my *h*. be
93 When other *helpers* fail, and

HELPLESS.
309 How *h*. nature lies
340 None but Jesus can do *h*.
399 To thee... I lift my *h*. heart
656 Hangs my *h*. soul on thee
899 And bid the *h*. live

HELPLESSNESS.
455 See my utter *h*.
497 My utter *h*. reveal
678 In my utter *h*.
739 All *h*., all weakness

HERALD, HERALDS.
181 Shall peace, the *h*., go
190 Hark! the *h*.-angels sing
767 Lo! the sacred *h*. stands
342 Hear the *heralds* of the gospel
342 Tender *h*.! Chase away
444 Bright *h*. of the eternal
810 Go forth, ye *h*. in my name
909 And send the *h*. forth
922 Forth with thy chosen *h*. come
929 Send forth thy *h*., Lord, to

HERITAGE.
229 bought with tears Thy *h*.
331 sold... Your *h*. above
811 His *h*. they toil to clear

HERMON.
200 Whiter than *H*.'s whitest

HEROD.
900 At night in *H*.'s dungeon cell

HIDE.
102 To *h*. thee from thy servant's
116 Darkness cannot *h*. from thee
123 Where can a creature *h*.
214 Thus might I *h*. my blushing
415 Let me *h*. myself in thee
454 Or *h*. for a moment my Lord from
548 O let me *h*. this aching head
651 *H*. in the hollow of thy hand
656 *H*. me, O my Saviour, *h*.
678 *H*. me, Jesus, till o'erpast
736 I *h*. me, Jesus, in thy name
1009 They *h*. themselves in heaven's
1014 *H*. us, hide us, Rocks and
1115 *H*. and bring us safe to land

HIDES.
38 He *h*. his face behind his wings
541 tower That *h*. my life above
596 He *h*. himself so wondrously
626 He *h*. the brightness of his face
686 And hovering, *h*. me in his
798 And *h*. our life above

HID 81 HOM

HIDING-PLACE.
1027 Be thou my only h.-p.

HIGH.
  5 Though h. above all praise
237 Our Jesus is gone up on h.
264 Christ, who now gone up on h.
270 Enthroned on h., almighty Lord
366 And lifts the soul on h.
594 That calls thee from on h.
747 Or take me to thee up on h.

HIGH PRIEST.
243 Jesus, our great H. P.
254 Of our H. P. above
322 There our H. P. appears
331 Jesus, our great H. P., Hath
390 In honor of my great H. P.
885 Thou art the great H. P.
1031 My merciful H. P.

HIGHWAY.
450 The king's h. of holiness
603 Go forth into the world's h.

HILL, HILLS.
 37 And lead us to thy holy h.
657 To that celestial h.
 98 Up to the hills where Christ is
285 From the celestial h. Light
703 Sink down, ye separating h.
745 To the h. I lift mine eyes
799 Thus on the heavenly h.
859 The bounds of the eternal h.
964 Before the h. in order stood
1036 E'en now we faintly trace, h.
1085 The h. leap up in gladness
1098 And let our h. and valleys

HINDERS, HINDRANCES.
1054 Which h. my joy and communion
690 What various hindrances we

HOARY.
605 His work my h. age shall
679 And when h. hairs shall

HOLD, HOLDS, HOLDETH.
401 I can h. out no more.
691 Blest when our faith can h.
737 Whom still I h., but cannot
523 Which holds, and will not let
746 Lo! be h. thee by thy hand
613 confident, Because it holdeth thee

HOLLOW.
373 The earth rings h. from
651 Hide in the h. of thy hand
866 Sleeps in the h. of his hand
1109 In the h. of his hand Our
1115 In the h. of thy hand Hide

HOLY.
 89 For 'tis a h. day
127 Thrice H.! thine the kingdom
131 H. as thou, O Lord, is none
136 Only thou art h.; there is
512 He wills that I should h. be

515 I shall be h. here
529 He wills that I should h. be
765 The h. to the holiest leads
932 Stay not till all the h.

HOLINESS.
  6 Spirit of h., On us descend
 14 His kingly crown is h.
 17 The beauty of his h.
 74 Make her in h. excel
131 Thy h. is all thine own
280 And every thought of h.
398 And perfect it in h.
428 The joys of h. below
502 Spirit of finished h.
529 That h. I long to feel
531 To real h. restored
532 To perfect h. and love
539 But inward h.
543 By perfect h. to appear
545 And taste, in h. divine
795 And perfect h. below
804 All the heights of h.
1056 put on thee In perfect h.
1064 Forgiveness and h. give

HOLY GHOST.
 30 say, The H. G. receive
 48 And God the H. G. declare
 49 Send down thy H. G., to be
118 And we confess the H. G.
270 The H. G. send down
272 I worship thee, O H. G.
275 The H. G. sent down from
275 Come, H. G., and fill the place
284 Come, H. G., in love
786 The H. G. receive

HOLY SPIRIT.
278 Come, H. S., come
269 Come, H. S., now descend
282 Grant us thy H. S., Lord
285 Come, H. S., come, With
808 Come down, thou H. S.
861 And here the H. S. rest
1108 O H. S.! who didst brood

HOMAGE.
 73 Your joyful h. pay
 77 This day be grateful h. paid
 87 When men to God their h. pay
121 And h. pay to thee
191 Yield to him the h. meet
294 My knee with humble h. bow
919 To pay their h. at his feet
1069 They their silent h. pay
1082 Still be the cheerful h. paid

HOME.
  4 To our eternal h.
 44 And, going, take thee to their h.
 64 That calls thy children h.
101 Happy the h. when God is there
108 I, perhaps, am near my h.
168 There is our h., our hope, our rest
244 up To their eternal h.
278 And make our hearts thy h.
283 Blessed Spirit, make thy h.

6

335 are waiting to welcome you *h.*
351 And thou art far from *h.* and
388 Has not for thee a *h.*
427 And grace will lead me *h.*
434 I did not love my *h.*
458 And fix in thee thy lasting *h.*
483 And take me *h.* to God
500 In my eternal *h.*
509 God only is the creature's *h.*
537 But make me, Lord, thy *h.*
539 When Jesus makes my heart his *h.*
546 And bring me *h.* to God
564 That fair *h.* is ours
633 We are not far from *h.*
636 Which drives us nearer *h.*
648 Our everlasting *h.* above
654 Straight to my *h.* above
659 So I but safely reach my *h.*
666 And then go *h.* my crown to
667 bliss Of an eternal *h.*
682 night...dark, and I am far from *h.*
703 And hasten to my *h.*
720 There our endless *h.* shall be
726 Safely to arrive at *h.*
743 my dear Lord will bring me *h.*
750 At evening in thy *h.*
786 He now is fitting up your *h.*
808 When thou shalt call us *h.*
873 To our *h.* beyond the sky
896 From thy Father's happy *h.*
909 And hasten to their *h.*
935 Hie thee to thy quiet *h.*
964 And our eternal *h.*
964 And our perpetual *h.*
988 But O, a brighter *h.* than ours
993 To be at *h.* with God
1026 In that heavenly *h.* to dwell
1033 Ten thousand to their endless *h.*
1039 There is a *h.* for weary souls
1052 Come to our peaceful *h.*
1053 I am nearer *h.* to-day
1054 *H.!* home! sweet, sweet home
1054 In hope of my glorious *h.*
1055 There is a blissful *h.*
1058 O *h.* of fadeless splendor
1063 We soon shall recover our *h.*
1070 And heaven, the heart's true *h.*
1072 My heavenly *h.* is bright and
1072 Let others seek a *h.*
1073 To our permanent *h.*
1078 And my abiding *h.*
1106 For the bright *h.* above
1111 Abroad, at *h.*, or in the deep

HOMES.
101 Lord, let us in our *h.* agree
652 Glad are the *h.* that sorrows
884 We read of *h.* in glory
892 And *h.* are bare and cold
901 For happier *h.* and brighter days
1106 That through our *h.* doth move

HOMEWARD.
91 Grant us thy peace upon our *h.*
518 It was thy love that *h.* led
694 I take my *h.* way in trust
903 Turn thee, brother; *h.* come
1001 Hastens *h.* to return

HOMELIEST.
597 On *h.* work thy blessing

HONEST.
29 Each in an *h.* heart

HONOR.
2 *H.* and power divine
51 Let all cry aloud, and *h.* the Son
51 All *h.* and blessing, with
139 Blessing and *h.*, praise and
144 Be to thee all *h.* paid
152 And *h.* him alone
595 Maintain the *h.* of his word
605 Nor could all worldly *h.* give
915 Thee *h.* and adore

HONORED, HONORS.
860 Be this, O Lord, that *h.*
1 The *honors* of thy name
154 The *h.* of their God
594 I'll lay my honors down
705 The *h.* of my God

HOPE.
12 Nor *h.* decline, nor love grow
28 In sure and certain *h.* rejoice
51 Cheered by *h.* and daily
150 *H.* and comfort from above
173 Thrice comfortable *h.*
208 The sinner's *h.*, let men deride
208 It cheers with *h.* the gloomy day
306 Ere life and *h.* forever fly
308 With trembling *h.* I see
313 Whence *h.* and comfort flow
353 Then *h.* may never beam on
391 Whose *h.*, still hovering round
394 Already springing *h.* I feel
411 With holy *h.* inflame
432 In *h.*, against all human hope
445 Whate'er by *h.*, by faith we
455 That I have any *h.* of heaven
474 Cheer it with *h.*, with love
479 *H.* to the end, in Jesus hope
510 In earnest *h.* I live
533 Till *h.* in full fruition die
542 Rejoicing now in earnest *h.*
550 *H.* still, and thou shalt sing
577 This *h.* supports us here
602 The *h.*, the trust, the purpose
612 Sweet to rejoice in lively *h.*
620 Hold on thy way with *h.*
640 The *h.* in which ye yearn
643 *H.* shall change to glad fruition
657 Thrice blessed, bliss-inspiring *h.*
663 Did not one radiant *h.* of bliss
663 That *h.* the sovereign Lord has
663 *H.* that unites the soul to heaven
703 When faith and *h.* shall cease
711 *H.* points the upward gaze
731 Waking *h.* within our bosoms
786 By holy, purifying *h.*
898 With words of high, sustaining *h.*
961 Our *h.* for years to come
966 And *h.* in full, supreme delight
967 I feel a strong immortal *h.*
960 In silent *h.* may lie
1016 *H.* restore and faith increase

1023 E'en to me the *h.* of heaven
1048 Where all his *h.* of glory lies
1056 Full of immortal *h.*
1058 Till *h.* be lost in sight
1058 Send *h.* before to grasp it
1113 And humbly *h.* for more
1114 Nor *h.* lends a ray, the poor
1117 Jesus, my only *h.* thou art

Blessed HOPE.
541 I thank thee for the *blessed h.*
850 O *blessed h.!* with this elate
1016 With that *blessed h.* before us
1030 O what a *blessed h.* is ours
1096 This *blessed h.* we owe

Glorious HOPE.
244 Rejoice in *glorious h.*
515 My hope is full, O *glorious h.*
539 What is our calling's *glorious h.*
542 O *glorious h.* of perfect love
797 This *glorious h.* revives

In HOPE.
82 *In h.* of one that ne'er shall
493 Rejoice *in h.*, rejoice with me
537 And now *in h.* rejoice
614 *In h.*, and love, and fear
676 O let my soul abound *in h.*
858 Here, *in h.* of glory blest
1054 Rejoicing *in h.* of my glorious

My HOPE.
325 On thee alone *my h.* relies
419 Be thou *my h.*, my joy, my
420 Here is *my h.*, my joy, my
421 *My h.* is built on nothing less
421 He then is all *my h.* and stay
427 His word *my h.* secures
458 Come, then, *my H.*, my Life
506 Nor from *my h.* remove
515 *My h.* is full, O glorious hope
595 Nor let *my h.* be lost
624 *My h.*, my all, my Saviour
642 *My h.* I cannot measure
759 *My h.*, my salvation, my all
962 And fix *my h.* on thee alone
1031 Provoke *my h.* or fear

Of HOPE.
67 So shall our sun *of h.* arise
184 To us a Child *of h.* is born
304 Without one cheering beam *of h.*
414 New tides *of h.* tumultuous roll
479 Prisoners *of h.*, lift up your
935 Aught *of h.* or joy foretell

HOPES.
67 We leave our mortal *h.* and fears
205 Where our earliest *h.* began
293 The *h.* that holy word supplies
308 My former *h.* are fled
314 Hence all our *h.* arise
365 What are thy *h.* beyond the grave
459 He whom I fix my *h.* upon
604 On whom my *h.* of heaven depend
616 With better *h.* be filled
628 The *h.* of earth indeed are gone

674 And all my *h.* decline
708 The *h.* of coming years
721 Christ, of all my *h.* the ground
749 Happy the man whose *h.* rely
752 With *h.* of heaven
766 To build our heavenly *h.* upon
783 Our *h.* and fears the same
942 All our *h.*, and prayers, and
949 year is gone... With all its *h.* and
992 On thee our *h.* depend
995 These lively *h.* we owe
1080 The *h.* that soothe, the fears
1088 The *h.* within me bounding

HOPELESS.
890 And turned to *h.* night
1001 Call us *h.* and unblest

HOREB.
200 Who once received on *H.*'s

HORN.
556 My *h.*, and rock, and buckler be

HORROR, HORRORS.
209 A *h.* of great darkness fell
412 My soul with inward *h.* shrinks
1082 No more a face of *h.* wear
180 With gloomy *horrors* overspread
358 O what eternal *h.* stand

HORSES.
1104 Some trust in *h.* trained

HOSANNA.
71 *H.* to the living Lord! Hosanna
76 *H.* to our King
776 Let him hear the loud *h.*
840 To sing, *H.* to the Lamb
882 *H.!* be the children's song
883 singing *H.* to his name

HOSANNAS.
73 Heaven with *h.* rings
77 And loud *h.* sung
185 Our glad *h.*, Prince of peace
277 *H.* languish on our tongues
874 Children, loud *h.* singing
883 Would their *h.* raise
901 *H.*, Lord, to thee we sing
908 shout *H.* to the Lord
1040 To him their loud *h.* raise

HOST.
47 Heaven's *h.* their noblest praises
118 Praised by all the heavenly *h.*
144 Join us with the heavenly *h.*
187 The glittering *h.* bestud the sky
315 The heavenly *h.* with joy confess
787 Behold the innumerable *h.*
907 And as the years, an endless *h.*
917 Let *h.* to host the triumph tell
1032 With that enraptured *h.* to
1077 The whole triumphant *h.*

HOSTS.
57 *H.* on high his power proclaim
120 Whom heavenly *h.* obey
131 By all thy heavenly *h.* adored

181 obey, Him. all the *h.* of heaven
205 Till amid the *h.* of light
239 And all the swarming *h.* of hell
245 With all the *h.* of God, in
247 There the *h.* of shining spirits
581 The *h.* of sin are pressing hard
639 Though *h.* encamp around me

HOSTILE.
155 keep From every *h.* power
584 For strong as is the *h.* shield
764 Fear not; though *h.* bands

HOUR.
371 And know his gracious *h.*
476 Jesus, in that important *h.*
520 Hasten the long-expected *h.*
569 triumph...Lasts but a little *h.*
630 And when the last dread *h.* is
667 Till life's last *h.* is fled

HOURS.
95 Great God, let all my *h.* be thine
470 All my goods, and all my *h.*
472 All, all my happy *h.*
970 Nor should we wish the *h.* more

HOUSE.
37 'Tis God's own *h.*, 'tis heaven's
45 The *h.* of God, the gate of heaven
65 Within thy *h.*, O Lord our God
69 Within thy *h.*, O God of grace
71 Return to this, thy *h.* of prayer
88 While we in thy *h.* appear
89 Come, in the *h.* of God appear
94 That in this *h.* have called upon
98 Now to thy *h.* will I resort
156 And in God's *h.* for evermore
338 Never from his *h.* to roam
633 And nearer to our *h.* above
759 And finding there the *h.* of God
763 A *h.* not made with hands
770 The *h.* of thine abode
855 In our Father's *h.* above
857 Who can call no *h.* their own
858 Here a *h.* of prayer and praise
861 choose not, Lord, this *h.* alone
871 We'll to his *h.* repair
963 In that eternal *h.* above
1053 Nearer my Father's *h.*
1056 We have a *h.* above
1063 The *h.* of our Father above
1072 My Father's *h.* is built on high
1078 There is my *h.* and portion fair
1116 My everlasting *h.* in heaven

HOUSEHOLD.
1106 Of holy *h.* love

HOUSELESS.
344 Thou who, *h.*, sole, forlorn

HOVER, HOVERING.
103 *H.* around us while we pray
194 They bend on hovering wing
733 Angels now are *h.* round us
776 Round each habitation *h.*
1001 *H.* round thy pillow

HUMAN, HUMANITY.
613 *H.* hearts and looks deceive me
665 The paths of our *humanity*

HUMBLE.
116 O may I bear some *h.* part
261 Inmate of a *h.* heart
289 While he can find one *h.* heart
527 Jesus, thine *h.* self impart
558 The *h.*, contrite heart
882 And find at last some *h.* place
1086 Our *h.*, thankful *h.*
1100 With *h.* heart, and bending knee

HUMBLED.
131 And, *h.* into nothing, own
387 *H.* to a little child

HUMBLY.
202 O who like thee so *h.* bore
382 Who *h.* comes to thee
389 And *h.* walk by faith with

HUMILITY.
202 So glorious in *h.*
351 The genuine, meek *h.*
443 By unfeigned *h.*
836 In meek *h.*

HUNGER, HUNGERED.
640 O happy, if ye *h.* As
732 Fainting by the way from *h.*
1066 *H.* now and thirst no more
640 As Jesus *hungered* then

HUNGERING, HUNGERINGS.
756 Seem *h.* and thirsting
487 Holy *hungerings* after heaven

HUNGRY.
55 the *h.* feed; From the gospel
242 He lives, my *h.* soul to feed
316 'Tis manna to the *h.* soul
326 Ho! all ye *h.*, starving souls
545 And feast my *h.* heart
836 Give to the *h.* from your

HURT.
623 who Can *h.* whom God delights

HUSBAND.
901 The wife regains a *h.* freed

HYMN, HYMNED.
22 One last *h.* of grateful praise
109 And, strengthened here by *h.*
109 May *h.* and prayer forever
137 Thine be the *h.* that rolls
652 tones which raise the heavenly *h.*
842 And *h.* the Saviour of mankind
1005 A *h.* of suppliant breath
874 Children...*Hymned* Thy praise.

HYMNS.
3 And *h.* of glory sing
43 And *h.* of praise we sing
60 Our grateful *h.* to raise
75 By *h.* of praise we learn

230 With *h.* of victory
705 And we in *h.* below
770 Her *h.* of love and praise
805 Christ to praise in *h.* divine
1104 And *h.* of peace conclude our
1105 Devoutly join in *h.* of praise
1108 Glad *h.* of praise from land

HYSSOP.
305 Nor *h.* branch, nor sprinkling

I.

I AM.
733 Glory to the great *I AM*
1073 To the great everlasting *I AM*
1075 Jehovah, great *I AM*
1077 Jehovah, Father, great *I AM*

IDOL, IDOLS.
267 Cast down every *i.*-throne
432 Though dear as life the *i.* be
462 The *i.* from my breast I'd tear
471 Tear the *i.* from our bleeding
471 Lo! at thy word our *i.* dies
549 The dearest *i.* I have known
624 Tear every *i.* from thy throne
33 To *idols*, which our wayward
404 With all my *i.* part
920 Thy voice their *i.* shall confound

IDLY.
607 Let none hear you *i.* saying

ILL, ILLS.
105 Forgive...The *i.* which I this day
156 Yet will I fear no *i.*
497 The first abhorred approach of *i.*
635 Let good or *i.* befall
93 *Ills* have no weight, and tears no
166 Of mortal *i.* prevailing

ILLUME, ILLUMINATE, ILLUMINES.
90 Thine the radiance to *i.*
488 Love my darkness shall *i.*
997 *I.* my dying bed
518 *Illuminate* my soul; Scatter
868 beams on the soul and *illumines*

IMAGE.
307 And stamp thine *i.* on my heart
409 Thy sacred *i.*, Lord, impart
458 Thine *i.* in my soul to see
464 May the world thine *i.* see
472 Me to thine *i.* now restore
495 And stamp thine *i.* on my heart
498 Thine *i.*, Lord, bestow
519 Diffuse thine *i.* through my
531 And stamp thine *i.* on my heart
681 Thine *i.* on earth to regain
701 express The *i.* of thine own
714 Thine *i.* ever fills my thought
733 Shall his glorious *i.* bear
783 His *i.* bear below
803 Love, thine *i.*, love impart
825 And let them in thine *i.* rise
894 The *i.* of thy love
900 Blots the bright *i.* stamped

987 Thine *i.* trace in every word
1054 And in thy dear *i.* arise
1116 O let me put thine *i.* on

IMMANUEL.
41 We're marching through *I.'s*
81 Hail, great *I.*. all divine
146 Bright seraphs learn *I.'s*
224 Join to praise *I.'s* name
246 Help to chant *I.'s* praise
319 Drawn from *I.'s* veins
460 But ransomed by *I.'s* blood
721 Safely reach *I.'s* ground
811 To cultivate *I.'s* lands
1064 The breadth of *I.'s* land
1065 But saints our *I.* sing
1067 Happy in *I.'s* love
1074 hand in hand to *I.'s* land

IMMENSITY.
1112 And lost in thine *i.*

IMMORTAL.
41 rise To that *i.* state
122 gavest...*I.* life to me
227 And bade us, *i.*, to heaven
628 But are not ours the *i.* years
989 to life *I.* in the skies

IMMORTALITY.
90 *I.* and light
740 Or *i.* endures
1000 *I.* thy walls
1049 Have won their *i.*
1050 in that word, 'Tis *i.*

IMMOVABLE.
763 Church...*I.* she stands

IMPOSSIBLE.
413 The things *i.* to men

IMPOSSIBILITIES.
432 Laughs at *i.*

IMPRESS.
146 Or *i.* of thy feet
429 Come, Holy Ghost, thyself *i.*

IMPRISONED.
422 Long my *i.* spirit lay

IMPROVE.
82 *I.* the day thy God hath
111 May we this life *i.*

INBRED.
240 Whose power our *i.* sin controls
486 Take away my *i.* sin

INCARNATE.
6 Come, thou *i.* Word
85 Almighty Son, *i.* Word
42 *I.* Deity, Let all the ransomed
71 Hosanna to the *i.* Word
190 Hail, *i.* Deity
191 Christ, the *i.* Deity
220 The *i.* God hath died for

229 Enter, i. God
302 blood, I. God, I fly
325 And hail the i. God
340 Lo! the i. God, ascending
534 I look to my i. God
605 I. Son of God
874 Though no more the i. God
1045 And following their i. God

INCARNATION.
853 In thy holy i.

INCENSE.
36 The i. of the heart may rise
46 Behold a cloud of i. rise
82 As grateful i. to the skies
252 With i. in his hands
805 praise ascend, Like i., to the
868 No i. is lighted, no victims
868 the heart is the altar whence i.
923 Sweet i. to his name shall
1082 Here in thy house shall i.
1110 Our i. of praise shall arise

INCORRUPT.
989 bodies...shall i. arise

INCREASE.
59 Let our faith and love i.
301 A large i. bestow
784 I. our faith, confirm
811 He kindly gives the wished i.
817 grace A large i. shall give
1085 All things with large i.

INDIA.
879 I. from I.'s sultry plain
930 From I.'s coral strand

INDUSTRY.
811 Their i. vouchsafes to
966 With serious i. and fear

INEBRIATE.
895 The lost i. to reclaim
899 To lift the poor i. up

INEFFABLE.
701 Thou sweetness most i.

INEFFABLY.
257 Creator... I. sublime
1063 with Jesus i. one

INFALLIBLE.
437 publish...The signs i.

INFANT.
102 Like i.'s slumbers, pure
189 Yonder shines the i. light
505 Soon as we draw our i. breath
439 E'en from my i. days
710 Prayer...That i. lips can try
723 By thy helpless i. years
854 I. voices j. tuned to swell
875 O Thou, whose i. feet were
919 And i. voices shall proclaim
987 Millions of i. souls compose

INFANTS.
828 Our i. in his arms he takes
877 When i. learn to lisp his name
885 I., and the glad throng
987 While i. in thy tender arms

INFANCY.
1048 From i. to age

INFECTED.
397 Make my i. nature pure

INFIRMITY, INFIRMITIES.
117 Pardon each i.
749 He healeth thine *infirmities*

INFLAME, INFLAMING.
658 Doth still my languid heart i.
701 And, seeking thee, themselves i.
702 heart, Inflaming it with love

INFLUENCE.
270 Thy heavenly i. give
279 Let us thine i. prove
280 He came sweet i. to impart
301 And shed its i. round
877 Almighty God, thine i. shed

INGRATITUDE.
551 My vile i. I mourn
1057 No base i. above

INIQUITY.
383 From all i. release
586 Thou hatest all i.

INNOCENCE.
418 Made up of i. and love

INSCRIBED.
208 I. upon the cross we see
437 My name i. in heaven

INSINCERE.
348 Dare not think him i.

INSPIRE.
5 To touch our lips, our souls i.
10 Come, Holy Ghost, their hearts i.
129 With love divine our hearts i.
261 Holy Ghost, our he'ris i.
238 Come, Holy Ghost, our souls i.
279 Come, Holy Ghost, our hearts i.
324 Salvation sha l i. our hearts
181 My consecrated heart i.
489 Every fainting so d i.
523 Tid thou into my soul i.
889 Lord, if thou wilt thyself i.

INSPIRES.
178 that all heaven's host i.
891 His grace alone i. our hearts

INSPIRED, INSPIRING, INSPIRATION.
781 The heart with love to God i.
987 By thy *inspiring* breath
297 book...By *inspiration* given

INSTRUCTED, INSTRUCTOR.
511 My well-*i.* soul
299 Divine *Instructor*, gracious Lord

INSULTED.
390 Stay, thou *i.* Spirit, stay

INTEMPERANCE.
895 What ruin hath *i.*

INTERCEDE, INTERCEDES, INTERCEDING.
438 lives above For me to *i.*
4 Sing how he *intercedes* above
264 *I.* in silence there
706 Since he for sinners *i.*
246 Ever for us *interceding*

INTERCESSOR.
1096 Kind *I.*, to thy love

INVITE, INVITES, INVITING.
348 Would he you to life *i.*
456 O that I could all *i.*
335 Now Jesus *invites* you, the Spirit
349 While God *i.*, how blest the
355 Lo! Jesus, who *i.*, Declares
370 'Tis love *i.* thee near
625 *I.* the helpless and the poor
718 He himself *i.* thee near
326 sounds with an *inviting* voice

INVITATION.
357 The *i.'s* given
364 The *i.* is to all
1088 I hear the *i.*

INWARD.
416 Till thou *i.* life impart
443 *I.* turn thine eyes, it saith

ISAAC.
471 And gave his *I.* back to God

ISAIAH.
274 Brightened *I.'s* vivid page

ISLAND, ISLANDS, ISLE, ISLES.
914 And answering *i.* sing
879 I, from *islands* of the main
911 Seaward far the *i.* brighten
939 Go to many a tropic *isle* In the
912 from the *isles* of the ocean, praise
944 Saviour, lo! the *i.* are waiting
978 The eternal *i.* established be

ISRAEL.
162 In *I.* are his mercies known
162 *I.* is his peculiar throne
163 When *I.*, of the Lord beloved
248 Now hail, strength of *I.'s* might
722 Thee, thy *I.'s* strength and hope
740 On *I.'s* God; he made the sky
745 He is *I.'s* sure defense
772 And for his *I.* cares
847 *I.'s* hosts triumphant go
927 The thousands of our *I.* see
935 Promised day of *I.*

951 Hath he our sinful *I.* spared
1104 And in the name of *I.'s* God

ISSUES.
543 And keep the *i.* of my heart

J.

JARS.
804 Bid our *j.* forever cease

JASPER.
564 Flash the streets with *j.*
1030 With *j.* glow thy bulwarks
1063 Her walls are of *j.* and gold

JEALOUS, JEALOUSY.
574 Arm me with *j.* care
543 And fill with godly *jealousy*

JEHOVAH.
9 Before *J.'s* awful throne
17 To sing the great *J.'s* praise
24 When *J.'s* work begun
25 Thank and praise *J.'s* name
669 Who sing *J.'s* praise
912 Praise to *J.* ascending on
920 I am *J.*, God alone
946 Sing to the great *J.'s* praise
1013 Jah! *J.!* Everlasting God
1091 Dread *J.!* God of nations

JERUSALEM.
89 Pray for *J.*
195 Light on thy hills, *J.*
595 And in the New *J.*
648 *J.*, the saints' abode
648 The New *J.* to find
648 To find the New *J.*
772 As round *J.*
775 Awake, *J.*, awake
821 *J.* breaks forth in songs
864 The New *J.* on high
926 *J.*, thy God is nigh
1031 To that *J.* above
1025 The New *J.* comes down
1044 *J.*, my happy home
1061 *J.*, the golden
1063 That lovely *J.* here

JESUS.
222 From *J.* shall not move
333 His name is *J.*, and he died
456 Only *J.* I pursue
456 Only *J.* will I know
588 Believe that *J.* reigns
600 Ye faithful souls, who *J.* know
684 There is a place where *J.* sheds
747 When *J.* no longer I see
747 If *J.* would dwell with me
754 I long to be like *J.*
798 So we may *J.* gain
802 Till we are in *J.* found
806 More and more in *J.* live
806 We who *J.* have put on
880 When *J.* was here among men
1054 And thrice precious *J.*, whose
1071 I long to be where *J.* is

JESUS'.
40 All may sit down at *J.'* feet
101 Happy the home where *J.'* name
332 and bless the sound of *J.'* name
356 In *J.'* love we know
442 What a heaven in *J.'s* name
453 they are talking of *J.'s* grace
456 and depth of *J.'* love
700 A sweeter sound than *J.'* name
733 precious Is the sound of *J.'* name
802 We are met in *J.'* name
805 Sing we, then, in *J.'* name
903 At *J.'* feet I lay
1063 Where *J.'s* beauties display

My JESUS.
302 My *J.* and my all
537 But O, *my J.,* come
697 *My J.* shall be still my theme
757 blessing to know that *my J.* is

Of JESUS.
51 The name all-victorious *of J.*
316 How sweet the name *of J.*
653 Take the name *of J.* with you
700 The love *of J.*, what it is
756 story... *Of J.* and his glory
1003 To the sight *of J.* go

Our JESUS.
256 Is to *our J.* given
332 'Tis heaven to see *our J.'s* face
650 *Our J.* shall from heaven
947 and might, Be to *our J.* given

To JESUS.
201 By friendly hands *to J.* led
369 I'll go *to J.*, though my sins
426 I came *to J.* as I was
765 Happy the souls *to J.* joined
798 Glory and praise *to J.* give

With JESUS.
37 There let us all *with J.* stand
570 *With J.* in my view
634 *With J.* by my side
754 I long to be *with J.*
1063 *With J.* ineffably one

JEWELS.
640 What are they but his *j.*

JOB.
274 Or *J.* endured the trying hour

JOHN.
510 O that I could, with favored *J.*

JOIN, JOINS.
792 O let us all *j.* hand in hand
806 *J.* us in one spirit, join
1033 E'en now by faith we *j.* our hands
1033 Our spirits, too, shall quickly *j.*
780 Who *joins* us by his grace

JOINED, JOINING.
30 Who in thy name are *j.*
587 Indissolubly *j.* To battle

758 I do find, we two are so *j.*
765 Happy the souls to Jesus *j.*
797 But we shall still be *j.* in heart
816 Inseparably *j.* in heart
842 Let earth and heaven be *j.*
592 labor give By *joining* it to thine

JORDAN.
171 When I tread the verge of *J.*
330 him again when we pass over *J.*
385 Like *J.'s* swelling stream
542 No more on this side *J.* stop
564 *J.* flows before us
622 Since God through *J.* leadeth
1037 While *J.* rolled between
1038 On *J.'s* stormy banks I stand

JOURNEY, JOURNEYS.
202 like thee, all my *j.* run
426 Till all my *j.'s* done
610 And crown my *j.'s* end
653 When our *j.* is complete
720 As we *j.* let us sing
739 I halt, till life's short *j.* end
758 how wondrous my *j.* will
878 Lead us all our *j.* through
879 All our earthly *j.* past
925 Come, let us anew our *j.*
1074 Come, let us anew our *j.*
1078 Now let the pilgrim's *j.* end
919 Doth his successive *journeys* run
1070 All *j.* end in welcome to

JOY.
24 Then amid eternal *j.*
69 The *j.* that from thy presence
125 Thy *j.* and glory still
236 Their everlasting *j.* to know
313 Where *j.* forever reigns
332 The *j.* of earth and heaven
414 And spread the *j.* around
442 What a *j.* I received
414 Earth has a *j.* unknown to
453 Their *j.* is to walk in the light
489 All our *j.* and all our peace
590 If *j.* shall at thy bidding fly
627 But *j.* shall come with early light
638 Boundless their *j.* above
639 His love thy *j.* increase
643 Were that *j.* unmixed with thee
653 It will *j.* and comfort give you
687 True *J.* of every human breast
687 Our *j.*, when sorrow fills the
686 'Tis equal *j.* to go or stay
702 And *j.* to all impart
712 Enter into my Master's *j.*
736 And *j.* and everlasting love
742 May it be *j.* to me
770 Beyond my highest *j.*
782 Nor *j.*, nor grief, nor time, nor
909 And everlasting *j.*
912 *J.* to the lands that in darkness
917 The holy *j.* prolong
952 O let our glorious *j.* be full
951 In glorious *j.* to live
985 Infinite *j.* or endless woe
1003 For the *j.* he sets before thee
1010 And all his *j.* shall know

JOY 89 JUD

1032 Give *j*. or grief, give ease or
1043 Where pure, essential *j*. is found
1070 Till morning's *j*. shall end the

Every JOY.
616 In *every j*. that crowns my days
663 And *every j*. that dies
1082 Eternal Source of *every j*.

My JOY.
442 Was *my j*. and my song
540 *My j*., my heaven on earth, be
736 In grief, *my j*. unspeakable

Of JOY.
21 Let the time of *j*. return
81 And fresh supplies *of j*. be shed
427 A life *of j*. and peace
553 A taste *of j*. divine
914 forth in sweetest strains of *j*.

With JOY.
43 *With j*. we lift our eyes
52 Fill our hearts *with j*. and peace
262 Fill my soul *with j*. divine
996 I may *with j*. appear

JOYS.
2 But all their *j*. are one
19 Jesus, thou soul of all our *j*.
41 And let your *j*. be known
41 May speak their *j*. abroad
41 Should constant *j*. create
53 *J*. which earth cannot afford
61 And let the thoughts of *j*. above
174 know of thee, or of the *j*. above
204 *J*. that through all time abide
234 But lo! what sudden *j*. we see
241 And all the *j*. I have
277 they go, To reach eternal *j*.
298 To *j*. divinely sweet
299 And life and everlasting *j*.
304 Angels, assist our mighty *j*.
318 Whose *j*. eternal flow
385 Happy they whose *j*. abound
418 Quick as their thoughts their *j*.
428 And then the *j*. of heaven
530 So near to heaven's eternal *j*.
564 Shedding *j*. untold
600 Superior to the *j*. below
612 Eternal *j*. my own
647 Earthly *j*. no longer please us
649 Though *j*. be withered all, and
662 Our dearest *j*., and nearest
701 In whom all *j*. are found
701 Surpassing all the *j*. we know
704 My God, the spring of all my *j*.
742 And fleeting *j*. resign
758 country I've found where true *j*.
765 Their mighty *j*. we know
774 And all the *j*. which mortals
805 Called we are their *j*. to prove
807 Where *j*. celestial thrill
807 And time our *j*. dispel
817 For fuller *j*. above
903 Rich are the *j*. which cannot die
952 Of saints, and let our *j*. abound
958 Their *j*., and griefs, and hopes

1014 Come to make our *j*. o'erflow
1031 Its *j*. as soon are past
1039 And *j*. supreme are given
1042 Hath *j*. substantial and
1044 When I thy *j*. shall see
1048 Eternal *j*. to share
1065 The *j*. of that holiest place
1075 From earth I rise and seek the *j*.
1088 The *j*. that round me wing

JOYFUL.
28 To him with *j*. voices give
40 And hear from him the *j*. sound
42 While earth repeats the *j*. song
56 O let the nations *j*.
66 And raise to Christ our *j*. strain
68 O then, aloud, in *j*. lays
89 And *j*. in the house of prayer
121 Of thee we make our *j*. boast
182 As with *j*. steps they sped
190 *J*., all ye nations, rise
191 Bright and *j*. is the morn
199 For which in *j*. strains we raise
230 Now let the heavens be *j*.
276 Where'er the *j*. sound is heard
323 Who knows the *j*. sound
495 bring near the *j*. hour, And
502 Hasten the *j*. day
551 And shed the *j*. light
613 Nay, rather with a *j*. heart
628 Then, Father, *j*. on my way
819 Hear from their lips the *j*.
827 *J*. that we ourselves are thine
858 To the *j*. sound reply
908 Shall hear the *j*. sound
910 soul shall hear the *j*. sound
1085 With *j*. hearts and voices

JUBILEE.
144 Praise with solemn *j*.
331 The year of *j*. is come
810 The glorious *j*. proclaim
882 This is the children's *j*.
921 Shall keep her last great *j*.
938 Hark! the song of *j*.
946 The *j*. of heaven
1016 Haste the joyful *j*.

JUDAH, JUDEA.
195 O'er *J*.'s sacred hills
195 O'er *J*.'s mountains rolled
874 *J*.'s ancient temple filling
195 Where wild *Judea* stretches far

JUDGE.
134 The *J*. of all the earth is just
244 Jesus, the *J*., shall come
387 *J*. of angels and of men
576 The *J*. is at the door
694 And then, our *J*., shall speak
787 And God, the *J*. of all, declare
968 If now the *J*. is at the door
996 And see the *J*., with glory
1014 While the frowning *J*. draws
1020 When I must stand before my *J*.
1021 Thou awful *J*. of quick and dead
1022 The *J*. ordained of quick and
1023 When the *J*. shall come at last

1023 O just *J.*, to whom belongs
1024 Thou *J.* of quick and dead
1027 When thou, my righteous *J.*
1028 The *J.* of man I see appear
1029 See the *J.* our nature wearing
1058 The *J.* is at the gate
1058 The *J.* that comes in mercy
1058 The *J.* that comes with might

JUDGE, (*verb*.)

50 For thou shalt *j.* the people
161 *J.* not the Lord by feeble sense
966 To *j.* the nations at thy bar
1023 Which shall *j.* the quick and
1024 To *j.* the human race

JUDGING.

1092 Watching invisible, *j.* unheard

JUDGMENT, JUDGMENTS.

105 Rise glorious at the *j.*-day
223 Follow to the *j.*-hall
336 small and great in *j.* stand
412 And sit in *j.* on my soul
485 *J.*, reason, bending low
941 when we stand in the *j.*
1017 When man to *j.* wakes
1021 And must I be to *j.* brought
1022 And in the day of *j.* save
1029 Day of *j.*, day of wonders
391 Lord, should thy *judgments*
396 Thy *j.*, too, which devils
1085 Thine awful *j.* are abroad
1096 Whose *j.* yet delay

JUST.

310 shall fallen man Be *j.* before his
389 'Tis *j.* the sentence... 'Tis *j.*
391 I must pronounce thee *j.* in death
410 Acknowledging how *j.* thou art
978 The memory of the *j.* appears
993 To live among the *j.*
1025 In death the wicked and the *j.*
1025 Nothing hath the *j.* to lose

JUSTICE.

127 *J.* and truth before thee stand
146 The *j.* or the grace
181 *J.* shall guard his throne
210 *J.* divine is satisfied
292 Reveals thy *j.* and thy grace
322 we adore Thy *j.* and thy grace
343 Ere the hand of *j.* falls
389 *J.* pursue, and mercy love
444 *J.* and mercy for thy life
632 Nor dare thy *j.* to arraign
735 While *j.* hears thy praying faith
915 And *J.* from her heavenly bower
1096 Though *j.* near thy awful

JUSTIFIES, JUSTIFIED, JUSTIFYING.

833 And *j.* your claim to heaven
367 soul is free, And thou art *justified*
283 Speak us freely *j.*
425 And speak me *j.*
1001 *J.* through faith alone
450 ever knew Thy *justifying*

K.

KEEP.

105 *K.* me, O keep me, King of
107 *K.* us from sin, O Lord, most
155 Our lives those holy angels *k.*
262 *K.* me, Lord, forever thine
356 And *k.* in all our way
434 'Tis he that still doth *k.*
455 *K.* me lest I turn again Out
455 Thy weakest servant *k.*
466 And *k.* us in thy way
556 Myself I cannot *k.*
682 *K.* thou my feet; I do not ask
915 And *k.* us to that day
1046 save And *k.* us to that day
1046 And he shall *k.* them still
1115 *K.* the souls whom now we

KEEPS, KEEPER, KEEPING, KEPT.

736 And *k.* my happy soul above
745 He thy quiet spirit *k.*
746 See the Lord, thy *Keeper*, stand
1010 Safe in his Saviour's *keeping*
106 praise to thee, who safe hast *kept*
585 *K.* by the power of grace divine
650 Thou who hast *k.* us to this hour

KEY, KEYS.

279 Unlock the truth, thyself the *K.*
241 The *keys* of death and hell

KILL.

166 The body they may *k.*
519 And *k.*, and make alive

KIND, KINDLY.

145 Praise the Lord, for he is *k.*
149 Is most wonderfully *k.*
176 How *k.* his precepts are
799 Whose *k.* designs to serve and
785 And let us always *kindly* think
806 *K.* for each other care

KINDNESS.

119 There's a *k.* in his justice
530 And *k.* in our bosoms dwell
635 And *k.* o'er thy lips is shed
859 If human *k.* meets return
950 In vain with lavish *k.*
1100 For all the *k.* thou hast
1103 For ages let thy *k.* last

KINDLE, KINDLES.

81 And *k.* there a pure desire
263 Let every high desire
264 *K.* there the gospel fire
269 *K.* our senses from above
247 *K.* a flame of sacred love
281 *K.* a flame of heavenly love
701 Then *kindles* love divine

KINDRED.

166 Let goods and *k.* go
248 Let every *k.*, every tribe
276 Till every *k.* call him Lord
707 The fellowship of *k.* minds

KIN 91 KNO

801 unite Our k. spirits here
916 Lo, every k.. every tribe
970 And bid our k. rise
973 To seek its k. sky
979 Thy k. and their graves
1055 Where k. minds shall meet

KING.

134 The Lord is K.! lift up thy
134 Your God is K.. your Father
140 O worship the K., all-glorious
190 Glory to the newborn K.
244 Rejoice, the Lord is K.
914 And own thee as their K.

KING of Glory.

14 Behold, the K. of glory waits
212 See there, the K. of glory see
237 Receive the K. of glory in
261 Take the K. of glory in
567 He with the K. of glory Shall
865 Great K. of glory, come
886 How once the K. of glory

KING of Kings.

14 The K. of kings is drawing near
48 Lord of hosts; the K. of kings
144 dim...behold the K. of kings
155 bands, Sent by the K. of kings
191 K. of kings, and Prince of Peace
247 K. of kings, and Lord of lords
256 The K. of kings, and Lord of
485 K. of kings, and wilt thou deign
653 K. of kings in heaven we'll crown
1093 Praises to the K. of kings

Our KING.

63 view The glories of our K.
69 O God, our K., whose sovereign
240 O Christ, our K., Creator, Lord
882 Hosanna to our K.
1059 Their God, our K. and Portion
1076 There dwells the Lord, our K.
1089 Protect...Great God, our K.
1097 So thou art still our K.

KINGS.

36 Whom k. adored in songs
218 That k. and prophets never knew
821 Which k. and prophets waited
937 Mightiest k. his power shall own

KINGDOM.

51 His k. is glorious, and rules over
148 Be the k. all thine own
166 His K. is forever
179 land of their sojourn...k. of love
181 His k. still increasing
244 His k. cannot fail
251 His k. over all maintains
268 Thy k. come, and Lett's
268 The k. of thy Christ prepare
330 Jesus, ride on,—thy k. is glorious
334 Now thy gracious k. bring
489 Bring thy heavenly k. in
585 The k. fixed within
545 Give me to prove the k. mine
583 The heavenly k. suffers force
597 And claim the k. of the earth
655 The k. that I seek is thine
669 He that unto God's k. comes
716 Thy k. come; thy will be done
716 And thine the k.. thine the
770 I love thy k., Lord
808 hasten Thy k. from above
808 travail Which makes thy k.
836 When thou shalt in thy k.
861 Thy k. come to every heart
879 In the k. of your Lord
880 For of such is the k. of
919 His k. spread from shore
1029 See the k. I bestow
1076 His k. still maintains

KINGDOMS.

563 K. rise and wane
763 For not like k. of the world
769 The k. are but one
938 And the k. of this world
938 Are the k. of his Son
1018 He claims the k. for his own
1018 The k. all obey his word
1108 The earth's extended k. lie

KINSMAN.

203 K., Friend, and elder Brother

KISS, KISSED.

251 K. the exalted Son
350 And k. his late-returning son
375 let us in, though late, to k. his
915 and Righteousness have kissed

KNEE, KNEES.

83 Ne'er may we bow the k. to idols
79 hearts of all that bent the k.
249 Every k. to him shall bow
658 And bow my faltering k.
615 Let every k. to Jesus bow
603 Your knees are faint, your souls
690 The weakest saint upon his k.

KNEEL, KNEELING.

43 While in thy house we k.
683 to the mercy-seat, fervently k.
750 Come, let us k. and pray
1105 Kneeling at thy gracious throne

KNIT.

1102 All hearts are k. in holy love
1107 As thou dost k. them, Lord, in

KNOCK, KNOCKETH, KNOCKING.

346 K.. and weep... knock—He knows
352 God calling yet! and shall he k.
377 Thou bidst us k. and enter in
376 How it knocketh, knocketh
28 He now stands knocking at the
376 Think you death will stand a-k.
403 Lord, I am k. at the gate

KNOW.

126 Thee to perfection who can k.
174 How little do we k. of thee
360 My son, k. thou the Lord
381 To k. thee who thou art

425 Thee only would I k.
437 How can a sinner k. His
456 Him to k. is life and peace
494 Thee only would I k.
524 Thee, only thee, resolved to k.
551 seek to k.. Shall know him and
630 Of those who k., or know him
722 Nothing k., or seek, beside
738 I k. thee, Saviour, who thou
744 And only thee to k.
1048 And k. as we are known
1059 And they that k. and see him
1079 Then, Lord, shall I fully k.

KNOWS.

372 Is here a soul that k. thee not
376 Jesus waited...But he k. thee
642 He k. the way he taketh

KNOWN.

63 name And joy to make it k.
121 every heart Is fully k. to thee
123 Lord, all I am is k. to thee
126 Only to thee, O God, is k.
332 What shall I do to make it k.
1021 Shall shortly be made k.
1050 Knowing as I am k.

KNOWLEDGE.

61 To ask the k. of thy word
123 O wondrous k., deep and high
239 The k. of myself bestow
290 year to year does k. soar
299 Here the fair tree of k. grows
441 And all your k. shall be
456 Other k. I disdain
501 do thy will, My k. would be
531 And in the k. of my Lord
669 My k. of that life is small
927 Their souls for lack of k. die
1098 Of k., truth, and thee

L.

LABOR.

116 They show the l. of thy hands
565 Fill brightest hours with l.
683 Go, l. on; spend and be spent
640 O happy, if ye l. as Jesus
648 Our l. this, our only aim
712 L. is rest, and pain is sweet
808 Accept these hands to l.
811 In the sweet l. of his love
819 Nor let them l., Lord, in vain
923 In this blest l. share a part
982 Life's l. done, as sinks the clay
1106 blessing, Were l. without rest

LABORS.

110 When each day's scenes and l.
598 We, to their l. entering in
606 My daily l. to pursue
810 And by your l. sinners live
816 That heaven Where all our l.
973 Our labors done, securely laid
975 All earthly l. done
1011 When shall my l. have an end

LABORED, LABORING.

517 Son...and l. for our good
362 Ye laboring, burdened, sin-sick

LABORER, LABORERS.

570 Are there not in the l.'s day
578 Laborers of Christ, arise
598 More l. for the Lord
816 Vineyard...Before his l. lies
818 The l. are few

LADDER.

640 What are they but the l.
690 Prayer climbs the l. Jacob

LADEN.

340 Come, ye weary, heavy-l.
728 Are ye weak and heavy-l.
732 Laboring and heavy-l.
1070 And l. souls by thousands

LAMB.

12 At the great supper of the L.
26 L. of God, for sinners slain
51 Fall down, and worship the L.
73 Worthy the L.. that once was
216 Might view the L. in his own
250 Thou art the ever-slaughtered L.
257 The L. upon his throne
312 Sinners, behold the L.
991 cry, Salvation to the L.
1007 Now thy little l.'s brief
1045 Ascribe their conquest to the L.
1060 The L. is all thy splendor
1063 The L. is their light and sun
1069 Shout the L., who died for all
1077 And sound...The slaughtered L.

Atoning LAMB.

221 Thou loving, all-a. L.
331 The all-a. L.; Redemption
430 wash in blood...Of the a. L.
435 know The all-a. L.
526 O, all-a. L. of God

Bleeding LAMB.

324 Salvation! O thou b. L.
483 Thou gracious, b. L.
1069 Glory to the b. L.

LAMB OF GOD.

210 The spotless L. of G. is slain
262 Lead me to the L. of G.
331 Extol the L. of G.
378 O L. of G., for sinners slain
393 O L. of G., I come! I come
526 O all-atoning L. of G.
631 Thou L. of G., thou Prince
754 The spotless L. of G.

Paschal LAMB.

216 P. L., by God appointed
259 Is our P. L. to-day
816 And eat the P. L.

LAMBS.

679 Like l. they shall still in
718 'Tis there, with the l. of thy

LAM 93 LAY

827 Hark, how he calls the tender *l.*
880 How he called little children as *l.*
887 Bear the *l.*, when they are weary
888 While the *l.* thy bosom share
892 And *l.* for whom the Shepherd bled
987 I take these little *l.*, said he

LAME.
1 And leap, ye *l.*, for joy
739 *L.* as I am, I take the prey

LAMENT.
379 Let me now my sins *l.*
412 Timely my sins *l.*
1001 Who can now *l.* the lot

LAMP, LAMPS.
290 As when the cloudless *l.* of day
297 Bright as a *l.* its doctrines shine
297 This *l.*, through all the tedious
345 Lest thy *l.* should fail to burn
930 benighted The *l.* of life deny
999 And the *l.* of his love is thy
1012 Which hangs like a *l.* in the tomb
1015 With my *lamps* well trimmed and
1034 Ye golden *l.* of heaven, farewell

LAND.
14 O blest the *l.*, the city blest
70 To every *l.* the earth around
148 Lord of every *l.* and nation
289 gospel...all our *l.* o'erspread
542 mountain-top See all the *l.* below
542 But now the *l.* possess
779 Scatter blessings o'er the *l.*
808 Through all this happy *l.*
873 Gently passing To the happy *l.* on
911 Proclaim To many a wakening *l.*
917 And over *l.*, and stream, and
920 grace proclaim In every *l.*, of
931 mercy To every *l.* below
933 The *l.* before you lies
941 From some far, forgotten *l.*
1010 Still through this *l.* of woe
1033 And reach the heavenly *l.*
1037 Death divides...heavenly *l.* from
1041 There is a *l.* mine eye hath
1051 Fair *l.*! could mortal eyes
1055 joyful feet...Amid that glorious *l.*
1071 Who would not seek the happy *l.*
1076 The goodly *l.* I see
1076 the wonders...Through all their *l.*
1089 Long may our *l.* be bright
1090 God bless our native *l.*
1093 Flow around this happy *l.*
1098 The *l.* we love the most
1100 This *l.* we fondly call our own
1109 Bold an unknown *l.* to try

LANDS.
908 And distant *l.* obey
912 See, from all *l.*, from the isles
922 We meet through distant *l.*
925 light shall shine on distant *l.*

LANDSCAPE.
180 Amid the verdant *l.* flow
1037 And view the *l.* o'er

LANE.
897 By *l.* and cell obscure

LANGUAGE, LANGUAGES.
222 What *l.* shall I borrow
689 thought be broken, *l.* lame
692 And all the powers of *l.* fail
980 In *l.* that no tongue can
79 People...Of various *languages*

LANGUID.
423 Who fixed his *l.* eyes on me
558 Look as when thy *l.* eye
647 Faith our *l.* spirits cheering

LANGUISH, LANGUISHING, LANGUOR.
646 Suffer not our hearts to *l.*
683 Come...disconsolate, where'er ye *l.*
747 Say, why do I *l.* and pine
969 And let me *l.* into life
1064 I *l.* and sigh to be there
852 weak, and *languishing*, and low
415 Could my zeal no *languor* know
612 When *l.* and disease invade

LATE.
373 *L.*, late, so late! and dark
412 Ere yet it be too *l.*

LAUNCH.
1038 Fearless I'd *l.* away
1109 We *l.* into the foaming deep

LAUREL.
1060 Thine is the victor's *l.*

LAVISH.
779 Then shall God, with *l.* hand
930 In vain with *l.* kindness

LAW.
142 justice stand To guard his holy *l.*
198 The giver of the *l.*
263 Be my *l.*, and I shall be
298 And every *l.* of sin reverse
305 Thy *l.* demands a perfect heart
391 Against thy *l.*, against thy grace
482 That blessed *l.* of thine
482 The *l.* of liberty...perfect law of
482 Thy nature be my *l.*
500 Give me to keep thy perfect *l.*
732 That by love's eternal *l.*
803 Write thy *l.* of love within
832 Its willing soul to keep thy *l.*
904 And thus thy *l.* of love fulfill
985 The *l.* gives sin its damning

LAWS.
57 *L.* which never shall be broken
200 The eternal *l.* of truth and right
292 Thy *l.* are pure, thy judgments

LAY, LAYS.
195 The high and solemn *l.*
68 Servants of God, in joyful *lays*
133 Come, O my soul, in sacred *l.*
744 In everlasting *l.*

1039 Cry aloud in heavenly *l.*
1077 I join the heavenly *l.*

LAZARUS.
417 O'er the grave where *L.* slept
723 O'er the grave where *L.* slept
1072 Although, like *L.*, sick and

LEAD.
110 O *l.* me onward to the skies
169 *L.* me a way I have not
171 *L.* me all my journey through
278 And *l.* us in the paths of life
465 *L.* us, Lord, from earth to heaven
487 Gently will he *l.* the weak
496 And *l.* me to thy holy hill
614 O *l.* us gently on until
646 Gently, Lord, O gently *l.* us
655 *L.* me by thine own hand
682 *L.*, kindly Light, amid the
718 *L.* me to my journey's end
885 *L.* us where thou hast trod

LEADS.
563 royal Master, *L.* against the foe
669 Christ *l.* me through no darker
907 And still it *l.*, as once it did
1112 Whose spirit *l.* believing souls

LEADER.
566 Lo! your *L.* from the skies
566 Follow where your *L.* trod
568 The Lord himself, thy *L.*
577 The Lord our *L.* is
577 And ever with our *L.* rest
648 *L.* of faithful souls, and Guide
720 Only thou our *L.* be
1045 Our gracious *L.* claims our praise
1061 And they who, with their *L.*

LEADETH, LEADING.
179 He *l.* my soul where the still
622 He *l.* me! O blessed thought
182 *Leading* onward, beaming bright

LED.
108 Thus far the Lord hath *l.* me on
182 Evermore be *l.* to thee
439 Whose love hath gently *l.* me on
1103 *L.* on by thine unerring aid

LEAF, LEAVES.
629 murmuring wind, the quivering *l.*
974 the withering *l.*, scarce whispers
977 And gay their silken *leaves* unfold
1088 The *l.* around me falling

LEAN, LEANED.
454 In him I am blest, I *l.* on his breast
667 hour of grief... Will *l.* upon its God
745 *L.* on thy Redeemer's breast
905 We *l.* on others as we walk
1012 And *l.* on the faith of his word
679 The soul that on Jesus hath *leaned*

LEAP, LEAPS.
1 And *l.*, ye lame, for joy
660 My heart would *l.* for joy

739 I *l.* for joy, pursue my way
703 My spirit *leaps* with inward joy

LEARN, LEARNING.
188 *L.* his name and taste his joy
205 *L.* thy love while gazing thus
495 Fain would I *l.* of thee, my
591 But *l.* what God is like
866 And let these *l.*, who here
24 *Learning* here, by faith and love

LEAVE.
455 And *l.* me not alone
475 Here, then, to thee thine own I *l.*
483 O never let me *l.* thy side
569 *L.* all to him, your Lord
596 And seems to *l.* us to ourselves
656 *L.*, O leave me not alone
660 Then *l.* me not when griefs
726 Prone to *l.* the God I love
889 Tender Shepherd, never *l.* us
1007 Lord, thou wouldst no longer *l.*

LEGACY.
503 tear of sorrow... *l.* of love
833 Accept your precious *l.*

LEGAL.
542 This moment end my *l.* years

LEGIONS.
193 Through all the shining *l.* ran
226 Jesus triumphs! countless *l.*
778 And scattered their *l.*, was

LEISURE.
675 And a heart at *l.* from itself

LENDETH.
901 *L.* his substance to the Lord

LENGTHEN, LENGTHENS.
668 And *l.* out my days
946 Who kindly *lengthens* out our
951 To God, who *l.* out our days
953 Who *l.* out our trials

LEPER, LEPERS, LEPROSY.
425 Touch me, and make the *l.* clean
527 Touch me, and make the *l.* clean
1099 The *l.* with his tainted life
40 *Lepers* and lame, and all were
305 The *leprosy* lies deep within
207 Purge out the inbred *l.*

LIBERTY.
149 In his justice... more than *l.*
331 Ye slaves... Your *l.* receive
407 And set my soul at *l.*
479 The day of *l.* draws near
482 The law of *l.* from sin
491 Set our hearts at *l.*
502 And bring the glorious *l.*
512 A pledge of *l.*
535 I ask... The *l.* from sin
736 In bonds, my perfect *l.*
983 breathe air of boundless *l.*
1056 A land of sacred *l.*

1089 Sweet land of *l.*
1089 Author of *l.*, To thee we sing
1098 valleys shout The songs of *l.*

LIE.
156 He makes me down to *l.*
971 ground Where you must shortly *l.*
972 Must *l.* as low as ours

LIFE.
1 New *l.* the dead receive
14 Let new and nobler *l.* begin
58 Endless *l.* in him possessing
64 Till *l.*, and love, and joy divine
93 ebbs out *l.'s* little day
106 I may of endless *l.* partake
135 Lord of all *l.*, below, above
227 Sad were the *l.* we may part
230 From death to *l.* eternal, From
232 Where *l.* is waking all around
246 *L.* is given through thy name
309 And give them *l.* divine
318 Thou art the *L.*:—the rending
323 Millions...here found *l.* and peace
337 Find on earth the *l.* of heaven
343 Soon your *l.* will pass away
358 There is a *l.* above, Unmeasured
377 The *l.* eternal give
453 new creation, a *l.* from the dead
466 That long as *l.* itself shall last
500 To die in thee is *l.* to me
558 *L.*, and happiness, and love Drop
586 gracious will....offers *l.* to all
602 And were this *l.* the utmost span
669 If *l.* be long, I will be glad
676 And love and *l.* before
719 By his death to *l.* restored
730 *L.*, and health, and peace
730 *L.* deriving from his death
740 While *l.*, and thought, and being
755 In thee is *l.* provided For all
773 *L.*, love, and joy, still gliding
791 In thee eternal *l.* we know
826 Till at thy will this *l.* is o'er
899 *L.* from the dead, Almighty
981 shall be clothed with endless *l.*
1005 Owning that *l.* and death Alike
1050 *L.* from the dead is in that word
1056 swallowed up Of everlasting *l.*
1070 strains are telling Of that new *l.*
1088 to glory. .and find true *l.* begin
1106 May they through *l.* go on

His LIFE.
58 Ye for whom *his l.* was given
259 He who gave for us *his l.*
407 Who gave *his l.* that I might live
1085 Who gave *his l.* for all

My LIFE.
389 But though *my l.* henceforth
500 *My l.* in thee, thy life in me
519 Jesus, *my L.*, thyself apply
637 *My l.*, my friends, my soul, I
675 Father, I know that all *my l.*
692 God of *my l.*, through all my
694 Lord Jesus Christ, *my L.*, my

Of LIFE.
358 'Tis not the whole *of l.* to live
531 Fullness *of l.* eternal find
656 Thou *of l.* the fountain art
664 My span *of l.* will soon be done
732 Light *of l.!* we walk in thee
1026 Lo, the day, the day *of l.*
1099 Thou Lord *of l.* and death

Thy LIFE.
289 And fill with all *thy l.* below
385 I shall *thy l.* receive
491 Let us all *thy l.* receive
519 More of *thy l.*, and more I have
584 My soul, weigh not *thy l.*
868 the power of *thy l.*-giving word
987 *Thy l.* I read, my gracious

LIFT, LIFTS, LIFTED.
21 Those that are cast down *l.* up
237 *L.* up your heads, ye heavenly
251 *L.* up your heart, *l.* up
542 hope...It *lifts* me up to things
657 It *l.* the fainting spirit up
169 power...*lifted up* my sinking

LIGHT.
33 Led by the *l.* thy grace imparts
72 at the creation, The *l.* first had
94 Turn...for us its darkness into *l.*
95 Whilst I enjoy the *l.*
104 sovereign word restores the *l.*
105 For all the blessings of the *l.*
116 Clad in *l.* and deathless bloom
163 A burning and a shining *l.*
204 beaming *L.* and love upon my
273 Enable with perpetual *l.* The
278 Come as the *l.*: to us reveal
279 And let there now be *l.*
284 Come, *L.* serene, and still
292 That see the *l.*, or feel the sun
295 Here *l.* descending from above
299 And still increasing *l.*
303 Till he his *l.* impart
349 While life prolongs its precious *l.*
375 No *l.* had we;—for that we do
375 let us in, that we may find the *l.*
426 I am this dark world's *L.*
445 Faith lends its realizing *l.*
477 I see from far thy beauteous *l.*
496 The darkness shineth as the *l.*
507 And God himself is *l.*
510 I look for many a lesser *l.*
516 As by the *l.* of opening day
546 morn the *l.* reveals, No light
552 Turned my darkness into *l.*
570 *L.* of the world! thy beams
620 At eve it shall be *l.*
640 the effluence of uncreated *L.*
644 By whose *l.* my soul shall
647 May our *l.* be always burning
672 Thy path unsullied *l.*
682 Lead, kindly *L.*, amid the
691 Shed o'er the world thy holy *l.*
694 Let me with joy behold the *l.*
845 Till he comes...In their golden *l.*
881 whose beams alone *L.* the
913 Let there be light

928 When will the promised *l.* arise
939 Pour the living *l.* of heaven
911 *L.* of nations, lead us o'er
1007 Now it dwells with thee in *l.*
1026 Day of unimagined *l.*
1058 The *l.* so new and golden
1061 What *l.* beyond compare
1063 A sure and a permanent *l.*
1064 arrayed With glory and *l.*

A LIGHT.
296 It gives a *l.* to every age
549 A *l.* to shine upon the road
611 Sometimes a *l.* surprises
975 vale... I see a *l.* within it shed

Everlasting LIGHT.
657 blaze of *everlasting l.*
768 with thee... thine *everlasting l.*
777 God, your *everlasting l.*
1014 Shines the *everlasting l.*

Glorious LIGHT.
694 Yea, like thyself, in *glorious l.*
940 Grant them, Lord, the *glorious l.*
942 promised... *Glorious l.* in latter

Heavenly LIGHT.
346 Wait till *heavenly l.* appears
809 Lord.. the *heavenly l.* divine
821 are our eyes... see this *heavenly l.*
902 For them that *heavenly l.* shall

In the LIGHT.
507 Walk *in the l.!* so shalt thou
507 Walk *in the l.!* and e'en
1065 And walk *in the l.* of the Lamb
1071 loyal hearts... Stand ever *in the l.*

My LIGHT.
397 On thee I call, *My l.,* my
496 Be thou *my l.,* be thou my way
639 In... temptation, *My l.,* my help

Of LIGHT.
86 This is the day *of l.*
296 Spirit *of l.!* explore, And
707 When sink the beams *of l.*
958 In the land *of l.* we dwell

Thy LIGHT.
262 Let *thy l.* within me shine
298 O send *thy l.* and truth abroad
428 Light in *thy l.* O may I see
481 Light in *thy l.* still may I see
1015 Where *thy l.* I do not see

With LIGHT.
145 Filled... new-made world *with l.*
267 Holy Ghost, *with l.* divine
808 And fill our souls *with l.*

LIGHTS, LIGHTED, LIGHTEN, LIGHTING.
805 *L.* in a benighted land
708 whose eyes Are *lighted* from
929 Shall we, whose souls are *l.*
273 And *lighten* with celestial fire

411 *L.* mine eyes with faith; my
731 *Lighting* up the steps to glory

LIGHTNING, LIGHTNINGS.
866 The *l.*-rifts disclose his throne
956 As the *l.* from the sky Darts
1052 Thunder thy clarion, and *l.* thy
1018 His *lightnings* flash, his thunders

LIKE, LIKENESS.
715 And make me all *l.* thee
775 Be *l.* your Lord, his word embrace
804 Make us... Altogether *l.* our Lord
631 O make me in thy *likeness* shine
1004 To his glorious *l.* wrought

LILY, LILIES.
875 How sweet the *l.* grows
875 The *l.* must decay
611 Who gives the *lilies* clothing

LIMB, LIMBS.
436 At cost of life and *l.,* I cling
905 And must these active *limbs* of

LINE, LINES.
342 message... Every *l.* is full of love
396 But I can read each moving *l.*
292 We read thy name in fairer *lines.*
289 adored For these celestial *l.*
837 Be written... ever-radiant *l.*

LINGER, LINGERS, LINGERED, LINGERING.
354 Then *l.* not in all the plain
668 And gladly *l.* out below
1088 But while I here must *l.*
92 Still the Spirit *lingers* near
909 Perchance thy weak... *lingered*
236 But we are *lingering* here
663 To lift the *l.* heart from

LION.
229 *L.* of Judah, hail! And
888 Let them be the *l.'s* prey

LIP, LIPS.
1008 Child... Thy *l.* and eye so bright
40 To touch thy servants' *lips* with
91 Guard thou the *l.* from sin, the
129 O may our *l.* confess thy name
151 My *l.* shall dwell upon thy
241 His *l.* with grace o'erflow
261 Hark, his gracious *l.* bestow
771 speak Through *l.* of humble clay
828 Since his own *l.* to us declare
994 Through these parched *l.* of thine

LISP.
148 May a mortal *l.* thy name
889 Taught to *l.* the holy praises

LISTEN, LISTENS, LISTENING.
45 And *l.* to the sacred word
771 Now *l.* to our cry
952 We *l.* for thy welcome voice
776 He who *listens* when we cry
133 Till *listening* worlds shall join

LIT 97 LOO

195 Calm on the *l.* ear of night
328 While *l.* thousands gathered
707 That *l.* ear to gain
865 Here may the *l.* throng

LITANY.
723 Hear our solemn *l.*

LITTLE.
174 How *l.* do we know of thee
722 Keep us *l.* and unknown
830 Let the *l.* ones come unto me
886 how holy His *l.* ones may be
888 Now these *l.* ones receiving
889 *L.* ones are dear to thee
956 wait, But how *l.*—none can know

LIVE.
42 Father, in whom we *l.*
101 And *l.* but for the skies
103 To *l.* more nearly as we pray
132 we at length with thee may *l.*
144 And in thee do all things *l.*
157 O Lord, we 'll *l.* to thee
234 Say, *L.* forever, wondrous King
277 shall we ever *l.* At this poor
281 'Tis thine to bid the dying *l.*
312 And bids the sinner *l.*
370 Thy Saviour bids me *l.*
385 And thou in me wilt *l.*
423 I die that thou mayst *l.*
426 And now I *l.* in him
470 I May to thy great glory *l.*
472 To thee O let me *l.*
490 Who in thee begin to *l.*
500 Jesus, I *l.* to thee, The
508 So shall we ever *l.* and move
520 Jesus hath died that I might *l.*
541 Shall *l.* to God at last
610 And make me *l.* to thee
761 mercy ever free, Shall while I *l.*
790 Together let us sweetly *l.*
805 We like them may *l.* and love
826 So unto thee I *l.* and die
835 And all may *l.* by thee
849 On earth to *l.* in thee
951 And henceforth *l.* and die to him
961 cease at once to work and *l.*
968 How then ought I on earth to *l.*
998 I would not *l.* alway; I ask

LIVES, LIVING.
126 What *l.* and moves, lives by
225 Jesus *l.* who once was dead
242 He *l.*, he lives, who once was
251 Who died, and *l.* to die no more
438 He ever *l.* above, For me to
1007 Where it *l.* may soon be living
500 *Living* or dying, Lord, I ask
609 might know Of *l.* thus to thee
1009 *L.* or dying, none were blest
1095 stand between...*l.* and the dead

LIVES, (plural of life).
129 Our holy *l.* thy power proclaim
701 And ever in our *l.* express
809 O let our *l.* to all around
1085 And with your *l.* adore him

LOAD.
137 To take our *l.* of sins away
176 Why should this anxious *l.* Press
311 to feel, And then the *l.* remove
312 He bore the mighty *l.*
413 my chain, Or e'er throw off my *l.*
495 O that my *l.* of sin were gone
754 frees us From the accursed *l.*
891 Each other's *l.* to share
967 Beneath its mountain *l.*
1078 My soul is lightened of its *l.*

LOADSTONE.
785 Touched by the *l.* of thy love

LOINS.
647 And our *l.* be girded round

LONG.
379 *l.* withstood...Long provoked
1015 *L.*, too long, in sin and sadness

LONG, LONGS, LONGING, LONG-INGS.
63 And shall we *l.* and wish in vain
419 For thee I *l.*, to thee I look
1071 paradise! I greatly *l.* to see
509 The love that *longs* for God
550 So *l.* my soul, O God, for thee
67 thou shalt bless our *longing* eyes
312 To him lift up your *l.* eyes
384 I am *l.* for thy favor
418 And *l.* hopes, and cheerful
631 My *l.* heart implores thy
1074 No *l.* we find for the
681 These passionate *longings* for

LONG-SUFFERING.
163 Be thou, *l.-s.*, slow to wrath
558 On me be all *l.-s.* shown

LOOK.
7 Jesus, we *l.* to thee
30 Met in thy name, we *l.* to thee
67 To thee we *l.*, on thee we call
252 sinners dare *L.* up to thine
307 Jesus, a word, a *l.* from thee
312 Jesus, we *l.* to thee; Where else
399 To thee I look, to thee, my Lord
423 never...Can I forget that *l.*
423 A second *l.* he gave, which said
426 *L.* unto me, thy morn shall rise
558 like Peter...Turn, and *l.* upon
606 And still to things eternal *l.*
722 Let us still to thee *l.* up
742 I *l.* to thee, I lay my hand
804 Jesus, Lord, we *l.* to thee; Let
880 That I might have seen his kind *l.*
949 eye Still *l.* on us in love

LOOKS, LOOKED, LOOKING.
505 discerning eye That *l.* to thee
426 I *looked* to Jesus, and I found
1094 To thee we *l.*, to thee we cried
555 on my guard, And *looking* up to
1024 And *l.* for our Lord

LOOM.
597 Thine is the *l.*, the forge, the

7

LORD.

435 truly say That Jesus is the *L.*
457 As *L.* and Master of the whole
567 And Christ is *L.* indeed
611 It is the *L.* who rises With
720 There our *L.* we soon shall see
755 no separation Between my *L.* and
785 Still let us own our common *L.*
840 One *L.* below, above
885 Thou art our holy *L.*
932 Proclaim, The *L.* is come
1006 Faith cries out, It is the *L.*
1050 Forever with the *L.!* Amen

LORE.

1099 Give wisdom's heavenly *l.*

LOSE. LOSING.

102 We *l.* ourselves in heaven above
566 We cannot *l.* our cause
591 And learn to *l.* with God
492 Well for him...all things *losing*

LOSS.

208 For this we count the world but *l.*
213 O may we count the world as *l.*
220 All things for him account but *l.*
471 All things for thee we count but *l.*
603 Thine earthly *l.* is heavenly gain
786 We for his sake count all things *l.*
798 And gladly reckon all things *l.*
1011 Our *l.* is his infinite gain

LOST.

392 *L.* and undone, for aid I flee
392 And *l.*, I am, till thou art mine
392 Lord, I am *l.*—but thou ha-t died
395 Jesus, when I have *l.* my all
411 Father, thy long-*l.* son receive
427 I once was *l.*, but now am found
495 Till I am wholly *l.* in thee
520 Let all I am in thee be *l.*
527 Till all I am is *l.* in thee
536 Till all I have is *l.* in thine
843 All it has won for us, the *l.*
880 Mourn for the *l.*,—but pray
892 To God the *l.* to bring

LOT.

685 And wheresoe'er my *l.* may be
691 Wheres'er our changeful *l.* is cast
696 That were indeed a dreadful *l.*
784 Give us in heaven a happy *l.*
801 Why hast thou cast our *l.* In
898 Go, share thy *l.* with him
1072 Be mine the happier *l.* to own
1087 To glory in your *l.* is comely
1088 resigning,—Its *l.* foreshadows

LOVE.

43 Where dwells eternal *L.*
49 Our *l.* shall never cease to glow
60 Let *l.* divine within us live
84 And fill my soul with heavenly *l.*
85 see him here, And *l.*, and praise
101 And *l.* fills every breast
119 Who would not *l.* thee with
119 Who then can that vast *l.* express

143 Whose *l.* is as great as his power
147 Yet I may *l.* thee too, O Lord
149 If our *l.* were but more simple
203 Saviour, who can *l.* like thee
205 *L.*, which bore the cross for us
205 Here we gather *l.* to live
211 Did e'er such *l.* and sorrow
214 And *l.* beyond degree
215 How vast the *l.* that him inclined
215 Was ever *l.* like thine
218 Sinners, whose *l.* can ne'er
251 rejoice In Jesus' mighty *l.*
262 Fill me with thy heavenly *l.*
272 Thy patient *l.*, at what a cost
279 Fountain of life and *l.*
304 He saw, and, O amazing *l.*
317 Thy ceaseless, unexhausted *l.*
323 Here *l.*, unchanging love, abounds
327 none but God such *l.* can show
332 O unexampled *l.!* O all-redeeming
337 All the life of glorious *l.*
351 The wonder, Why such *l.* to me
384 *L.* of God, so pure and changeless
401 my one desire...Thy only *l.* to
411 All *l.* be paid to thee
442 peace Of a soul in its earliest *l.*
416 A faith that sweetly works by *l.*
450 Nothing but *l.* shall I receive
457 not speak Of any other *l.* but
457 Nothing desire...But thy pure *l.*
474 move In me, till all my life be *l.*
476 noth ng May dwell but thy pure *l.*
476 My every act, word, thought, be *l.*
481 Let all my hallowed hea*rt* be *l.*
491 *L.* divine, a l love excelling
504 That did not work by *l.*
501 That *l.* divine may rule my breast
533 And all my soul be *l.*
536 *L.* only can the conquest win
540 The *l.* of Christ to me
540 God only knows the *l.* of God
586 O may I *l.* like thee
610 The *l.* that through all trouble
642 In heavenly *l.* abiding
699 That I may *l.* thee more
701 Thy wondrous *l.* adore
701 Thee may we *l.* alone
706 *L.* is the sacred fire within
707 There is a *l.* that never fails
719 Shows us his eternal *l.*
725 More *l.*, O Christ, to thee, More
733 Wondering at the *l.* that crowned
738 'Tis *L.!* 'tis Love! thou diedst
789 sight, When those who *l.* the Lord
780 *L.* is the golden chain that binds
797 binds Our hearts In Christian *l.*
801 And all thy gracious *l.* proclaim
802 More and more let *l.* abound
843 Only *l.* to us is given
853 *L.* the proof that Christ we know
897 When shall *l.* freely flow
830 And *l.* from God supreme
868 And *l.* fill the air with fragrance
167 All his wondrous *l.* proclaim
970 To keep us from our *l.*
1047 Though thou take what most we *l.*
1036 There *l.* shall have its perfect
1051 Precious Jesus, whose *l.* cannot

1073 By *l.* we still rise And look
1079 *L.* thee with unsinning heart
1084 Praise...For the *l.* that crowns

Boundless LOVE.
294 All nature sings thy *boundless l.*
312 Thy *boundless l.* shall set us free
316 I would thy *boundless l.* proclaim
510 things Thy *boundless l.* can give

Everlasting LOVE.
28 Let the feast Be *everlasting l.*
37 And sing thine *everlasting l.*
221 Thy sovereign, *everlasting l.*
480 sing Thy *everlasting l.* to man

His LOVE.
5 Then be *his l.* in Christ proclaimed
27 All that see and share *his l.*
183 And wonders of *his l.*
247 Resting in *his l.* and favor
304 *His l.* can ne'er be told
437 *His l.* surpassing far
512 A token of *his l.* he gives
530 dwell with God, to taste *his l.*
540 Stronger *his l.* than death and hell
546 *His l.* was all my song
572 *His l.* and light Fill all my
588 What can *his l.* withstand
621 For thou hast known *his l.*
747 While blest with a sense of *his l.*
761 Shall but *his l.* display
787 And speak *his l.* abroad
833 And thus *his l.'s* intent expressed
919 Dwell on *his l.* with sweetest
1020 I must not taste *his l.*

In LOVE.
270 *In l.* eternal dwell
437 In heaven, who dwell *in l.*
509 Is there less power *in l.*
586 Let all be wrought *in l.*
784 And perfect us *in l.*
791 And be forever lost *in l.*

Is LOVE.
150 God is wisdom, God *is l.*
208 In shining letters, God *is l.*
358 And all thy life *is l.*
379 God *is l.!* I know, I feel
518 And all my heart *is l.*
738 Thy nature and thy name *is L.*
739 Thy nature and thy name *is L.*
783 God *is l.*, and all his saints
799 And all the air *is l.*

My LOVE.
327 I meet the object of *my l.*
411 fix *My l.* entire on thee
552 That *my l.* is weak and faint
762 O may *my l.* to thee Pure
1020 You forever shall *my l.* and

Of LOVE.
12 We first received the pledge *of l.*
128 Eternal depth *of l.* divine
224 Hark! the voice *of l.* and mercy
279 The depths *of l.* divine
325 How rich the depths *of l.* divine
326 Rivers *of l.* and mercy here
348 After all his flow *of l.*
359 Redeemer, full *of l.*
440 All the life and heaven *of l.*
455 Much *of l.* I ought to know
488 Jesus, full *of l.* divine
521 A heart...full *of l.* divine
521 Thy new, best name *of L.*
529 In all the depths *of l.* divine
573 The dignity *of l.*
743 And all the forms *of l.* he wears
751 Thou art the sea *of l.*
781 the heart *Of l.*, we offer thee
786 And the sweet task *of l.*
955 patience of hope, and the labor *of l.*

Perfect LOVE.
7 In hope of *perfect l.*
199 Who joy in God with *perfect l.*
378 The love, the *perfect l.* of God
486 Cast it out by *perfect l.*
491 Glory in thy *perfect l.*
502 Spirit of *perfect l.*
506 guide Into thy *perfect l.*
513 expire. Cast out by *perfect l.*
523 inspire The *perfect l.* unknown
526 And find the pearl of *perfect l.*
529 And bless me with thy *perfect l.*
538 And depth, of *perfect l.*
542 O glorious hope of *perfect l.*
638 They rest in *perfect l.*
715 Till thou thy *perfect l.* impart
801 And rise renewed in *perfect l.*
837 O may thy pure and *perfect l.*
848 Fill us with thy *perfect l.*
1022 Give *perfect l.* for conscious
1048 Where all is *perfect l.*

Redeeming LOVE.
319 *Redeeming l.* has been my
433 The depth of all-*redeeming l.*
438 His all-*redeeming l.*, His
483 But rest in thy *redeeming l.*
540 The greatness of *redeeming l.*
761 His dear *redeeming l.*, His
818 proclaim Thine all-*redeeming l.*
794 Who rest in thy *redeeming l.*
983 With praises of *redeeming l.*

Thy LOVE.
9 Vast as eternity *thy l.*
19 lives employ In setting forth *thy l.*
46 Shed in our hearts *thy l.* abroad
52 Let us each, *thy l.* possessing
55 Let us all, *thy l.* possessing
64 Come, Lord, *thy l.* alone can
70 And saints on earth *thy l.* proclaim
81 To show *thy l.* by morning light
104 My God, how endless is *thy l.*
113 The bosom of *thy l.*
128 How vast *thy l.*, how great thy
157 And by *thy l.* we live
159 *Thy l.* our path surround
221 O let *thy l.* my heart constrain
274 Proclaimed *thy l.* and taught thy
282 Much more wilt thou *thy l.* display
283 Fill me with *thy l.*

LOV 100 LYR

593 Just as I am— *thy l.* unknown
469 heart And fill it with *thy l.*
449 E'en life itself, without *thy l.*
429 Short of *thy l.* I would not stop
464 Happy only in *thy l.*
476 In suffering be *thy l.* my peace
476 In weakness be *thy l.* my power
477 To taste *thy l.*, be all my choice
477 I am *thy l.*, thy God, thy All
522 The virtue of *thy l.*
541 My soul upon *thy l.* I cast
544 *Thy l.* can find a thousand
554 *Thy l.* so free, so sweet
616 *Thy l.* my thoughts shall fill
683 Better than life itself *thy l.*
869 Now, Jesus, now *thy l.* impart
836 And all *thy l.* to me
987 trace *Thy l.* in every line
1086 offer For all *thy l.* imparts

To LOVE.
63 We long *to l.* as angels do
196 O give us hearts *to l.* like thee
433 What shall I do my God *to l.*
458 *To l.* my God I only live
703 And death must yield *to l.*
708 What we have ceased *to l.*
783 Teach us *to l.* each other, Lord

With LOVE.
271 Inspire our souls *with l.*
650 Our hearts *with l.* to thee
702 heart, Inflaming it *with l.*
780 His bosom glow *with l.*
1043 And filled *with l.*, and lost

LOVES.
261 Still he *l.* the earth he leaves
327 Ah! who that *l.* can love enough
651 And still he *l.* and guards
707 When earthly *l.* decay
886 forget me, Because he *l.* me so
1088 The *l.* to which I cling

LOVED.
434 'Twas he that *l.* my soul
442 He hath *l.* me, I cried
513 And thou art *l.* alone
649 *L.* with an everlasting love
682 Which I have *l.* long since
700 None but his *l.* ones know
756 story That I have *l.* so long
758 For Jesus hath *l.* me, I cannot
783 to love As we are *l.* by thee
872 Thou hast *l.* us, love us still
886 save me, Because he *l.* me so
1026 When they who, unseen, have *l.*
1029 *L.* and served the Lord below

LOVER, LOV'ST.
32 *L.* of souls! thou know'st to prize
119 O Jesus, *L.* of mankind
442 And the *L.* of sinners adore
626 Jesus, *L.* of my soul
552 Say, poor sinner, *lov'st* thou me

LOVING.
37 And for thy *l.*-kindness wait
135 Yet to each *l.* heart how dear

169 The heaven of *l.* thee alone
469 And every *l.* heart
633 His *l.*-kindness shall break
676 Thy *l.*-kindness hath a charge
749 Whose *l.*-kindness crowns
856 With thy wonted *l.*-kindness

LOVELY, LOVELIEST.
695 *L.* art thou, and full of grace
500 Jesus...The *loveliest* and best

LOW, LOWEST.
548 My head is *l.*, my heart is sad
642 My heart may *l.* be laid
197 In vain we search the *lowest* deeps

LOWLY, LOWLINESS.
202 And learn of thee, the *l.* One
501 Still to the *l.* soul He doth
510 find...in thee, The *L.* and the
521 O for a *l.* contrite heart
675 And a work of *l.* love to do
801 *L..* meek, in thought and word
851 With *l.* thankful hearts, we praise
932 Stay not till all the *l.* Triumphant
394 With thy meek *lowliness* to fill
527 O give me *l.* of heart

LOYAL.
1071 Where *l.* hearts and true

LULL, LULLED.
681 And *l.* me to sleep on thy breast
1069 *Lulled* with the transporting

LURE.
568 voices That *l.* thy soul astray

LURKS.
373 Death...And *l.* in every flower
409 I feel Evil still *l.* within

LUST.
477 Nor let one darling *l.* survive
859 Death to each fleshly *l.*

LUSTER.
135 We ask no *l.* of our own
201 cross...Adds more *l.* to the day
286 With *l.* shining more and more
594 That prize...shall new *l.* boast
809 lives...With purest *l.* shine
815 And let them in thy *l.* glow
824 And let their *l.* still increase
307 star of Bethlehem shed A *l.*
977 rising from the tomb, With *l.*
980 sun...Sheds mellow *l.* o'er the scene

LYRE, LYRES.
36 The *l.* of Hebrew bards was strung
70 Awake, my tongue; awake, my *l.*
193 legions...strung and tuned the *l.*
229 Each angel sweeps his *l.*
658 trembling hand and dropping *l.*
195 angels, with their sparkling *lyres*
235 Then take your golden *l.*
1057 'Mid the angelic *l.* above
1073 Join...Hearts, voices, and *l.*

M.

MADE.
118 power alone All is *m*., and
144 Since by thee were all things *m*.
586 iniquity, But nothing thou hast *m*.
1085 Who *m*. us very good

MADNESS.
107 No cherished *m*. vex the soul

MAGNIFY.
34 never cease to laud and *m*.
384 *M*. them all in me
472 Shall *m*. my Maker's name
847 *M*. thy dying word

MAIDENS.
16 Young men and *m*., raise

MAIN.
145 How to rise above the *m*.
1112 Lord of the wide, extensive *m*.

MAJESTY.
119 Terrible *m*. is thine
206 I see God descend in *m*.
248 To him all *m*. ascribe
322 What *m*. and grace Through
409 Do thou thy *m*. reveal
412 disclosed in *m*. severe
413 In *m*. come down
527 Beam forth with mildest *m*.
710 that reach The *M*. on high
1013 Robed in dreadful *m*.
1029 Judge.. Clothed in *m*. divine
1112 O'erawed by *m*. divine

MAKER.
38 We would adore our *M*. too
112 And wide proclaim his *M*.'s praise
133 In all our *M*.'s grand designs
186 *M*., and Monarch, and Saviour of
412 I view my *M*. face to face
740 I'll praise my *M*. while I've
962 Almighty *M*. of my frame
1086 He only is the *M*. Of all things
1114 We fly to our *M*.,—Save, Lord

MALADY.
532 My inbred *m*. remove

MALICE.
790 He comes, of hellish *m*. full

MAN.
26 *M*., the well-beloved of Heaven
160 And led me up to *m*.
188 Peace...Reaching far as *m*. is
207 who smote in *M*. for man the
217 The *M*. of sorrows weeps in
249 See the *M*. of sorrows now
665 Thou *M*. of grief, who once
737 Art thou the *M*. that died for me
813 A *m*.! an heir of death! a slave
944 Thee, as *M*. for sinners slain
959 And, in his highest honor, *m*.

MANGER.
182 To that lowly *m*.-bed
182 At that *m*. rude and bare
191 From the *m*. to the throne
192 And in a *m*. laid

MANGLED.
339 See his body *m*., rent
340 Bruised and *m*. by the fall

MANHOOD.
231 *M*. to deliver, manhood didst put
373 in sudden night On *m*.'s middle

MANIFEST.
199 Christ deigns to *m*. to-day

MANKIND.
70 To all *m*. thy love make known
192 Glad tidings...To you and all *m*.
261 Still he calls *m*. his own
332 What thou for all *m*. hast done
364 For God hath bidden all *m*.
387 Of *m*. the life and light
433 grace...It reaches all *m*.
528 That all *m*. thy truth may see
755 life provided For all *m*. and me
795 In them let all *m*. behold
822 arms...Would all *m*. embrace
831 Sent to disciple all *m*.
926 Shall all *m*. together view
1098 Lord, while for all *m*. we pray

MANNA.
59 Still on heavenly *m*. feeding
62 Whose word, like *m*. showered
72 The heavenly *m*. falls
316 'Tis *m*. to the hungry soul
776 He who gives us daily *m*.
847 Eat we *m*. from above
849 O *M*. sent from heaven

MANSION.
242 He lives my *m*. to prepare
328 A nobler *m*. waits the just
968 secure A *m*. in the skies
986 Our *m*. in the skies
999 to the grave; and, its *m*.
1056 Our glorious *m*. in the sky
1059 A *m*. with the blest
1060 O one, O only *m*.
1072 heavenly *m*. shall be mine
1072 heavenly *m*. mine shall be
1072 My heavenly *m*. is secure
1072 A heavenly *m*. near the throne
1072 heavenly *m*. stands for me

MANSIONS.
167 From blissful *m*. ever bright
236 gone up...To *m*. in the skies
237 He claims these *m*. as his right
294 And points to *m*. in the sky
335 Or waft you to *m*. of glory
652 Large are the *m*. in thy
659 title clear To *m*. in the skies
681 Away to the *m*. above
879 In the *m*. of the blest
963 May *m*. for themselves prepare

MAN 102 MEE

1011 Escaped to the m. of light
1026 In those m. to abide
1027 heaven's resounding m. ring
1053 Nearer...Where the many m. be

MANTLE.
92 Night her solemn m. spreads
578 love A m. round your breast

MARBLE, MARBLES.
311 Thou, by thy voice, the m. rend
215 The solid marbles rend

MARCH, MARCHING.
87 the stupendous m. Of vast
699 And m., with courage in thy
1050 A day's m. nearer home
1074 We m. hand in hand to
568 *Marching* as to war, With

MARGIN.
1033 And we are to the m. come

MARINER.
1114 the m. cherish, Who cries

MARK, MARKS.
310 If he our ways should m.
956 arrow flies...the m. to find
202 How beauteous were the *marks*
1014 By the m. received for me

MARRIAGE.
430 Till summoned to the m.-feast
801 Meet at the m. of the Lamb
1107 Cana's hall To bless the m. day

MART.
929 In crowded m., by stream or

MARTHA.
609 Serve with careful M.'s hands

MARTYR, MARTYRS.
141 Thee the noble m. band
1061 And all the m. throng
10 Prophets and *martyrs* hear the
130 With all the m.' noble host
569 So shall thy saints and m. raise
805 Such as in the m. glowed
911 The m.' ashes, watched
952 truth for which the m. bled
1010 road...saints and m. trod

MARY.
540 sit With M. at the Master's feet
609 Serve with...loving M.'s heart

MASTER.
51 your M. proclaim, And publish
170 A suffering life my M. led.
197 O Lord and M. of us all
460 Thee, my new M., now I call
573 That I my heavenly M. know
607 Loud and long the M. calleth
647 Him our Lord and M. call
857 By wise m.-builders squared
955 stand still till the M. appear

MAZE, MAZES.
762 While life's dark m. I tread
477 Through all its latent *mazes*

MEADOW.
231 Bloom in every m., leaves on

MEAN, MEANER, MEANEST.
243 All are too m. to speak his worth
153 Thus while the *meaner* creatures
698 Thanks to thy name for m. things
69 Might I enjoy the *meanest* place
592 Worth to my m. labor give

MEANS.
831 Honor the m. ordained by thee

MEASURE, MEASURES.
143 love...neither knows m. nor
149 Than the m. of man's mind
962 Teach me the m. of my days
884 We come, with simple *measures*

MEDIATOR.
1004 Deck the M.'s crown

MEDICINE.
736 The m. of my broken heart
1060 And m. in sickness

MEEK, MEEKLY, MEEKNESS.
495 Give me thy m. and lowly mind
700 O joy of all the m.
754 like Jesus, M.. loving, lowly
374 All the day long he *meekly*
54 Hear with *meekness*, Hear thy
202 marks...in thy m. used to shine
586 learn...With m. to reprove
631 In lowly m. may I rest
873 May we walk in love and m.

MEET, (verb.)
7 We m. on earth for thy dear sake
22 There we all may m. again
22 Though we here should m. no
40 here, when two or three shall m.
41 Jesus, where'er thy people m.
86 Come down to m. us here
89 Where all are wont to m.
580 Christ comes...m. with him
711 dear a spot As where I m.
755 We go to m. the Lord
765 Shall m. thee in the skies
786 Go on, we'll m. you there
796 Yet shall we m. again
797 And hope to m. again
807 When shall we m. again
807 Soon shall we m. again
839 M. and remember me
860 To all who here shall m. be
881 We hope to m. again
945 Come down and m. us now
954 tie on. him in the sky
956 Never more to m. us here
1011 There those who m. shall part
1011 And those long parted m. again
1064 O when shall we m. in the air
1078 I come to m. thee in the skies

MEET, (adverb.)
669 when grace hath made me *m.*
808 Make, O make us *m.* for thee
954 take to glory all Who *m.* for glory

MEETING.
719 For our glorious *m.* there
796 Our *m.*-time, the eternal day
796 Our *m.* place, the eternal throne
1002 We would, at this solemn *m.*
1046 O what a joyful *m.* there

MELODY, MELODIOUS.
874 temple filling With the *m.*
952 And sing with cheerful *m.*
726 Teach me some *melodious* sonnet
865 Here may thy word *m.* sound
1067 Hark, their songs *m.* rise

MELT, MELTS, MELTED, MELTINGS.
209 *M.* and reclaim my wandering
214 And *m.* mine eyes to tears
285 O *m.* this frozen heart
404 And *m.* my hardness down
461 Hence our hearts *m.*, our eyes
558 Let thy mercy *m.* me down
1088 hopes...All *m.*, like stars of even
366 that power which *melts* the heart
385 Yet, when *melted* in the flame
851 The *meltings* of a broken heart

MEMBER, MEMBERS.
806 Every *m.* feel its share
800 Church...On all her *members*
992 And when the *m.* die

MEMORIAL, MEMORIALS.
108 Some fresh *m.* of his grace
845 Sweet *memorials*,—till the Lord

MEMORY.
470 Take my *m.*, mind, and will
549 peaceful hours...sweet their *m.*
700 Nor can the *m.* find A sweeter
833 In solemn *m.* of the dead
836 And mind and *m.* flee
850 We keep the *m.* adored
914 strains...In *m.* of thy love
974 'Tis like the *m.* left behind
978 But the sweet *m.* of the good
902 Blest be thy *m.*, and blest

MEMORIES.
115 How such holy *m.* cluster
708 The tender *m.* of the past

MEN.
938 Ye *m.* of God, arise! His
1085 *M.*, the dear objects of his grace

MERCHANDISE.
829 Of wisdom's costly *m.*

MERCY.
14 *M.* is ever at his side
50 O God, to us show *m.*
110 Ask *m.* in the Saviour's name
127 *M.* witholds thy lifted hand
127 Thy willing *m.* flies apace
149 There's a wideness in God's *m.*
149 There is *m.* with the Saviour
161 clouds...big with *m.*, and
202 And *m.* with thy life-blood
208 He brings us *m.* from above
276 Bid *m.* triumph over wrath
335 When God in great *m.* is coming
335 And prove that his *m.* is
336 For *M.* still lingers and calls
343 Hear, O sinner, *m.* hails you
345 Hasten, *m.* to implore
349 *M.* is found, and peace is given
371 'Tis *m.* speaks to-day
380 But with thee is *m.* found
407 *M.* I ask to seal my peace
412 If yet...*m.* may be sought
420 That *m.* they may taste, and live
420 *M.*, free, boundless mercy, cries
420 *M.* is all that's written there
422 'Tis *m.* all! let earth adore
428 Thy grace and *m.* prove
543 In me thine utmost *m.* show
546 I know thy *m.* cannot fail
557 Thine utmost *m.* show
559 And *m.*, mercy, I implore
649 *M.*'s full power I then shall
670 Be thy dear *m.* given
915 *M.* and Truth, that long were
1001 Grace hath opened *m.*'s door
1002 *M.* still is on the throne
1073 And the burden is, *M.* divine
1091 Thou hast *m.* more abounding
1094 To thee for *m.* call
1107 This *m.* we implore

His MERCY.
11 *His m.* is forever sure
150 But *his m.* waneth never
254 address *His m.* and his power
335 And prove that *his m.* is
343 Seek *his m.* while you may
360 Then shalt thou find *his m.* sure
467 render...For all *his m.*'s store
589 *His m.* now implore
704 If Jesus shows *his m.* mine
761 *His m.* ever free, Shall while

Of MERCY.
110 On me with beams *of m.* shine
285 on...soul With beams *of m.*
343 'Tis the voice *of m.* calls
379 Depth *of m.!* can there be
449 His acts *of m.* and of grace
726 Streams *of m.*, never ceasing
824 Jesus, the word *of m.* give
891 Our work *of m.* bless

Thy MERCY.
43 *Thy m.* and thy truth reveal
119 On all thy works *thy m.*'s beams
154 *Thy m.* never shall remove
160 *Thy m.* lent an ear
274 *Thy m.* let the sinner find
382 cannot doubt *Thy m.* is for me
384 Let *thy m.* light on me
508 aspires, For all *thy m.*'s store

MER 104 MIL

528 That I *thy m.* may proclaim
546 I know *thy m.* cannot fail
558 And let *thy m.* melt me down
616 *Thy m.* o'er my life has flowed
649 Father, *thy m.* never dies
681 The arms of *thy m.* display
693 For all *thy m.* I will give
851 *Thy m.* and thy strength bestows
858 Here reveal *thy m.* sure
944 And *thy m.* manifold

MERCIES.

8 Eternal are thy *m.*, Lord
20 Lord, thy *m.* never fail
25 For his *m.*, firm and sure
41 Thy former *m.* here renew
60 Thy *m.* we'll review
98 thy house...To taste thy *m.*
99 His *m.* multiplied
99 Minutes came quick, but *m.*
103 New *m.*, each returning day
101 And morning *m.* from above
139 Whose *m.* over all rejoice
140 Thy *m.*, how tender! how firm
145 For his *m.* shall endure
160 When all thy *m.*, O my God
170 How do thy *m.* close me
172 Whose *m.* are so great
270 And all thy *m.* crown
317 Faithful, O Lord, thy *m.* are
359 And all thy faithful *m.* prove
391 Are not thy *m.* large and free
433 I see thy *m.* rise
491 All thy faithful *m.* crown
524 And make thy faithful *m.* known
709 I love to think on *m.* past
729 For that love whose tender *m.*
738 Thy *m.* never shall remove
786 Jesus...Whose *m.* never end
956 Thanks for *m.* past received
1081 These various *m.* from above
1113 We praise thee for thy *m.* past

MERCIFUL.

439 make known, How *m.* thou
503 I dare believe Thee *m.* and
531 O God, most *m.* and true

MERCY-SEAT.

41 There they behold thy *m.-s.*
61 Before thy *m.-s.*, O Lord
85 As we thy *m.-s.* surround
89 Bend at thy *m.-s.*
117 How beautiful thy *m.-s.*
182 Ever seek the *m.-s.*
238 Which, at the *m.-s.* of God
683 Come to the *m.-s.*, fervently
684 retreat...found beneath the *m.-s.*
956 We meet in coming to the *m.-s.*
1096 Still open is the *m.-s.*

MERIDIAN.

1034 Nor the *m.* sun decline

MERIT, MERITS.

273 Praise to thy eternal *m.*
854 All the Saviour's dying *m.*
1004 Thine the *m.* of his blood

216 By thy *merits* we find favor
246 Help to sing our Saviour's *m.*
322 Mingles his *m.* with his tears
416 No *m.* or good works to plead
689 Fear not; his *m.* must prevail
1096 O let thy *m.* plead above

MESSAGE.

21 Send some *m.* from thy word
233 They with the angels' *m.* speed
301 That all who hear thy *m.*, Lord
336 Her *m.*, unheeded, will
342 Sinners, will you scorn the *m.*
364 My *m.* as from God receive
756 never heard The *m.* of salvation
929 Hear not the *m.* sent from thee

MESSENGER, MESSENGERS.

681 O when will the *m.* come
167 They come, God's *messengers* of
931 billows flow, Bear *m.* of
939 Go, ye *m.* of God

MESSIAH.

189 Now proclaim *M.*'s birth
868 And *M.*, the King, who shall
907 star leads To the *M.*'s feet
930 nation Has learned *M.*'s name
937 When beneath *M.*'s sway
1013 wailing, Shall the true *M.* see
1069 before God and his *M.* fall

MIDNIGHT.

78 No *m.* shade, no clouded
135 Our *m.* is thy smile withdrawn
180 And all my *m.* hours defend
191 It came upon the *m.* clear
217 'Tis *m.*; and on Olives' brow
604 Let *m.* be ashamed of noon
633 break...The *m.* of the soul
636 illume The *m.* of the soul
750 When *m.* veils our eyes
917 A solemn *m.* song
954 Upstarting at the *m.* cry

MIDST.

7 Thou in the *m.* of us shalt be
30 We wait...Thee in the *m.* to find
791 Thee in the *m.* we wait to feel

MIDSUMMER.

747 The *m.* sun shines

MIGHT.

48 All *m.* and love we render
140 O tell of his *m.*, and sing of
151 Lord our God is clothed with *m.*
452 The mighty glory in their *m.*
554 onward In the Spirit's *m.*
587 Stand, then, in his great *m.*
639 His *m.* thy heart shall strengthen
1077 All *m.* and majesty are thine

MILITANT.

1033 His *m.* embattled host

MILK.

326 Salvation...Like floods of *m.* and
362 Buy wine, and *m.*, and gospel

MIL 105 MOR

542 Rivers of *m.* and honey rise
1061 With *m.* and honey blest
1076 There *m.* and honey flow

MILLENNIAL.
955 The *m.* year Rushes
1025 The grand *m.* reign begun

MIND.
524 The *m.* which was in thee impart
527 O let thy *m.* within me dwell
528 The *m.* which was in Christ
531 O let me gain my Saviour's *m.*
586 O arm me with the *m.*, Meek
675 I ask thee for a present *m.*
675 And a *m.* to blend with outward
795 O let them all thy *m.* express

MINE.
173 good...I know it shall be *m.*
222 I joy to call thee *m.*
422 Jesus, with all in him, is *m.*
425 But art thou not already *m.*
427 God...Wilt be forever *m.*
447 I am my Lord's, and he is *m.*
462 Whate'er I fondly counted *m.*
467 I owe To thee whate'er is *m.*
488 I am thine and thou art *m.*
488 Jesus, Saviour, thou art *m.*
512 When God is *m.* and I am his
536 my God, I know, I feel thee *m.*
610 the sweet hope that thou art *m.*
655 Not *m.*, not mine the choice
674 I fear to call thee *m.*
742 If I may call thee *m.*
961 And certified that thou art *m.*
1042 'tis enough that thou art *m.*
1047 make thee Some day all *m.* own

MINISTERS, MINISTRY.
130 Thy *m.* are living flame
817 converting power... *m.* attend
926 Comfort, ye *m.* of grace
831 And own thy glorious *ministry*

MINUTE.
565 Give every flying *m.* Something

MIRACLE, MIRACLES.
223 Mark that *m.* of time
730 I 'm a *m.* of grace
589 adore His *miracles* of grace

MIRTH.
69 Exceeds a thousand days of *m.*
509 And dissipating *m.*
968 No room for *m.* or trifling
1087 benefits forgot, Amid your *m.*

MISERY.
145 eye Looked upon our *m.*
317 And help our *m.*
490 Full of sin and *m.*
737 My sin and *m.* declare
898 redeem A breaking heart from *m.*
968 A moment's *m.* or joy; But O
996 soul to save From endless *m.*

MISSION.
643 Soon shall close thy earthly *m.*
818 laborers...Their *m.* fully prove

MISSOURI.
933 Before *M.*'s fountains, Rehearse

MISTS.
111 The *m.* of error and of vice
200 sweeps the lingering *m.* away

MOAN.
68 He hears the uncomplaining *m.*
557 To thee I make my *m.*: Let
994 parched lips...no more... *m.*
1006 Wherefore should I make my *m.*

MOCK, MOCKING.
356 Why... *m.* the sons of God
569 The Lord shall *m.* them from
249 *Mocking* thus the Saviour's claim

MOLD.
450 *M.* every purpose of the soul
473 *M.* as thou wilt thy passive clay
793 O let us take a softer *m.*

MOLEST.
97 No evil shall *m.*: Under the
684 And sin and sense *m.* no more

MOMENT, MOMENTS, MOMENTARY.
365 He'll in a *m.*, call thee hence
366 concerns depend...upon a *m.*'s
473 from this *m.* live or die To serve
948 Each *m.* brings it near
955 arrow is flown,—the *m.* is gone
968 A *m.*'s misery or joy; But O
576 How swift its *moments* fly
664 The passing *m.* say; As
977 The *momentary* glories waste

MONARCH, MONARCHS.
83 And reign sole *M.* in my breast
755 richer Than *m.* on his throne
868 No *m.* kneels praying to
155 Which of the *monarchs* of the

MONEY.
340 Without *m.*, Come to Jesus
362 *M.* ye need not bring, nor price

MOON, MOONS.
57 Sun and *m.* rejoice before him
188 The *m.* takes up the wondrous
145 And the *m.* to shine by night
292 Sun, *m.*, and stars, convey thy
293 The *m.* forgot her nightly tale
724 Sun, *m.*, and stars forgot
1058 That knows no *m.* nor sun
777 Waning *moons* no more shall
919 Till *m.* shall wax and wane

MOORED.
187 Now safely *m.*, my perils o'er

MORE.
474 *M.* shouldst thou have, if I had

MORIAH.
195 And brighter on M.'s brow
868 The pomp of M. has passed

MORN.
116 May the m. in heaven awake us
159 From m. till noon—till latest
546 Soon as the m. the light revealed
546 And when the m. the light reveals
682 And with the m. those angel faces
982 How bright the unchanging m.

MORNING.
93 Heaven's m. breaks, and earth's
98 Lord, in the m. thou shalt hear
103 New every m. is the love
110 And as each m.'s sun shall rise
113 angels guard...Till m. light
231 Welcome, happy m.! age to
233 The m. kindles all the sky
354 sun Sinks ere thy m. is
750 Come at the m. hour
925 Let the glad m. bless our
932 The m. light is breaking
940 May the m. chase the night
974 But soon the m.'s happier light
984 The m. break, and pierce the
1059 The m. shall awaken

MORNINGS.
948 Nor many m. rise Ere all
998 The few lurid m. that dawn

MORTAL, MORTALS, MORTALITY.
133 What m. verse can reach
240 Hast deigned a m. form to wear
240 A m.'s painful lot to bear
241 No m. can with him compare
427 And m. life shall cease
630 When Power divine, in m. form
646 When this m. life is ended
758 No m. doth know what be
45 And mortals find his earthly
87 In courts by m. trod
153 Ye m., catch the sound
243 glorious names...ever m. knew
244 M., give thanks and sing
261 Christ, awhile to m. given
965 diseases...To hurry m. home
1035 M., behold the sacred seat
741 Farewell, mortality; Jesus is

MOSES.
4 song Of M. and the Lamb
199 When M. and Elias met
274 When glory beamed from M.
680 And sing the song of M.
735 God's hands or bound...As M. or
1037 Could we but climb where M.

MOTH.
647 M. and rust are there unknown
902 Which m. or rust shall ne'er
959 And grief shall like a m. consume

MOTHER, MOTHERS.
147 No m. half so mild Bears
552 Can a m.'s tender care Cease
658 Thy love, with all a m.'s care
1065 Zion...The m. of spirits
768 Mothers cease their own to

MOUNT.
648 We travel to the m. of God
657 And scale the m. of God

MOUNT, (verb.)
61 on wings...M. upward to the
443 M. to Christ, my glorious Head
969 Lend, lend your wings! I m.
1011 And m. with his spirit above
1019 And m. above the fiery void

MOUNTAIN.
180 Or on the thirsty m. pant
198 Lord, lead us to the m. height
199 Which Christ upon the m. shows
200 High on the m. here with
354 Flee for thy life, the m. gain
522 This m. sin, remove
523 faith...Which doth the m.
542 I stand, and from the m. top
582 See on the m.-top The
715 Then let me on the m.-top
763 A m. that shall fill the earth
767 On the m.'s top appearing
912 Loud from the m.-tops echoes
1061 And fly to the m. of God
1089 From every m. side Let

MOUNTAINS.
132 Ere m. reared their forms
168 And m. down the gulf be hurled
181 Before him, on the m.
310 The m., in thy wrath
369 sin Like m. round me
446 faith that doth m. move
501 faith...As m. to remove
509 If m. can be moved by faith
518 And make the m. flow
773 Let m. from their seats
863 The m. in their places stood
896 His m. lift their solemn
1015 O'er the distant m. breaking
1019 m. are on mountains hurled

MOURN.
21 Comfort those who weep and m.
111 To m. for errors past
275 O leave us not to m. below
370 He sees thy softened spirit m.
370 Thy Father calls,—no longer m.
381 Help us to look on thee, and m.
414 In pensive silence m.
458 I only live my sin to m.
536 No longer then my heart shall m.
671 Blessed are they that m.
869 And they who m., and they
880 M. for the lost,—but call
967 Thou bidd'st me m. in calm
970 Why do we m. for dying friends
1094 M. with our mourning land

MOURNS, MOURNED.
546 My soul in darkness m.
618 That e'er have mourned the chief

MOURNER, MOURNERS.

45 And wipe away the *m.'s* tear
65 Here give the *m.* rest
68 He lifts the *m.* from the dust
102 Be every *m.'s* sleep to-night
154 Thou giv'st the *m.* rest
203 He can mark each *m.'s* tear
346 Weep—he loves the *m.'s* tears
487 Happy *m.*, hear, and see
625 Did ever *m.* plead with thee
630 And lonely watch the *m.* keeps
898 Thy neighbor? Pass no *m.* by
959 But give the *m.* rest
1026 Blessed...patient *mourners*
1045 Once they were *m.* here

MOURNFUL, MOURNFULLY, MOURNING.

1 The *m.*, broken hearts rejoice
331 Ye *m.* souls, be glad
489 Every *m.* sinner cheer
967 hope, Which bears my *m.*
845 E'en now we *mournfully* enjoy
110 And, *mourning* o'er my guilt and
403 Thou bidd'st the *m.* soul
424 Why...Go *m.* all their days
578 Go...Where *m.* hearts deplore
767 Cease thy *m.*; Zion still is
1002 to-day we're filled with *m.*
1003 ended, All thy *m.* days

MOUTH.

139 And fillest every *m.* with good
443 In thy *m.* and in thy heart
823 Now let them from the *m.* of God
926 And what his *m.* in truth

MOVE.

42 In whom we are, and *m.*
124 In whom we are, and *m.*, and
461 And by thee *m.*, and in thee live
913 Dove....*M.* o'er the waters' face
916 Spirit.. *M.* on the formless void

MOVES.

126 What lives and *m.*....from thee
396 And nothing *m.* this heart of
707 And *m.* the hand which moves

MULTIPLY.

817 And *m.* the faithful race
940 *M.* and still increase

MURMUR, MURMURS, MURMURING.

506 Never to *m.* at thy stay
610 heart, From every *m.* free
622 Nor ever *m.* nor repine
667 That will not *m.* nor complain
692 Shall check the *m.* and the sigh
845 Hush, be every *m.* dumb
658 Its feeble *murmurs* melt away
531 Then every *murmuring* thought
628 So shall each *m.* thought
632 O let no *m.* thought arise

MUSIC.

70 And swell your *m.* to the skies
194 And still their heavenly *m.* floats

195 angels...lyres, Make *m.* on the
257 heavenly anthem drowns All *m.*
316 So shall the *m.* of thy name
332 name the sinner hears...'Tis *m.*
398 name, Is *m.* in a sinner's ear
444 Draw *m.* from each chiming star
670 word...Its *m.* shall the lone heart
692 To join the *m.* of the skies
702 Thy name is *m.* to the heart
807 spirits dwell, There may our *m.*
1070 The *m.* of the gospel leads us
1089 Let *m.* swell the breeze

MUTE.

122 Shall I be *m.*, great God, alone
195 shall Christian tongues be *m.*

MUTUAL.

783 With *m.* love inflame
797 Our *m.* burdens bear
803 *M.* love the token be

MYRRH.

186 *M.* from the forest, and gold

MYSELF.

91 May I give *m.* to thee
409 I strive To give *m.* away
573 obedient...I must *m.* appear
742 I give *m.* to thee; Thy love
966 To thee, against *m.*, to thee

MYSTERIES, MYSTERY.

257 bends...At *m.* so great
213 And in the *mystery* of thy death
256 to know The *m.* of his love
422 'Tis *m.* all! the Immortal dies
423 Such is the *m.* of grace
504 give me skill Each *m.* to explain
538 to understand The *m.* unknown
540 They cannot reach the *m.*
851 Author of this great *m.*

MYSTERIOUS.

161 God moves in a *m.* way
174 *M.* deeps of providence
632 For though *m.* now thy ways
723 By the dread *m.* hour

MYSTIC.

806 Who thy *m.* body are
844 Breaking thus one *m.* bread
853 banquet...Of his *m.* flesh and
924 Spirit...Unites in *m.* love

N.

NAIL, NAILED, NAILS.

212 Pointed the *n.*, and fixed the
423 And helped to *n.* him there
941 Of the *n.*, the thorn, the spear
215 Saviour of mankind *Nailed* to
219 See...The cruel *nails* they drive
339 Driven the *n.* that fixed him

NAKED.

643 *N.*, poor, despised, forsaken
996 Go, clothe the *n.*, lead the blind

NAME.

1 Jesus! the *n.* that charms
17 And bless his holy *n.*: His
44 The sweetness of thy saving *n.*
68 Blest be that *n.*, supremely
107 Master...Whate'er our *n.* or sign
256 Their *n.*, an everlasting name
314 Jesus, no other *n.* than thine
316 How sweet the *n.* of Jesus sounds
316 Dear *n.!* the rock on which I
319 No other *n.* but thine
332 Jesus.. No other *n.* is given
398 Thy *n.*, thy all-restoring name
428 My *n.* is written on his hands
506 To thee and thy great *n.*
521 Write thy new *n.* upon my heart
528 Hallow thy great and glorious *n.*
595 will he own my worthless *n.*
650 That still thy gracious *n.* we
651 Lord hath called me by my *n.*
653 O the precious *n.* of Jesus
697 No music's like thy charming *n.*
736 Thy mighty *n.* salvation is
736 To me, with thy great *n.*, are
737 Thyself hast called me by my *n.*
737 reveal Thy new, unutterable *n.*
754 I love the *n.* of Jesus, Immanuel
775 Nor bear his hallowed *n.* in vain
791 Are we not met in thy great *n.*
822 Jesus! the *n.* high over all
852 The *n.* by heaven and earth
874 Echo with thy glorious *n.*
911 proclaim...The one availing *n.*
1023 Spare me for thine own great *n.*
1027 What if my *n.* should be left

His NAME.

142 I love *his n.*, I love his word
145 Let us sound *his n.* abroad
188 Learn *his n.*, and taste his joy
197 our dead Are burdened with *his n.*
242 He lives, all glory to *his n.*
276 And grants *his n.* to know
435 show The virtue of *his n.*
751 *His n.* abroad is poured
757 doth rejoice at the sound of *his n.*
822 latest breath...but gasp *his n.*
896 To crown his head, or grace *his n.*

Jesus' NAME.

29 sends From heaven, in *Jesus' n.*
141 trust is all thrown on *Jesus's n.*
248 All hail the power of *Jesus' n.*
332 And bless the sound of *Jesus' n.*
421 But wholly lean on *Jesus' n.*
582 standard.. In *Jesus' n.* I lift
700 A sweeter sound than *Jesus' n.*
733 precious is the sound of *Jesus' n.*
802 We are met in *Jesus' n.*
805 Sing we, then, in *Jesus' n.*

Thy NAME.

7 *Thy n.* salvation is, Which
20 Who in *thy n.* are joined
70 Shall hear, and in *thy n.* rejoice
88 Here we come *thy n.* to praise
330 *Thy n.* shall be praised in the
377 And write *thy n.* upon my heart
606 Forth in *thy n.*, O Lord, I go
656 Just and holy is *thy n.*, I am
715 unless Thou tell *thy n.* to me
737 Tell me *thy n.*, and tell it now
738 Thy na're and *thy n.* is Love
1097 And ever bless *thy n.*

NAMES.

191 N. most awful, names most
213 Join all the glorious *n.* Of
787 Whose *n.* are writ in heaven
907 The brightest *n.* that earth can

NARROW.

61 That from the safe and *n.* way
182 Keep us in the *n.* way
262 Keep me in the *n.* way
300 O gladly tread the *n.* path
450 I'll pursue The *n.* way
455 lest I turn again Out of the *n.* way
667 A faith that keeps the *n.* way
873 Guide us... In the *n.* way of truth
889 May we walk the *n.* way
966 Lo! on a *n.* neck of land

NATION.

773 While every *n.*, every shore
821 Let every *n.* now behold Their
918 Bid every *n.* hail the light
926 Go into every *n.*, go; Speak
932 A *n.* in a day
932 Flow thou to every *n.*, Nor
987 Every *n.*, every clime, Shall

NATIONS.

50 That so throughout all *n.* Thy
50 O let the *n.* joyful Their
50 And on the earth all *n.* Shall
63 And tell the wondering *n.* round
77 blessings .. On *n.* yet unborn
153 Echo...Through all the *n.* round
231 Show thy face.. bid the *n.* see
292 Till Christ has all the *n.* blessed
331 Let all the *n.* know, To earth's
582 To all the *n.* call
779 shine, Till the *n.* from afar
867 When God the *n.* shall survey
910 Great God, the *n.* of the earth
915 The *n.* all whom thou hast
921 To groaning *n.* haste the hour
921 To thee let all the *n.* flow
925 Though now the *n.* sit beneath
925 Ye *n.*, catch the kindling ray
928 All *n.* bow to thy command
932 Bring tidings...Of *n.* in
936 Jesus' love the *n.* fires
942 Come and bless bewildered *n.*
944 story Be it to the *n.* told
1077 The ransomed *n.* bow
1088 Lord of the *n.*, thus to thee
1101 The angry *n.* rush to arms
1101 Thy law the angry *n.* own

NATIVE.

648 Contending for our *n.* heaven
874 temples .. honors of our *n.* place
1088 Toward heaven, thy *n.* place
1098 O hear us for our *n.* land

NATURE.
7 From n.'s path we turn aside
122 n.'s loud acclaim...nature's debt
127 And when created n. dies
130 N. and grace, with all their
130 Still restless n. dies and
139 N.'s expanse before thee
215 Hark! how he groans, while n.
247 We shall see Him, in our n.
306 In vain, alas! is n.'s aid
394 No more her power let n. boast
43i Turn back our n.'s rapid tide
514 Make haste to bring thy n. in
521 Thy n., gracious Lord, impart
531 Thy n. to my soul impart
547 We, for whose sake all n. stands
681 Thy n. I long to put on
876 Hear us, who thy n. share
916 If sang...When n. rose to view
969 Cease, fond n., cease thy strife
1025 N.'s end we wait to see
1072 All n. sink and cease to be
1041 Thy hand all n. hails
1093 Hark! the voice of n. sings

NAUGHT.
75 great to speak the world from n.
331 Ye who have sold for n. Your
436 N. have I of my own, Naught
492 E'en himself doth count as n.
800 our wretched strength for n.
936 Him who spake a world from n.

NAVIES.
1104 Our n. spread their flags abroad

NEAR.
102 It is not night if thou be n.
185 Yet to each loving heart how n.
216 I might now perceive thee n.
255 Weak...he still is n., To lead
299 Be thou forever n.
395 If haply I may feel thee n.
309 And may I still draw n.
549 To God with faith draw n.
629 still whispering, Thou art n.
629 Living and dying, thou art n.
645 Suffering Son of man, be n. me
681 O Jesus, in pity draw n.
695 And ever let me feel thee n.
746 Keeper, stand Omnipotently n.
776 Showing that the Lord is n.
791 And we shall then behold thee n.
815 Draw n., O Son of God, draw
1021 O let me feel thee n.
1071 Jesus...To feel and see him n.
1111 faith exults to know thee n.

NEARER.
103 road To bring us daily n. God
497 Thee may I always n. feel
724 N., my God, to thee
1053 I am n. home to-day Than

NEED, NEEDFUL, NEEDY.
340 fitness...Is to feel your n. of him
372 knows thee not, Nor feels his n.
568 He knows thine hourly n.

596 leave...Just when we n. him
760 I n. thee every hour, Most
69 All needful grace will God
492 Still the one thing n. choosing
327 Arise, ye needy...he'll forgive
340 Come, ye sinners, poor and n.

NEGLIGENT.
547 heaven to obtain, How n. we live

NEIGHBOR, NEIGHBORS.
898 Who is thy n.? He whom
758 now I'm in care my neighbors

NERVE, NERVES.
594 Awake, my soul, stretch every n.
601 brace thy heart and n. thine arm
208 And nerves the feeble arm for

NEW.
453 My soul's n. creation, a life
470 Take my heart, but make it n.
481 In love create thou all things n.
491 Finish then thy n. creation
502 And all things n. become
916 The n. creation shall ascribe

NEWBORN.
195 first proclaim the n. light
949 come...The n. year to bless

NEWNESS.
829 N. of life our calling now

NEWS.
193 angels flew...To bear the n.
243 By thee the joyful n. Of
331 The n. of heavenly grace
810 The joyful n. to all impart

NIGH.
51 And still he is n.; his presence
79 in trouble thou wert n.
335 God in great mercy is coming so
370 sees...When no one else is n.
403 I know That thou art ever n.
550 When thou, O Lord, wast n.
570 For thou art always n.
651 Still n. me, O my Saviour
677 For while thou, my Lord, art n.
747 were he always thus n., Have
760 lose their power When thou art n.
1090 Thou who art ever n., Guarding

NIGHT.
77 O what a n. was that which
90 Bringing up from mortal n.
92 N. her solemn mantle spreads
95 N. unto night his name repeat
102 Abide with me when n. is
105 Glory to thee, my God, this n.
111 The n. of sin disperse
114 Through all the hours of n.
114 Or if this n. should prove my last
116 Though the n. be dark and
336 To sink...gloom of eternity's n.
349 soon, approaching n....blot out
375 so late! and dark and chill the n.

564 Leave behind the *n.*
565 Work, for the *n.* is coming
589 With lighted hearts all *n.*
613 The *n.* of sorrow endeth there
617 Should he come at *n.* or morning
661 sunshine...Without it all is *n.*
682 The *n.* is dark, and I am far
682 O'er moor...till The *n.* is gone
691 Chase the dark *n.* of sin away
707 sleeps Beneath the wing of *n.*
708 And what was day is *n.*
737 With thee all *n.* I mean to stay
744 spent...Our *n.* in praise and
767 Has thy *n.* been long and
778 Arise, for the *n.* of thy sorrow is
833 In that sad, memorable *n.*
918 Fast as ye bring the *n.* of death
952 How many pass the guilty *n.*
1015 Spent the *n.*, the day at hand
1022 This weary, restless, dangerous *n.*
1026 And there shall be no more *n.*
1028 reigns. And scatters *n.* away
1047 *N.* shall end in day
1049 There is no *n.* in heaven
1063 Which never is followed by *n.*

NIGHTS, NIGHTLY.
292 And *n.* and days, thy power
705 And comforts of my *n.*
138 And *nightly* to the listening
1050 And *n.* pitch my moving tent

NOD.
151 Ye nations, wait his *n.*; And
866 The universe obeys his *n.*

NOISE.
457 I'll bid this world of *n.* and show
769 thy dwellings...From *n.* and
1079 Loud as many waters' *n.*

NOON, NOONTIDE.
78 But sacred, high, eternal *n.*
565 Work through the sunny *n.*
777 Find eternal *n.* in me
135 Our *noontide* is thy gracious
958 And the *n.* of glory eternally

NORTH.
909 And, Keep not back, O *N.*
919 From *n.* to south the princes meet

NOTES.
58 Hark! the *n.* of angels, singing
301 angels...when...your highest *n.*
429 Not all the *n.* by angels heard
764 vie with Gabriel...In *n.* almost
821 And tuneful *n.* employ
852 But all the *n.* which mortals
1033 And the grateful *n.* prolong

NOTHING.
67 Lord, we are *n.* in thy sight
119 Who less Than *n.* am
486 Let me in o *n.* fall
525 Now let me into *n.* fall
607 There is *n.* I can do
608 There's *n.* here deserves my

NUMBER, NUMBERED.
431 Into that happy *n.*, Lord
961 *Numbered* among thy people, I

O.
OAK.
859 The beauty of the *o.* and pine

OATH.
421 His *o.*, his covenant, and blood
1075 I on his *o.* depend

OBEDIENT, OBEDIENTLY, OBEDIENCE.
67 Thy creatures bend the *o.* knee
397 And bid the *o.* waters flow
432 *O.* faith, that waits on thee
573 But first, *o.* to his word
894 To form in our *o.* souls
917 kingdoms be *O.*, mighty God
1024 be found *O.* to thy word
1113 winds retire, *O.* to thy will
720 Lord, *obediently* we'll go, Gladly
471 His faith by his *obedience* showed
485 Into glad *o.* brought

OBEY.
69 glorious hosts of heaven *o.*
325 *O.*, and be forever blest
359 We would thy word *o.*, And
360 Thy father's God *o.*
400 I fain would now *o.* the call
442 happy...Who the Saviour *o.*
475 But let me all thy words *o*
605 To hear thy dictates, and *o.*
609 That I may long *o.*
676 Whom all in y times *o.*
1012 O teach us thy will to *o.*
1053 Here...May we cheerfully *o.*
1109 Whom winds and seas *o.*
1115 Lord, whom winds and seas *o.*

OBLATION, OBLATIONS.
185 Vainly we offer each ample *o.*
389 Will mult.plied *oblations* please

OBSTRUCTS.
926 Whate'er *o.* obstructs in vain

OCEAN.
159 Thy power is in the *o.* deeps
187 The *o.* yawned and rudely
326 Rivers of...In a rich *o.* join
358 'Twere vain the *o.'s* depths to
773 L not may the troubled *o.* roar
866 The rolling *o.*, rockest with
882 light O'er earth and *o.* fly
931 Roll on, thou mighty *o.*
978 So, through the *o.*-tide of years
1069 Rivers to the *o.* run
1092 Shouting in chorus, from *o.*
1108 Who bidd'st the mighty *o.* deep
1111 If life's wide *o.* calm or roar

ODOR, ODORS.
794 Smell the sweet *o.* of our prayers
186 *Odors* of Eden and offerings
774 Their blossoms fragrant *o.* give

O'ERCOME.
413 Thou canst o. this heart
583 I have o. for your
587 Ye may o. through Christ

OFFENSE, OFFENSES.
800 The world's o., his people's
391 And past *offenses* pain my eyes
1083 All o. purge away

OFFERING, OFFERINGS.
250 An o. in the sinner's stead
250 Thy o. still continues new
278 Let our whole soul an o. be
474 O God, what o. shall I give
863 But in thy sight our o. stands
884 Father, accept our o.
186 Odors of Edom and *offerings*
484 My o. all be offered through
889 May we our thank-o. bring
897 Mean are all o. we can
923 Our prayers and o. gladly

OFFICE.
806 Never from our o. move

OFFSPRING.
827 Thine let our o. be

OIL.
81 Like holy o., to cheer my head
156 My head thou dost with o. anoint
684 The o. of gladness on our heads
954 O. in your vessels take

OLD.
502 When o. things shall be done
679 E'en down to o. age all my
756 To tell the o., old story
1107 O bless, as erst of o., The

OLIVE.
618 O Thou, who in the o.
626 Although the o. yield no oil

OLIVES', OLIVET.
217 'Tis midnight; and on O. brow
197 And faith has yet its *Olivet*

OMISSION.
511 O may the least o. pain

OMNIPOTENT, OMNIPOTENCE.
127 The power o. is thine
413 Stretch out thine arm o.
679 Upheld by my gracious, o. hand
133 *Omnipotence*, with wisdom
168 Secure in his o.
523 The o. of love
1018 Girt with o. and grace
1110 O. walks on the deep
1113 servants... Their help, O.

ONE.
101 When o. their wish, and one
463 Peace... in being o. with thee
463 May thy will and mine be o.
463 O. for evermore with thee

789 And gathered into o.
789 We all partake the joy of o.
790 But make us of o. mind and
790 And keep us o. in thee
792 Fast in o. mind and spirit
796 Still o. in life and one in death
801 Didst thou not make us o.
804 Make us of o. heart and mind
806 Many are we now and o.
975 O. will be with me there

ONWARD.
563 O., then, ye people
566 O., then, ye hosts of God
640 O happy... If o. ye will tread
855 O. to our home we move
932 river... Pursue thine o.
1044 Blest seats... I o. press to you
1070 O. we go, for still we hear
1074 But o. we move, And still

OPEN.
326 gates... Stand o. night and day
377 O. mine eyes to see thy face
377 O. the door of faith and love
403 O., and take me in
791 With o. hearts and hands we

OPPOSE, OPPOSES, OPPOSERS.
269 enter in, Whatever may o.
680 In vain our march *opposes*
268 Let him *opposers* all o'errun

OPPRESSED, OPPRESSION.
236 With sin and care o.
364 Come, all ye souls by sin o.
369 Come with your guilt and fear o.
382 No longer let me be o.
450 O. by sins, I lift mine eye
857 rest To the heart by sin o.
929 And the o. forever weep
1061 Sinks heart and voice o.
181 He comes to break *oppression*
777 Never shall you feel o.
1091 Save thy people from o.
1093 Never feel o.'s rod

OPPRESSOR.
154 Beneath the proud o.'s frown
778 The o. is vanquished, and Zion

ORACLES.
34 A thousand o. divine
291 And search the o. divine

ORB, ORBS.
1034 And thou, refulgent o. of day
138 Amid the radiant *orbs* be found
146 Those mighty o. proclaim thy
881 When the o. that people space
1025 Let those ponderous o. descend

ORDINANCE.
831 And bless the o. divine
848 In thine o. appear

ORIENT.
195 Clothed with its o. fires

ORIGINAL.
112 And to its great *o.* The
138 heavens ...great *O.* proclaim

ORPHAN, ORPHANS.
178 face...stills the sighing *o.'s*
401 The *o.* clasps a father found
1062 *Orphans* no longer fatherless

OURSELVES.
368 Give us *o.* and thee to know
945 Give up *o.*, through Jesus'

OUTCAST, OUTCASTS.
559 me ...An *o.* from thy face
857 door, For the *o.* and the poor
32 Gather the *outcasts* in, and save
451 And claimed the *o.* as thy

OUTSTRETCHED.
213 holy Lord...With *o.* arms
560 With *o.* hands, and

OVERCAME, OVERCOMETH, OVERCOMING.
226 By his death he *o.*
567 To him that *overcometh,* A
985 O for an *overcoming* faith To

OVERFLOW, OVERFLOWING.
679 rivers of sorrow shall not *o.*
353 And sins, an *overflowing* tide

OVERTHROW, OVERTHROWN.
569 Who madly seeks to *o.*
478 thee, who hast *overthrown*

OWE.
1079 Not till then, how much I *o.*
1084 These to thee, my God, we *o.*

P.

PACIFIED.
455 And art thou *p.*
531 My God, in Jesus *p.*

PAGAN.
939 O'er the *p.'s* night of care

PAGE, PAGES.
206 What glory gilds the sacred *p.*
876 And read in every *p.*...promise
229 O may these heavenly *pages* be

PAID.
210 'Tis finished! all the debt is *p.*
567 Sinners, his life for you he *p.*
367 Thy debt is *p.*, thy soul is free
378 Surety, who all my debt hast *p.*

PAIN.
49 How transient is our present *p.*
215 O Lamb of God, was ever *p.*
522 But thine the deadly *p.*
345 your affliction, or banish your *p.*
337 By his *p.* he gives you ease

346 *P.* in endless bliss expire
347 Greedy of eternal *p.*, O ye
471 In *p.*, you travel all your days
281 Renewed thy sacred *p.*
406 What *p.*, what labor, to secure
422 Died for me, who caused his *p.*
505 A soul inured to *p.*, To hardship
511 sin A *p.* to feel it near
572 And *p.* for him is sweet
616 In every *p.* I bear...find delight
619 When worn with *p.*, disease, and
620 We smile at *p.*, while thou art near
631 When *p.* o'er my weak flesh
634 And, free from *p.*, thy glories sing
643 In thy service, *p.* is pleasure
645 By thy more than mortal *p.*
646 In the hour of *p.* and anguish
663 who...Could bear his lot of *p.*
665 Through fellowship of *p.*
668 A few more years in *p.*
674 relief For every *p.* I feel
689 If *p.* afflict, or wrongs oppress
728 O what needless *p.* we bear
737 I rise superior to my *p.*
760 I need thee every hour, In joy or *p.*
797 When...part, It gives us inward *p.*
801 And bear each other's *p.*
813 Since in all *p.* thy tender love
885 While in our mortal *p.*
460 O the *p.*, the bliss of dying
984 Nor *p.*, nor grief, nor anxious fear
1003 Bear a momentary *p.*
1020 To linger in eternal *p.*
1043 The *p.* of life shall then be o'er
1057 No slightest touch of *p.*
1064 No *p.* the inhabitants feel
1067 Torturing *p.*, and heavy woe
1072 Nor *p.* nor death can enter

PAINS, PAINED.
100 night in sighs, And restless *p.*
154 Thou know'st the *p.* thy servants
180 Thy bounty shall my *p.* beguile
570 Regardless of the *p.* I feel
612 'Tis sweet to look beyond my *p.*
621 He bade my *p.* remove
723 O by all the *p.* and woe
836 Remember thee, and all thy *p.*
911 By thy *p.* and consolations
976 The *p.*, the groans, the dying strife
1035 And *p.*, and groans, and griefs
477 My heart is *pained,* nor can it be

PALACE, PALACES.
648 That *p.* of our glorious King
747 A *p.* a toy would appear
1053 The *p.* of angels and God
1073 In the *p.* of God, the great King
871 salvation shone Through...*palaces*

PALESTINE.
195 The answering hills of P.

PALM, PALMS, PALMY.
195 Her silent groves of *p.*
914 The *p.* of victory thine
1010 He bears the shining *p.*
1011 *Palms* of victory, Crowns of glory

PAL 113 PAR

1032 And conquering p. they bear
1046 P. in our hands we all shall
1069 P. they carry in their hands
930 From many a *palmy* plain

PALSIED.
1099 The p. and the lame

PANG, PANGS.
202 And death...Was p., and scoff
358 There is a death, whose p.
629 stooped to share...sharpest p.
630 One thought shall every p. remove
663 And every p. that wrings the
203 When the *pangs* of trial seize us
200 Unutterable p. were thine
223 O the p. his soul sustained
796 Our farewell p., how sharp
839 Those p. he would not flee

PANOPLY.
587 The p. of God
599 In p. of truth complete

PANT, PANTS, PANTING.
180 Or on the thirsty mountain p.
326 Ho! ye that p. for living streams
382 Only for thy love I p.
419 P. for the cooling water-brook
490 See, I p. in thee to rest
508 Thine, wholly thine, we p. to be
457 Which *pants* to have no other will
496 prove my heart, it p. for thee
840 Each heart that p. for thee
944 P. for thee each mortal breast
1068 P. to view his glorious face
490 Jesus, see my *panting* breast

PARADISE.
257 Fair flowers of p. extend
260 Christ hath opened p.
351 In Christ to p. restored
382 And be of p. possessed
512 I am his, Of p. possessed
514 To love's sweet p.
515 in my heart A constant p.
520 Thy presence makes my p.
542 And all the fruits of p.
731 'Tis p. when thou art here
757 hath found it, hath p. found
758 The souls that believe in p.
802 Of our p. possessed
825 And then transplant to p.
834 Not p., with all its joys
847 Thou hast opened p.
983 They find with Christ in p.
986 bloom, A plant of p.
999 But the mild rays of p.
1006 He to p. is fled
1032 And trees of p.
1041 home...Within the p. of God
1060 O p. of joy! Where tears
1071 O p.! O paradise
1076 With all the fruits of p.

PARCHED.
678 O'er a p. and weary land
977 P. by the sun's directer ray
994 Through these p. lips of thine

PARDON.
220 P. for all flows from his side
312 P. and peace abound
325 Here p., life, and joy divine
342 P. to each rebel sinner
351 A p. written with his blood
362 P. and peace in Jesus find
372 bought his p. on the tree
386 P. I accept unbought
398 In p., Lord, my cure begin
412 If yet, while p. may be found
412 Her p. to secure
412 died To make that p. sure
423 It seals my p. too
444 His voice proclaims my p. found
445 P., and holiness, and heaven
535 I ask the blood-bought p.
557 Again my p. seal, Again
613 And in thy p. and thy care
645 Write upon my heart the p.
736 P., and holiness, and heaven
833 P., and holiness, and heaven
831 P. and peace to dying men
943 Give the p. of our sins
957 P. of our sins renew
968 Ah! write the p. on my heart
1023 thief Spakest p. and relief
1092 Give to us p. and peace, O Lord

PARDONED.
418 Who feel the joys of p. sin
531 P. of all that I have done
985 If sin be p., I'm secure

PARDONING.
35 To us thy p. love extend
88 While we pray for p. grace
110 With p. mercy richly blest
258 Manifest thy p. love
258 To thy p. grace receive them
262 Speak thy p. grace to me
305 Lord, let us hear thy p. voice
359 Haste to your p. God
377 Now let me find my p. Lord
391 So let thy p. love be found
406 And taste thy p. grace
428 blest by...God of p. love
438 reconciled, His p. voice I hear
546 felt...Saviour's p. blood
733 Manifests his p. favor
735 And magnify thy p. love
848 Thou thy p. grace declare
851 Thy p. mercy we receive
862 seek thy p. grace, Cast
1027 Thy p. voice O let me hear

PARENT, PARENTS.
112 soul its heavenly P. sing
101 And *parents* hold him dear
101 Where p. love the sacred word
172 pity of the Lord...as tender p.
282 If earthly p. hear Their children

PART, (*separate*.)
22 Christians, brethren, ere we p.
511 From Thee that I no more may p.
521 neither life nor death can p.
695 Then willingly with all I'd p.

782 Nor life, nor death can p.
790 O do not suffer him to p.
796 Yet must we p., and parting weep
797 When we asunder p., it gives
816 Shall never p. again

PART, PARTS, (portion.)

174 In p. we know thy will
425 Unless thou wash...no p. in thee
510 love...Be mine this better p.
596 hard...To rise and take his p.
780 sigh, And with him bear a p.
791 Though but in p. we know thee
847 And never act our *parts*

PARTED, PARTING, PARTINGS.

261 Saviour, p. from our sight
94 With one accord our *parting* hymn
581 He'll take thee at thy p. breath
725 This be the p. cry My heart shall
855 Now in p., Father, bless us
974 So gently flows the p. breath
980 Such is the Christian's p. hour
1009 world...Where p. is unknown
1062 Where *partings* are no more

PARTAKERS.

782 P. of the Saviour's grace

PARTNER, PARTNERS.

552 P. of my throne shall be
662 *partners* of our blood...divide
805 P. of like precious faith
893 The p. of thy grace

PARTNERSHIP.

719 For our p. in light

PASCHAL.

246 P. Lamb, by God appointed
259 Is our P. Lamb to-day
846 And eat the P. Lamb
847 Where the p. blood is poured
847 P. Victim, paschal Bread

PASS, PASSED, PASSING, PAST.

220 Behold him, all ye that p. by
384 P. me not, O
781 And when by turns we p. away
433 grace...So wide it never *passed*
132 Each *passing* moment so to spend
960 The glory of a p. hour
25 *Past*, and present, and to be

PASSAGE.

631 Nor count the p. strange or
657 And force your p. to the skies
1004 Wait thy p. through the shade

PASSION.

285 Each evil p. overcome
383 By thy p. on the tree, Let
617 And since, by p.'s force
645 By thy last mysterious p.
854 True Recorder of his p.
869 storm Of earthborn p. dies
875 And stormy p.'s rage
895 From p.'s fearful strife

1003 Struggle through thy latest p.
1013 All the tokens of his p.
1014 By the tokens of his p.

PASSIONS, PASSIONATE, PASSIONLESS.

309 The p. to recall. And upward bid
309 Then shall our p. and our
455 And all my restless p. sway
490 Earthly p. far remove
703 My p. hold a pleasing reign
792 Our wild, unruly p. bid
681 *passionate* longings for home
1059 crown of...*passionless* renown

PASSOVER.

230 p. of gladness...passover of God

PASTOR, PASTORS.

823 not...small import The p.'s care
992 into thy hands Our p. we resign
812 *Pastors* and teachers hence arise
812 P. and people shout thy praise

PASTURE, PASTURES.

180 The Lord my p. shall prepare
718 The p. I languish to find
888 Never from thy p. roving
156 in *pastures* green; he leadeth me
158 He feeds in p. large and fair
179 I feed in green p., safe-folded I
642 Green p. are before me
759 To feed them in p. of love
761 gently glide Through p. green
872 In thy pleasant p. feed us
888 Feed in p. ever vernal
1007 And the lovely p. see That
1061 The p. of the blessed Are

PATH.

135 Sheds on our p. the glow of day
140 And dark is his p. on wings of
150 All the p. in which we rove
163 And O, when gathers on our p.
179 I seek—by the p. which my
313 feet abide, Nor from thy p. depart
344 Come, and make my p. your choice
360 Nor choose the p. to heaven
389 Must take the p. thyself hast
457 That p. with humble speed I'll
464 May I tread the p. he trod
507 thy p. shall be Peaceful, serene
510 lesser light About my p. to shine
614 We know not what the p. may be
629 No p. we shun, no darkness
642 My p. to life is free
655 Choose out the p. for me
682 I loved to choose and see my p.
742 Whether my p. shall lie 'Mid
999 Nor tread the rough p. of the
1015 Show the same p. to heaven
1088 The light my p. surrounding

PATHS.

160 When in the slippery p. of youth
171 Thy p. I cannot trace
180 Though in the p. of death I tread

PAT 115 PEA

269 Turn from the *p.* of life aside
329 And all her flowery *p.* are peace
560 Give me in all thy *p.* to tread
862 If from thy *p.* our souls...stray
875 child .The *p.* of peace have trod
1103 Secure the *p.* of life we tread
1112 'Tis here thine unknown *p.* we

PATHWAY.
202 That lit thy lonely *p.*, trod
644 Tread its *p.* to the skies
679 When through fiery trials thy *p.*
687 Be thou our *p.* to the skies

PATIENCE.
146 We read thy *p.* still
269 With *p.* firm and purpose high
597 In truth and *p.* wrought
619 Grant *p.*, rest, and kind relief
623 With steadfast *p.* arm my breast
631 With lamb-like *p.* arm my breast
729 *P.* gives, and consolation
955 By the *p.* of hope, and the labor
1014 Partners in his *p.* here
1054 Endue me with *p.* to wait

PATIENT.
196 What *p.* love was seen in all
202 So *p.*, through a world of woe

PATRIARCH, PATRIARCHS.
36 Sat weary by the *p.*'s well
225 *Patriarchs* from the distant ages

PATTERN.
500 So let thy life our *p.* be
804 To thy Church the *p.* give
1045 For his own *p.* given

PAUL.
274 Which made *P.*'s heart with
580 Lay *P.* and Silas bound
585 victory...I long with *P.* to share

PAVEMENT.
863 He spreads its *p.*, green and
1034 The *p.* of those heavenly courts

PAVILION, PAVILIONED.
660 In thy *p.* to abide
140 *Pavilioned* in splendor, and

PAY, PAYS, PAID.
559 For I have naught to *p.*
951 Our hearts to *p.* thee all thy
322 debt...Upon the cross he *pays*
210 'Tis finished! all the debt is *paid*
367 Thy debt is *p.*, thy soul is free
378 Surety, who all my debt hast *p.*

PEACE.
30 Speak *p.* into our hearts, and say
60 Beam *p.* into each heart
74 Let *p.* within her walls be found
89 God send his people *p.*
94 Call us, O Lord, to thine eternal *p.*
101 agree, This blessed *p.* to gain

108 *P.* is the pillow for my head
178 And *p.* and joy which never end
184 And *p.* abound below
192 And to the earth be *p.*
194 When *p.* shall over all the earth
225 Knows the everlasting *q.*
246 *P.* is made 'twixt man and God
262 Life and *p.* to me impart
271 Give *p.* and joy, for we are thine
284 *P.*, when deep griefs o'erflow
290 voice Spreads heavenly *p.* around
337 *P.*, unspeakable, unknown
344 *P.* that ever shall endure
348 To procure your *p.* with God
397 *P.*, righteousness, and joy impart
399 Restore my inward *p.*
428 That all-comprising *p.* bestow
437 We all his unknown *p.* receive
450 I'll go, for all his paths are *p.*
463 *P.* I ask—but peace must be
487 Bless with late but lasting *p.*
532 Which bought for me the sacred *p.*
561 No *p.* we have, no joy we see
577 And dwell in endless *p.*
614 And heavenly *p.* be won
623 Speak to my warring passions, *P.*
639 The Lord will give thee *p.*
651 *P.*, doubting heart! my God's
681 And pine to recover my *p.*
725 Sought *p.* and rest; Now
752 What *p.* of mind
767 *P.* and joy shall now attend thee
773 In sacred *p.* our souls abide
773 Sweet *p.* thy promises afford
777 *P.* and righteousness shall reign
780 In one another's *p.* delight
789 A *p.* to sensual minds unknown
802 Constant joy, and lasting *p.*
807 When will *p.* wreathe her chain
841 Our *p.* is made with Heaven
868 Till faith bring the *p.* to the
869 The *p.* that dwelleth without end
914 fruits Of grace and *p.* divine
981 Shall *p.* and hope no more arise
1021 And make my *p.* with God
1092 Give to us *p.* in our time. O Lord
1092 *P.* to the nations, and praise to
1102 Give *p.*, O God, give peace again
1108 And give, for wild confusion, *p.*

In PEACE.
383 And bid us go *in p.*
410 And bid me die *in p.*
609 Kept *in p.* by Jesus' name
862 Grant us to walk in *p.* and love

Of PEACE.
107 Teach us the way *of p.* to prize
337 Find in Christ the way *of p.*
371 You live, devoid *of p.*
799 Blest are the sons *of p.*
821 And words *of p.* reveal
1052 Come to the land *of p.*

PEACE *on earth.*
26 *P. on earth* to man forgiven
188 *P. on earth*, good-will from
195 *P. on earth*; good-will to men

Perfect PEACE.
170 Will keep me still in *perfect p.*
178 mind... is kept in *perfect p.*
455 O preserve in *perfect p.*
463 Now thy *perfect p.* impart
495 And fill me with thy *perfect p.*
521 And keep our minds in *perfect p.*
542 And keeps his own in *perfect p.*
753 Gather....And keep in *perfect p.*
755 yonder, In *perfect p.* and rest
1010 He dwells in *perfect p.*
1115 Keep our souls in *perfect p.*

Thy PEACE.
86 *Thy p.* our spirits fill
94 Grant us *thy p.* upon our
94 Grant us *thy p.*, Lord, through
418 *Thy p.* and love my portion be
855 Saviour, still *thy p.* bestow
862 *Thy p.* to shed, thy joy to bring

With PEACE.
634 Fills my sad soul *with p.*
729 Fills my soul *with p.* and joy
870 *With p.* their hearts to fill
1098 *With p.* our borders bless

PEACEFUL.
95 And bring a *p.* night
158 An honored life, a *p.* end
549 What *p.* hours I once enjoyed
590 Kept *p.* in the midst of strife
627 Whose days a *p.* tenor keep
659 roll Across my *p.* breast
676 but I With *p.* heart will say
980 When all is *p.* and serene

PEARL, PEARLS.
526 And find the *p.* of perfect love
1004 *P.* of price by Jesus bought
186 Gems of the mountain, and *pearls*

PEN.
700 Nor tongue nor *p.* can show

PENITENT, PENITENCE.
259 How the *p.* forgiven
404 bestow The *p.* desire
868 faith bring the peace to the *p.*
60 True *penitence* impart
177 'Mid tears of *p.* we knelt
320 When *p.* has wept in vain
1096 mercy-seat To *p.* and prayer

PENITENTIAL.
45 To hush the *p.* sigh
67 And dry our *p.* tears
147 worship thee with...*p.* tears
372 grief, And *p.* pain
405 Let floods of *p.* grief
709 to shed The *p.* tear
752 And e'en the *p.* tear is
852 Let humble, *p.* woe
932 waking To *p.* tears
1058 Let *p.* sorrow To heavenly

PENTECOST, PENTECOSTAL.
272 With thee each day is *P.*
286 As on the day of *P.*, Descend

499 In me renew thy *P.*
275 We wait the *pentecostal* powers
278 Come...With *p.* grace

PEOPLE.
13 And count thy *p.'s* triumph mine
513 rest...To all thy *p.* known
641 Will clothe his *p.* too
861 Here, when thy *p.* seek thy face
865 crown...This *p.* as thine own
922 Has called thy *p.* from afar
1027 I love to meet thy *p.* now

PERDITION.
345 Lest *p.* thee arrest

PERFECT.
23 Make us *p.* in his will
46 And guide into thy *p.* will
136 *P.* in power, in love, and
432 And *p.* me in love
448 Till *p.* I am found in thee
464 Give me, Lord, the *p.* mind
474 Thy glory to the *p.* day
494 speak...And *p.* me in love
497 And long to see the *p.* day
507 In which is *p.* day
514 nature in, And *p.* us in love
521 *P.*, and right, and pure, and
646 Lead us in thy *p.* way
825 Till all thy *p.* mind they gain
924 And *p.* all our souls in one

PERFECTED, PERFECTING, PERFECTION.
46 And *p.* in love below
493 be pure, And *p.* in love
806 *Perfecting* the saints below
126 Thee to *perfection* who can know
525 Now let me gain *p.'s* height
532 This mark of true *p.* find

PERFUME.
179 With *p.* and oil thou anointest
919 His name like sweet *p.* shall rise
970 flesh of Jesus...left a long *p.*
986 And gladden with thy sweet *p.*

PERIL, PERILS.
373 Its *p.* every hour
1092 Praise him who saved...from *p.*
103 New *perils* past, new sins

PERISH.
343 Haste...You must *p.* if you stay
360 Then shalt thou *p.* in thy sins
369 But, if I *p.*, I will pray
369 I can but *p.* if I go; I am
626 And *p.* all the bleating race
927 They *p.*, whom thyself hast

PERPETUAL.
104 *P.* blessings from thy hand
104 Demand *p.* songs of praise
341 Flows...In a full *p.* tide
964 And our *p.* home

PERPLEX.
777 Shall no more *p.* your ways

PESTILENCE.
949 Defend our land from p.
1095 And p., with rapid stride

PETER.
543 broke Unfaithful P.'s heart
558 False to thee, like P., l
558 Would fain, like P., weep

PETITION, PETITIONS.
610 Let this p. rise
688 Thy wings shall my p. bear
239 Hear, and my weak *petitions*

PHYSICIAN.
306 And is no kind p. nigh
206 There is a great P. near
398 The good, the kind P., thou
1064 P. of souls, unto me

PIERCE, PIERCED.
265 P. the clouds of nature's night
380 P. this bleeding, broken heart
339 *Pierced* him with a soldier's
381 Have p. a thousand, thousand
627 Though with a p. and broken
637 The hand my cruel sins had p.
854 Look on him we p., and grieve
1013 P. and nailed him to the tree
338 On his *pierced* body laid, Justice
847 Flowing from his p. side
1107 flowed Forth from thy p. side

PIETY.
899 To temperance, truth, and p.
902 Their works of p. and love
903 The seeds which p. and love

PILGRIM.
171 P. through this barren land
308 It marks the p.'s way
344 Weary p., hither come
346 P., burdened with thy sin
346 Holy p., what for thee
590 O may we lead the p.'s life
620 Poor p., lift in hope thy head
643 Swift shall pass thy p. days
693 A p. in a land unknown
718 While I am a p. here
864 The p. heirs of guilt and woe
914 Light of the lonely p.'s heart
980 The p. on his gloomy road
1036 Our p. host shall safely land
1048 Heaven, the Christian p.'s home
1078 How happy is the p.'s lot
1088 Come, p., come away

PILGRIMS.
564 P. to your country
640 O happy band of p.
648 Strangers and p. here below
1010 But we, poor p., wander
1060 refreshment To p. far away
1067 P. in this vale of tears
1068 Cease, ye p., cease to mourn
1070 Singing to welcome the p.
1074 But strangers and p. ourselves
1089 Land of the p.' pride
1100 To this fair land the p. trod

PILGRIMAGE.
80 Our p. will soon be trod
788 Here in their house of p.
1010 one...Whose p. is o'er

PILLAR, PILLARS.
37 The p. and the flame of fire
163 The cloudy p. glided slow
171 Let the fiery, cloudy p., Lead
564 Burns the fiery p.
1036 God's fiery p. for our guide
119 hell, and heaven's strong *pillars*
215 And earth's strong p. bend
328 P. of earthly pride decay
863 And heaved its p. one by one

PILLOW, PILLOWS.
108 Peace is the p. for my head
1004 Hovering round thy p., bend
1008 Buds on thy p. laid
1114 Aroused by the shriek...thy p.
976 Feel soft as downy *pillows* are

PILOT.
1110 And faith in our P. shall be

PINE, (tree.)
859 The beauty of the oak and p.

PINE, PINING.
273 Or long for thy return to p.
326 that pant...And p. away and die
550 For thee...My thirsty soul doth p.
631 For thee my thirsty soul doth p.
1015 Far away from thee I p.
1073 heart...If for Jesus it p.
849 Give us, for thee long *pining*, To

PIOUS.
75 We blest and p. grow
709 Blest is the p. house

PISGAH.
515 The promised land, from P.'s top
688 Till, from Mount P.'s lofty

PIT, PITFALLS.
543 If near the p. I rashly stray
927 The p. its mouth hath opened
905 Life's twilight path, with *pitfalls*

PITY.
201 Look down in p., Lord, we pray
214 Amazing p.! grace unknown
340 Full of p., love, and power
391 Show p., Lord, O Lord, forgive
404 With softening p. look
953 fig-tree down, The p. of the Lord
1092 Show forth thy p. on high

PITYING.
145 He hath with a p. eye Looked
157 Since thou a p. ear didst
304 With p. eyes the Prince of
417 Saviour, look with p. eye
558 Jesus, let thy p. eye Call
634 Soon as thy p. face Shone
900 To look on those with p. eye

968 Jesus, vouchsafe a p. ray
1022 O Son of man, so p. found
1094 With p. eye behold our need

PLACE, PLACED.
170 But lo! a p. he hath prepared
303 God is in this and every p.
595 Appoint my soul a p.
696 To me remains nor p. nor time
696 While p. we seek, or place we
801 cast our lot in the same age and p.
805 One in every time and p.
806 *Placed* according to thy will

PLAGUE.
1005 And let the p. be stayed

PLAIN.
98 path of duty straight, And p.
161 interpreter...he will make it p.

PLAIN, PLAINS.
80 The p., the stream, the wood
354 Then linger not in all the p.
882 Hosanna...spread from p. to
313 Lead to the blissful *plains*
908 rivers of..flow o'er the bright p.
1038 O'er all the wide-extended p.
1057 While o'er the happy p. they

PLAINTIVE.
399 Then listen to the p. sound

PLAN, PLANS.
321 Which drew the wondrous p.
809 Except the Lord conduct the p.
895 Our *plans* and efforts bless

PLANETS.
138 And all the p. in their turn

PLANT, PLANTS.
301 The rising p. destroy
986 We p. thee here, with tears
611 Which, like the *plants* that throw
1081 The p. in beauty grew

PLEA.
124 His blood's availing p.
369 Perhaps he will admit my p.
385 This, only this, is all my p.
385 Of love, this shall be a l my p.
392 I give up every p. beside
393 Just as I am, without one p.
553 This all my hope, and all my p.
725 This is my earnest p.

PLEAD.
98 Christ is gone, To p. for all his
235 He lives, his people's cause to p.
238 Forever doth for sinners p.
242 He lives, to p. for me above
378 I p. with thee, my suit to gain
436 I dare in faith to p.
438 His precious blood, to p.
438 Five bleeding wounds... p.
625 For whom the Saviour deigns to p.
819 We p. for those who plead for
1080 Lord, in thy name thy servants p.

PLEADS.
73 And now he p. our cause above
243 And now it p. before the throne
259 P. for us, and hears our cry
425 For me the blood of sprinkling p.
612 Where Jesus p. above

PLEADERS, PLEADING.
819 Successful p. may they be
225 Holiest hearts for ages *pleading*
239 If now I find thee p. there
246 There for sinners thou art p.
250 P. thy death for sinners now
711 prayer...in earnest p. flows
727 Ever p., ever crying, Lord
735 Father, regard thy p. Son

PLEASANTNESS.
329 Her ways are ways of p.

PLEASE, PLEASED, PLEASING.
19 To p. our God alone
175 To love and p. thee more
675 But to p. thee perfectly
45 Well *pleased* his people's voice to
695 For I am p. with none beside
23 fulfill What is *pleasing* in his
502 I do...Well p. in thy sight
637 P. or painful, dark or bright
675 a mind intent on p. thee

PLEASURE.
173 But in his p. rest
324 Salvation! What p. to our ears
367 Lovers of p. more than God
419 life itself...No lasting p.
456 Him to know...p. without end
662 Each p. hath its poison too
726 And I hope, by thy good p.
1055 Where each new scene fresh p.

PLEASURES.
41 Drink endless p. in
356 And p. springing from the well
366 And p. never die
456 All thy p. I forego
516 Its p. can no longer please
516 So earthly p. fade away
617 Vain are all terrestrial p.
695 The p. of the world I flee
751 sea...Where all my p. roll
757 True p. abound in the
777 P. without end shall flow
814 Or the world's p., or its praise
899 And p. pure, refined
973 All earthly p. will be o'er
1032 Who taste the p. there
1042 The sacred p. of the soul

PLEDGE.
12 We first received the p. of love
82 Is the dear p. of glorious rest
398 The measure and the p. of love
410 The p. thou wilt at last receive
421 The p. of joys to come
461 That p. of love forever there
512 A p. of liberty
630 A p. that storms shall cease

PLENTY, PLENITUDE.
1061 And p. fills the plain
1085 With p., and with peace
276 O Spirit...In all thy *plenitude*
351 The p. of gospel grace
488 Proved thy p. of grace
532 Thy Spirit's p. impart

PLOW.
1086 We p. the fields and scatter

PLUCK, PLUCKS, PLUCKED.
588 who Shall p. you from his
651 Nor earth, nor hell shall p. me
453 I trust in his word; none *plucks*
25 *Plucked* from the destroyer's

PLUNDERERS.
62 And p. of the air

PLUNGE, PLUNGED.
420 By faith I p. me in this sea
527 And p. me in the purple flood
529 And p. me, every whit made
304 *Plunged* in a gulf of dark
319 And sinners, *plunged* beneath
423 Aud p. me in despair

POINT, POINTS, POINTING.
287 Comforter...p. our souls above
962 A little p. my life appears
966 A p. of time, a moment's space
300 light Now *points* to his abode
115 *Pointing* up to that fair heaven

POISON.
662 Each pleasure hath its p. too

POLE.
138 spread the truth from p. to pole
257 From p. to pole, that wars
358 Or pierce to either p.
288 All the wide world, to either p.
922 Along the line to either p.
930 It spreads from p. to pole
938 He shall reign from p. to pole

POLISHED.
865 And shine like p. stones

POLLUTE, POLLUTED.
111 O may no gloomy crime P.
130 How shall *polluted* mortals dare

POOL.
397 I wait the moving of the p.

POOR.
1 The humble p. believe
68 In him the p. may safely trust
102 enrich the p. With blessings
154 And raise the p. that fall
393 Just as I am—p., wretched
464 P., unfriended, or unknown
872 P. and sinful though we be
893 Thy face...in thy p. would see
896 And not the p. despised
897 spent, Like his, upon the p.
897 The p. are with us still
904 He that hath pity on the p.
904 A liberal portion to the p.

PORT.
585 Just as the p. is gained
1111 When in the tempting p. they

PORTAL, PORTALS.
225 O to enter that bright p.
879 met...At the p. of the sky
14 Fling wide the *portals* of your
193 Down through the p. of the sky
237 Dragged to the p. of the sky
868 Whose p. were marble, whose

PORTION.
363 I am thy p.; come to me
401 My life, my p. thou
462 My p. thou, my treasure
494 Thou...My p. here below
540 This only p., Lord, be mine
638 May he our p. here
695 Yet Jesus shall my p. be
962 O be a nobler p. mine
996 happiness or woe...my p. be
1068 Thy better p. trace
1075 And him my only p. make

POSSESS.
233 Our hearts p., on thee we wait
401 Come, and p. me whole
457 P. it thou, who hast the right
474 Guard thou thine own, p. it
476 O may thy love p. me whole

POSSESSION.
402 Saviour take P. of my
777 Still in undisturbed p.

POUR.
274 On us thy Holy Spirit p.
936 But the Lord will shortly p.
1085 Who doth upon us p. His

POVERTY.
170 Inured to p. and pain
655 Choose...My p. or wealth
893 What can my p. bestow

POWER.
17 earth shall feel his saving p.
18 And here in saving p. descend
39 Thy saving p. and love display
65 With p. reach every heart
81 And every p. find sweet employ
167 And by thine own almighty p.
191 he shall bear P. and majesty
243 Thine is the p.; behold we sit
251 Extol his kingly p.
276 Give p. and unction from above
288 Thy word is p. and life
319 blood shall never lose its p.
336 What p. then, O sinner, will
437 The sacred p. we prove
461 Thou giv'st the p. thy grace to
489 Fill us with thy glorious p.
495 would, but thou must give the p.

513 Saviour, now the p. bestow
523 The faith shall bring the p.
535 The sin-subduing p.
556 Jesus, be thou my p.
587 And in his mighty p., Who in
677 confessed in all thy saving p.
797 But there's a p. which man
736 In weakness, my almighty p.
761 His all-protecting p. displayed
822 P. into strengthless souls he
861 Still by the p. of his great name
979 That manifests the Saviour's p.
994 'Twill then be raised in p.
1005 When earth all helping p.
1017 What p. shall be the sinner's stay
1058 'Midst p. that knows no limit
1112 Whose p. the wind and sea
1112 Amazing heights of boundless p.

All POWER.
245 All p. to our great Lord
582 All p. to him be given. He
588 All p. to him be given; Believe
830 All p. is trusted in my hands

His POWER.
47 Let all within us feel *his* p.
68 Above the heavens *his* p. is
181 *His* p., increasing, still shall
651 I own *his* p., accept the sign
876 Sing of the wonders of *his* p.

Of POWER.
6 Spirit *of* p.
18 Thou God *of* p., thou God of love
26 God *of* p., and God of love
284 Speak the word *of* p. to me
502 Spirit *of* p. within
818 let them speak thy word *of* p.

POWER *divine*.
309 Can aught but p. *divine*
319 And formed by p. *divine*
396 But p. *divine* can do the deed
499 Reveal thy p. *divine*
620 believe...His love and p. *divine*
867 While p. *divine* his word
1107 His gracious p. *divine*, The

Thy POWER.
125 O God, *thy* p. is wonderful
126 High is *thy* p. above all
218 'Tis finished! Son of God, *thy* p.
286 Descend in all *thy* p.
319 I'll sing *thy* p. to save
368 *Thy* p. to us make known
406 I now should feel *thy* p.
477 To feel *thy* p., to hear thy voice
499 Reveal *thy* p. divine
512 O may *thy* p. the blood apply
535 So arm me with *thy* p.
682 So long *thy* p. hath blest
854 Let us feel *thy* p. applying
861 *Thy* p. and goodness here
1103 *Thy* p. we see, thy greatness

POWERS.
104 I yield my p. to thy command
106 That all my p., with all

120 To thee the p. on high
155 With all the heavenly p.
270 Their wondrous p. impart
478 That all my p., with all
485 All my p. shall wait on thee
574 O may it all my p. engage
582 The p. of hell surround
705 My life, with all its active p.
721 Still for thee my p. employ
740 Praise shall employ my nobler p.
742 Thy love...Claims all my p.
899 Be all their p. inclined

POWERFUL.
171 Hold me with thy p. hand
894 grace....All-p. from above

PRACTICE.
39 Reduce to p. what we hear

PRAISE.
4 His endless p. proclaim
8 fill the world with loudest p.
13 His tribute of immortal p.
15 They p. thee still; and happy
19 Thee let us p., our common
25 P. him, ye who know his love
27 P. him, praise him, evermore
27 P. the Lord, his mercies trace
50 p. thee, Let all the people praise
57 P. the Lord, ye heavens adore
59 Then we'll give thee nobler p.
77 And p. on every tongue
97 All p. to him who dwells in
99 Till we shall p. thee as we
101 And p. is wont to rise
106 All p. to thee, who safe hast kept
118 P. shall aye be brought to thee
120 Thy constant p. recite
121 To thee the p. designed
153 P., ye the Lord, ye immortal
285 But thine shall be the p.
316 Accept the p. I bring
324 To thee the p. belongs
330 We will p. him again when we
385 And give the p. to him
449 To God the voice of grateful p.
451 And ceaseless p. to thee is
458 Shall speak thy co-extended p.
467 P. him, ye saints, the God
484 And all my spotless life be p.
506 For thine immortal p.
531 But breathe unutterable p.
600 And only live to love and p.
611 Accept our feeble p.
658 And filled my lips with p.
676 And p. thee more and more
683 P. with my heart, my mind
706 Then shall my lips in endless p.
715 And prayer in endless p.
731 P., my soul, the King of heaven
740 I'll p. my Maker while I've
759 eternity....Re-echoes the p. of
760 To build....And his eternal p.
777 And your gates shall all be P.
798 Again in Jesus, p. we join
820 And p. thee evermore on high
847 P. we Christ, whose blood was

PRA 121 PRA

870 Are met for p. and prayer
946 All p. to him belongs
995 Saviour, accept the p. Of
1036 And prayer be lost in p.
1069 God, the glorious Saviour, p.
1070 When the p. of heaven I hear
1084 P. to God, immortal praise
1084 Let thy p. our tongues employ
1103 The tribute of exulting p.

His PRAISE.
3 Come, sound his p. abroad
133 And let his p. employ thy tongue
172 My soul repeat his p.
226 They shall join his p. to sing
589 And now show forth his p.
782 And show his p. below
871 And let his p. be great

Of PRAISE.
24 Songs of p. their powers employ
71 Shall swell the sound of p. again
779 With the voice of p. resound
807 Our songs of p. shall close

Our PRAISE.
49 Our p. shall never cease to flow
107 Our p. to thy pure glory sing
321 And well deserves our p.

Thy PRAISE.
12 Increase thy p., improve our
55 To thy p. and glory live
100 Lord of my life, O may thy p.
148 Shall thy p. unuttered lie
160 To utter all thy p.
193 Thy p. shall never end
257 Thy p. shall never fail
508 And gladly sing thy p.
608 Awhile show forth thy p.
692 grateful powers shall sound thy p.
705 Shall spread thy p. abroad
706 Nor will I cease thy p. to sing
724 thoughts Bright with thy p.
725 latest breath Whisper thy p.
744 Too short to sing thy p.
953 O let us all thy p. declare
1082 Well may thy p. our lips employ
1084 Let thy p. our tongues employ

To PRAISE.
81 To p. thy name, give thanks
88 Here we come thy name to p.
91 Teaching us to p. aright
282 And all unite to p. thy name
466 Turn thou our prayers to p.
786 And join with us to p. his love
889 Join to p. our Lord and King

PRAISES.
12 And wear our p. as thy crown
50 Thy p. let them sing
106 High p. to the eternal King
137 Thy p. ring through earth and
139 In p. every hour employ
188 Heaven and earth his p. sing
233 Help us to render p. due.

246 Loudest p., without ceasing
304 The Saviour's p. speak
340 Sing the p. of the Lamb
692 Thy tuneful p., raised on high
729 With my mouth thy p. sing
734 Evermore his p. sing
744 We long thy p. to repeat
754 To sing with saints his p.
788 Thy p. they prolong
870 Long may they sing thy p.
876 And loudest p. give
885 Sound we thy p. high, And
919 And endless p. crown his head
1093 P. to our God belong

PRAISED, PRAISING.
129 Thy name be p. for evermore
484 Thy name be p. on earth
192 throng Of angels, praising God

PRAY.
15 O happy souls that p.
43 Lord, teach our hearts to p.
223 Learn of Jesus Christ to p.
382 for sinners...I humbly p.
438 The Father hears him p.
480 So shall we p. and never cease
506 I want a heart to p., To pray
517 As taught by thee in faith I p.
543 And stir me up to p.
589 P., without ceasing, pray
621 While I have breath to p.
689 they live should Christians p.
706 When God inclines the heart to p.
710 Lord, teach us how to p.
735 In Jesus' power and spirit p.
745 faithful soul p. always; pray
750 home, Around its altar, p.
762 Now hear me while I p.
769 sweet accord Of souls that p. to
856 Hear thy servants as they p.
884 O teach us how to p.
890 but p., Pray to our God above
1024 care, And stir us up to p.
1047 While I breathe I p.
1096 And gives us time to p.

PRAYS, PRAYED, PRAYING.
217 The suffering Saviour p. alone
221 Sinners, he p. for you and me
512 Redeemer lives, And ever p. for
710 And cry, Behold he p.
157 To thee, O Lord of life, we prayed
201 P. to behold the light of day
682 I was not ever thus, nor p.
753 The praying spirit breathe

PRAYER.
79 And offered p. with holy hands
79 And not a p., a tear, a sigh
79 Yet one p. more;—and be it one
101 Happy the home where p. is
181 To him shall p. unceasing
252 Or offer their imperfect p.
255 deigns Our every p. to heed
264 Granted is the Saviour's p.
264 Sighs the unutterable p.
283 O thou that hearest p., Attend

PRA 122 PRE

399 listen to...a poor sinner's p.
567 armor...Each piece put on with p.
584 With p. and crying strong, Hold
589 every want In instant p.
597 And p., by thee Inspired and
599 He takes the trustiest weapon, p.
658 Thy mercy heard my infant p.
672 his ear Attends the softest p.
689 P. is appointed to convey
706 P. is the breath of God in man
707 That power is p., which soars
709 hours...In humble, grateful p.
710 P. is the soul's sincere desire
711 Sweet is the p. whose holy
713 With p. and praise agree
715 souls be cast In never-ceasing p.
717 'Tis the time for earnest p.
718 Jesus loves to answer p.
722 God of love, who hearest p.
725 Hear thou the p. I make
735 O wondrous power of faithful p.
738 Be conquered by my instant p.
750 P. is the Christian pilgrim's staff
771 chosen few Awake to earnest p.
793 Regard thine own eternal p.
800 O may that holy p., His
819 Attentive to our earnest p.
858 Here to meet for praise and p.
880 Their holy hands in humble p.
906 He thy gentlest p. can hear
919 To him shall endless p. be made
991 Thy ceaseless p. be heard
1080 All thine are ours by p.
1105 And listen to our heartfelt p.

In PRAYER.

160 To form themselves in p.
546 In p. my soul drew near
616 Or seek relief in p.
717 If we look to God in p.
728 carry Every thing to God in p.
861 scattered souls may blend in p.
1043 While here he kneels in p.

My PRAYER.

98 To thee will I direct my p.
369 Perhaps will hear my p.
505 And know thou hear'st my p.
686 Inspire, and then accept, my p.
738 My p. hath power with God
742 To thee direct m. p.

Of PRAYER.

41 may we prove the power of p.
45 sacred hour, the hour of p.
199 The voice of p., the hymn
417 By thy lonely hour of p.
589 besiege...With all the power of p.
597 For one brief hour of p.
688 Sweet hour of p., sweet
690 who that knows the worth of p.
710 The path of p. thyself hast
717 If we live a life of p.
752 that which calls...The hour of p.

Our PRAYER.

33 Thine ear hath heard our p.
89 Our p. shall never cease

278 Spirit Divine, attend our p.
785 And know our p. is heard
1094 King of nations, hear our p.

PRAYERS.

46 The p. of saints to heaven
197 Through him the first fond p. said
407 In answer to a thousand p.
408 Dear Lord, to thee our p. ascend
702 To thee our p. ascend
797 We pour our ardent p.
806 Accept the p. that thousands
922 Our p. assist; accept our

PREACH, PREACHER.

32 Open the door to p. thy word
276 To p. the reconciling word
608 And p. thee, too, as love knows
822 P. him to all, and cry in death
823 May they...Jesus, whom they p.
825 And p. the death by which
843 P. the glad news so free
942 Men may p., but till thou
944 of the preacher Speed the foot

PRECEPTS.

176 How kind his p. are
293 Its truths divine and p. wise
902 Make all the p. of his word
1100 O spread thy truth's bright p.

PRECIOUS.

181 souls...Were p. in his sight
224 O what pleasure Do these p.
510 I ask for all the p. things
653 O the p. name of Jesus
768 Thou art p. In his sight
1014 Christ, to all believers p.

PREPARE.

246 There thou dost our place p.
443 Could I but my heart p.
457 And for thys If p. the place
574 And O, thy servant, Lord, p.
586 My simple, upright heart p.
672 He shall p. thy way
846 Their faithful hearts with us p.
848 Thou our faithful hearts p.
858 Thou thy people's hearts p.
880 beautiful place he has gone to p.
926 A voice that loudly calls,—P.
926 P. your hearts, for God is nigh
957 Then, O my Lord, p. My
1024 Our cautioned souls p.
1028 P., my soul, to meet him
1028 And thus p. to meet him
1051 P. me, dear Saviour, for glory

PREPARES, PREPARING.

225 God has promised, Christ p. it
843 Thy love p. with God
1071 Lord In love p. for me
1105 Here, in earth's home preparing

PREPARED.

19 O Christ, who hast p. a place
170 But lo! a place he hath p.
319 Lord, I believe thou hast p.

564 glories Hath our God p.
580 Christ comes, we stand p.
921 Long ages have p. thy way
1028 His presence...On those p.
1030 The heaven p. for me
1031 P., by grace divine, For

PRESENCE.

7 Thy promised p. claim
14 Let me thy inner p. feel
18 feel The p. of our God
30 Let us thy p. feel
39 Thy p., gracious God, afford
43 Nor from thy p. cast away
51 his p. we have: The great
67 And humbly now thy p. claim
88 May we feel thy p. near
93 I need thy p. every passing
123 In vain...To shun thy p.
128 O fix thy sacred p. there
165 His p. guards his people's path
168 With his unclouded p. blest
291 So shall my heart his p. prove
455 Thy p. let me always find
457 O let thy sacred p. fill
474 This house still let thy p. fill
498 bestow Thy p. and thy love
501 Lord, we thy p. seek
512 His p. makes me free indeed
531 I shall not in thy p. move
537 Thy p., Lord, the place shall
551 So shall his p. bless our souls
610 Thy p. through my journey shine
685 Thy p., Lord, fills every place
700 And in thy p. rest
747 His p. disperses my gloom
759 O thou, in whose p. my soul
831 We now thy promised p. find
860 Jehovah's p. can confine
861 And be it with thy p. filled
991 And all in Jesus' p. reign
1028 His p. sheds eternal day
1030 And with his glorious p. here
1054 And feel in the p. of Jesus
1054 Though oft from thy p. in
1083 In thy p. to abide
1110 Forever thy p. is near

PRESENT.

211 That were a p. far too small
896 Her costliest p. brought

PRESENT, (verb.)

7 P. we know thou art, But O
40 Yet God is p. in this place
121 P. alike in every place
163 Thus p. still, though now unseen
366 The p. we should now redeem
389 P. for past can ne'er atone
574 To serve the p. age, My
633 Nor p. things, nor things to come
650 And felt thee p. in the flame
717 God is p. every-where

PRESENT, PRESENTING.

134 He will p. them at the throne
859 We but p. thee with thine own

98 *Presenting,* at the Father's
946 To thee p., through thy Son

PRESERVE, PRESERVED, PRESERVER.

23 And p. us day and night
62 P. it from the passing feet
825 P. them for thy glorious cause
1100 Great God, p. us in thy fear
798 *Preserved* by power divine
1103 P. by thee for ages past
112 found My kind *Preserver* near

PRESS, PRESSED.

201 P. onward in the path he trod
478 Still to p. forward in thy way
594 Awake...And p. with vigor on
643 Life with trials hard may p. me
665 P. onward to that blest estate
1074 And p. to our permanent place
548 Once *pressed* and blessed by thee
667 not shrink, Though p. by every

PRESSING.

92 P. onward to the prize
205 P. onward as we can
321 supplies...While p. on to God

PREVAIL, PREVAILS.

207 Should strive and should p.
289 gospel...Shall mightily p.
440 Bless me; for I will p.
458 I will not, till my suit p.
546 Rise, Lord, and help me to p.
569 nor hell...Against us shall p.
936 the work...Ever mighty to p.
239 If now for me *prevails* thy

PREY.

235 The grave hath lost its p.
790 He seizes...As his own lawful p.
889 protect...Lest we fall an easy p.

PRICE.

336 No p. is demanded, the Saviour
415 In my hand no p. I bring
469 Who bought us with a p.
843 Thine was the bitter p.
941 Of the precious p. that bought

PRIDE.

7 Not in the name of p. Or
107 And its rebellious p. control
411 These clouds of p. and sin dispel
497 P. in its earliest motions did
511 first approach to feel Of p.
527 Save me from p....the plague
601 Nor let thy foolish p. rebel
682 spite of fears, P. ruled my will

PRIEST, PRIESTS, PRIESTHOOD.

250 Our everlasting P. thou art
697 In thee, my P., will I rejoice
800 One P. before the throne
814 When from the p. or pastor's lips
542 With Jesus' *priests* and kings
834 And let the p. themselves believe
250 Thy *priesthood* still remains

PRINCE, PRINCES.
24 When the P. of peace was born
166 The P. of darkness grim
184 His name shall be the P. of peace
558 Saviour, P., enthroned above
804 Show thyself the P. of peace
826 Hence, P. of darkness! hence
1016 Come, thou blessed P. of peace
1076 Triumphant...The P. of peace
972 Princes, this clay must be your

PRINTS.
261 See, he shows the p. of love
1077 He shows his p. of love

PRISON, PRISONS.
580 Paul...Bound, and in p. sang
589 Our p. is this earth
976 Fond of our p. and our clay
1011 A soul out of p. released
1072 When from this earthly p. free
608 Our fathers, chained in prisons
717 And p. would palaces prove

PRISONER, PRISONERS, PRISONED.
1 He sets the p. free
185 He comes, the p. to release
740 And grants the p. sweet release
822 Jesus the p.'s fetters breaks
1000 P., long detained below
479 Prisoners of hope, lift up your
493 My fellow-p. now, Ye soon
231 Loose the souls long-prisoned
266 P. souls deliverance find

PRIZE.
92 Pressing onward to the p.
113 May we set out to win the p.
476 Dauntless to the high p. aspire
547 wings...To fly and take the p.
560 Oft I begin to grasp the p.
566 Waves before you glory's p.
577 Till, of the p. possessed, We
583 And take the glorious p.
594 'Tis his own hand presents the p.
501 That p., with peerless glories
640 Shall win so great a p.
627 To patient faith the p. is sure
687 In death our everlasting p.
688 To seize the everlasting p.
832 And laboring for the p. in heaven
983 The bliss unmixed, the glorious p.
1033 friends...have obtained the p.
1016 And keep the p. in view
1068 Press onward to the p.

PROCLAIM.
231 Throughout the world p.: The
825 Or send them to p. the word
841 Here their common faith p.
861 Here, when thy messengers p.
991 Thou dost thy Lord p.

PROCLAMATION.
1016 Let the glorious p.

PRODIGAL.
411 The p., with streaming eyes

PROFANE.
457 Henceforth may no p. delight

PROFIT.
285 The p. will be mine
672 No p. canst thou gain By

PROLONGS.
108 Thus far his power p. my days
319 While life p. its precious light
749 The Lord...P. thy feeble breath

PROMISE.
33 Lord, Wilt keep thy p. still
57 Never shall his p. fail
71 Where we thy parting p. claim
161 His p. all may freely claim
177 And found his p. true
282 We plead the p. of thy word
337 God's original p. this
361 And every p. in his word
391 light on some sweet p. there
393 Because thy p. I believe
395 The fullness of thy p. prove
479 Lord Is ever to his p. just
494 And let me now the p. prove
506 The p. is for me
522 Come, O my God, the p. seal
532 Thy faithful p. seal
529 The p. by thy mercy made
534 The faithful p. of the Lord
546 I called each p. mine
563 We have Christ's own p.
569 As true as God's own p. stands
595 Firm as his throne his p. stands
625 Does not the p. still remain
668 I believe...Thy every p. true
740 And none shall find his p. vain
828 He still the ancient p. keeps
876 The p. made to earliest youth
945 And p., in this sacred hour
1036 Forth to the land of p. bound
1050 The p. of that faithful word

PROMISES, PROMISED.
210 The precious p. are sealed
317 A thousand p. declare Thy
506 God hath kept His p. to men
709 And all his p. to plead
769 And thy rich p. in me fulfil
114 Lord, take me to my promised
1015 In thy bright and p. land

PROPHET, PROPHETS.
35 Our P., Priest, Redeemer, Lord
40 Not here, as to the p.'s eye
213 Great P. of our God
316 Jesus...My P., Priest, and King
843 Nor p. nor evangelist Preach
1073 With the p. we soar
10 Prophets and martyrs hear the
36 And p. praised with glowing
120 And p. crowned with light
218 foretold By p. in the days of old
225 P., psalmists, seers and sages
279 moved by thee The p. wrote
450 The way the holy p. went
595 Where p.' word, and martyrs'

821 P. and kings desired it long
912 Long by the p. of Israel foretold

PROSPECT, PROSPECTS.
930 Ceylon...Though every p. pleases
1051 O may the p. fire Our
747 Sweet *prospects*, sweet birds, and
1039 To brighter p. given

PROSPERS, PROSPERITY, PROSPEROUS.
436 He p. day by day His work
13 Thy saints in full *prosperity*
89 Zion, in all thy palaces, P.
163 brightly shines the *prosperous*
722 Save us in the p. hour

PROSTRATE.
139 P. before thy face we fall
147 By p. spirits day and night
147 P. before thy throne to lie
340 Your Redeemer p. lies
369 P. I'll lie before his throne
380 P. at thy feet I fall
394 My soul before Thee p. lies
653 Falling p. at his feet
674 cleave to thee, Though p. in the
1069 P. on their faces fall

PROTECT, PROTECTS, PROTECTED.
624 P. me through my life's short
678 Still p. me with thy love
931 P. them from all harm
1089 P. us by thy might, Great God
1108 P. them wheresoe'er they go
170 Jesus *protects*; my fears, be gone
651 The Lord p., forever near
772 So God p. and covers them
1097 Thy providence *protected* them

PROTECTING, PROTECTION.
71 O Saviour, with p. care
360 Seek his p. care by night
616 While thee I seek, p. Power
790 Us into thy *protection* take
987 P. they may find in thee
1101 Thy kind p. still implore
1109 Under thy p. we Our souls

PROVE.
323 Come, then, and p. its virtues too
433 O may I to the utmost p. The
472 I wait thy perfect will to p.
488 Let me live and die to p. Thine
525 I wait to p. thy perfect will
541 But can it be that I should p.
783 And seek that grace to p.
789 The gift...We all delight to p.

PROVERB.
705 A p. of reproach—and love

PROVIDE, PROVIDER, PROVISION.
141 The Lord will p.
175 Will here all good p.
1083 God, our Maker, doth p.
164 Thy great *Provider* still is near
826 The rich *provision* taste

PROVIDENCE.
27 Praise his p. and grace
148 For thy p., that governs
161 Behind a frowning p.
169 Thy ruling p. I see
174 Mysterious deeps of p.
179 O what shall I ask of thy p.
617 In thine all-gracious p.
664 A thousand ways has P.
745 Kept by watchful p.
933 His p. is leading, The
946 His p. hath brought us

PROVOKED.
379 Long p. him to his face

PUBLISH, PUBLISHES.
51 And p. abroad his wonderful name
201 Thee may I p. all day long
437 And p. to the sons of men The
802 P. we his praise below
138 And *publishes* in every land

PULSE.
376 Say not 'tis thy p. is beating
788 Derive its p. from thee, the heart
836 Yea, while a breath, a p. remains
965 And every beating p. we tell

PURCHASE, PURCHASED.
46 Take the dear p. of thy blood
275 The p. of our dying Lord
378 Take the dear p. of thy blood
411 Saviour, thy p. own
490 Take the p. of thy blood
833 To p. life and peace for you
924 The p. of thy passion claim
1003 Show the p. of his merit
124 His blood demands the *purchased*
330 the Lamb, who has p. our pardon
460 P. and saved by blood divine
547 crown He p. with his blood
826 Another Lord hath p. me

PURE.
46 And p., as thou thyself art pure
54 Full and p. for evermore
107 O may our hearts be p. within
131 Holy and p. is God alone
131 The rock of p., almighty love
205 Through thy cross made p. and
230 Our hearts be p. from evil
476 nothing in my soul...but thy p.
491 P. and spotless let us be
493 We shall in heart be p.
495 I cannot rest till p. within
501 Blest are the p. in heart
501 O give the p. and lowly heart
514 And p. as those above
614 sorrow...That make the spirit p.
656 Make and keep me p. within
762 my love to thee P., warm, and
807 love freely flow P. as life's river
837 O may thy p. and perfect love
884 Then, where the p. are dwelling
886 To show how p. and holy His
954 Ye p. in heart, obtain the grace
1071 I want to be as p. on earth

PURER, PUREST.

280 *P.* and worthier thee
389 How in thy *p.* eyes appear
291 Fill all my life with *purest* love
729 *P.* joys do daily bring

PURGE, PURGES, PURGED, PURGING.

425 *P.* my iniquity
668 blood... Which *purges* every stain
244 When he had *purged* our stains
775 Be *p.* from every sinful stain
983 no further test... Of *purging* fires

PURIFY, PURIFIES, PURIFIED, PURIFYING.

318 Inform the mind And *p.* the heart
446 A faith that *purifies* the heart
539 casts out sin And *p.* the heart
81 When grace has *purified* my heart
899 By grace restored and *p.*
1083 There, forever *p.*, In thy
425 Thy *purifying* blood apply, And

PURITY.

131 And when thy *p.* we share
147 power, And awful *p.*
280 Spirit of *p.* and grace
503 to impart the spotless *p.*
522 I want thy life, thy *p.*
527 Thy spotless *p.* bestow
545 Bless me with *p.* of heart
832 O God of grace and *p.*

PURPOSE, PURPOSES.

459 Mold every *p.* of the soul
564 Till each yearning *p.* spring
742 Be this my *p.* high To serve
161 His *purposes* will ripen fast

PURSUE.

878 Jesus help us to *p.*; Lead
950 With diligence may we *p.*

PURSUITS.

365 Vain man thy fond *p.* forbear
685 Whate'er *p.* my time employ

Q.

QUELL, QUELLS.

244 He all his foes shall *q.*
342 Fearful hearts, they *q.* your fears
604 No fears to *q.*, no soul to save
297 And *quells* our rising fears

QUENCH, QUENCHED.

511 And *q.* the kindling fire
633 Shall *q.* the spark divine
381 And *quenched* in death those
688 fiery dart, and *q.* with Jesus' blood
830 *Q.* from the soul's bright

QUICKEN, QUICKENS, QUICKENED.

270 *Q.* our souls, our guilt remove
668 *Q.* my mortal frame
101 And *quickens* all my drowsy
899 *Quickened* by thee, Be all their

QUICKENING.

7 O may thy *q.* voice
29 Father, thy *q.* Spirit send
35 To us thy *q.* power extend
86 Send forth thy *q.* breath
221 In us a *q.* spirit be
277 With all thy *q.* powers
285 feel Thy *q.* influence
406 O let me hear thy *q.* voice
432 Thy *q.* word shall raise
461 Till thou thy *q.* Spirit breathe
560 Lord, stir up thy *q.* power
835 And feel the *q.* Spirit move
972 Grant us the power of *q.* grace

QUIET.

291 When *q.* in my house I sit
982 A holy *q.* reigns around

R.

RACE.

68 Look down upon the human *r.*
278 salvation... Wide as the human *r.*
287 fill... With love to all our *r.*
810 Where'er the human *r.* is found
876 And turn the rising *r.*
885 Thou mightest save our *r.*
894 Saviour flew To bless a ruined *r.*
926 O lift ye up the fallen *r.*
943 favor To our ruined, guilty *r.*
1023 Then the Lord of all our *r.*

RACE. (to run.)

218 'Tis finished! yes, the *r.* is run
336 thee in darkness to finish thy *r.*
478 Uphold me in the doubtful *r.*
594 A heavenly *r.* demands thy zeal
594 Have I my *r.* begun
648 Patient the appointed *r.* to run
721 Till I close my earthly *r.*
758 So this is the *r.* I'm running
956 Many souls their *r.* have run
991 The battle's fought, the *r.* is won

RADIANT.

211 His head with *r.* glories crowned
253 That we may join that *r.* host
261 Wide unfold the *r.* scene

RAGE.

166 His *r.* we can endure
569 Dread not his *r.* and power
659 Then I can smile at Satan's *r.*
706 And envy *r.* in vain
812 'Midst all the *r.* of hell they stand
813 Yea, let men *r.*; since thou wilt
1047 How the powers of darkness *R.*
1101 And *r.*, and noise, and tumult

RAIMENT.

200 And watch thy glistering *r.* glow
1062 ten thousand in sparkling *r.*

RAIN, RAINS.

611 shining, To cheer it after *r.*
1080 The former and the latter *r.*

RAI   127   REA

1081 And sent the early *r*.
1084 The early and the latter *r*.
1086 And soft refreshing *r*.
354 The *rains* descend, the winds are

RAINBOW.
135 Our *r*. arch thy mercy's sign

RAMS.
389 Thousands of *r*. his favor buy

RUN.
54 May we *r*., nor weary be
606 And *r*. my course with even joy

RANSOM, RANSOMS.
35 A *r*. for our souls hath found
148 Came to *r*. guilty captives
215 'Tis done! the precious *r*.'s paid
219 Our *r*. thus is made complete
238 Thou hast for all a *r*. paid
312 Our *r*.-price be fully paid
333 Their *r*. from the death of sin
338 Justice owns the *r*. paid
378 My *R*. and my Peace
423 This blood is for thy *r*. paid
605 To him who for my *r*. died
743 My *r*. from the dreadful guilt
985 But Christ, my *r*., died
999 Whose God was thy *r*., thy
749 And *ransoms* thee from death

RANSOMED.
4 Ye *r*. sinners, sing
25 Let the *r*. thus rejoice
235 With him shall rise the *r*.
248 Ye *r*. from the fall
331 Return, ye *r*. sinners, home
347 Why, ye *r*. sinners, why
488 Nor let that *r*. sinner die
449 And all my *r*. powers combine
473 Thy *r*. servant, I Restore
493 Ye *r*. sinners, hear
694 Among the *r*. of thy grace
734 *R*., healed, restored, forgiven
842 Let all the *r*. sons of men
844 That our *r*. souls are thine
909 With songs thy *r*. shall return
927 O claim them for thy *r*. ones
930 Till o'er our *r*. nature
947 Join all ye *r*. sons of grace
990 Their *r*. spirits soar
1027 To take thy *r*. people home
1043 To thee the *r*. seed shall come
1060 Thy *r*. people raise

RAPTURE.
54 Sharing then in *r*. greater
83 My opening eyes with *r*. see
147 What *r*. will it be, Prostrate
789 What height of *r*. shall we know
842 With *r*. we lift up our head
1013 With what *r*. Gaze we on
1026 What will be the bliss and *r*.
1064 My fullness of *r*. I find
1071 All *r*. through and through
1073 By hope we the *r*. implore
1089 My heart with *r*. thrills

RAPTURES, RAPTURED, RAPTUROUS.
447 And tell its *r*. all abroad
705 And sweeter *r*. rise
823 forever live In *r*. or in woe
295 Saviour's face; Our *raptured*
66 every heart with *rapturous*
442 O the *r*. height Of that
1065 When, caught in the *r*. flame

RAVENS.
641 And he who feeds the *r*.

RAVISHED.
261 *R*. from our wishful eyes
542 It gives my *r*. soul a taste
721 Part from thee my *r*. soul
1032 Jesus... Before my *r*. eyes

RAY.
112 With every brightening *r*.
173 A *r*. of heavenly light appears
185 To clear the mental *r*.
422 Thine eye diffused a quickening *r*.
709 May its departing *r*. Be calm
913 day Sheds not its glorious *r*.
997 And with a *r*. of love divine
1100 casts her soft and hallowed *r*.

RAYS.
31 shine With never-fading *r*.
119 Thou shin'st with everlasting *r*.
201 At once he saw the pleasant *r*.
230 The Lord in *r*. eternal Of
613 Thy *r*. outshine the sun
837 Shines forth so full, so free, in *r*.
902 Whose cheering *r*. illume
1039 There *r*. divine disperse the

READY.
335 And now Christ is *r*. your
340 Jesus *r*. stands to save you
350 All things ready... come away
357 All things are *r*., Come
364 All things in Christ are *r*. now
535 Made *r*. in thy powerful day
543 *R*. prepared and fitted here
555 For each assault... *r*. may I be
884 All things are *r*., come away

REALM, REALMS.
211 Where the whole *r*. of nature
580 Meet for thy *r*. in heaven
765 Thee in thy glorious *r*. they
48 our eyes To those bright *realms*
65 In *r*. beyond the skies
137 Along the *r*. of upper day
191 From the highest *r*. of heaven
313 only way... To *r*. of endless day
661 Her portion in those *r*. of bliss
981 In those dark, silent *r*. of night
1067 High in yon *r*. of light
1068 To *r*. of endless peace

REAP, REAPS.
579 a tear, Shall *r*. with many a song
598 Would *r*. where they have strown
73 And *reaps* the fruit of all his

REAPER, REAPERS.
602 The r.'s song among the sheaves
933 Wide fields...Invite the r.'s toil
575 The angel *reapers* shall descend
598 More r. for white harvest fields
644 Only waiting, till the r.
644 Quickly, r., gather quickly

RE-ASCEND, RE-ASCENDS.
118 R., immortal Saviour
261 Christ...*Re-ascends* his native

REASON.
445 Unseen by r.'s glimmering ray
756 And that is just the r. I tell
890 For r.'s light divine, Quenched

REBEL, REBELS.
391 Let a repenting r. live
519 Still with the r. strive
917 Till not one r. heart remains
220 To bring us *rebels* back to God
325 For guilty r., lost in sin
371 stands His r. to receive
380 Worst of r. have I been
412 To redeem even r. like me
735 And speaks thy r. up to heaven
771 Till r. shall obey

REBELLIOUS, REBELLION.
146 To save r. worms
321 contrived a way To save r. man
390 For many long r. years
409 I feel *rebellion* still alive

REBUKE.
1114 R. the destroyer, Save, Lord

RECALL, RECALLS, RECALLED.
543 R. me by that pitying look
971 When God *recalls* his own
1006 God r. the precious loan
971 God has *recalled* his own

RECEIVE.
318 He would all the world r.
393 Just as I am—thou wilt r.
407 O that I could my Lord r.
469 Jesus, thine own at last r.
471 And soon with thee shall all r.
539 My heart would now r. thee
758 And when I'm to die R. me.
806 Let us still r. of thine
828 R. them, Lord, into thine arms
835 The tokens...O let us all r.
872 Thou hast promised to r. us
945 Thee...Let all our hearts r.
1007 Thou dost now with joy r. it

RECEIVED.
810 Freely from me ye have r.
904 Freely we have r. from thee

RECLINE.
510 with favored John, R. my weary
635 on thy care, Blest Saviour, I r.
754 I on his breast r.

RECONCILES, RECONCILED, RECONCILING.
311 Jesus' precious blood...r. to God
88 Show thy *reconciled* face
109 God and sinners r.
428 without a cloud...The Godhead r.
438 My God is r.; His pardoning
439 testify...In Jesus r.
440 thy child, Late in Jesus r.
1001 R. by grace below
219 That holy *reconciling* tide
291 O may the r. word
558 Speak the r. word
792 Speak but the r. word
804 By thy r. love, Every

RECOMPENSE.
602 Comes, day by day, the r.
904 And lo! his r. is sure
977 If heaven must r. our pains

RECORD, RECORDS, RECORDER.
32 And prove the r. true
337 O believe the r. true
291 Talk o'er the *records* of thy will
854 True *Recorder* of his passion

REDEEM, REDEEMS.
75 'Twas greater to r.
234 Born to r., and strong to save
407 Lord receive Who did the world r.
412 To r. even rebels like me
453 so good to r. The weakest
539 R. me from all sin
754 He doth my soul r.
898 Perhaps thou canst r.
936 Jesus, mighty to r.

REDEEMED.
188 Souls r. and sins forgiven
205 We in thee r., complete
510 The fullness which thy own r.
522 Ask...To be r. from sin
850 By Christ r., in Christ
967 R. from death, and grief, and
991 R. from earth and pain
1043 The Lord's r., their heads shall
1114 In thy strength, thy *redeemed*

REDEEMING.
42 thanks...For thy r. grace
52 Triumph in r. grace
84 R. grace and dying love
210 The great r. work is done
260 Love's r. work is done
319 R. love has been my theme
338 Love's r. work is done
350 The wonders of r. grace
438 His all-r. love, His
433 The depths of all-r. love
450 I'll point to thy r. blood
483 But rest in thy r. love
540 The greatness of r. love
761 His dear r. love
789 All praise to our r. Lord
794 Who rest in thy r. love
798 For his r. grace
798 our boast Of his r. power

RED 129 REI

818 Thine all-*r*. love
877 To seek *r*. grace
983 With praises of *r*. love

REDEEMER.
1 My great *R*. praise
8 Let the *R*.'s name be sung
14 *R*. come! I open wide
23 To that great *R*.'s praise
64 Come, great *R*., come
88 Through the dear *R*.'s name
186 Guide where our infant *R*.
206 Shines in my *R*.'s face
216 And my *R*. know
223 Your *R*.'s conflict see
242 I know that my *R*. lives
278 offering be To our *R*.'s name
299 Here the *R*.'s welcome voice
300 bed Where the *R*. lay
325 *R*., let me call thee mine
348 What could your *R*. do
355 O blest *R*., come
359 *R*., full of love, we would
367 To earth the great *R*. came
374 Jesus, *R*. of mankind
401 Gracious *R*., take, O take
424 conscience...In the *R*.'s blood
442 'Twas a heaven below My *R*.
512 I know that my *R*. lives
521 A heart...My great *R*.'s throne
681 And see my *R*. and die
697 Thou dear *R*., dying Lamb
733 My *R*. from all sin
757 My *R*. to know, to feel his
800 The slain, the risen Son, *R*.
801 Away to our *R*.'s breast
823 Their own *R*. see
861 Here will the world's *R*. reign
867 Here let the great *R*. reign
909 Again in thy *R*. trust
923 When our *R*. shall be known
927 Nor know they their *R*. nigh
947 And shout to the *R*.'s praise
991 Lodged...In thy *R*.'s breast
1003 To thy great *R*.'s breast
1012 We know the *R*. can save
1025 At his *R*.'s beck
1032 only bliss...In the *R*.'s breast

REDEMPTION.
148 For thy rich, thy free *r*.
271 And full *r*. bring
315 grace, Which in *r*. shine
330 And sing of *r*. forever and
331 *R*. in his blood
336 *R*. is purchased, salvation
467 And by *r*. thine
526 I seek *r*. through thy blood
792 Who seek *r*. in thy blood
843 *r*. cost, All our redemption won
928 And deem that our *r*.
940 And *r*., Freely purchased
952 And triumph in *r*. found

REED, REEDS.
254 The bruisèd *r*. he never breaks
901 wilt not break the bruisèd *r*.
487 Bruisèd *reeds* he ne'er will break

REFINE, REFINING.
396 Thy Spirit can from dross *r*.
496 Wash out its stains, *r*. its dross
518 *Refining* fire, go through my

REFRESH, REFRESHED, REFRESHING, REFRESHMENT.
52 O *r*. us, Traveling through
129 *R*. us with thy pleasant streams
646 O *r*. us Traveling through this
106 And hast *refreshed* me while I
769 They pass *r*. the thirsty vale
550 my soul...for...thy *refreshing*
176 And sweet *refreshment* find
813 Will still my sure *r*. prove

REFUGE.
67 Their common trust and *r*. see
158 O be that *r*. mine
168 God is our *r*. and defense
208 The sinner's *r*. here below
305 Our only *r*. is thy grace
333 This thought my *r*. still shall
341 Here the lost a *r*. find
386 But to thy wounds for *r*. flee
533 O let not this last *r*. fail
556 My help and *r*. in distress
656 Other *r*. have I none
678 Be my *r*. and my rest
679 To you, who for *r*. to Jesus
728 Precious Saviour, still our *r*.
773 God is the *r*. of his saints
871 A *r*. in distress
890 And to the *r*. flee
979 for me May such a blissful *r*. be
1098 Be thou her *r*. and her trust

REFUSE.
347 Will ye still *r*. to live
625 And thou *r*. that mourner's

REGARD.
371 Sinners, the voice of God *r*.
506 I want a true *r*., A single

REGIONS.
290 New *regions* blest, new powers
313 The *r*. of unclouded light
696 But *r*. none remote I call
727 In those high and holy *r*.
1000 All the *r*. of the sky

REGISTER, REGISTERED.
945 And *r*. our names on high
902 Forever *registered* above

REIGN.
6 Come, and *r*. over us, Ancient
52 *R*. with Christ in endless day
76 o'er his Church Eternally to *r*.
83 And *r*. sole monarch in my
148 Blessed be thy gentle *r*.
152 And he...For evermore shall *r*.
181 His *r*. on earth begun
184 His *r*. no end shall know
229 And *r*. in light
235 To *r*. in endless day
240 And *r*. through ages without end

9

256 They r. with him above
257 His r. shall know no end
320 Shall r. with him in heaven
334 Born to r. in us forever
476 And r. without a rival there
488 serve thee....below, And r. with
499 And in me live and r.
519 R. in me, Lord; thy foes control
621 And r., my Saviour, reign alone
919 Jesus shall r. where'er the sun
928 O come and r. o'er every land
930 Creator, In bliss returns to r.
966 to live And r. with thee above
993 To r. with thee on high
1016 When thou comest back to r.
1034 Where I shall r. with God

REIGNS.
17 And r. in glory there
66 Who r., and shall forever reign
134 He r.! ye saints, exalt your
142 The Lord Jehovah r.
183 Joy to the world! the Saviour r.
246 He r. supreme in heaven
256 He r. o'er earth and heaven
436 O'er all my mind be r.
507 Who r. in light above
521 Where Jesus r. alone
582 He ever r. the same
663 Who r. above the skies
1038 There God the Son forever r.
1069 Him who r. enthroned on high
1075 Who r. enthroned above
1077 The God who r. on high

REJECT, REJECTED, REJECTION.
706 foolish builders....R. it with
76 Christ is that Stone *rejected* once
853 In thy trial and *rejection*

REJOICE.
7 And bid our inmost souls r.
11 Come ye before him and r.
21 Let us all r. in thee
134 O earth, and all ye heavens, r.
219 In thee we will r.
241 R., the Lord is King
251 Ye sons of men, r.
287 And bid the mournful saint r.
332 To bid their hearts r.
419 This work shall make my heart r.
641 I cannot but r.
664 Shall in eternity r.
693 My soul shall still in God r.
711 When God has made the heart r.
712 stay, And bid my heart r.
742 O bid my heart r., Be thou
747 And makes all within me r.
757 And my heart doth r. at the
759 And in thee I will ever r.
801 R. with them that do rejoice
952 Let us r., give thanks, and sing

REJOICES, REJOICING.
296 My soul r. to pursue
4 Sing on, *rejoicing* every day
85 Welcome....And these r. eyes
905 And, r., self deny

RELEASE, RELEASES, RELEASED.
334 From our fears and sins r. us
368 Convince....And freely then r.
495 My heart from every sin r.
559 Speak, O speak the kind r.
613 I welcome the r.
943 Every burdened soul r.
1010 Who sent him calm r.
1033 And eager long for our r.
754 He from them all *releases*
22 There *released* from toil and pain
528 O that I now, from sin r.

RELENT, RELENTINGS.
329 Hearts of stone, r., relent
375 the Bridegroom will r. Too late
379 Kindled his *relentings* are

RELICS.
984 And give these sacred r. room

RELIEF.
241 He flew to my r.
302 soul obeys...And runs to this r.
304 amazing love! He ran to our r.
314 R. alone is found in Jesus'
320 His hand that brings r.
408 Thy sovereign grace can give r.
618 Send us down blest r.
674 Thy word can bring a sweet r.
688 My soul has often found r.
752 No words can tell what sweet r.

RELIEVE.
406 And all my wants thou wouldst r.
715 Shepherd Divine, our wants r.
872 Thou hast mercy to r. us

RELIGIOUS.
81 Let my r. hours alone
1021 live With what r. fear

RELY, RELYING, RELIANCE
359 We would on thee r.
523 Lord, if on thee I dare r.
648 Who would on thee alone r.
661 Courage, my soul! on God r.
672 Thou on the Lord r.
769 Who only will on thee r.
771 Our souls on thee r.
727 Lord, on thee alone r.
639 Place on the Lord *reliance*

REMAINS.
519 Scatter the last r. of sin

REMEMBER.
75 Thus, Lord, while we r. thee
113 O may we all r. well
114 In mercy, Lord, r. me
531 R., Lord, my sins no more
552 Yet will I r. thee
619 Dear Lord, r. me
660 My God, r. me
670 R. them, like her, through
833 And thus, my friends, r. me
836 I will r. thee
839 Meet and r. me

853 May we, Lord, *r.* thee
927 *R.* Lord, thy dying groans
961 Jesus, in death *r.* me
1102 *R.* not our sin's dark stain

REMEMBRANCE, REMEMBRANCER.
840 sacred sign To our *r.*
853 In *r.*, Lord, of thee
854 Come, *Remembrancer* divine

REMISSION.
341 Here the guilty, free *r.*

REMNANT.
285 The *r.* of our days
419 And fill the *r.* of my days
962 And spend the *r.* to thy praise

REMORSE.
344 In *r.* for guilt who mourn

REMOVE.
28 Come quickly...Nor ever hence *r.*
113 And we from time *r.*
114 mine eyes Since thou wilt not *r.*
401 possess...Nor hence again *r.*
482 Whence it may ne'er *r.*
483 Never will I *r.* Out of
483 like thee, Before I hence *r.*
751 I cannot live if thou *r.*
757 this prove, till w.th joy I *r.*
963 But all, before they hence *r.*
991 And bade thee suddenly *r.*
1020 despair To see my God *r.*
1065 O when shall we sweetly *r.*

REND, RENDS.
215 The solid marbles *r.*
311 Thou, by thy voice, the marble *r.*
413 O that thou wouldst the heavens *r.*
224 See! it *rends* the rocks asunder

RENDER.
467 What shall I *r.* to my God
883 But shall we only *r.* The

RENEW.
86 Our failing strength *r.*
264 Life divine in us *r.*
476 Hourly within my soul *r.*
482 And all my soul *r.*
503 My fallen soul *r.*
505 Almighty to *r.*
709 The prospect doth my soul *r.*
916 When thou shalt all *r.*

RENEWS, RENEWED.
686 And keep till he *r.* my heart
245 Till all the earth, *renewed*
292 In souls *r.* and sins forgiven
521 A heart in every thought *r.*
536 And all *r.* I am

RENOUNCE, RENOUNCING.
647 Here would we *r.* them all
708 And thus, when we *r.* for thee
371 *Renouncing* every sin
685 *R.* every worldly thing

REPENT, REPENTING.
311 O that I could *r.*
365 *R.*, thine end is nigh
375 No light had we;—for that we do *r.*
379 Now incline me to *r.*
404 O that I could *r.*
391 Let a *repenting* rebel live

REPENTANCE, REPENTANT.
189 Sinners wrung with true *r.*
340 True belief and true *r.*
368 *R.* unto life bestow
410 tears Which from *r.* flow
414 With deep *r.* I'll return
558 *R.* to impart
412 And early, with *repentant* tears
449 Gave my *r.* soul to prove
723 When, *r.*, to the skies

REPORT.
590 Help us, through good *r.* or ill

REPOSE.
82 draw from Christ that sweet *r.*
92 All things tell of calm *r.*
92 Till in heaven our souls *r.*
97 May we with calm and sweet *r.*
105 O let my soul on thee *r.*
110 And wearied nature seeks *r.*
116 an evening blessing, Ere *r.* our
477 Inly I sigh for thy *r.*
477 When it hath found *r.* in thee
776 What can shake thy sure *r.*
807 Our hearts will ne'er *r.*
979 A calm and undisturbed *r.*
980 To sink into that soft *r.*
986 And share thy long *r.*
990 O be like theirs my last *r.*
993 And wake in glorious *r.*
1052 But pure *r.* and love
1055 To sweet *r.* in heaven
1067 Calm and undisturbed *r.*

REPRIEVE.
951 Indulged another kind *r.*
968 While God prolongs the kind *r.*

REPROACH.
619 for thy sake, upon my name *R.*
814 All hail, *r.*; and welcome, pain

REPROBATES.
451 Hast made the *r.* thine

REPROVE.
432 Thou never wilt *r.*
511 If I stray...that moment, Lord, *r.*
586 With meekness to *r.*

REQUEST.
504 Grant, then, this one *r.*

REQUIRE, REQUIRES.
457 This, only this, will I *r.*
489 Nothing more can we *r.*
494 Thee I restlessly *r.*
537 What more s' all I *r.*
508 The sole return thy love *requires*

RESCUE, RESCUES, RESCUED.
207 second Adam... to the r. came
381 Lover of souls! to r. mine
541 And r. this poor soul of mine
681 Appear, to my r. appear
753 Swift to my r. come
1074 troubles... come to our r., and
734 *Rescues* us from all our foes
118 *Rescued* from our misery

RESERVE.
161 Without r. give Christ your heart

RESIDE, RESIDES, RESIDING, RESIDENCE.
499 And in my heart r.
748 I long to r. where thou art
1066 God *resides* among his own
189 God with man is now *residing*
751 If God his *residence* remove

RESIDUE.
473 Myself, my r. of days, I
946 Our r. of days or hours

RESIGN.
60 May we our wills r.
128 Our flesh, soul, spirit, we r.
155 And when our spirits we r.
389 Though I to thee the whole r.
392 Here, then, to thee I all r.
397 Here, then, to thee I all r.; To
401 My friends, my all, r.
462 Gladly I all for thee r.
469 Our souls and bodies we r.
537 Come as thou wilt, I that r.
654 I wou'd my all r.
961 I shall into thy hands r.
1042 What sinners value I r.

RESIGNED.
464 To thy gracious will r.
521 A heart r., submissive, meek
615 Be every wish r.
616 *R.* when storms of sorrow lower
747 My all to his pleasure r.

RESIGNATION.
632 Calm r. we implore

RESOLVE, RESOLVED.
369 And make this last r.
369 I can but perish... am *resolved* to
462 *R.* to seek my all in thee
737 To know It now r. I am

REST.
45 The hour that yields the spirit r.
72 We reach the r. remaining
78 But there's a nobler r. above
81 Sweet is the day of sacred r.
82 Is the dear pledge of glorious r.
90 Emblem earnest of the r.
103 Fit us for perfect r. above
109 Here find the r. of God's own
113 Upon our beds to r.
114 Lord, take me to thy promised r.
280 heart Wherein to fix his r.
281 And give the weary r.
284 *R.*, which the weary know
331 Let us find our r. in thee
344 *R.*, eternal, sacred, sure
358 O where shall r. be found
359 O come, and I will give you r.
370 Regain thy long-sought r.
380 Give the weary wanderer r.
491 Let us find that second r.
495 *R.* for my soul I long to find
500 To die is endless r.
513 Lord, I believe a r. remains
513 O that I now the r. might know
513 To me the r. of faith impart
524 Take us into thy people's r.
528 Enter into the promised r.
531 Jesus, the sinner's r. thou art
534 A perfect r. from sin
568 Nor dream of peaceful r.
572 O r. at Jesus' feet
627 There is a day of sunny r.
636 surges rise And r. delay to come
643 Heaven will bring me sweeter r.
647 Seek our only r. in Jesus
652 Come... and I will give you r.
663 Bid us to seek a purer r.
718 Lord, I come to thee for r.
845 weary ones... Enter on their r.
857 May thy Spirit here give r.
879 Each one entering into r.
971 And entered into r.
982 When sinks a weary soul to r.
983 Enter into immediate r.
994 *R.* for the toiling hand
1001 Jesus is their endless r.
1006 child... to early r. is gone
1011 His r. he hath sooner obtained
1032 And find its long-sought r.
1039 There is an hour of peaceful r.
1045 Possess the promised r.
1052 For here the soul shall find its r.
1055 And is there, Lord, a r.
1065 O when shall we enter our r.
1070 *R.* comes at length, though life
1071 Who doth not crave for r.
1071 Who would not be at r. and free

Eternal REST.
73 The type of heaven's *eternal r.*
400 soul return... To her *eternal r.*
753 turn again To my *eternal r.*
801 Away to our *eternal r.*
816 return To our *eternal r.*
1059 Short toil, *eternal r.*

Everlasting REST.
61 provides An *everlasting r.*
178 to find An *everlasting r.*
512 bliss And *everlasting r.*
540 find in thee My *everlasting r.*
542 peace And *everlasting r.*
1024 to secure An *everlasting r.*

Heavenly REST.
101 And one their *heavenly r.*
659 In sons of *heavenly r.*
887 Bring them to thy *heavenly r.*
1058 And claim my *heavenly r.*

My REST.

170 Who, who shall violate *my r.*
456 Here will I set up *my r.*
533 Forever here *my r.* shall be
636 *My r.* in toil, my ease in pain
998 There sweet be *my r.* till he bid

Of REST.

72 O day *of r.* and gladness
72 graces...From this our day *of r.*
85 Welcome, sweet day *of r.*
86 This is the day *of r.*
362 It tells me of a place *of r.*
549 return, Sweet messenger *of r.*
1000 Welcome to a land *of r.*
1008 Rise to thy home *of r.*
1030 The land *of r.*, the saints' delight
1058 bring us To that dear land *of r.*

Thy REST.

82 Return, my soul, enjoy *thy r.*
236 And lead us to *thy r.*
388 There, sweet shall be *thy r.*
487 Turn again to God, *thy r.*
681 And gather me into *thy r.*
1008 Go to *thy r.*, fair child

REST, (verb.)

88 May we *r.* this day in thee
113 O may we in thy bosom *r.*
408 Our spirits *r.* in thee
426 Come unto me and *r.*
436 Here I can firmly *r.*
447 Now *r.*, my long-divided heart
548 *R.* in thee and be still
616 That heart will *r.* on thee
617 Author of good, we *r.* on thee
633 And *r.* upon his name
638 They *r.* in perfect love
638 And let us *r.* before thy throne
661 Nor can they *r.* below
745 *R.* in him, securely rest
787 My weary soul would *r.*
843 Here we would *r.* midway
957 And we shall be with those that *r.*
967 For them that *r.* in thee
984 *R.* here, blest saint, till from
988 Fair spirit, *r.* thee now
992 *R.* from thy labor, rest
1040 But now from all their labors *r.*
1115 *R.*, on thee alone reclined

I REST.

500 In thy blest love *I r.*
541 *I r.* in thine almighty power
613 how blest...When in thy love *I r.*

To REST.

102 my last thought, how sweet *to r.*
291 Oft as I lay me down *to r.*
646 Bid us in thine arms *to r.*
681 And give me *to r.* from all sin
748 There only I covet *to r.*

RESTING-PLACE.

388 But not a *r.-p.* above
426 I found in him a *r.-p.*
888 Let them find a *r.-p.*

986 Then shall we seek thy *r.-p.*
1052 God, Thy holy *r.-p.*

RESTLESS.

153 Thou *r.* globe of golden light
364 Ye *r.* wanderers after rest
388 O cease...On *r.* wing to roam
535 My *r.* soul cries out, oppressed
537 That still my soul may *r.* be
550 Why *r.*, why cast down, my
675 I would not have the *r.* will

RESTORE.

156 My soul he doth *r.* again
290 Flow to *r.*, but not destroy
398 Art willing to *r.* them now
409 And now my soul *r.*
473 I *R.* to thee thine own
557 Again my soul *r.*
676 Almighty to *r.*
680 To which thou shalt *r.* us
759 *R.* and defend me, for thou
761 with sweet accord The lost *r.*
767 God, thy God, will now *r.* thee
974 Its glory shall *r.*
999 took thee, and he will *r.* thee
1015 To *r.* me to my home
1099 *R.* and quicken, soothe and

RESTORES, RESTORED.

179 *R.* me when wandering
103 *Restored* to life, and power, and
259 How the lost may be *r.*
491 Perfectly *r.* in thee
558 Let me be by grace *r.*
789 And bids us, each to each *r.*
904 For more than all shall be *r.*
1085 when we wandered *R.* us

RESTRAIN, RESTRAINED, RESTRAINING.

813 The Spirit's course in me *r.*
1084 Should thine altered hand *r.*
1102 The wrath of sinful man *r.*
967 *Restrained* from passionate
678 *Restraining* me from sin

RESURRECTION.

225 Sing the *r.* song
230 The day of *r.!* Earth
230 in rays eternal Of *r.* light
232 This *r.*-day
232 Joy in his *r.* take
600 His *r.'s* power declare
665 To know thy *r.* power
829 partake Of *r.* life
853 In thy glorious *r.*
1039 We feel the *r.* near

RETREAT.

553 This only safe *r.*
684 There is a calm, a sure *r.*
713 The calm *r.*, the silent shade
973 In this our last *r.*
1055 nor ever roam From...serene *r.*

RETRIBUTION.

1059 O happy *r.*

RETURN.

315 Hasten, sinner, to *r*.
362 *R.*, ye weary wanderers, home
370 *R.*, O wanderer, return
400 When shall my soul *r*.
458 God of my life, what just *r*.
491 Suddenly *r.*, and never
512 Thou wilt *r.* and claim me
548 glad To see thy child *r*.
549 *R.*, O holy Dove, return
553 Hast thou not said, *R.*
554 Yet mercy calls, *R.*
621 *R.*, my soul, to God, thy rest
686 *R.*, and walk in Christ, thy Way
814 Thus shall meet till his *r*.
1006 but he Never shall *r.* to me
1068 Soon our Saviour will *r*.

RETURNING.

420 *R.* sinners to receive
647 Waiting for our Lord's *r*.
706 Prayer... *R.* whence it came
710 sinner's voice, *R.* from his
1015 On his bright *r.* way

REVEAL.

7 But O thyself *r*.
18 Here to our hearts thyself *r*.
19 Jesus, thyself in us *r*.
30 But O thyself *r*.
39 Father, in us thy Son *r*.
435 *R.* the things of God
455 More and more thyself *r*.
481 Still to my soul thyself *r*.
494 Son of God, thyself *r*.
515 Come, O my God, thyself *r*.
522 Now to my waiting soul *r*.
712 Talk with us, Lord, thyself *r*.
737 Wilt thou not yet to me *r*.
791 Jesus, attend; thyself *r*.
868 And *r.* to each heart its
1005 Where Jesus is pleased to *r*.

REVEALS, REVEALED, REVEALING.

303 Till he his glorious self *r*.
597 worlds... *Revealed* and ruled by
943 Come, and, by thyself *revealing*

REVERE.

604 That I no more *r.* his name

REVERENCE, REVEREND.

38 A solemn *r.* checks our songs
151 Ye sons of earth, in *r.* bend
328 And joy and *r.* filled the place
866 True wisdom is with *r.* crowned
972 The tall, the wise, the *reverend*

REVIVE, REVIVES, REVIVED, REVIVING.

508 Turn, and *r.* us, Lord, again
771 O Lord, thy work *r*.
977 *R.* with ever-during bloom
234 Jesus, the dead, *revives* again
294 *R.* my heart and cheeks my fear
662 life.. *r.* and springs again
428 *Revived*, and cheered, and blest
85 Welcome to this *reviving* breast

REVOKES.

189 Justice now *r.* the sentence

REVOLT.

379 Now my soul *r.* deplore

REWARD.

49 Art our exceeding great *r*.
319 Nor me a blood-bought, free *r*.
494 My exceeding great *r*.
565 Never yield... Your divine *r*.
607 Rich *r.* he offers free
609 I find his service my *r*.
609 Till they gain their full *r*.
816 And lo! we see the vast *r*.
897 They lose not their *r*.
902 Shall meet a sure *r*.
954 Made ready for your full *r*.
990 Like theirs my last *r*.
991 remove To thy complete *r*.

RICH, RICHER, RICHNESS.

158 How *r.* a lot is thine
175 While Christ is *r.*, can I be poor
357 Come, *r.* and poor, come, old and
452 The *r.* in flattering riches trust
234 A thousand drops of *richer* blood
755 Though poor, I shall be *r*.
932 Nor in thy *richness* stay

RICHES.

299 Exhaustless *r.* find
329 True *r.*, and immortal praise
335 In *r.*, in pleasures, what can
356 *R.* unsearchable in Jesus'
540 Its *r.* are unsearchable
822 taste... The *r.* of his grace
828 extends The *r.* of his grace

RIGHT.

469 His sovereign *r.* assert
475 Thou only hast done all things *r*.
502 witness... That all I do is *r*.
596 But *r.* is right, since God is God
596 And *r.* the day must win
606 Thee will I set at my *r.* hand
631 Shall I be found at thy *r.* hand
680 see thee stand at God's *r.* hand
694 And set me then upon thy *r*.
1018 Our Lord, who now his *r*.
1058 To diadem the *r*.
1058 Let *r.* to wrong succeed

RIGHTEOUS.

278 Where all the *r.* go
310 Not the *r.*—Sinners Jesus
418 Now *r.* through thy grace I
966 And suffer all thy *r.* will
982 How blest the *r.* when he dies

RIGHTEOUSNESS.

50 judge... In truth and *r*.
98 guide my feet in ways of *r*.
156 Within the paths of *r*.
164 Let him his *r.* impart
183 The glories of his *r*.
245 earth, renewed in *r*.
268 The earth in *r.* renew

355 Let him that thirsts for r.
378 The Lord, my R.
385 boast, Their works of r.
422 And clothed in r. divine
443 But the r. of faith
446 We have no outward r.
452 The Lord, my R., I praise
475 Glad to fulfill all r.
486 Cut it short in r.
487 Fill with all his r.
515 The glorious crown of r.
522 Thy r. brought in
542 There dwells the Lord, our R.
570 On thee, bright Sun of r.
665 In r. complete
739 The Sun of r. on me
743 I'd sing his glorious r.
761 lead In paths of r.
822 His only r. I show
841 put on The r. of God
915 Before him R. shall go
934 In r. to reign
937 R., and joy, and peace
966 And wake to r.
1004 Thine the r. of God
1019 Shall stand in Jesus' r.
1042 And stand complete in r.
1076 The Lord our R., Triumphant

RISE.

41 Yea, and before we r. To
113 And when we early r., And
212 loosed from flesh and earth, I r.
223 Saviour, teach us so to r.
229 Rise, glorious Conqueror,
231 third morning, r., my buried
337 R. into the life of God
376 'Tis thy Saviour...R., and let me
440 R. eternal in my heart
464 R. with him to live with God
514 wait, Till thou shalt bid us r.
519 That I with thee may r.
557 Wilt thou not bid me r.
947 Thither he bids us r.
995 my dust, Till he shall bid it r.
1000 Rests in hope again to r.
1015 R., my soul, from sleep awaking
1029 R. to life from earth and sea
1051 How would our spirits long to r.
1088 invitation, And fain would r. and

RISING.

877 And turn the r. race

RISEN.

223 Christ is r.; he meets our
226 Yes, the Lord has r. to-day
227 For Jesus hath r., and man
230 For Christ the Lord hath r.
232 Thy Lord has r. long
233 Proclaim, The Lord is r. indeed
235 The Lord is r. indeed
237 Our Lord is r. from the dead
259 Christ, the Lord, is r. again
260 Christ, the Lord, is r. to-day
272 My r. Lord, for aye were lost
600 If r., indeed, with him ye are
829 A r. Lord our trust

RITE, RITES.

833 He left his death-recording r.
837 grace! Which in this sacred r.
848 In the r. thou hast enjoined
830 Rites cannot change the heart

RIVAL.

476 And reign without a r. there
718 And without a r. reign

RIVER, RIVERS.

168 There is a r. pure and bright
255 Joys like a r. come
504 Flows the gladdening r.
930 From many an ancient r.
41 There, from the rivers of his
180 Where peaceful r., soft and slow
326 R. of love and mercy here
389 R. of oil, and seas of blood
679 The r. of sorrow shall not
888 Drink the r. of thy grace
998 Where the r. of pleasure flow
1032 R. of life divine I see
1068 R. to the ocean run

ROAD.

321 To tread the heavenly r.
530 Shall aught beguile me on the r.
549 So purer light shall mark the r.
573 lead...family in the celestial r.
699 length of the celestial r.
1040 O may we tread the sacred r.

ROAM, ROAMED.

434 I loved afar to r.
434 I seek no more to r.
909 Where'er they rest or r.
1018 While through this world we r.
1054 from thy presence in sadness I r.
1055 And live and love, nor ever r.
344 Long hast roamed the barren

ROBE, ROBED, ROBES.

133 To form a r. of light divine
140 Whose r. is the light, whose
650 When, robed in majesty and
1024 When, r. in majesty and power
1032 They all are r. in spotless
322 Lays his bright robes of glory by
593 In robes of victory through the
1007 Clothed in r. of spotless
1046 In r. of white arrayed
1049 All holy in their spotless r.
1061 Are clad in r. of white
1066 Washed their r. by faith below
1069 All in whitest r. arrayed

ROCK.

131 Established on the r. of peace
131 The r. that never shall remove
311 The r. in sunder cleave
317 thy mercies...A r. that cannot
362 See from the R. a fountain rise
421 On Christ, the solid r., I stand
678 As a great r. extends its shade
732 From the stricken R. are flowing
748 To lie at the foot of the r.

764 Built on a *R.*, with idle rage
766 Yet on this *R.* the Church
992 We gather round our *R.*
1053 On the *r.* of the shore of death
1108 From *r.* and tempest, fire and foe

ROCK *of ages.*
170 What can the *R. of ages* move
415 *R. of ages*, cleft for me
633 Be thou, O *R. of ages*, nigh
750 At noon, beneath the *R. of ages*
776 On the *R. of ages* founded
1019 Stand, as the *R. of ages*, sure
1060 Upon the *R. of ages* They

ROCKS, ROCKY.
233 Vainly with *r.* his tomb was
304 O for this love let *r.* and hills
396 The *r.* can rend; the earth can
1014 Men on *r.* and mountains calling
1089 My native country...I love thy *r.*
1089 Let *r.* their silence break, The
1109 *R.*, and storms, and deaths defy
957 On this wild *rocky* shore

ROD.
3 Nor dare provoke his *r.*
156 For thou art with me, and thy *r.*
177 How gentle was the *r.*
179 Thy *r.* shall defend me, thy staff
310 We sink beneath his *r.*
478 Or smile, thy scepter or thy *r.*
667 Beneath the chastening *r.*
761 My failing flesh his *r.* Shall
939 Take the wonder-working *r.*

ROOF.
863 He hung its starry *r.* on high
865 Beneath this *r.*, O deign to show

ROOM.
361 his word Declares there yet is *r.*

ROOT, ROOTED, ROOTING.
301 May it take *r.* in every heart
803 *R.* out every seed of ill
953 Then dig about the *r.*
518 *Rooted* and fixed in God
489 *Rooting* out the seeds of sin

ROSE, ROSES, ROSY.
875 The *r.* that blooms beneath the
977 And sweeter than the virgin *r.*
1008 Fresh *roses* in thy hand
373 Our eyes have seen the *rosy* light

ROUGH, ROUGHER.
213 And the *r.* way that thou hast
496 If *r.* and thorny be the way
509 Though *r.* and strait the road
1074 The *rougher* the way, the shorter

ROUSE.
509 The thought of God will *r.*
890 *R.* them to shun that dreadful

ROVE, ROVING.
868 And *r.*, my soul, no more
519 Then shall my feet no longer *r.*

554 And let me *r.* no more
712 While here o'er earth we *r.*
753 Suffered no more to *r.*
321 Grace taught my *roving* feet
554 How oft my *r.* thoughts depart

ROYAL, ROYALLY.
248 Bring forth the *r.* diadem
842 Table spreads, How *r.* is the
914 The praises of thy *r.* name
152 Full *royally* he rode

RUIN, RUINED.
169 I ever into *r.* run But
570 Nor fear the *r.* spread below
890 Mourn for the *ruined* soul
1019 And on that *r.* world look

RULE, RULES.
6 Now *r.* in every heart
50 Shall thy just *r.* confess
334 *R.* in all our hearts alone
485 *R.* here, Lord, and rule alone
891 This blessed *r.* to keep
183 He *rules* the world with truth and
244 He *r.* o'er earth and heaven
630 He *r.* the seraph and the worm

RULER.
280 Sovereign *R.*, Lord of all
931 O thou eternal *R.*
1020 Thou *R.* of my heart
1090 *R.* of wind and wave
1101 Great *R.* of the earth and

RULEST, RULETH, RULING.
673 What though thou *r.* not
51 God *ruleth* on high, almighty to
673 And *r.* all things well
616 Thy *ruling* hand I see

RUN, RUNS, RAN.
54 May we *r.*, nor weary be
606 And *r.* my course with even
302 soul obeys...And *runs* to this
304 He ran to our relief

S.

SABAOTH.
166 Lord *S.* is his name

SABBATH.
75 The Lord of *S.* let us praise
78 Lord of the *S.*, hear our vows
80 Sweet is the light of *S.* eve
80 The endless *S.* of our God
82 Another *S.* is begun
82 How sweet a *S.* thus to spend
87 Hail to the *S.* day
87 Thy *S.*, the stupendous march Of
92 Twilight ray Of the holy *S.* day
92 At the holy *S.'s* close
92 Where the *S.* ne'er shall close
349 No *S.'s* heavenly light shall rise
513 The *S.* of thy love

534 The true eternal S. see
1044 And S. has no end

SABBATHS.
78 Thine earthly S., Lord, we love
88 Thus may all our S. prove
92 Saviour, may our S. be
1082 And circling S. bless our

SABBATIC.
946 And bring the grand S. year

SACRAMENTAL.
831 The s. seal apply
833 To crown the s. feast

SACRIFICE.
43 nor cast away The s. we bring
46 Grateful, accepted s.
47 Ceaseless, accepted s.
78 And own as grateful s.
99 Our evening s.
103 God will provide for s.
106 To pay thy morning s.
110 My morning s. I bring
210 Accomplished is the s.
211 I s. them to his blood
223 God's own s. complete
243 conscience needs No s. beside
250 A s. for guilty man
339 Made his soul a s.
364 That precious, bleeding s.
372 Accept the grateful s.
381 That made thy soul a s.
417 By thy one great s.
438 The bleeding S. In my behalf
467 Offer the s. of praise
471 Jesus, accept our s.
474 A holy, living s.
483 bring Our s. of praise
508 Our s. receive
562 And make the s. complete
592 or do, Is one great s.
708 Poor is our s., whose eyes
723 O'er the dreadful s.
794 Our s. of praise approve
800 Our S. is one
836 O Lamb of God, my S.
846 And share his s.
919 With every morning s.
920 Vain s. for human guilt
946 powers A s. to thee
951 A living s. divine
1095 Accept the s. we bring
1113 that life, Thy s. shall be

SACRIFICIAL.
306 And in that s. blood

SAD, SADDEN, SADDENED, SADNESS.
302 How s. our state by nature is
426 Weary, and worn, and s.
652 come... When the s. heart is weary
929 scene, That makes us *sadden*
267 Cheer this *saddened* heart of
265 Holy Ghost, dispel our *sadness*

652 Come unto me... who droop in s.
1095 the scene Of s. and of dread

SAFE.
116 We are s. if thou art nigh
158 There is a s., a secret place
169 And s. beneath thy wings to rest
170 S. in thy arms I lay me down
346 S. from all the lures of vice
625 And he is s., and must succeed
672 So, s., shalt thou go on
676 S. in thy sanctifying grace
762 O bear me s. above
1111 O keep them s. at Jesus' side

SAFELY, SAFETY.
242 He lives to bring me s. there
23 And all our souls in *safety* keep
394 Lead me where peace and s. reign
698 Or what's my s., or my health
1100 In s. through their dangerous

SAFEGUARD.
114 The s. of thy might

SAGES.
189 S., leave your contemplations

SAIL, SAILED.
636 Toward heaven we calmly s.
1114 When through the torn s. the
593 And *sailed* through bloody seas
1011 Who s. with the Saviour beneath

SAINT.
573 A s., indeed, I long to be
984 Rest here, blest s., till from

SAINTS.
46 O let us all be s. indeed
57 God hath made his s. victorious
66 And s. on earth, with saints
200 Those glorious s. of other days
225 S. all longing for their heaven
253 The s. are at his feet
424 Dost thou not dwell in all thy s.
451 For this the s. lift up their voice
467 Praise him, ye s., the God of
563 treading Where the s. have trod
585 Nor all the s. in heaven
598 And prayers of s. were sown
619 Thou, with the s. at thy right
600 a place, Among thy s. a seat
666 How happy are the s. above
787 The s. on earth and all the dead
788 The s. below and saints above
799 The s. are blest above
847 And in thee thy s. shall rise
862 Where dwell thy s. before
870 Yet, Lord, where'er thy s. apart
870 Here, Saviour, deign thy s. to
946 appear To s. on earth forgiven
948 Awake, ye s., and raise your
949 the faith Which s. of old
954 With all his s. ascend
954 Shall soon the s. receive
983 The s. who die of Christ possessed
992 Go, take with s. thy place

998 Where the s. of all ages in
1004 S. in glory perfect made
1013 Thousand thousand s. attending
1027 Among thy s. let me be found
1034 There all the millions of his s.
1037 Where s. immortal reign
1040 The s. in countless myriads
1045 The s. above, how great their
1046 glorious company, When s.
1067 Dwell the raptured s. above
1069 S. and angels joined in one
1069 S. begin the endless song
1069 Next the s. in glory they
1093 S. and angels join to sing
1102 Where s. and angels dwell above

795 Thy power unto s. show
810 An'l teach them where s.
821 Who bring s. on their tongues
824 let the priests...put s. on
890 S.! O salvation! The
948 love That shows s. nigh
951 Unto s. wise, Oil in your
991 And still to God s. cry
991 S. to the Lamb
1083 To his uttermost s.
1026 King...Cometh with s.
1069 All s. from him came
1088 A sinner to s.
1097 To them s. gave
1097 From whom s. came

SAKE.
156 E'en for his own name's s.
547 We, for whose s. all nature stands
619 If, for thy s., upon my name
820 With every sin for thy dear s.
897 If given for the Saviour's s.
952 We can, O Jesus, for thy s.

SALEM'S.
234 Lo! S. daughters weep around
417 tears...Over S. lost abode
723 tears...Over S. loved abode

SALT.
564 flock of Jesus, S. of all the earth

SALVATION.
42 And cry, S. to our God
42 S. to the Lamb
51 Ascribing s. to Jesus, our King
58 Sweet the theme, a free s.
108 With sweet s. in the sound
165 S. to the Lord belongs
195 S. comes to-day
246 Thou didst free s. bring
262 Seal s. on my heart
312 S. in his name is found
314 This is s.'s only source
315 S. well deserves the praise
322 And pours s. down
323 S. like a river rolls
324 S.! O the joyful sound
326 S. in abundance flows
327 Of him who did s. bring
332 By which we can s. have
336 Redemption is purchased, s. is free
345 Ere s.'s work is done
359 thine arms...And find s. there
411 Life and s. bring
448 I taste s. in thy name
512 He brings s. near
535 Thou hear'st me for s. pray
569 S. shall for you arise
582 S., happiness, and heaven
626 The God of my s. praise
639 God is my strong s.
641 The theme of God's s.
686 The grace that sure s. brings
707 To bring s. down
763 We trust our whole s. here
771 O come, and bring s. near
777 You shall name your walls S.

Full SALVATION.
21 Full s. to each heart
388 With *full* s. blest
522 With *full* s. bless
643 Know, my soul, thy *full* s.
798 Preserved...To *full* s. here

Great SALVATION.
8 The *great* s. loud proclaim
278 And make the *great* s. known
451 To us the *great* s. brought
491 Let us see thy *great* s.
715 With all thy *great* s. bless
779 Make thy *great* s. known
854 Now reveal his *great* s.

His SALVATION.
5 And *his* s. ours
442 O that all *his* s. might see
871 How bright has *his* s. shone
883 When *his* s. bringing
1104 In *his* s. is our hope

Of SALVATION.
453 The day *of* s. that lifts up
775 The garment *of* s. take
912 Shouts *of* s. are rending the
932 Blest river *of* s.
943 Give the knowledge *of* s.
1012 The light *of* s. we trust

Our SALVATION.
57 Praise the God of *our* s.
72 On thee, for *our* s.
680 The praise of *our* s.
851 Author of *our* s., thee

Thy SALVATION.
13 Let *thy* s. visit me
431 Let *thy* s. roll
491 Visit us with *thy* s.
633 Who wait for *thy* s., Lord
697 And *thy* s. seek
720 O my God, how *thy* s.
1104 Till *thy* s. shall appear

SAME.
399 If still the s. thou art
734 Praise him, still the s. as ever
763 A thousand years the s.
782 The s. in mind and heart
1077 Who was and is the s.

SANCTIFY, SANCTIFIES, SANCTIFYING.
289 Diffuse...And s. the whole
470 All my actions s.
480 Send him our souls to s.
517 If thou my nature s.
518 And s. the whole
679 To s. to thee thy deepest distress
808 To s. thy people Through
924 seals Them one, and *sanctifies*
543 jealousy And *sanctifying* fear
795 And wait thy s. word

SANCTIFIED.
46 Present us s. to God
107 whose groans and tears Have s.
472 All s. by spotless love
482 And, s. by love divine
536 While s. by grace
784 lot With all the s.

SANCTITY, SANCTITIES.
482 Thy spotless s.
864 Hath one pervading s.
671 Baptized into the *sanctities*

SAND, SANDS.
421 All other ground is sinking s.
930 Roll down their golden s.
238 were sinners more Than *sands*

SARDIUS.
1060 The s. and the topaz

SATAN.
32 From sin and S.'s power
141 When S. appears to stop up
158 And S., roaring for his prey
185 prisoner to release, In S.'s
231 Loose souls...bound with S.'s
497 S. and sin are always near
526 S., with all his arts, no more
563 S.'s host doth flee
568 Till S.'s host is vanquished
570 Though sin and S. still are near
583 S., the world, and sin, tread down
584 Nor suffer S.'s deadliest strife
588 S. shall be subdued
624 Save me from sin and S.'s power
659 Then I can smile at S.'s rage
667 Nor S.'s arts beguile
677 Sin and S. I defy
689 The world, with sin and S.
690 And S. trembles when he sees
713 From scenes where S. wages
736 My light, in S.'s darkest hour
822 And bruises S.'s head
911 In vain is S.'s boast Of
918 Set up thy throne where S. reigns
923 Where S. long hath held his
928 Let S. from his throne be hurled
937 S. and his host, o'erthrown

SATANIC.
645 In that dark S. hour

SATISFY, SATISFIED.
509 Yet nothing less can s.
175 With this will I be *satisfied*

388 And every longing s.
741 Jesus has s.; Jesus is mine
794 eat Thy dainties, and be s.

SAVAGE.
919 And s. tribes attend his word

SAVE.
51 almighty to s.; And still he is
66 he bled, To s. us from eternal
116 Thou canst s., and thou canst heal
157 O s., in our distress we said
322 swiftly didst thou move To s.
349 And none be found to hear or s.
359 come...And I will s. you all
377 Thou canst...this moment s.
387 Jesus! hear and s.
391 Yet s. a trembling sinner, Lord
398 Art able now our souls to s.
415 Thou must s., and thou alone
417 By thy power the lost to s.
476 And s. me, who for me hast died
509 'Tis not enough to s. our souls
522 done! thou dost this moment s.
524 A world to s. from endless woe
541 Assured...through life wilt s.
543 Save. Jesus, or I yield, I sink
551 His arm...Is also strong to s.
556 Myself I cannot s.
678 To s. me in the trying hour
844 To his love who died to s.
886 The Lord came down to s. me
1005 We call on thee to s., Father
1046 But Christ will to the utmost s.
1075 And he shall s. me to the end
1092 S. us in mercy, O save us from
1113 Nor impotent to s.
1114 S., Lord, or we perish

SAVES, SAVEST.
218 Hail him who s. you by
740 He s. the oppressed, he feeds
796 Which s. us to the uttermost
154 Thou sav'st the souls whose
691 Thou s. those that on thee call

SAVED.
28 Yield to be s. from sin
319 Church of God Are s., to sin
331 And, s. from earth, appear
364 And freely now be s. by grace
374 Be s., be saved by grace
449 S. me when sinking in
450 Because I was not s. from sin
508 Made, and preserved, and s. by
535 nor will I rest, Till I am s.
746 Till thou art s. from sin
765 And s. by grace alone
820 He shall be s. who trusts

SAVING.
39 Thy s. power and love display
44 The sweetness of thy s. name
68 His s. name let all adore
236 O by thy s. power So
301 message, Lord, Its s. power may
374 Display thy s. power
485 The s. power, impart

651 Show forth in me thy s. power
865 Here, Lord, display thy s. power
890 And show his s. love

SAVIOUR.

26 S. of offending man
102 Sun of my soul, thou S.
258 Give us to the bleeding S.
270 Grant, S., what we more
322 The mighty S. comes
347 God, your S., asks you why
348 Now, e'en now, your S. stands
349 No S. call you to the skies
350 Ready your loving S. stands
381 Pass me not, O gracious S.
437 How can my gracious S. show
445 Save us, a present S. thou
450 What a dear S. I have found
495 S. of all, if mine thou art
514 S. from sin, we thee receive
522 My present S. thou
600 There your exalted S. see
643 What a S. died to win thee
719 He our loving S. is
731 Thus the risen S. whispers
742 S., who died for me, I
742 S., with me abide
762 Blest S., then, in love
794 S. of all, to thee we bow
795 And thee their utmost S.
807 Take us, dear S.
811 S. of men, thy searching eye
826 Thou, faithful S., bidd'st me
872 S., like a shepherd lead
872 Blessed Lord and only S.
888 S., who thy flock art feeding
896 She loved her S., and to him
916 To whom that S. came
934 Let all their bleeding S. know
936 Sons of God, your S. praise
941 S., sprinkle many nations
992 S., into thy hands Our
1000 Thus the mighty S. speaks
1029 Glorious S., Own me in
1031 There my exalted S. stands
1069 Each before his S. stands

My SAVIOUR.

209 My S.! every mournful word
212 Who, who, my S., this hath done
242 He lives, my S., still the same
412 Of my S. possessed, I was
447 On thee, my S. and my God
450 Till late I heard my S. say
531 O when wilt thou my S. be
635 'Tis to my S. I would live
643 They have left my S., too
713 My S.! thou art mine
713 glories... Which in my S. shine
996 Or with my S. dwell
1015 O my S., When wilt thou
1041 Apostles...Around my S. stand

Our SAVIOUR.

255 none like thee, Our S. and
561 To make our S.'s glory known
577 We follow .Our S. and our
648 And meet our S. in the skies

844 Since our S. broke the bread
843 Let us now our S. find

Thy SAVIOUR.

376 'Tis thy S. knocks, and cri'th
758 Rise, follow thy S., and bless

The SAVIOUR.

14 The S. of the world is here
187 But one alone the S. speaks
192 The S., who is Christ the Lord
195 The S. now is born
215 Behold the S. of mankind
299 And view the S. there
333 I know the S. died for me
343 Haste, O sinner, to the S.
361 The S. calls to-day
368 And to the S. turn
379 There for me the S. stands
398 And art thou not the S. still
533 For me the S. died
651 And shout to prove the S.
700 The S. of mankind
729 Christ, the S. of the lost
812 The S., when to heaven he
917 But over all the S. reigns
960 To meet the S. they adore
1003 Lo! the S. stands above

SAVIOUR'S.

18 And bless the S. precious name
58 Raising high the S. name
61 Help us to see the S. love
63 Come ye that love the S. name
169 fly But to my loving S. breast
277 Come, shed abroad a S. love
331 appear Before your S. face
457 In which my S. footsteps shine
561 To make our S. glory known
578 And wrap the S. changeless love
668 spread The common S. name
720 Sing our S. worthy praise
727 Loves her S. praise to show
783 And glorify our S. grace
823 And filled a S. had is
818 In memory of the S. love
841 All who bear the S. name
844 Which the S. death declare
846 The bleeding S. name
849 Water...From out the S. heart
854 All the S. dying merit
873 Nearer to our S. side
893 My S. voice is heard
897 If given for the S. sake
916 rejoice To hear a S. name
932 And seek the S. blessing
956 Fill us with a S. love
991 Thou seest thy S. face
1001 Place him at the S. feet
1018 And glory decks the S. face
1012 And in my S. linage rise
1077 Before the S. face

SCALES.

309 And make the s. of error fall

SCARS.

1013 Gaze we on those glorious s.

SCATTER, SCATTERS, SCATTERING.
489 S. all our guilty gloom
790 wolf...To s., tear, and slay
822 Jesus' name...*scatters* all our
384 blessing Thou art *scattering* full
943 S. all the night of nature

SCATTERED.
411 Unite my s. thoughts, and fix
778 And s. their legions, was
903 seeds...Have s. here below
911 And from that s. dust, Around
929 A s., homeless flock, till all

SCENES.
275 Thou didst such glorious s.
661 O happy s. above the sky

SCEPTER.
14 His s., pity in distress
243 Thy s. and thy sword, Thy
253 A palmy s. in each hand
257 Whose power a s. sways
268 And to thy s. all subdue
371 Bow to the s. of his word
917 Now wave the s. of thy reign
933 Thy s. shall obey
940 Sway thy s., Saviour, all

SCIENCE.
597 The worlds of s. and of art
866 And S. walks with humble feet

SCORN.
167 Thou didst not s. thine angel's
202 humbly bore The s., the scoffs
213 In love of thee and s. of self
342 Sinners, will you s. the message
344 Long hast thou borne...world's s.
356 Above your s. we rise
591 Then learn to s. the praise of men
592 Thou didst not s. our earthly
813 What, then, is he whose s. I
827 Nor s. their humble name
1078 Blest with the s. of finite good

SCORNS, SCORNED.
254 Nor s. the meanest name
677 Nobly *scorned* to bow the knee

SCOURGE, SCOURGED.
209 The s., the thorns, the deep
283 Sin has *scourged* me; bring me

SCREEN, SCREENED.
163 Be thoughts of thee a cloudy s.
645 S. me from the adverse power
678 And s. my naked head
748 And *screened* from the heat of

SCROLL.
938 He shall reign, when, like a s.
1017 shriveling like a parched s.
1033 Shriveling like a parched s.

SEA.
119 O God, of good the unfathomed s.
149 mercy, Like the wideness of the s.
174 Thy way is in the s., Thy paths
317 A vast, unfathomable s.
363 Life seems a dark and stormy s.
371 Like a rough s., that cannot rest
431 soon shall reach the boundless s.
613 Upon life's wildest s.
636 If, on a quiet s., Toward
858 While the s. shall gird the land
863 The s., the sky; and all was good
863 Lord, 'tis not ours to make the s.
908 From s. to sea, from shore to
930 Till, like a s. of glory, It
988 Or the fullness of the s.
958 torrent...That bears us to the s.
978 As, 'mid the ever-rolling s.
1019 And make the greedy s. restore
1019 The greedy s. shall yield her dead
1037 Death, like a narrow s., divides
1108 For those in peril on the s.
1110 And measured the depths of the s.
1112 Whose power the wind, the s.
1112 We own thy way is in the s.
1113 The s., that roars at thy command
1115 Bid them walk on life's rough s.

SEAS.
3 He gave the s. their bound
153 Shout to the Lord, ye surging s.
187 Once on the raging s. I rode
389 Rivers of oil, and s. of blood
396 The s. can roar; the mountains
659 bathe my weary soul in s. of
966 'Twixt two unbounded s. I stand
1035 The earth and s. are passed away

SEAMAN.
1114 Nor hope lends a ray the poor s.

SEAL.
51 Lord, from thy word remove the s.
128 And s. the abode forever thine
266 S. of truth, and Bond of union
383 The sinner's pardon s.
395 The s. of thine eternal love
401 O take And s. me ever thine
407 Mercy I ask to s. my peace
455 And s. me for thine own
460 And now I set the solemn s.
461 S. thou my breast and let me
480 And show and s. us ever thine
519 And s. me thine abode
559 Love me freely, s. my peace
562 Till death thy endless mercies s.
726 Here's my heart, O take and s. it
801 O may thy Spirit s. Our souls
829 the worth Of this the outward s.
831 The sacramental s. apply
848 S. our souls forever thine
988 His s. was on thy brow

SEALS, SEALED.
841 The Spirit s.; and faith puts on
841 *Sealed* when he was glorified
316 S., by signs the chosen know
837 By blood and suffering s.

SEAMLESS.
197 The healing of the s. dress

SEARCH, SEARCHING, SEARCHER.
97 eyes With strictest s. survey
291 And s. the oracles divine
295 O may we s. with eager pains
496 S., prove my heart, it pants for
496 O thou, to whose all-*searching*
79 But thou, soul-s. God! hast
811 Saviour of men, thy s. eye
402 *Searcher* of hearts, in mine Thy

SEASON, SEASONS.
699 Nor think the s. long
952 For us suffice the s. past
95 To turn the *seasons* round
561 Where are the happy s. spent
957 A few more s. come
1081 The rolling s., as they move
1085 By him the rolling s. In

SEAT.
15 O glorious s.! thou God, our
244 He took his s. above
245 High on his holy s., He bears
253 Jesus. Upon his heavenly s.
723 From thy s. above the sky, Hear
744 And ceaseless sing around thy s.
879 have reached that heavenly s.

SEATS, SEATED.
37 And take our s. at thy right hand
340 While the blissful s. of heaven
749 Till we take our s. above
1044 Blest s.! through rude and
1068 haste away To s. prepared above
246 *Seated* at thy Father's side
600 S. at God's right hand again
1114 Now s. in glory, the mariner

SECRET, SECRETS.
439 The s. of thy love reveal
441 A s. chord that mine will bear
453 Thy s. to me shall soon be made
501 The s. of the Lord is theirs
675 Or s. thing to know
737 The s. of thy love unfold
1021 Yes, every s. of my heart
1023 Every s. brought to light
123 sight surveys...The *secrets* of

SECTS.
806 Names, and s., and parties fall

SECURE.
158 He rests s. in God
169 S. within thine arms I lie
175 Who made my heaven s.,
418 Lord, how s. and blest are
595 And he can well s. What I've
635 S. of having thee in all
669 In thy tabernacle hide, S.
795 S. I am while thou art mine
772 His faithful people stand s.
773 S. against a threatening hour
807 S. from worldly woes
888 Only there s. from harm
941 the shadow...may we dwell s.
969 I stand, S., insensible
972 And are we still s.

1025 Rests s. the righteous man
1076 He keeps his own s.

SECURES, SECURED, SECURELY.
141 Yet one thing s. us, whatever
123 *Secured* by sovereign love
97 thy wings shall they *securely*
176 His saints s. dwell
1056 fabric...It stands s. high
1109 In the hollow...Our souls s. rest

SEE.
15 With warm desires to s. my God
49 We then shall s. thee as thou art
81 Then shall I s., and hear, and
105 'tis heaven above To s. thy face
230 hearts pure...That we may s.
247 We shall s. him as he is
363 From all I love, enjoy, and s.
501 pure in heart...they shall s. God
545 And God forever s.
714 I s. thee not, I hear thee not
803 Thee the unholy cannot s.
880 I shall s. him and hear him
886 And though I cannot s. him
1079 When I s. thee as thou art

SEED.
29 And let the s. thy servant sows
62 O God, by whom the s. is given
248 Ye chosen s. of Israel's race
289 The true immortal s.
301 word is cast Like s. upon the
301 Let not...This holy s. remove
575 Sow in the morn thy s.
817 The s. shall surely grow
819 Teach them to sow the precious s.
826 Among thy s. a place I claim
911 Shall spring a plenteous s.
1010 The precious s. of weeping
1086 scatter The good s. on the land

SEEDS.
305 The s. of sin grow up for death
857 And the s. of truth be sown

SEEK.
21 Shall we s. the Lord in vain
21 Now we s. thee, here we stay
29 To s. thee, all our hearts dispose
37 We come, great God, to s. thy
86 Lift up our hearts to s. thee there
240 To them who s. thee ever near
318 Must s. him, Lord, by thee
343 Bids you haste to s. the Saviour
353 And haste to s. in Christ thine
360 S. him while he is near
361 come without delay, And s. the
370 return And s. thy Father's face
371 guilt forgive Of those that s. his
411 I'll return And s. my Father's
491 Nothing would I s. but thee
510 And still I s., 'mid many fears
553 Hast thou not bid me s. thy face
650 S. ye my face Without delay
688 And since he bids us s. his face
691 To them that s. thee thou art
700 How good to those who s.
725 Now thee alone I s., Give

873 Those who s. thee in their youth
906 S. him, for he may be found
941 When we s. them Let thy Spirit
944 The they s., as God of heaven

SEEN.
445 and God is s. by mortal eye
516 Now I have s. the Lord
596 He is least s. when all...power
708 Till thou art s., it seems to be
714 Yet though I have not s.
793 When thou art s. in us below
1059 Shall then be s. and known

SEER, SEERS.
864 When to the exiled s. were given
268 The ancient *seers* thou didst

SEIZE, SEIZES, SEIZED.
382 This the crown I fain would s.
413 And s. me for thine own
753 Thine own this moment s.
790 He *seizes* every straggling soul
192 dread Had seized their troubled

SELF.
263 Perish s. in thy pure fire
303 Till he his glorious s. reveals
477 Chase this s.-will through all
505 A s.-renouncing will

SELFISHNESS.
7 Not in the name of...s. we meet
559 For my s. and pride Thou
590 Let grace our s. expel

SEND.
41 He will s. down his heavenly
607 Here am I., s. me, send me
992 S. whom thou wilt, but

SENSE, SENSES.
123 Thou know'st the s. I mean
445 The things unknown to feeble s.
571 Superior s. may I display
626 And when the joys of s. depart
662 How strong it strikes the s.
969 Steals my *senses*, shuts my sight

SENTENCE.
342 Every s., O how tender
389 'Tis just the s. should take
963 Their righteous s. to receive

SEPARATION.
755 It makes no s. Between

SEPULCHRAL.
723 By the sad s. stone

SERAPH.
56 With his s. train before him
148 Grand beyond a s.'s thought
192 Thus spake the s.; and forthwith
195 When nightly burst from s. harps
351 The sight that veils the s.'s face
422 In vain the firstborn s. tries
480 Outsoar the firstborn s.'s flight

485 Breathing around the s. fire
640 He rules the s. and the worn
658 melt away Into a s.'s song
707 That eye is fixed on s. throngs

SERAPHS.
48 And s. shout the Triune God
224 Tune your harps anew, ye s.
692 The glowing s. round thy throne
860 those bright courts where s.'s
870 Immortal s. glow
964 With s., thrones, and powers

SERAPHIC.
193 And sweet s. fire
244 With pure s. joy
414 S. transport wings the sound
489 Light of life, s. fire
969 my ears With sounds s. ring

SERAPHIM.
10 Angels and s. proclaim
40 Nor s. responsive cry
40 Send forth the s., O Lord
865 the song Of s. above
999 heardst was the s.'s song

SERENE.
12 S. I laid me down
549 Calm and s. my frame
1039 And all s. in heaven

SERPENT, SERPENTS.
229 have trod The s. down
479 Jesus who on the s. treads
810 Be wise as *serpents*, where you

SERVANT.
170 The s. is above his Lord
414 I'll ask a s.'s place
463 Let thy happy s. be One
467 Thy lawful s., Lord, I owe
592 S. at once, and Lord of all
603 Should not the s. tread it still
742 Thy faithful s. be Thine
976 O would my Lord his s. meet
991 S. of God, well done
1047 thy trouble, O my s. true
1059 And each true-hearted s.

SERVANTS.
41 But s. of the heavenly King
51 Ye s. of God your Master
241 And take his s. up To
282 And let thy s. share Thy
414 While s. of my Father share
459 That calls thy willing s. home
811 See where the s. of the Lord
824 Jesus, let all thy s. shine
1033 For all the s. of our King
1036 And all the s. of our God
1107 wine The wondering s. drew
1113 How are thy s. blest, O Lord

SERVE.
105 To s. my God when I awake
205 Here we learn to s. and give
360 S. him with all thy heart and

SER 144 SHE

473 To s. my God alone
475 S. with a single heart and eye
480 And s. thee as thy hosts above
491 S. thee as thy hosts above
498 That we may s. thee here below
567 Ye that are men, now s. him
572 Lord, if I may, I'll s. another
573 I and my house will s. the Lord
669 To love and s. thee is my share
741 To s. thee till I die
744 Who live to s. our God alone

SERVICE.
15 Their constant s. there
112 And in thy s. I would spend
468 Then life shall be thy s., Lord
470 Claim me for thy s., claim
602 And ours the grateful s. whence
605 I own thy right To every s.
643 In thy s. pain is pleasure
825 And fit for thy great s. make

SET, SETTING.
296 truths...They rise, but never s.
110 And at my life's last *setting* sun
709 And spend the hours of s. day

SETTLE.
401 S. and fix my wavering soul
483 S., confirm, and 'stablish me

SEVER.
492 O that we our hearts might s.
807 Meet ne'er to s.

SHADE.
111 mists of error....s. the universe
155 And s. us with their wings
163 In s. and storm, the frequent
232 The s. and gloom of life are fled
284 S., 'mid the noontide glow
451 In sin and error's deadly s.
507 tomb No fearful s. shall wear
546 But now when evening s.
647 Early dawn and evening s.
931 And death's black s. no more
961 Walk...through dreadful s.
986 A land of deepest s.
1082 opening light and evening s.

SHADES.
97 The deepest s. no more disguise
113 The evening s. appear
115 Silently the s. of evening
128 Soon as the evening s. prevail
267 Chase the s. of night away
298 Dispel the s. of night
416 Triumph o'er the s. of night
704 In darkest s., if thou appear
873 Thus, when evening s. shall
943 Borders on the s. of death
1100 Dispels the s. of error's night

SHADOW.
97 Under the s. of thy wings Shall
105 Keep me. Beneath the s.
656 defenceless head With the s.
791 Beneath thy s. let us sit

964 Under the s. of thy throne
1041 There rests no s., falls no

SHADOWS.
93 breaks, and earth's vain s. flee
103 Within all s. standest thou
424 And see the s. fade
620 Though earthborn s. now
628 afflictions.. Like s. of the night
644 Only waiting till the s.
652 Come unto me, when s,
664 As lengthening s. o'er the mead
716 S. with his wings thy head
907 As s. cast by cloud and sun
1039 The evening s. quickly fly
1052 From s. come away
1059 The s. shall decay
1070 And life's long s. break in

SHAKE, SHAKES, SHAKEN.
310 Her rooted pillars s.
679 all hell should endeavor to s.
775 S. off the dust that blinds thy
989 voice This rending earth shall s.
162 He *shakes* the heavens with loud
224 S. the earth, and veils the sky
994 sound That s. the silent chamber
1029 All the powers of nature, *shaken*

SHAME.
88 Take away our sin and s.
351 The guiltless s., the sweet distress
391 My lips with s. my sins confess
423 Unawed by s. or fear
483 And never put to s.
591 Jesus won the world through s.
595 Nor will he put my soul to s.
101 Take up thy cross, nor heed the s.
619 I'll hail reproach, and welcome s.
638 what if...Christ's, Is earthly s, or
736 lo! from sin, and grief, and s.
736 In s., my glory and my crown
766 Nor can we suffer s.
850 The s., the glory, by this rite

SHARON.
195 And S. waves in solemn praise
870 And here, like S.'s odors sweet
875 sweet the breath.. Of S.'s dewy

SHEAF, SHEAVES.
644 Have the last s. gathered home
579 And bring his golden *sheaves*
607 Who will bear the s. away
808 angels gather Their s. of golden
1085 The golden s. of harvest
1087 Bearing your s. along

SHED.
270 His love within us s. abroad
378 O let thy Spirit s. abroad
405 He s. those tears f r thee
411 Jesus s. his blood for me
498 the Saviour's love S. in our
540 O that it now were s. abroad
833 My blood so freely s. for you
838 The cup...That was for sinners s.
850 His life-blood s. for us we see

SHEEP.
11 And for his *s.* he doth us take
46 Before thy *s.*, great Shepherd, go
431 I was a wandering *s.*
434 The Shepherd sought his *s.*
434 No more a wandering *s.*
465 These thy frail and trembling *s.*
790 The *s.* he never can devour

SHELTER, SHELTERED, SHELTERING.
320 We have no *s.* from our sin
750 Sweet is that *s.* from the sun
964 Our *s.* from the stormy blast
861 Close *sheltered* in thy bleeding
1105 S. by thee from every harm
1103 O still thy *sheltering* arm extend

SHEPHERD.
23 Brought the S. of the sheep
44 Great S. of the chosen few
46 Before thy sheep, great S., go
156 The Lord's my S., I'll not want
179 The Lord is my S., no want
434 I did not love my S.'s voice
642 My S. is beside me
748 Thou S. of Israel, and mine
759 Where dost thou, dear S.
759 Dear S., I hear and will
761 My S.'s mighty aid
790 Jesus, great S. of the sheep
793 Under one S. make one
897 See Israel's gentle S. stands
872 Saviour, like a *s.* lead us
885 S. of tender youth
888 With the *s.'s* kindest care
889 Tender S., never leave us
927 S. of souls, with pitying
1007 Tender S., thou hast stilled
1070 Kind S., turn their weary

SHEPHERDS.
189 S., in the fields abiding
192 While *s.* watched their flocks

SHIELD.
69 God is our *s.*, he guards our way
96 God's guardian *s.* was round
140 Our S. and Defender, the Ancient
171 Be thou still my strength and *s.*
316 My *s.* and hiding-place
427 He will my *s.* and portion be
555 Lest I...cast my *s.* away
588 hold On faith's victorious *s.*
588 Believe, hold fast your *s.*, and
599 And faith's broad *s.* before him
626 I never will give up my *s.*
653 name of Jesus...As a *s.* from
1075 My *s.* and tower

SHIELD, SHIELDS, (*verb.*)
167 O *s.* us in the last dread hour
448 And *s.* me in the threatening
465 S. us through our earthly strife
678 And *s.* me with thy power
728 In his arms he'll take and *s.* thee
1108 Our brethren *s.* in danger's hour
876 And *shields* from every harm

SHINE.
50 Cause thou to *s.* upon us
64 Now, Saviour, let thy glory *s.*
93 S. through the gloom and point
198 His face *s.* wondrous fair
267 S. upon this heart of mine
279 shall know, If thou within us *s.*
266 As makes a world of darkness *s.*
428 Upon my heart to *s.*
474 Here let thy light forever *s.*
489 S. in my drooping heart
498 And then in glory *s.*
519 S. to the perfect day
584 And on thy head shall quickly *s.*
620 His light shall round thee *s.*
702 S., Lord, on every heart
704 The opening heavens around me *s.*
743 My soul shall ever *s.*
890 Where God had bid it *s.*
893 Dost thou exalted *s.*
978 urns...Of golden light forever *s.*
978 They still *s.* on from age to age
981 And *s.* in everlasting day
1046 Our face like his shall *s.*
1054 I long...Lord, in thy beauties to *s.*
1059 servant Shall *s.* as doth the day
1063 And lo! by reflection they *s.*

SHINING.
304 Down from the *s.* seats above
416 S. to the perfect day
641 A season of clear *s.*, To cheer
777 God shall rise, and, *s.* o'er you
1016 But, in heavenly vesture *s.*

SHIP.
1011 Where all the *s.'s* company meet
1109 storms...defy, With Jesus in the *s.*

SHIPWRECK.
1004 Not one...Ever suffered *s.* there

SHOCK.
168 His people smile amid the *s.*

SHONE.
146 Which of the glories brighter *s.*
196 What grace, O Lord, and beauty *s.*
274 flame of living fire Which *s.*
507 Because that light hath on thee *s.*

SHORE.
8 praise shall sound from *s.* to shore
22 Yet there is a brighter *s.*
153 And *s.* reply to shore
330 Zion...having gained the blest *s.*
577 rest, On yonder peaceful *s.*
696 free from care On any *s.* since God
721 When I touch the blessed *s.*
752 Lord, till I reach that blissful *s.*
816 Who meet on that eternal *s.*
914 Come, blessed Lord, let every *s.*
931 waft them safe to the destined *s.*
938 When it breaks upon the *s.*
941 All along each distant *s.*
975 And I shall tread the eternal *s.*
1011 Hard toiling to make the blest *s.*
1033 bands On the eternal *s.*

1037 Should fright us from the s.
1038 Can reach that healthful s.
1041 A land upon whose blissful s.
1049 For they who gain that s.
1060 Thou hast no s., fair ocean
1070 fields and ocean's wave-beat s.
1073 we soar To the heavenly s.
1115 Land us on the heavenly s.

SHORES.
1098 O guard our s. from every foe

SHORT.
333 When time seems s. and death is
669 life... If s., yet why should I be
950 How s. the term of life appears
964 A thousand ages...S. as the watch

SHORT-SIGHTED.
514 mind Of man, s.-s. man, can

SHOULDER.
191 On his s. he shall bear

SHOUT.
8 And s. for joy the Saviour's name
139 And s., ye morning stars, for joy
563 Hell's foundations quiver At the s.
566 Join that glorious train Who s.
688 And s. while passing through
934 mountains The sacred s. shall fly
1015 S. all the people of the sky
1030 And s. and wonder at his grace
1061 The s. of them that feast

SHOUTS, SHOUTING.
322 Midst s. of loftiest praise
589 In s., or silent awe, adore
921 The joyous s. from land to land
1011 All with s. cry out, "Tis he
1025 S. with all the sons of God
1027 With s. of sovereign grace
1041 With shouting each other they
1092 S. in chorus, from ocean to ocean

SHOW.
833 Do this my dying love to s.

SHOWER, SHOWERS.
295 As a gracious s. descend
817 Now, then, the ceaseless s.
936 Lo! the promise of a s.
181 He shall descend like showers
384 S., the thirsty land refreshing
551 As s. that usher in the spring

SHRINE.
109 We cannot at the s. remain
447 While to that sacred s. I move
820 Its sacred s. it fixes there
862 And write thy name upon its s.
875 Within thy Father's s.

SHROUDED.
115 O the s. and the lonely

SHUDDER.
1004 S. not to pass the stream

SHUDDERS, SHUDDERING.
363 When nature shudders, loath to
630 And shuddering nature waits her

SHUN, SHUNNING.
223 S. not suffering, shame, or loss
358 Teach us that death to s.
555 And s. the paths of sin
571 By shunning every evil way

SHUT.
214 sun...hide, And s. his glories in
376 a-knocking Where the door is s.
753 And s. me up in God
954 With God eternally s. in

SICK, SICKENS, SICKNESS.
21 Heal the s., the captive free
102 Watch by the s., enrich the poor
564 S., they ask for healing
578 Go where the s. recline
1099 The s. with fevered frame
509 And sickens it of passing shows
283 And all our sickness heal
655 Choose thou...My s. or my health
717 In our s. or our health
977 Or broke by s. in a day
977 Let s. blast, or death devour
1038 S. and sorrow, pain and death
1061 No s. or sorrow shall prove
1105 Where s. lurked, and death

SICKLE.
602 not be our lot to wield The s. in

SIDE.
32 Thy feet, thy hands, thy s.
111 Not fearing...with Christ on our s.
230 no shelter...But in thy wounded s.
533 my rest...Close to thy bleeding s.
631 Close by thy s. still may I keep
675 While keeping at thy s.
897 For thou hast placed us s. by side

SIGH.
370 He hears thy humble s.
553 hears Contrition's humble s.
605 I would not s. for worldly joy
624 Then shall I s. and weep no more
710 Prayer is the burden of a s.
740 When each can feel his brother's s.
997 And the last s. that shakes the

SIGHS.
78 No s. shall mingle with the songs
100 While many spent the night in s.
351 The s. that waft your souls to
408 With s. and prayers and tears
673 God hears thy s. and counts thy
702 O Jesus, Saviour, hear the s.
1023 Lo, my s., my guilt, my shame
1028 And s. are unavailing
1067 S. no more shall heave the breast

SIGHING.
181 To give them songs for s.
651 The s. ones that humbly seek
755 Where there shall be no s.

SIGHT.

98 Thou art a God before whose s.
123 Thy all-surrounding s. surveys
132 Past, present, future, to thy s.
174 And bless thee for the s.
201 Receive thy s., the Saviour said
249 O what joy the s. affords
430 When faith in s. shall end
533 Till faith to s. improve
564 veil be lifted, Till our faith be s.
574 Arm me...As in thy s. to live
577 Till faith shall end in s.
643 Faith to s., and prayer to praise
657 shall see The beatific s.
715 Where faith in s. is swallowed up
787 Whose faith is turned to s.
821 But died without the s.
822 We, too, before thy gracious s.
843 One s. alone we see
902 Who, walking in his s.
913 S. to the inly blind
966 Where faith is sweetly lost in s.
1035 Lo, what a glorious s. appears
1067 saints...Far beyond our feeble s.

SIGN, SIGNS, SIGNED.

429 Abba...Nor can the s. deceive
831 Effectual make the sacred s.
844 Saviour, witness with the s.
851 The sacred, true, effectual s.
146 Known through...thousand *signs*
861 Be mighty s. and wonders done
341 *Signed* when our Redeemer died

SIGNAL.

52 So, whene'er the s.'s given
1004 Wait to catch the s. given

SILENCE.

293 And deepest s. hush on high
526 My flesh...Shall s. keep before
665 Then, O my soul, in s. wait
959 Turn not in s. from my tears

SILENT.

38 And praise sits s. on our tongues
47 And s. bow before his face
115 Living in the s. hours

SILK, SILKEN.

901 Softer than s. are iron chains
977 And gay their *silken* leaves unfold

SILOAM.

875 By cool S.'s shady rill How

SILVER.

329 Wisdom to s. we prefer
859 The gold and s. make them thine

SIMPLE.

149 If our love were but more s.
868 More s. and lowly the walls that

SIN.

41 see his face And never, never s.
102 Let him no more lie down in s.
205 Gazing thus our s. we see
207 When all was s. and shame
214 Maker, died, For...creature's s.
267 Long hath s., without control
347 Will ye still in s. remain
363 When against s. I strive in vain
365 S. kills beyond the tomb
392 Lord, I am s.—but thou art love
450 Nothing but s. have I to give
482 sanctified...Forever cease from s.
497 The slightest touch of s. to feel
503 make, An end of all my s.
514 Saviour from s., we thee receive
511 From all indwelling s.
523 possible...Should live and s. no
536 Come, O my Saviour, cast out s.
541 From s. forever cease
543 In each approach of s. alarm
544 From inbred s. to fly
557 And bid me s. no more
559 seal my peace And bid me s. no
571 O may I still from s. depart
586 My whole of s. remove
588 Believe, till freed from s.'s
643 Rise o'er s., and fear, and care
716 And as we those forgive Who s.
784 Whate'er of s. in us is found
798 Which saves...Till we can s. no
803 Utterly abolish s.
848 All the power of s. remove
884 From s. and sorrow free
916 behold A world by s. destroyed
1008 Ere s. could wound thy breast
1039 weary souls By s. and sorrow
1043 And s. shall never enter there
1044 Nor s. nor sorrow know
1049 There is no s. in heaven
1071 I want to s. no more
1114 When s. in our hearts its wild

SINS.

26 Take, O take our s. away
95 My s. might rouse his wrath to
106 Disperse my s. as morning dew
212 My s. have caused thee, Lord
221 Take all, take all my s. away
244 And all our s. destroy
246 All our s. on thee were laid
311 Grant me my s. to feel
339 Yes, thy s. have done the deed
339 No ; with all my s. I part
365 Thy s., how high they mount
367 Your s. were all on Jesus laid
368 And take our s. away
382 Heal me...O take my s. away
383 By thy dying...Take all our s.
407 E'en now my s. remove
423 I saw my s. his blood had spilt
444 O Lord in dust my s. I own
502 day Which shall my s. consume
531 Remember, Lord, my s. no more
612 grace divine My s. on Jesus
645 Take my s. and fears away
648 Through thee, who all our s. hast
694 And sorely with my s. oppressed
751 I lay my s. on Jesus
775 No longer in thy s. lie down
945 blood apply Which takes our s.

957 wash me...And take my s. away
1022 Our s. are written, every one

SINNING.
491 Take away our bent to s.

SINFUL, SINFULNESS.
83 One s. thought, through all
136 Though the eye of s. man thy
147 Bears ..With me, thy s. child
213 The s. world that lies below
287 Turn us....From every s. way
281 S. though my heart may be
784 ground Of every s. heart
823 For you and all the s. race
275 to us reveal Our *sinfulness* and

SINLESS.
532 Thy s. mind in me reveal
614 And, till in heaven we s. bow
999 may die, for the S. hath died

SINNER.
221 Would Jesus have the s. die
323 Suited to every s.'s case
357 O s., come, the Saviour waits
382 Wilt thou cast a s. out
460 Grant one poor s. more a
517 Surely I shall, the s. I
586 hate the sin...still the s. love
966 A s. born to die
992 A s. saved by grace
996 not have One wretched s. die

SINNERS.
84 That s. may with angels join
98 S. shall ne'er be thy delight
128 S., a vile and thankless race
219 And O to thee may s. turn
220 Come, s., see your Saviour die
221 S., he prays for you and me
222 Lord, hast suffered...for s. gain
238 Lord I believe were s. more
312 look to thee; Where else can s. go
347 S., turn; why will ye die
347 Why, ye ransomed s., why
347 Why, ye long-lost s., why
351 Come, O ye s., to the Lord
398 S. of old thou didst receive
405 Did Christ o'er s. weep
450 Then will I tell to s. round
493 Ye ransomed s., hear
522 Jesus! The name to s. dear
548 Thou that hast for s. died
861 And dying s. pray to live
961 Because thou didst for s. die
999 And s. may die, for the Sinless
1028 But s., filled with guilty fears

SINAI.
206 When on S.'s top I see
787 word Which God on S. spoke

SINCERE.
154 mercy...From men of heart s.
372 We bow...And think ourselves s.
439 And followed, with a heart s.
573 And serve with heart s.

SING.
1 O for a thousand tongues to s.
6 Help us thy name to s.
26 To thee we now presume to s.
41 Let those refuse to s. Who
50 Thy praises let them s.
63 angels do, And wish like them to s.
85 And sit and s. herself away
106 Who all night long unwearied s.
130 mortals dare To s. thy glory
140 And gratefully s. his wonderful
140 O tell of his might, and s. of
148 Who can s. that wondrous song
183 And heaven and nature s.
219 And s. till time shall be no more
224 Join to s. the pleasing theme
259 We, too, s. for joy, and say
269 S., ye heavens,—and earth, reply
330 And s. of his love, his salvation
480 And s. with all the saints in light
485 All shall s. their gracious Lord
563 Men and angels s.
621 To s. thy praise in endless day
654 I travel calmly on, And s. in
661 Then shall my cheerful spirit s.
680 Shall s. like those in glory
697 Then will I s. more sweet, more

SINGS, SINGING, SANG.
408 All heaven thy glory s.
641 surprises The Christian while he s.
138 Forever *singing* as they shine
144 S. everlastingly To thee
259 S. evermore on high
934 When shall the voice of s.
1031 Jerusalem...With s. I repair
189 Ye who *sing* creation's story

SINGLENESS.
281 That we in s. of heart

SINK, SINKS.
401 I s., by dying love compelled
543 Save, Jesus, or I yield, I s.
583 The world must s. beneath the
632 Nor let us s. in deep despair
673 Still s. thy spirits down
496 When *sinks* my heart in waves

SIT, SITS.
16 upon the throne.. shall forever s.
85 And s. and sing herself away
540 O that I could forever s.
657 And by his side s. down
244 He *sits* at God's right hand
357 Through him who now in glory s.
866 Beyond the heavens he s. alone

SKY.
17 framed the globe: he built the s.
87 arch Of yon unmeasured s.
230 From earth unto the s. Our
255 to guide His people to the s.
443 Head, And bring him from the s.
574 soul to save...fit it for the s
618 And thou, that, when the starry s.
630 Shines sweetly in the vaulted s.

972 We'll rise above the *s.*
990 Shall call them to the *s.*
1072 Far, far above the starry *s.*

SKIES.
146 By thousands through the *s.*
159 Thy power...reaches to the *s.*
261 Following thee beyond the *s.*
416 Christ, whose glory fills the *s.*
600 Ye soon shall meet him in the *s.*
640 Look upward to the *s.*
642 B ight *s.* will soon be o'er me
816 reward Which waits us in the *s.*
846 cross...Shall lift us to the *s.*
923 his hand hath spread the *s.*
939 Where the *s.* forever smile
947 To meet him in the *s.*
952 But humbly lift them to the *s.*
952 And far above these nether *s.*
1019 By faith we now transcend the *s.*
1034 decline Amid those brighter *s.*
1041 Its *s.* are not like earthly skies
1073 And look down on the *s.*
1074 hurry our souls to the *s.*
1110 Thou, who hast spread out the *s.*

SKILL.
146 orbs ..Their motions speak thy *s.*
148 Works with *s.* and k ndness
161 mines Of never-failing *s.*
169 I have no *s.* the snare to shun
504 Though thou shouldst give me *s.*
509 Yet vain were *s.* and valor

SLAIN, SLAY.
2 Worthy the Lamb...was *s.* for
26 Lamb of God, for sinners *s.*
76 And numbered with the *s.*
253 Lamb of God, Once *s.* on earth
381 On thee, whom we have *s.*
382 Lamb of God, for sinners *s.*
386 Standing now as newly *s.*
420 Before the world's foundation *s.*
423 For I the Lord have *s.*
456 Christ, the Lamb of God, was *s.*
890 Mourn for the thousands *s.*
930 The Lamb for sinners *s.*
934 And him who once was *s.*
1013 Once for favored sinners *s.*
1019 The earth no more her *s.*
288 sword, To *slay* the man of sin

SLAVE, SLAVES.
900 A rescued soul, a *s.* no more
831 Ye *slaves* of sin and hell
461 Make *s.* the partners of thy

SLEEP.
96 shield...In my defenseless *s.*
97 For thou dost never *s.*
100 In gentle *s.* I close my eyes
102 When the soft dews of kindly *s.*
103 Through *s.* and darkness safely
105 I, ere I *s.*, at peace may be
105 And may sweet *s.* mine eyelids
105 S., which shall me more vigorous
108 I lay my body down to *s.*
155 And, unconcerned, we sweetly *s.*

170 He smooths...and gives me *s.*
228 In the tomb, And *s.* the night
556 Whose eyelids never *s.*
576 This is no time for thee to *s.*
576 O *s.* not, dream not, but arise
750 I *s.*, but my heart waketh
952 We will not let our eyelids *s.*
973 Shall *s.* the years away
979 But there is still a blessed *s.*
986 Here *s.* thou, till our longer race
1108 calm amidst its rage didst *s.*

SLEEPS, SLEEPER, SLEEPING, SLEPT.
159 Thine eye of mercy never *s.*
372 And bid the *sleeper* rise
984 Can reach the peaceful *s.*
1010 The form of one now *sleeping*
112 I *slept*, and I awoke and found
165 I laid me down and *s.*...I woke

SLIDE.
745 Nor suffer thee to *s.*

SLIGHT, SLIGHTED.
347 Will ye *s.* his grace, and die
353 That call...mayst not always *s.*
1092 Thy ways all holy, and *slighted*

SLIPPERY.
160 When in the *s.* paths of

SLOTH.
96 Pardon, O God, my former *s.*
106 Shake off dull *s.*, and joyful
576 Thou hast no time to lose in *s.*

SLUGGISH.
209 Awake, my *s.* soul, awake
547 Awake, my *s.* soul
547 Lord, shall we live so *s.* still

SLUMBER, SLUMBERS.
186 Angels adore him, in *s.*
352 And still my soul in *s.* He
555 shake This *s.* from my soul
560 Chase this dread *s.* from
979 To be for such a *s.* meet
984 To *s.* in the silent dust
990 those Who *s.* in the Lord
96 Who doth my *slumbers* keep
714 When *s.* o'er me roll
745 Careless *s.* cannot steal

SMILE.
168 His people *s.* amid the shock
287 vale of death, A *s.* of glory wear
542 Favored with God's peculiar *s.*
561 No peace we have...but in thy *s.*
609 Supported by his *s.*; Joyful
643 And, while thou shalt *s.* upon
643 What a Father's *s.* is thine
657 Nor heed its scornful *s.*
691 Glad when thy gracious *s.* we
776 Thou mayst *s.* at all thy foes
796 We'll *s.* upon the troubled past
980 That *s.* upon his wasted cheek
998 And the *s.* of the Lord is the

SMI 150 SON

1068 Because thy s. was fair
1101 Thy s. is life, thy frown is death
1103 Whose favored s. upholds them
1117 O could I catch one s. from thee

SMILES.
306 See in his heavenly s. appear
414 The Saviour s.; upon my soul
627 The light of s. shall till again
675 To meet the glad with joyful s.
722 From the world's pernicious s.
811 And s. on the peculiar race
852 And thy forgiving s. impart
919 Its bright and gladdening s.
1002 With thy s. of love returning
1054 and s. of thy face
1060 And s. have no alloy

SMILING, SMILINGS.
161 Behind...He hides a s. face
177 How soon we found a s. God
438 Where Jesus shows a s. face
1027 To see thy s. face
751 The *smilings* of thy face

SNARE, SNARES.
662 And every sweet a s.
160 And through the pleasing *snares*
457 With all its glittering s.
570 Ten thousand s. my path
905 Amid the s. misfortune lays

SNOW.
46 blood shall wash us white as s.
305 blood can make us white as s.
425 And wash me white as s.
503 And I am white as s.
527 Wash me, and I am white as s.
1066 Blood that washes white as s.
1086 He sends the s. in winter

SOAR.
624 My ransomed soul shall s. away
639 To s. to endless day
890 And hence in spirit may we s.
1032 And s. to worlds on high

SOBER.
505 I want a s. mind
1058 Be s. and keep vigil

SOCIAL, SOCIETY.
1051 What s. joys are there
787 In such *society* as this My

SOD.
1012 Must mingle again with the s.

SOFT, SOFTEN, SOFTENING.
891 S. be our hearts their paths to
813 Shall I ...*Soften* thy truth, or
559 And let me feel thy *softening*

SOIL.
578 dew...Already cheers the s.
653 And promise clothes the s.
959 Visit every s. and see

SOJOURN, SOJOURNS, SOJOURNERS.
179 Through the land of their s.
1031 A stranger...I calmly s. here
1073 He only *sojourns* here
864 But we, frail *sojourners* below

SOLD.
927 Thy people, Lord, are s. for
1013 Those who set at naught and s.

SOLDIER, SOLDIERS.
568 Go forward, Christian s.
593 Am I a s. of the cross
565 Onward, Christian *soldiers*
566 S. of the cross, arise
567 Stand up...Ye s. of the cross
587 S. of Christ, arise
588 S. of Christ, lay hold
825 Train up thy hardy s.

SOLITUDE.
223 All is s. and gloom
709 I love in s. to shed The
973 Our cold remains in s.

SON.
51 cry aloud, and honor the S.
118 S. of man and Son of God
170 The S. of God, the Son of man
184 To us a S. is given
191 Unto us a S. is given
198 Hear my beloved S.
210 This is my S., O hear ye him
220 The Father's co-eternal S.
327 God to you his S. hath given
432 But thou wilt form thy S. in me
439 Father, in me reveal thy S.
464 mind Of thy well-beloved S.
480 Thou hast in honor of thy S.
627 The anointed S. of God makes
670 O S. of Mary, S n of God
677 Stand, O S. of man, confessed
800 The slain, the risen S.
830 Impart The nature of thy S.
834 Father, in these reveal thy S.
841 The S. of God came down to die
841 The Father gives the S.
925 Lo! the S. of God is come
1024 The immortal S. of man

SONS.
186 and best of the s. of the morning
241 compare Among the s. of men
251 witness...That we are s. of God
356 lea The sacred s. of grace
540 The first-born s. of light
776 Still supply thy s. and daughters
829 We'd walk as s. of God
916 And if the s. of God rejoice
920 How many of the s. of men
932 The s. of earth are waking
1066 Foremost of the s. of light

SONG.
4 Awake, and sing the s. Of
8 In every land beg n the s.
10 And swell the loud triumphant s.

33 God, our strength, to thee our s.
42 While earth repeats the joyful s.
58 Join the everlasting s.
74 And pour the grateful s.
80 And we shall join the ceaseless s.
99 new joys Do a new s. require
146 humble part In that immortal s.
148 Who can sing that wondrous s.
160 A grateful s. I'll raise
185 And every voice a s.
194 That glorious s. of old
217 Is borne the s. that angels know
230 Let earth her s. begin
248 We'll join the everlasting s.
258 On every lip a s.
273 This may be our endless s.
294 For love like this, O let my s.
315 And still the s. renew
319 Then in a nobler, sweeter s.
441 Loud is the s. the heavenly
469 And take up every thankful s.
563 your voices In the triumph-s.
690 Our cheerful s. would oftener
692 The s. shall wake with opening
724 Still all my s. shall be
742 Be thou my s.
744 The new, eternal s.
759 My comfort by day, and my s.
763 voice Of her unending s.
800 One s. ascendeth to the skies
917 Soon may the last glad s. arise
1034 millions...Shall in one s. unite
1049 All holy in their s.
1069 Saints, begin the endless s.
1085 A s. of happy love

SONGS.
2 Come, let us join our cheerful s.
8 In s. of praise divinely sing
20 Deign our humble s. to hear
20 There, in joyful s. of praise
24 S. of praise awoke the morn
41 Then let our s. abound
48 we raise Our hearts in solemn s.
64 How should our s., like those
70 To s. of joy my soul inspire
73 In loftiest s. of praise
76 Let s. of triumph hail the morn
78 The s. which from thy servants
104 Demand perpetual s. of praise
169 Give sweeter s. than lips can
171 S. of praises I will ever give
183 Let men their s. employ
275 Come, Holy Spirit, raise our s.
332 New s. do now his lips employ
467 We sing the s. of heaven
551 Like morning s. his voice
653 And his s. our tongues employ
726 Call for s. of loudest praise
852 Far, far above our humble s.
876 Come, sing in joyful s. of praise
886 My sweetest s. I'll raise
946 Demands our choicest s.
995 accept...Of these our humble s.
1070 Angelic s. are swelling O'er
1076 And sing in s. which never end
1082 Demand successive s. of praise
1085 sing s. of love and praise

SOOTHE, SOOTHES, SOOTHING.
167 To s. our sorrow, calm our fear
281 'T is thine to s. the sorrowing
380 S., O soothe this troubled breast
878 Gently s. each impulse wild
316 name of Jesus...soothes...sorrows
436 And s. away my pains
706 Prayer s. the troubled breast
284 Come...With soothing power
898 Thy s. hand may press

SORROW.
125 shall pain Or s. make thee
183 No more let sin and s. grow
211 S. and love flow mingled
218 And yet our eyes with s. see
255 In all our s., all our fear
320 When s. swells the laden breast
311 Come, in s. and contrition
502 Liberty from s., fear, and sin
578 And where the sons of s. pine
611 Then s., touched by thee, grows
614 O teach us to endure The s.
629 And s. crown each lingering
638 to bear All that of s., grief
641 Set free from present s.
653 Child of s. and of woe
654 Through s. or through joy
683 Earth has no s. that Heaven
773 Arise, for the night of thy s.
780 When s. flows from eye to
797 From s., toil, and pain
875 Will shake the soul with s.'s
896 For s.'s children comfort find
898 He who drinks the cup When s.
905 The sum of human s. less
973 Through s.'s night, and danger's
1008 Or s. wake the tear
1011 And s. and sin are no more
1017 And the end of s. Shall
1055 Or s. entrance find
1057 Nor s.'s least alloy
1059 Brief s., short-lived care
1063 Away with our s. and fear
1065 Where s. and death are no more
1068 Fly from s., care, and pain
1083 Free from s., free from sin

SORROWS.
1 name...That bids our s. cease
154 When s. bow the spirit down
231 Speak his s. ended, hail
294 There Jesus bids my s. cease
381 O Thou who hast our s. borne
396 To hear the s. thou hast felt
412 To give those s. weight
412 Behold the s. of my heart
441 All my s. are his own
551 chase...The s. of the night
619 In all my s., conflicts, woes
628 No s. dim celestial love
640 The s. ye endure, The
665 Didst all our s. bear
674 On thee, when s. rise
728 who will all our s. share
754 He all my s. shares
944 Fruitful let thy s. be
971 Then let our s. cease to flow

SORROWED, SORROWING, SORROWFUL.

651 thou on earth hast wept And s.
627 God has marked each *sorrowing*
664 seek In s. paths below
666 saints...Who once went s. here
856 And always *sorrowful* we live

SOUGHT.

434 'T was he that s. the lost
441 Found me when I s. him not
726 Jesus s. me when a stranger

SOUL.

119 Who would not his whole s. and
124 Father, to thee my s. I lift
211 Love so amazing...Demands my s.
365 Reflect, thou hast a s. to save
416 Visit thou this s. of mine
439 Mine inmost s. expose to view
438 And to my inmost s. make known
470 Take my s. and body's powers
472 My s. and all its powers
474 my God, thou hast my s.: No
476 O grant that nothing in my s.
482 My s. shall then, like thine
482 S. of my soul remain
495 To lay my s. at Jesus' feet
497 O that my tender s. might fly
552 Hark, my s.! it is the Lord
556 My s. to thee alone, Now
571 A never-dying s. to save
619 I lift my s. to thee; In all
656 Jesus, Lover of my s.
751 I rest my s. on Jesus
754 This weary s. of mine
788 Derive...Its life from thee, the s.
854 power applying Christ to every s.
866 Then, Saviour, then my s. receive
996 Who diedst thyself my s. to save
1000 angels sing, As they bear the s.
1012 His s., which in heaven had birth
1068 So a s. that's born of God
1116 But ere my s. from earth remove

SOULS.

29 And put our s. in frame
60 And fill our s. with praise
66 Our s. are his immortal breath
78 To that our laboring s. aspire
182 Bring our ransomed s. at last
219 Our s. are saved alive
269 Within these s. of thine to rest
356 Of life, our s. o'erflow
561 By the s. that love him One
607 While the s. of men are dying
715 O let our s. on thee be cast
801 O may thy Spirit seal our s.
811 Marks the dear s. he calls his
819 Teach them immortal s. to gain
823 They watch for s. for which
823 For s. which must forever live
825 take The s. we here present to
858 But the s. that are buried in
882 His praise, to whom our s. belong
951 Our s. and bodies shall be thine
958 Our s. to thee commend
1046 Our s. are in his mighty hand

1085 The s. he died to save
1109 Under thy protection we Our s.
1113 death...Shall join our s. to thee

SOURCE.

67 Eternal S. of truth and light
91 God, the s. of life and light
127 From thee, great S. of being
129 Thou S. of life and holy love
265 Come, thou S. of joy and gladness
313 Jesus, thou S. divine
394 To thee, her S., my spirit flies
474 O S. of life! live, dwell, and
1020 Jesus, thou S. of all my joys

SOVEREIGN.

9 His s. power, without our
47 Still hear and do thy s. will
63 The S. of your hearts proclaim
139 And hail thee s. Lord of all
152 And he, as s. Lord and King
161 And works his s. will
302 But there's a voice of s. grace
322 Great S., we adore Thy
369 undone Without his s. grace
433 And depth of s. grace
451 Glory to God, whose s. grace
460 And own thy s. right in
703 Love...The s. of the rest
916 new creation...To s. love
918 S. of worlds! display thy power
948 Awake, and praise that s. love

SOW, SOWS.

817 The word of life we s.
579 And he who *sows* with many
(See Seed.)

SOWER, SOWING, SOWN.

55 Bless the s. and the seed
687 S. of life's immortal seed
1081 In earth...The s. hid the grain
731 *Sowing* much and reaping none
573 The late or early *sown*

SPAN.

602 And were this life the utmost s.
661 My s. of life will soon be done
959 My life is but a s.
962 My days are shorter than a s.

SPANGLED.

128 And s. heavens, a shining

SPARE, SPARES.

379 Me he now delights to s.
735 And Jesus forces me to s.
953 Yet doth he us in mercy s.
959 O s. me yet, I pray; Awhile
1091 Correct...Then let thy mercy s.
953 And *spares* us yet another year

SPARK, SPARKS, SPARKLE.

969 Vital s. of heavenly flame
973 The vital s. shall lie
973 For o'er life's wreck that s. shall
1009 Whose *sparks* fly upward to
1062 Then eyes with joy shall *sparkle*

SPARROW.
148 Wings an angel, guides a s.
151 not...Disturb the s.'s nest

SPEAK.
54 S., and let thy servants hear
406 O s., and I shall live
557 S., and my soul shall live
712 S. to our hearts, and let us feel
712 And bear thee inly s.
738 S. to my heart, in blessing speak
738 S., or thou never hence shalt
742 For thou the word must s.
911 Still, still, though dead, they s.
918 S., and the world shall hear
918 S., and the desert shall rejoice
1021 take heed,—To all I s. or do

SPEAKS, SPAKE.
1 He s., and, listening to his voice
151 He s., and in his heavenly height
552 Jesus s., he speaks to thee
759 He s.! and eternity, filled with
24 When he *spake* and it was done

SPEAR.
219 And see! the s. hath pierced
723 Piercing s., and torturing scorn
1005 When s., and shield, and crown

SPEECH, SPEECHLESS.
710 Prayer is the simplest form of s.
1099 Gave s., and strength, and sight
293 disciples...with *speechless* joy
351 The s. awe that dares not
531 adore, With s. wonder, at

SPEED.
354 O s. thee, speed thee on thy way
576 Up, then, with s., and work
663 lingering heart...s. its flight

SPHERE, SPHERES.
135 Center and soul of every s.
929 Look from thy s. of endless
1034 soul, that springs beyond thy s.
229 Claim for thine own the *spheres*
1076 The listening s. attend

SPIRES.
195 Crowned with her temple s.
1036 And the bright city's gleaming s.

SPIRIT.
84 Come, sacred S., from above
120 Blest S., one with God above
166 The S. and the gifts are ours
274 Where is that S., Lord, which
276 O S. of the living God, In all
347 God, the S., asks you why
350 Ready the S. of his love
355 The S. in our hearts is
356 The S. we receive Of wisdom
384 Pass me not, O mighty S.
438 His S. answers to the blood
480 Send us the S. of thy Son
499 Walk in the S. even here
524 With thy meek S. arm our breast
589 Still let the S. cry In all
618 By thy meek S., thou, of all
643 Think what S. dwells within
745 My soul the S. feels
793 And breathe the S. of thy love
878 In our hearts the S. mild
900 Thy gracious S., we implore
924 Come, Lord, thy glorious S. cries
936 Lord will shortly pour All the S.
1001 Them the S. hath declared

Eternal SPIRIT.
250 By the *eternal* S. made
309 'Tis thine, *eternal* S., thine
331 By thine own *eternal* S.

Thy SPIRIT.
268 On all the earth *thy* S. shower
282 O let *thy* S. now Descend
406 lie, Till thou *thy* S. give
432 Thou wilt *thy* S. give
559 But if thou *thy* S. shed
686 If with me now *thy* S. stays
771 *Thy* S. then will speak
795 If now *thy* S. move my breast
819 And free *thy* S.'s living power
826 *Thy* S. now shall live w.thin
832 O may *thy* S. gently draw
1013 the gladness Of *thy* S. feel in

SPIRIT, (*human*.)
165 Thou, Lord, my s. didst sustain
474 My s., soul, and flesh receive
474 Thou hast my s.; there display
515 Thou only canst my s. fill
520 And be in s. one
661 Her portion...My s. longs to know
681 O when shall my s. be there
969 angels say, Sister s., come away
982 Light from its load the s. flies
1012 The s. of man never dies

SPIRITS.
342 Waiting s., speed your way
648 On thee alone our s. stay
671 full of strength...human s. are
684 There is a scene where s. blend
765 And thence our s. rise
787 Behold the s. of the just
807 Where kindred s. dwell
1032 I see a world of s. bright
1109 We on his love our s. stay

SPIRITUALLY.
347 S. dead in sin

SPLENDOR, SPLENDORS.
1106 Veiled in the softened s.
194 peace...Its ancient *splendors*
925 And hail the s. of the day

SPOIL, SPOILS, SPOILED, SPOILER.
1091 Save from s. thy holy place
758 Great *spoils* I shall win from
1002 O'er the s. that death has won
234 Sing how he *spoiled* the hosts of
902 Or *spoiler* take away

SPOKEN.
57 Praise the Lord, for he hath s.
777 Hear what God the Lord hath s.
1064 For Jesus hath s. the word

SPOKESMAN.
735 In honor of our S. there

SPOT, SPOTLESS.
320 In vain Over some foul, dark s.
714 And earth hath ne'er so dear a s.
209 darkness fell On thee...spotless
483 And then my s. soul receive
522 And s. love and peace
523 And all my s. life shall show
532 And all my s. life shall tell
623 With s. love and lowly fear
764 free indeed. And s. here below
808 Clothe us in s. raiment
1071 pure...As on thy s. shore

SPRING.
122 And all the mingling sounds of s.
231 Earth...clothing her for s.
232 bright blossom...Of an eternal s.
977 Fairer than s. the colors
994 But bright shall be your s.
1037 There everlasting s. abides
1080 And still, now s. has on us
1081 The s.'s sweet influence, Lord
1082 The flowing s., at thy command
1084 All that s. with bounteous

SPRING, (fount.)
323 love abounds, A deep, celestial s.
337 Insatiate to this s. I fly
440 S. of life, thyself impart
577 From heaven's eternal s.
656 S. thou up within my heart
701 My God, the s. of all my joys
721 Christ, the s. of all my joy
774 A sacred s., at thy command
812 The s. whence all these blessings

SPRINKLE, SPRINKLES, SPRINKLED.
527 S. me, Saviour, with thy blood
911 Saviour, s. many nations
438 blood...*sprinkles* now the throne
281 And by thy *sprinkled* blood

SPURN, SPURNED.
353 S. not the call to life and
102 some...have *spurned* to-day
627 And s. of men, he goes to die

SQUANDERED.
906 S. life's most golden hours

STAFF.
179 Thy rod shall defend me, thy s.
685 Our shepherd...Our s. and song

STAGGER.
529 No more I s. at thy power

STAIN, STAINS.
305 Can wash the dismal s. away
751 wash...Till not a s. remains

1102 Remember not our sin's dark s.
302 Our sin, how deep it *stains*
307 The deepest s. of sin efface
319 plunged...Lose all their guilty s.
754 To wash my crimson s.

STALL.
180 his bed with the beasts of the s.
626 The empty s. no herd afford

STAMMERING.
47 praise thee with a s. tongue
319 poor lisping, s. tongue Lies

STAMP.
475 But let me all thy s. receive
525 And s. me with thy Spirit's seal
803 thine image...S. it now on every
848 S. us with the stamp divine

STAND.
236 That we may s. in that dread
567 S. up, stand up for Jesus
679 help thee, and cause thee to s.
751 S. but in him, as those have
805 We for Christ, our Master, s.

STANDS.
459 That s. between us and thy love
772 On every side he s., And for
1056 It s. securely high
1063 She s. as she ever hath stood

STANDARD.
582 The s. of your God

STANDARD-BEARER.
582 His s.-b., I To all

STAR.
182 Did the guiding s. behold
182 Where they need no s. to guide
187 One s. alone, of all the train
189 Ye have seen his natal s.
217 The s. is dimmed that lately
292 In every s. thy wisdom shines
300 Bright was the guiding s. that
416 Day-s. in my heart appear
443 And gain the Morning S.
604 Bright Morning S., lid
654 Let not my s. of hope Grow
701 art my soul's bright morning s.
752 From blush of morn to evening s.
759 The s. that on Israel shone
778 o'er thy hills dawns the day-s.
779 Hail her as their guiding s.
781 As s. by star grows dim
842 S. of our sorrow's troubled
907 O Father, may that holy s.
914 S. of the coming day
918 O bid the morning s. arise
935 See that glory-beaming s.
935 Higher yet that s. ascends
939 And the S. of Jacob rise
974 The rising s. appears
981 Nor day-s. gild the darksome
1060 Thus s. by star declines
1086 He lights the evening s.

STARS.

- 38 Where s. revolve their little
- 57 Praise him, all ye s. of light
- 107 So when the evening s. appear
- 115 Like the s. when storms are past
- 138 While all the s. that round her
- 139 And shout, ye morning s., for joy
- 248 Crown him, ye morning s. of light
- 516 light...The s. are all concealed
- 547 And s. their courses move
- 628 The s. of heaven are shining
- 644 Till the s. of heaven are
- 644 Holy, deathless s. shall rise
- 698 And call the s. my own
- 815 Still hold the s. in thy right
- 863 The morning s. together sang
- 916 It sang the morning s. for joy
- 1009 Nor sink those s. in empty night
- 1014 See the s. from heaven falling
- 1019 We, while the s. from heaven
- 1034 Ye s. are but the shining dust
- 1069 Let the morning s. reply

STARVE, STARVING.

- 414 I s., he cries, nor can I
- 335 Why will you be *starving*, and

STATE.

- 502 I ask no higher s.; Indulge
- 636 Teach us, in every s., To make
- 1000 God save the s.

STATION, STATIONS.

- 59 When we reach our blissful s.
- 249 Jesus takes the highest s.
- 613 Joy to find in every s.
- 1015 Keep me in my lowly s.
- 97 angels...Their constant *stations*

STATUTES.

- 765 For he that in thy s. treads
- 788 Thy s. are their song

STAY.

- 167 God willeth you with us to s.
- 206 Here I would forever s.
- 345 S. not for the morrow's sun
- 352 God calling yet! I cannot s.
- 369 For if I s. away, I know I
- 402 He calls...And yet from him I s.
- 648 On thee alone our spirits s.
- 691 O Jesus, ever with us s.
- 712 Here...my God, vouchsafe to s.
- 730 With my Saviour will I s.
- 741 Here would I ever s.; Jesus is
- 950 If thou permit our s.
- 998 I ask not to s. Where storm
- 1006 God forbids his longer s.
- 1038 Would here no longer s.

STAYS, STAYED.

- 633 Blest is the man...That s. himself
- 170 Lord, on whom my soul is *stayed*
- 178 The mind which still on thee is s.
- 450 mind Be every moment s.
- 529 On thee, O God, my soul is s.
- 643 I have s. my heart on thee

STEADFAST, STEADFASTLY.

- 180 My s. heart shall fear no ill
- 518 My s. soul from falling free
- 616 My s. heart shall know no fear
- 631 With s. eye mark every step
- 649 On this my s. soul relies
- 672 Fix on his work thy s. eye
- 772 S., and fixed, and sure
- 536 Till *steadfastly* by faith I stand

STEER.

- 648 Thither our steady course we s.

STEP, STEPS.

- 201 And with firm s. and words
- 283 S. by step where Christ has trod
- 682 distant scene; one s. enough for
- 155 Angels...attend Our *steps*
- 179 Still follow my s. till I meet
- 180 My weary, wandering s. he leads
- 296 My soul rejoices to pursue The s.
- 313 Direct our s., thou gracious Guide
- 356 Angels...all our s. attend
- 385 His s. I at a distance see
- 483 On thee my feeble s. I stay
- 560 With s. unwavering, undismayed
- 564 Forward...S. and voices joined
- 594 Forget the s. already trod
- 724 S. unto heaven; All that
- 745 He thy feeble s. shall stay
- 761 My willing s. shall lead In
- 887 Guide their s. and help their
- 891 We would, O Lord, thy s. pursue
- 946 While on in Jesus' s. we go

STEPHEN.

- 680 We each, as dying S.

STEWARDS.

- 892 As s. true receive

STILL, STILLED.

- 623 Say to my trembling heart, Be s.
- 1004 *Stilled* Its tossings, hushed its

STING, STINGS.

- 93 Where is death's s.? where
- 234 ask the monster, Where 's thy s.
- 260 Where, O Death, is now thy s.
- 623 O Death! where is thy s.? Where
- 969 O Death, where is thy s.
- 979 Death hath lost his venomed s.
- 985 And where, O Death, thy s.
- 985 Death has no s. beside
- 989 And where, O Death, thy s.
- 999 And death has no s. for the
- 371 A thousand *stings* within your

STIR.

- 543 And s. me up to pray
- 562 And still s. up thy gift in me
- 786 O let us s. each other up

STONE.

- 76 The S. the builders set at naught
- 76 That S. has now become The sure
- 76 Christ is that S., rejected once
- 260 Vain the s., the watch, the seal

STO   156   STR

303 And break my heart of s.
321 Grace...in heaven the topmost s.
368 And break these hearts of s.
378 And break my heart of s.
558 look...And break my heart of s.
724 My rest a s., Yet in my dreams
857 On this s., now laid with prayer
861 This s. to thee in faith we lay
(See Corner-Stone.)

STONES, STONY.
451 Hath animated senseless s.
857 Here be living s. prepared
883 The s., our silence shaming
350 Just now the stony to remove
540 In this poor s. heart
550 The s. shall depart

STOOPS, STOOPED.
164 In mercy s. to hear thy cry
325 S. to our vile abode
400 And s. to ask my love
147 For thou hast stooped to ask of
315 How low he s., how high

STORE, STORES.
474 Small as it is, 'tis all my s.
713 A boundless, endless s.
903 joys...With God laid up in s.
904 As thou hast blest our various s.
1083 But the fruitful ears to s.
33 For them shall earth its stores
1084 For the s. and gardens yield
1084 From her rich, o'erflowing s.

STORM.
161 And rides upon the s.
187 The s. was loud, the night
187 And, through the s. and danger's
354 The s. is gathering in the west
541 I rest me till the s. be past
616 The gathering s. shall see
630 Hushed with a word the raging s.
631 The s. swept by, nor left a trace
635 Nor fear the coming s.
642 The s. may roar without me
656 Hide me...Till the s. of life is
676 And let the s. that does thy work
676 And let the s. that speeds me
678 For O the s. is high
731 With us when the s. is sweeping
998 Where s. after storm rises
1090 Through s. and night
1113 The s. is laid, the winds retire

STORMS.
153 Thunder, and hail, and fire, and s.
177 'Mid raging s., exults to find
225 Soon the s. of time shall cease
403 Though s. his face obscure
418 Should s. of wrath shake
476 And when the s. of life shall
613 And when life's fiercest s. are
643 S. may howl and clouds may
659 Let s. of sorrow fall
772 In s. and hurricanes abide
773 When s. of sharp distress
957 A few more s. shall beat

973 The s. of earth shall beat
1039 Where s. arise and ocean rolls
1052 And s. no more have sway

STORMY.
33 In trouble's dark and s. hour
41 That rides upon the s. sky
551 And stills the s. wave
611 O who could bear life's s. doom
634 Shone through my s. fears
681 From every s. wind that blows
1038 On Jordan's s. banks I stand

STORY.
189 Listen to the wondrous s.
204 All the light of sacred s.
225 Death and sorrow, earth's dark s.
330 let us tell the glad s., And sing
442 And the s. repeat, And the
572 To tell the s., To show the glory
727 Changeless sounds, wondrous s.
756 I love to tell the s. Of unseen
880 When I read that sweet s. of old
884 We hear the wondrous s.
886 I love to hear the s. Which
914 Of thy cross the wondrous s.
1016 Earth can now but tell the s.
1079 Looking o'er life's finished s.

STRAIN, STRAINS.
34 And asks our noblest s.
66 Ascend for him our cheerful s.
449 And praise thee in a bolder s.
1016 Let each heart repeat the s.
8 To every land the strains belong
61 Our humble s. attend
65 Till higher s. our tongues
73 And earth, in humbler s.
83 And join the s. which angels
146 And try their choicest s.
692 Soon shall I learn the exalted s.
819 In humble s. thy grace implore
1070 Sweet the truths those blessed s.

STRAIT.
717 Then, my soul, in every s.

STRANGER, STRANGERS.
372 A s. to the blood which bought
439 A s. to the gospel hope
726 Jesus sought me when a s.
740 He helps the s. in distress
781 S. nor foe art thou
1031 A s. in the world below
1072 While here, a s. far from home
648 Stranger and pilgrims here below
855 Bless us here, while still as s.
1071 But s. and pilgrims ourselves

STRAY, STRAYED.
262 Let me never from thee s.
354 O far from home thy footsteps s.
356 Ye simple souls that s.
118 That I from thee may never s.
468 That I from thee no more may s.
478 Nor suffer me again to s.
496 If in this darksome wild I s.
511 If to the right or left I s., That

646 When in devious paths we s.
655 Else I must surely s.
686 If to the right or left I s., His
762 Nor let me ever s.
784 If to the right or left we s., Leave
929 In pity look on those who s.
1008 In waywardness to s.
1095 We turn who oft have strayed

STRAYING.
683 light of the s., Hope of the
892 lambs...Are s. from the fold

STREAM.
323 Whoever...May of this s. partake
420 I drank Of that life-giving s.
431 While down the s. of time we
731 When we cross the chilling s.
762 When death's cold, sullen s.
773 There is a s. whose gentle flow
774 And pours its limpid s. around
774 Flow, wondrous s., with glory
956 Bear us down life's rapid s.
964 Time, like an ever-rolling s.
1033 Though now divided by the s.
1053 Is the deep and unknown s.
1107 Bless with the holier s. that

STREAMS.
72 With soul-refreshing s.
128 How wide thy healing s. are
168 Whose s. make glad the heavenly
317 Its s. the whole creation reach
912 S. ever copious are gliding along
1033 Are there celestial s., Where
1087 The s. rejoice

STREET, STREETS.
1009 In crowded s., by restless couch
1044 And streets of shining gold
1060 The s. with emerald blaze

STRENGTH.
15 They go from s. to strength
108 And gives me s. for days to come
141 No s. of our own, nor goodness
162 God is the s. of every saint
166 Did we in our own s. confide
201 And aided by new s. from thee
251 Jesus...In glorious s. arrayed
276 Souls without s., inspire with
413 For everlasting s. is thine
452 The most gigantic s. of man
461 Who thence their life and s.
466 We trust not in our native s.
556 But s. in thee I surely have
567 And s. to strength oppose
587 Who in the s. of Jesus trusts
589 From s. to strength go on
648 From s. to strength we travel
670 But not with s. like thine
675 So I ask thee for the daily s.
707 When human s. gives way
727 S. we crave to burst our chain
737 And when my all of s. shall fail
739 On thee alone for s. depend
762 grace impart, S. to my fainting
769 journey on from s. to strength

773 And give new s. to fainting
814 Give me thy s., O God of
851 bread...express The s. through
891 His arm the s. imparts
920 Put on thy s., the nations
985 Joyful, with all the s. I have
1043 Thine own immortal s. put
1076 Though nature's s. decay
1097 not their number, nor their s.
1117 S. of my failing flesh and

His STRENGTH.
177 And in his s. confide
567 Stand in his s. alone
587 With all his s. endued
601 His s. shall bear thy spirit

My STRENGTH.
496 My s. proportion to my day
624 Be thou my s., be thou my
608 Till I my s. renew
676 Go not from me, O my S.
694 My s. by day, my trust by
718 Every hour my s. renew
752 Then is my s. by thee renewed
959 Awhile my s. restore

Our STRENGTH.
19 And all our s. exert
566 God, our s. and shield is near
862 Our s., our comfort, and our
873 Be our s., for we are weakness

Thy STRENGTH.
448 So in thy s. shall I go on
814 Give me thy s., O God of
920 Put on thy s., the nations shake
952 And bid us in thy s. rejoice
1114 Arise in thy s., thy redeemed

STRENGTH to STRENGTH.
15 They go from s. to s.
567 And s. to s. oppose
589 From s. to s. go on
648 From s. to s. we travel
769 journey on from s. to s.

STRENGTHEN, STRENGTHENS.
478 S. my feet with steady
543 Surround, sustain, and s. me
670 So s. us to pray
679 I'll s. thee, help thee, and
811 And strengthens their unwearied

STRENGTHENED, STRENGTHEN- ING.
109 And, s. here by hymn and prayer
670 As thou wert s. in thy woe
869 Be s. as they pray
154 Thy strengthening hands uphold
631 In me thy s. grace be

STRIFE.
86 The waves of s. be still
259 Who for us endured the s.
400 Ah! what avails my s.
441 Safe with him from earthly s.
444 O smile and heal the s.

565 See, the s. will soon be done
567 The s. will not be long
608 friend and foe in all our s.
618 Saw the dread s. begun
664 Soon will the toilsome s. be o'er
713 I flee, From s. and tumult far
829 Would be at constant s.
885 Healer of s.
916 sound Shall quell the deadly s.
1040 Wage to the end the glorious s.
1056 We urge the restless s.

STRING, STRUNG.
633 Bid every s. awake
703 And sound from every joyful s.
819 'Tis *strung* and tuned for endless

STRIVE, STRIVING, STROVE.
60 When with heart and voice we s.
277 In vain we s. to rise
326 And vainly s. with earthly toys
353 God's Spirit will not always s.
409 I would be thine; but while I s.
497 Still may I s., and watch, and pray
805 S. we, in affection strive
949 And help us all with sin to s.
1058 S., man, to win that glory
166 Our *striving* would be losing
264 S. till he cast out sin
347 He, who all your lives hath *strove*
450 The more I s. against its power

STROKE.
618 Blest Saviour, if the s. must fall

STRONG.
21 Make them s. in faith and hope
366 Though s., and young, and gay
440 S., and permanent, and clear
453 So s. to deliver, so good to redeem
479 O ye of fearful hearts, be s.
569 Fear not, be s.' your cause
587 S. in the strength which God
737 When I am weak, then I am s.
742 word...That makes me s.
866 The Lord our God alone is s.
890 Call to the s., the free
1108 Eternal Father! s. to save

STRONGLY.
263 By thee may I s. live

STRONGHOLDS.
636 Sin's s. it now o'erthrows

STRUGGLE, STRUGGLES.
566 soon be done; Then s. manfully
775 Arise, and s. into light
900 Who s. with that fatal chain
1003 S. through thy latest passion
1022 To s. onward into light
957 A few more *struggles* here

STRUGGLEST, STRUGGLING, STRUGGLINGS.
737 In vain thou s. to get free
109 May *struggling* hearts that seek
383 Every s. soul release

163 Bid this s. heart be still
399 The *strugglings* of my will

STUBBORN.
311 And break my s. heart
381 subdue, And break my s. heart
390 Though I have steeled my s. heart
396 To take this s. heart away
617 Too oft, with s. will, We

STUMBLING-BLOCK.
486 Every s.-b. remove
544 Shall every s.-b. remove
573 The s.-b. remove
804 Every s.-b. remove

STUPID.
396 To stir this s. heart of mine

SUBDUE, SUBDUES, SUBDUED.
281 S. the power of every sin
285 This stubborn will s.
309 The stubborn will s.
381 s., And break my stubborn heart
536 The strength of sin s.
172 His power *subdues* our sins
210 Death, hell, and sin...*subdued*
243 news...Of hell s., and peace with
339 Break, by Jesus' cross s.

SUBMIT, SUBMISSION.
371 S. to him, your sovereign Lord
495 O that I could at last s.
632 With meek *submission* may we
1054 O give me s., and strength as my

SUBSTANCE.
606 Whose eyes mine inmost s. see

SUCCESS.
6 And give thy word s.
891 And granted us s.
891 And grant us good s.
895 To crown them with s.

SUCCESSION.
130 Thy being no s. knows
812 So shall the bright s. run

SUCCOR.
157 we prayed, And did for s. flee
181 He comes with s. speedy To
222 And for my s. flying
312 Tempted souls, they bring you s.
506 My s. and salvation, Lord
678 Thou hast my s. been
739 My soul its life and s. brings
900 And send them s. from on high
1095 to thee, O Lord, We now for s. fly
1097 Whose s. they implored

SUFFER.
181 succor...To those who s. wrong
207 Inspire To s. and to die
216 Thou didst s. to release us
256 They s. with their Lord below
487 If with Christ thou s. here
627 For all his children s. here

629 Content to s. while we know
657 Who s. with our Master here
1003 S., with thy Lord to reign

SUFFERED.
32 to sinners cry, I s. this for you
194 The world has s. long
222 What thou, my Lord, hast s.
367 For you he s. pain
381 Reveal the charity...That s. in
442 He hath s. and died
454 For me he hath s., for me
723 S. once for man below
951 And strangely s. us to live

SUFFERER, SUFFERERS.
921 That he who once a s. bled
1057 Shall Jesus' *sufferers* know
1066 S. in his righteous cause

SUFFERING.
170 A s. life my Master led
178 Aid in s. and distress
476 In s. be thy love my peace
487 Christ his s. son shall own
624 My s. time shall soon be o'er
671 sanctities Of s. and of prayer
676 No s. while it lasts, is joy
816 are o'er, Our s. and our pain

SUFFERINGS.
315 The s. which he bore
493 Who Jesus' s. share
506 Or wish my s. less
632 For all our keenest s. here
638 Christ's s. shared below
645 In my s. to sustain
694 O let thy s. give me power
695 Thy s. I embrace with thee
840 Thy s., Lord, each sacred sign
846 our faith employ, His s. to record
853 In thy s. on the tree
854 All his s. for mankind
927 The meed of all thy s. these
1032 O what are all my s. here
1066 They have all their s. past

ALL-SUFFICIENT.
401 Thou *all-s*. art
736 Thou *all-s*. Love divine
1075 Whose *all-s*. grace Shall

SUGGESTIONS.
141 But when such s. our

SUIT.
239 My earnest s. present, and gain
440 Lo! to his my s. I join
523 not let go Till I my s. obtain
718 Come, my soul, thy s. prepare

SULTRY.
36 Nor where at s. noon, thy
180 When in the s. glebe I faint

SUMMER.
602 Nor ours to hear, on s. eves
644 For the s.-time is faded

747 My s. would last all the year
1080 The s. sun and air
1081 S. nor winter fails
1082 The s. rays with vigor

SUMMONS, SUMMONED.
52 Glad the s. to obey
74 With joy the s. we obey
459 Until the final s. come
589 His s. cheerfully obey
967 For me thou wilt the s. send
979 Waiting the s. from on high
1029 How the s. Will the sinner's
959 Ere I am *summoned* hence away

SUN.
69 God is our s., he makes our day
77 O what a s., which broke this day
92 Gently as life's setting s., When
95 Then shall my s. in smiles
107 Now doth the s. ascend the sky
111 The s. itself is but thy shade
112 See how the morning s. Pursues
113 And view the unwearied s.
138 The unwearied s., from day to day
145 Caused the golden-tressed s.
161 The rolling s. stands still
204 When the s. of bliss is beaming
214 Well might the s. in darkness
292 The rolling s., the changing light
293 Almighty Lord, the s. shall fail
413 And bid the s. stand still
427 The s. forbear to shine
478 I thank Thee, uncreated S.
565 Work in the glowing s.
620 And ere thy s. shall set in death
704 And thou my rising s.
724 The s. gone down, Darkness be
747 If thou art my s. and my song
858 While the s. and moon endure
956 While, with ceaseless course, the s.
980 And when the s., with cloudless
1014 S. and moon are both confounded
1063 No need of the s. in that day
1068 S., and moon, and stars decay
1072 And s. and moon refuse to shine
1079 When has sunk you glaring s.

SUNBEAMS.
80 And soft the s. lingering

SUN OF RIGHTEOUSNESS.
99 Then the S. *of* r.
96 Bright S. *of* r., arise
110 O S. *of* r., divine
190 Hail the S. *of* r.
292 Great S. *of* r., arise
411 O S. *of* r., arise
416 S. *of* r., arise
428 Eternal S. *of* r.
570 On thee, bright S. *of* r.
739 The S. *of* r. on me
824 As the bright S. *of* r.
940 S. *of* r., arising

SUN *and* MOON.
57 S. *and* m. rejoice before him
292 S., m., and stars convey thy

724 S., m., and stars forgot
788 S., m., and stars are firmly
858 While the s. and m. endure
1014 S. and m. are both confounded
1068 S., and m., and stars decay
1072 And s. and m. refuse to shine

SUN'S.
68 From the s. rising to its rest

SUNSET.
565 Under the s. skies
974 The s. beam is cast

SUNSHINE.
149 And our lives would be all s.
620 And bid the s. smile
661 This is the s. of the soul

SUNS.
8 Till s. shall rise and set no more
133 Ten thousand s. around him
708 Where s. unsetting light the s.
777 Ye, no more your s. descending
1011 It hath no need of s. to rise
1081 Thou gav'st refulgent s. to shine

SUNDERED.
684 Though s. far, by faith they

SUP, SUPPER.
28 But s. with us, and let the feast
12 At the great *supper* of the Lamb
350 Haste to the s. of my Lord
357 Come to the s. spread

SUPPLIANT.
201 When the blind s. in the way
706 The humble s. cannot fail
1005 Hear, hear our s. breath

SUPPLICATION, SUPPLICATIONS.
265 Hear, O hear, our s.
690 breath...To heaven in s.
1091 Hear thy people's *supplications*

SUPPLY, SUPPLIES.
55 Now s. thy people's need
466 Lord will all our need s.
617 Thy hand alone s.
617 Let mercy still s.
736 In want my plentiful s.
145 His full hand *supplies* their need
255 S. our every need
286 The power that gave it still s.
321 And new s. each hour I meet
326 Lord, we are come to seek s.

SUPPORT, SUPPORTS, SUPPORTING.
391 Some sure s. against despair
421 S. me in the whelming flood
418 S. my weakness with thy might
496 O let thy hand s. me still
605 Its sure s., its noblest end
656 Still s. and comfort me
742 S., defend, and guide
95 'Tis he *supports* my mortal

740 The Lord s. the fainting mind
997 Lay thy *supporting* hand

SURE, SURETY.
207 Most s. in all his ways.
49 A *surety* of thine endless love
438 Before the throne my S. stands

SURGES.
636 But should the s. rise
957 And s. swell no more
978 'Galust which the s. of the main

SURVEY, SURVEYS.
594 A cloud...Hold thee in full s.
1019 While we s. the awful scene
811 King of saints his work *surveys*

SUSTAIN, SUSTAINS, SUSTAINED, SUSTAINING.
165 Thou, Lord, my spirit didst s.
753 My feeble mind s.
411 He *sustains* the hidden life
980 S. and cheers his languid
658 *Sustained* my childish days
508 Thy all-*sustaining* power we

SWALLOW, SWALLOWED.
490 S. up my soul in love
927 To s. up its careless prey
420 My sins are *swallowed* up in thee
431 Be lost and s. up in thee
481 My will be s. up in thee
715 Where faith in sight is s. up
1056 And hasten to be s. up

SWATHING-BANDS.
192 All meanly wrapped in s.-b.

SWAY.
197 We own thy s., we hear thy call
245 He bears the righteous s.
519 Who would not own thy s.
672 Thou every-where hast s.
712 bounding heart shall own thy s.
908 Assert thy rightful s.
928 shall reign with illimitable s.
1081 We own and bless thy gracious s.

SWEAT.
221 Thy bloody s., thy grief and
383 And bloody s., we pray
811 They their s., and blood, and pain

SWEET.
101 where Jesus' name is s. to every
161 But s. will be the flower
205 earth's bitter things grow s.
461 then pain is s., and life and
612 'Tis s. to look beyond my pains
669 For, if thy work on earth be s.
678 Thy s., refreshing grace
692 A work so s., a theme so high
697 name, Nor half so s. can be
712 Labor is rest, and pain is s.
717 S. prospects, sweet birds, and
752 My God, is my hour so s.
1026 S. and joyful it will be

SWEETS, SWEETENS.
299 Sublimer s. than nature knows
208 And *sweetens* every bitter cup

SWEETNESS.
149 In the s. of our Lord
611 Breathes s. out of woe
612 If such the s. of the stream
700 Jesus.. With s. fills the breast
747 Have all lost their s. to me
849 Thy s., never wasting

SWELLING.
171 Bear me through the s.

SWIFT, SWIFTLY.
352 Shall life's s. passing years
1015 S. to hear, and slow to roam
332 How *swiftly* didst thou move To
678 O how s. didst thou move
936 Now the word doth s. run

SWORD.
6 Gird on thy mighty s.
288 Is sharper than a two-edged s.
311 Thou, by thy two-edged s.
418 on thy thigh thy conquering s.
538 The sharpness of thy two-edged s.
569 He girdeth on his s.
584 the hostile shield, Thy s. is
599 The Spirit's s. is in his hand
847 Death's dark angel sheathes his s.
938 Sheathed his s.; he speaks — 'tis
953 When justice bared the s.
1096 Who yet suspends the lifted s.

SWORN.
348 By his life, your God hath s.
1075 He by himself hath s.
1080 And thou hast s. to hear

SYMBOL, SYMBOLS.
92 S. of the peace within
844 Still these *symbols* witness gave

SYMPATHY, SYMPATHIZE, SYMPATHIZING.
254 Touched with a s. within
801 To join with softest s.
806 Touched with softest s.
675 To soothe and *sympathize*
487 Touched with *sympathizing* care
797 flows The s. tear
894 O may our s. hearts

T.

TABERNACLE.
660 And in thy t. hide
864 Must seek a t. where
1056 This t., sink below

TABLE.
156 A t. thou hast furnished me
179 In the midst of affliction my t.
834 The King of heaven his t. spreads
812 When he the t. spreads
855 As we from thy t. go

TABOR.
206 T.'s glorious steep I climb

TAINTED.
1095 Walks forth with t. breath
1113 And breathe in t. air

TAKE, TAKETH, TAKEN.
386 Coming, as at first I came, To t.
450 and thou, blest Lamb, Shalt t. me
461 T. my poor heart, and let it be
470 T. my soul and body's powers
601 T. up thy cross
676 T. from me any thing thou wilt
833 T., eat, this is my body given
1012 He gave, and he *taketh* away
223 Who hath *taken* him away
1002 Thou didst give, and thou hast t.
1002 Thou hast t. but thine own
1006 God hath t. him away

TALE.
122 tells, O Lord, the wondrous t.
933 Rehearse the wondrous t.
956 And when life's short t. is told

TALENTS.
955 And our t. improve, By

TARES.
1083 Wheat and t. together sown
1083 In the fire the t. to cast

TARRY, TARRIED.
340 If you t. till you're better
1107 For he who *tarried* at their side

TASK, TASKS.
19 And still the pleasing t. pursue
607 Take the t. he gives you gladly
622 And when my t. on earth is
597 From daily *tasks* set free

TASTE, TASTED, TASTING.
84 Never did angels t. above
88 Here afford us, Lord, a t.
221 May t. the grace that found out
420 That mercy they may t. and
666 But now they t. unmingled love
757 That...the fullness...this is the t.
822 O that the world might t. and see
853 Wine of gladness...May we t. it
1030 We more than t. the heavenly
686 If I have *tasted* of thy grace
849 O let us, freely *tasting*, Our

TAUGHT.
40 Nor as he in the temple t.
443 righteousness of faith Hath t.
897 Yet thou hast t. us, Lord
905 Till t. by him who for our
941 none has t. them Of his love

TEACH.
23 May he t. us to fulfill
207 Should t. his brethren, and
273 T. us to know the Father, Son
230 came in tongues...To t.

TEA 162 TEM

760 I need thee every hour; T. me
812 Jesus, now t. our hearts to
820 T. all nations my commands
881 T. the way of truth and right
892 To t. the way of life and peace
956 T. us henceforth how to live
1022 And t., O teach us by thy grace

TEACHABLE. TEACHER.
481 Humble, and t., and mild
328 Yes, sacred *Teacher*, we will
499 T. and heavenly Guide
735 If thou, my God and T.

TEAR.
401 To t. my soul from earth away

TEAR.
41 songs abound, And every t. be dry
203 Jesus wept! that t. of sorrow
234 Come, saints, and drop a t. or two
570 And wipe the falling t.
405 Each sin demands a t.
604 No t. to wipe, no good to crave
611 thou who driest the mourner's t.
627 And numbered every secret t.
637 never cause...child a needless t.
654 Though seen through many a t.
666 And joy without a t.
695 Nor count it worthy of a t.
706 music in a groan...beauty in a t.
710 Prayer...The falling of a t.
711 And dried the bitter t.
879 Every t. and pain gone by
1067 Every t. is wiped away

TEARS.
93 His have no weight, and t. no
157 Our eyes no longer drowned in t.
212 Still let thy t., thy groans, thy
232 And the sad t. death makes us
234 Break off your t., ye saints, and
256 But only let that path of t. Lead
327 I shed my t. and make my moan
342 Chase away the falling t.
351 The t. that tell your sins forgiven
405 The Son of God in t.
410 O for those humble, contrite t.
415 Could my t. forever flow
417 By the bitter t. that flowed
423 But now my t. are vain
441 T. of such pure and deep delight
455 T. of joy mine eyes o'erflow
478 Give to mine eyes refreshing t.
548 hath shed Both t. and blood
553 hand, indulgent, wipes the t.
611 And he who has but t. to give
627 The lids that overflow with t.
634 Save the sweet dew of t.
723 By the boiling t. that flowed
759 And smile at the t. I have shed
762 Wipe sorrow's t. away
770 Church...For her my t. shall fall
794 And treasure up our gracious t.
828 With flowing t. and thankful
852 In t. of godly sorrow flow
911 Human t. for thee are flowing
919 With all its mourners' t.

971 Why should our t. in sorrow flow
974 Whose eyes are bathed in t.
986 Who shall forbid...our t. of love
988 The eye long dimmed by t.
1022 For all the t. thy people shed
1023 sinner cease From her t. and
1038 they shall rise and find their t.
1049 And t. are of those former things
1057 There gushing t. are wiped away
1060 Where t. are ever banished
1062 That brimmed with t. of late

TEARFUL. TEARLESS.
363 With t. eyes I look around
1039 There faith lifts up the *tearless*
1059 The t. life is there

TEMPER. TEMPERS.
163 To t. the deceitful ray
268 What lovely *tempers*, fruits of
600 Your faith by holy t. prove

TEMPERANCE.
895 The cause of t. is thine
899 To t., truth, and piety

TEMPEST.
351 The rising t. sweeps the sky
399 And bid the t. cease
551 His voice commands the t.
620 When t. clouds are dark on
636 Blest be the t., kind the storm
656 While the t. still is high
678 A covert from the t. be
764 The threatening t. blows
787 The t., fire, and smoke
978 So through the t. and the gloom
1011 Outflying the t. and wind
1039 And views the t. passing by
1067 There no angry t. blows
1113 When by the dreadful t. borne
1114 through the torn sail the wild t.

TEMPESTS.
667 When t. rage without
709 While here by t. driven
763 And t. are abroad
928 E'en now, when t. round
931 holdest...The t. of the ocean
957 And we shall be where t. cease
1074 The t. that rise shall
1090 When the wild t. rave
1111 When t. rock the groaning
1115 Save, till all these t. end

TEMPLE.
11 your heart; Make it a t., set
40 Nor as he in the t. taught
43 That glorious t. in the skies
56 seraphim Filled his t., and
71 our secret soul to be A t. pure
74 Thy chosen t., Lord, how fair
87 Thy t. is the arch of yon
189 In his t. shall appear
410 Come, and in thy t. stay
479 The Lord will to his t. come
489 Make me his t. and abode
501 And for his t. and his throne
501 A t. meet for thee

519 A t. built by God
764 The Christian t. stands
774 Beside thy t. cleaves the
792 And build the t. of our God
820 We 'd keep his t. pure
856 To this t., where we call thee
857 For the t. near thy throne
858 Here to thee a t. stand
861 To thee this t., Lord, we build
862 Enter thy t., glorious King
862 In that great t. built above
863 perfect world...Was the first t.
863 A humbler t., made with
864 Yet he beheld no t. there
864 God and the Lamb its t. are
864 With purer light our t. cheer
865 crown This t. as thy home
866 And let these halls thy t. be
868 We rear not a t., like Judah's
869 O Thou, whose own vast t. stands
870 rear This t., Lord, to thee
870 A living t. rear
874 Though a t. far less glorious
1082 While in thy t. we appear
1083 Come to God's own t., come
1091 From thy t. in the skies

TEMPLES.

15 Thine earthly t. are
36 In every clime Shall t. rise
489 To thy human t. come
491 Never more thy t. leave
679 hoary hairs shall their t. adorn
800 From different t. though it rise
815 Be t. of the Holy Ghost
859 To dwell in t. made with hands
865 While t. stand and men adore
867 Accept our t. for his own
868 Shall be t. to God, everlasting
871 These t. of his grace
910 The t. of thy praise

TEMPT, TEMPTED.

69 Not tents of ease...t. my feet
209 Conspired to t. God's only Son
741 T. not my soul away: Jesus
1088 angels o'er me T. sweetly to
342 Tempted soul, they bring you
543 And still my t. soul stand by
715 To all thy t. followers give

TEMPTER.

93 thy grace can foil the t.'s power
165 The t. to my soul hath said
223 Ye that feel the t.'s power
417 Of the subtle t.'s power
505 looks to thee....And sees the t.
626 And basely to the t. yield
688 And oft escaped the t.'s snare
722 From the flattering t.'s power
723 Of the insulting t.'s power
899 The t.'s power withstand

TEMPTATION, TEMPTATIONS.

555 Lest I into t. fall
624 In fierce t.'s darkest hour
645 By thy most severe t.
651 And guard in fierce t.'s hour

680 Through torrents of t.
716 Into t. lead us not
1051 Though now my t. like billows
254 He knows what sore temptations
640 The manifold t. That
653 If t. round you gather
760 T. lose their power When

TENDER, TENDERNESS.

127 Each evening shows thy t. love
140 Thy mercies how t.! how
177 How t. is thy hand, O
254 His heart is made of tenderness
351 The unutterable t.
410 O for that t. of heart
417 By the t. that wept
420 Thy heart still melts with t.
559 Shed thy love, thy t.
670 Let thine own word of t.
888 Let thy t. so loving

TENEMENT, TENEMENTS.

45 And this frail t. decays
328 Decay, then, tenements of dust

TENT, TENTS.

1050 Yet nightly pitch my moving t.
1116 And glad I'll drop this t., to find
69 Not tents of ease nor thrones of
759 Say, if in your t. my Beloved

TERRESTRIAL.

138 Move round the dark t. ball
248 every tribe On this t. ball
647 Vain are all t. pleasures
1033 Let all the saints t. sing

TERRIBLE.

162 How t. is God in arms
1092 God the All-T.! thou who

TERROR, TERRORS.

208 It takes its t. from the grave
308 My t. now begins
629 What t. can confound me
1023 Day of t., day of gloom
162 When terrors rise and nations
227 Vain were the t. that gathered
252 Bright t. guard thy seat
787 Not all the t. of the Lord
814 Only thy t., Lord, restrain
976 Nor feel the t. as she passed

TEST.

197 We t. our lives by thine
983 For them no further t. remains
1020 And pass the solemn t.

TESTIFY.

435 And t. to all mankind
439 Would he not t. of thee
532 Saviour, I long to t.

THANK.

222 language shall I borrow To t.
520 Saviour, I t. thee for the grace
889 May we our t.-offerings bring
1086 We t. thee, then, O Father

THA 164 THO

THANKS.
13 O render t. to God above
42 Give t. to God on high
42 ransomed race Render in t.
51 And t. never ceasing for
99 Let warmest t. arise
296 Lord, everlasting t. be thine
472 my every breath in t. and
493 Let us give t. and sing
692 And mean the t. I cannot
713 The t. I owe thee, and the love
884 Their voice of t. would raise
985 Immortal t. be paid
1077 Give t. to God on high
1087 And joyful t. proclaim

THANKFUL, THANKFULNESS, THANKLESS.
19 Compose into a t. frame
26 Thee with t. hearts we prove
70 To thee I'll raise my t. voice.
283 make thy home in my t. heart
476 O knit my t. heart to thee
610 Give me a calm, a t. heart
827 We bring them, Lord, in t.
854 Bring to every t. mind
949 Thy t. people praise thee
1083 Come, ye t. people, come
214 Dissolve my heart...*thankfulness*
347 Why, ye *thankless* creatures

THANKSGIVING, THANKSGIVINGS.
232 life...One long t. be
1087 In loud t. raise
1110 In joyous t. to thee
23 Loud *thanksgivings* to our God

THAW.
396 And t., with beams of love

THEME, THEMES.
118 Thou art every creature's t.
160 The pleasing t. renew
208 The angel's t. in heaven above
727 Know no t. of nobler song
756 story..."T will be my t. in glory
764 Loved t. of many a sacred song
852 The t. demands immortal
8 Your lofty *themes*, ye mortals
58 Sacred t. to you belong

THIEF.
319 The dying t. rejoiced to see
617 There no t. can ever enter
1023 Thou, who to the dying t.

THINE.
222 O make me t. forever
241 thousand hearts... should all be t.
302 T. is the work and only thine
393 Now to be t., yea, thine alone
409 I would be t.; but, Lord, I feel
460 Lord, I am t., entirely thine
460 T. would I live, thine would I die
465 T. forever! God of love
468 heart....And in ke it always t.
469 Our all...no longer ours but t.
470 Now, O God, t. own I am
472 T., wholly thine, shall be
474 No longer mine but t. I am
476 T., wholly thine, alone I am
488 Jesus, all I have is t.
490 T. we are, thou Son of God
500 I ask but to be t.
508 T., wholly thine, we pant to be
757 My God, I am t.; what a comfort
760 O make me t. Indeed
762 from this day Be wholly t.
875 To keep us still t. own
892 All that we have is t. alone
1005 in life and death, T., only thine
1015 When shall I be wholly t.
1080 T., too, by right, and ours by

THINK.
383 T. on us who think on thee
470 All I think, or speak, or do
592 And all I t., or speak, or do
606 In all I think, or speak, or do
789 E'en now we t. and speak the
793 We all shall t. and speak the

THIRST, THIRSTS.
326 may quench your raging t.
311 He that drinks need t. no more
399 That I may t. no more
426 My t. was quenched, my soul
461 I t., thou wounded Lamb
540 I t., I faint, I die to prove
545 Me with that restless t. inspire
691 And t. our souls from thee to fill
819 Our burning t. assuage
355 him that *thirsts* for righteousness
362 Ho! every one that t., draw nigh

THIRSTING, THIRSTY.
732 T. for the springs of water
944 T., as for dews of even
180 Or on the *thirsty* mountains pant
323 Come, t. souls, and bless the Lord
384 Showers, the t. land refreshing
550 For thee...my t. soul doth pine
551 And cheer the t. ground
631 For thee my t. soul doth pine
683 A t. land, whose springs are dry
936 cloud...Hangs o'er all...t. land

THORN, THORNS, THORNY.
1005 for our sake The t., the rod
183 Nor *thorns* infest the ground
211 Or t. compose so rich a crown
222 With t., thine only crown
256 The head, once crowned with t.
339 Crowned with t. his sacred head
708 Its joys are but the treacherous t.
742 my path...'Mid t. or flowers
496 Though rough and *thorny*...way
620 Thy t. path awhile

THOUGHT.
102 Be my last t. how sweet
137 Our every t., our every song
476 thy boundless love...No t. can
488 Every t., design, and word
616 Thy love the power of t. bestowed
673 Far, far above thy t. His
685 One t. shall fill my soul with
655 My sweetest t. henceforth shall

968 Nothing is worth a t. beneath
1051 Bear every t. above
1053 One sweetly solemn t.

THOUGHTS.
7 And worldly t. forget
47 To thee may all our t. arise
83 My t., O God, ascend to thee
97 And heavenly t. refreshed
103 New t. of God, new hopes of
123 My t. lie open to thee, Lord
159 Lead all our t. to thee
160 Ere yet my feeble t. had learned
317 Where all our t. are drowned
369 In whose breast a thousand t.
372 Our inmost t. perceive
418 Quick as their t. their joys
616 To thee my t. would soar
705 My t. shall then to nobler
839 If tender t. within us burn
968 No matter which my t. employ

THOUGHTFUL, THOUGHTLESS.
675 I ask thee for a t. love
966 And deeply on my t. heart
901 Spare, Lord, the *thoughtless*
929 The t. young, the hardened

THREE.
16 Him T. in One, and one in Three
35 Mysterious Godhead! T. in One
72 To thee, blest T. in One
91 God, the blessed T. in One
130 almighty T., the eternal One
136 God in T. persons, blessed Trinity
139 Co-equal, co-eternal T.
198 The chosen t., on mountain
199 How with the t. disciples there
470 One in T., and Three in One
913 Blessed and holy T., Glorious
1076 Before the great T. One

THREESCORE.
1032 I suffer on my t. years

THRIVE.
575 Thou know'st not which shall t.

THRONE.
2 Of him who sits upon the t.
16 Who sits upon the t., And shall
58 Jesus fills the t. on high
97 Whose t. is in the vast abyss
127 Yet, nearer to thy sacred t.
135 Before thy ever-blazing t.
144 Spirits blest, before the t.
148 From the highest t. of glory
148 Leave thy footstool, take thy t.
152 majesty Upon his holy t.
185 Let every heart prepare a t.
216 Will he forsake his t. above
225 Saints shall stand before the t.
247 Seated on his lofty t.
334 Raise us to thy glorious t.
647 On the things around the t.
650 And seated on his glorious t.
673 Proclaim, God sitteth on the t.
683 waters flowing Forth from the t.

811 High on his everlasting t.
867 And will he, from his radiant t.
916 tribe Assembling round the t.
968 The inexorable t.
1001 Bear him to the t. of love
1018 Descending on his great white t.
1019 And share the everlasting t.
1023 Summon all before the t.
1040 Lo! round the t. a glorious
1047 Shall be nearer my t.
1053 Nearer the great white t.
1066 Therefore are they next the t.
1069 Stand before yon dazzling t.
1079 When I stand before the t.
1106 A t. without thy blessing

Eternal THRONE.
422 Bold I approach the *eternal* t.
1013 High on thy *eternal* t.
1025 Around the *eternal* t.
1066 Nearest the *eternal* t.

Father's THRONE.
176 Haste...heavenly *Father's* t.
251 High on his *Father's* t.
322 Priest...Before his *Father's* t.
408 Around thy *Father's* t. on high
422 He left his *Father's* t. above
688 And b.ds me at my *Father's* t.
797 Before our *Father's* t. We pour

His THRONE.
40 The Lord upon *his* t. appears
41 accord, While ye surround *his* t.
142 *His* t. is built on high
261 Though returning to *his* t.
322 Down from *his* t. on high
621 I'll hasten to *his* t.
743 Exalted on *his* t.
776 Rising to *his* t. on high
789 When round *his* t. we meet
800 Ere to *his* t. he passed
876 To him who left *his* t. above
984 Break from *his* t., illustrious

Thy THRONE.
20 When round *thy* t. we sing
35 Before *thy* t. we sinners bend
43 Before *thy* t. we bow, O thou
49 For us around *thy* t. of grace
83 Eternal King, erect *thy* t.
148 Leave thy footstool, take *thy* t.
236 And round *thy* t. unceasingly
415 And behold thee on *thy* t.
485 Henceforth take it for *thy* t.
517 Who always see thee on *thy* t.
587 My heart shall be *thy* t.
619 And when before *thy* t. I stand
723 Bending from *thy* t. on high
801 Before *thy* t. appear
859 when we bring them to *thy* t.
870 Though round *thy* t., above
881 God of love, who from *thy* t.
996 And when thou comest on *thy* t.
1065 And rise to a share in *thy* t.

THRONE of Grace.
439 sprinkles now the t. *of grace*
498 Behold the t. *of grace*

THRONES.

553 See at thy *t. of grace*
717 They who seek the *t. of grace*

THRONES.
10 By all the powers and *t.* in
38 And ranks of shining *t.* around
162 Kingdoms and *t.* to God belong
289 And give us *t.* above
917 Let *t.*, and powers, and kingdoms

THRONED.
119 High *t.* on heaven's eternal
135 Lord of all be'ng! *t.* afar
387 *T.* above celestial things
444 Or, *t.* in floods of beamy day
694 When, *t.* above the skies

THRONG.
74 As here thy servants *t.*
192 Appeared a shining *t.*
248 O that with yonder sacred *t.*
253 A great and countless *t.*
563 Join our happy *t.*
697 With all thy favored *t.*
744 A bright, harmonious *t.*
754 with Jesus Amid the heavenly *t.*
1001 See they *t.* the blissful shore
1049 Behold that blessed *t.*
1062 *T.* up the steeps of light

THUNDER, THUNDERS.
140 His chariots of wrath the deep *t.*
153 *T.*, and hail, and fire, and storms
379 Lets the lifted *t.* drop
555 The *t.* of thy power
725 Direct thy vengeful *t.'s* aim
787 Not to the *t.* of that word
1030 The *t.* of that awful word
142 The *thunders* of his hand
225 When, amidst earth's closing *t.*
814 let winds blow, or *t.* roar
866 And *t.* voice the name of God
938 Loud as mighty *t.* roar
1019 While twice ten thousand *t.*
1029 Louder than a thousand *t.*
1079 Loud as *t.* to the ear

THYSELF.
91 Thou dost give *t.* to me
106 And with *t.* my spirit fill
239 Give me *t.*, or else I die
397 And pour *t.* into my heart
520 But give *t.* to me
530 gifts alas.. Unless *t.* be given
543 And make me like *t.* below
545 Less than *t.* cannot suffice
715 Till thou *t.* bestow
1084 Love thee for *t.* alone

TIDE.
181 The *t.* of time shall never
187 Death-struck, I ceased the *t.* to
413 Thou only can't drive back the *t.*
597 Around us rolls the ceaseless *t.*
773 Trembles and dreads the *t.*
953 The *t.* that hurries thoughtless

TIDINGS.
138 Confirm the *t.* as they roll

226 Joyful *t.*! Yes, the Lord is risen
235 angels... The joyful *t.* bear
342 *T.* bear without delay
414 Through all the courts the *t.* flew
821 How sweet the *t.* are! Zion
910 Lord, when shall these glad *t.*
926 Glad *t.* unto all we show
932 Each breeze Brings *t.* from
939 Bear the *t.* round the hall
941 Haste, O haste, and spread the *t.*

TIE., TIES.
741 Break every tender *t.*, Jesus is
768 Every human *t.* may perish
797 Blest be the *t.* that binds Our
419 And I am thine by sacred *ties*
663 writes... By faith's endearing *t.*
663 And trust to holier *t.*
805 Dear *t.* of mutual succor bind
960 How slender all the fondest *t.*
975 All human *t.* resigned must be

TIME, TIMES.
294 Till *t.* and nature are no more
349 Soon, borne on *t.'s* most rapid
576 *T.* hurries past thee like the
576 Thou hast no *t.* to lose in sloth
576 Thy *t.* is almost o'er
615 Since all the varying scenes of *t.*
713 echo... When *t.* shall be no more
948 On all the wings of *t.* it flies
951 O may we all the *t.* redeem
955 our *t.*, as a stream, Glides swiftly
964 *T.*, like an ever-rolling stream
970 tending upward... As fast as *t.*
1009 Beyond the flight of *t.*
1060 Thou hast no *t.*, bright day
637 My *times* are in thy hand

TITLE.
219 Own his *t.*, praise his name
385 Other *t.* I disclaim
659 When I can read my *t.* clear

TOIL.
22 There released from *t.* and pain
80 Nor will our days of *t.* be long
486 Till *t.*, and grief, and pain shall
547 ants See how they *t.* and strive
561 Forward.. Through the *t.* and
572 Jesus' feet There *t.* seems
575 Thou canst not *t.* in vain
578 health Repay your arduous *t.*
579 said to his *t.* he goes, His seed
584 Who all your *t.* foreknew
593 I'll bear the *t.*, endure the pain
603 *T.* on, and I in my toil rejoice
609 Nor feel my happy *t.*
731 With us when we *t.* in sadness
811 Je us, the r *t.* d lighted sees
825 Indeed to *t.* and patient pain
801 strength in parts our only *t.*
992 Now *t.* and confl a *t.* o'er
1032 And smile at *t.* and pain
1017 But that *t.* shall make thee Some
1058 *T.*, man, to gain that light
1067 Passed this scene of *t.* and pain

TOILS.

577 the day When all our *t.* shall
708 Its noblest *t.* are then the scourge
770 Till *t.* and cares shall end
811 He rests well pleased their *t.* to
816 Where all our *t.* are o'er
957 A few more *t.*, a few more tears
971 Their *t.* are past, their work is
986 And heavier *t.* shall close
1001 They from all their *t.* are freed

TOILED, TOILING, TOILSOME.

1026 Who for Christ have *t.* and
994 Rest for the *toiling* hand
709 Thus, when life's *toilsome* day is
1055 While *t.* years are given

TOKEN, TOKENS.

512 A *t.* of his love he gives
32 Show us the *tokens* of thy love
424 bring...The *t.* of thy grace
867 With choicest *t.* of thy grace
1014 Mark the *t.* Of his heavenly

TOMB.

90 First, for man, the dismal *t.*
108 And wait thy voice to rouse my *t.*
223 Early hasten to the *t.*
228 Deep in our Saviour's *t.*
228 Fearless we lay us in the *t.*
233 Vainly with rocks his *t.* was
234 The rising God forsakes the *t.*
336 not heard in the vale of the *t.*
365 Sin kills beyond the *t.*
373 Halt feebly to the *t.*
410 My body in the *t.*
507 Walk in the light! and e'en the *t.*
957 Asleep within the *t.*
965 stand thick...push us to the *t.*
970 convey Their bodies to the *t.*
972 Still walking downward to the *t.*
973 Are marching to the *t.*
974 Descending to the *t.*
977 Yet these, new rising from the *t.*
981 No future morning light the *t.*
984 Unveil thy bosom, faithful *t.*
998 no, welcome the *t.!* Since Jesus
999 sorrows and darkness...the *t.*
1023 Shrouding every human *t.*
1039 Beyond the confines of the *t.*
1054 thy dear image arise from the *t.*

TOMBS.

972 Hark! from the *t.* a doleful

TO-MORROW.

357 come, *T.* may not be
361 *T.* it may be too late

TONGUE.

84 And every *t.* confess thee, Lord
107 Curb thou for us the unruly *t.*
146 And love command my *t.*
148 Break, my *t.*, such guilty silence
196 Escaped thy silent *t.*
319 this poor lisping, stammering *t.*
442 *T.* can never express
546 His praises tuned my *t.*
705 Nor shall my *t.* alone proclaim
719 O 'tis more than *t.* can tell
813 Soften truth, or smooth my *t.*
1016 Onward roll from *t.* to tongue
1040 Of every *t.* redeemed to God

TONGUES.

1 O for a thousand *t.*, to sing
2 Ten thousand...are their *t.*
9 earth, with her ten thousand *t.*
243 Our *t.* shall bless thy name
270 Though on our heads no *t.* of fire
271 New *t.* impart to speak the
275 When, with thy fiery, cloven *t.*
276 Give *t.* of fire and hearts of love
280 He came in *t.* of living flame
283 Answer not with *t.* of light
304 And all harmonious, human *t.*
504 Had I the gift of *t.*
815 And let all *t.* confess their
849 O tune our *t.*, and set in frame
995 nobler soun l...our immortal *t.*
1034 Let thy praise our *t.* employ
1089 Let mortal *t.* awake

TOPSTONE.

859 May raise the *t.* in its day

TORMENT, TORMENTS.

1030 awful word Would so *t.* my
371 Can you in endless *torments*

TORRENT.

193 The impetuous *t.* ran
958 How swift the *t.* rolls

TORTURE.

202 Yet love through all thy *t.*

TOSSED.

187 The wind that *t.* my foundering
344 Ye who are *t.* on beds of pain
393 Just as I am, though *t.* about
1039 When *t.* on life's tempestuous
1114 O Jesus, once *t.* on the breast

TOUCH, TOUCHED.

197 We *t.* him in life's throng and
201 And *t.* the darkened lids, and say
374 *T.* with thine all-victorious blood
713 There, if thy Spirit *t.* the soul
1099 And lo, thy *t.* brought life and
820 His heart that's *touched* with all

TOWER, TOWERS.

141 In this our strong *t.* for safety
541 The name of Jesus is my *t.*
934 High *t.* and lowly dwelling
1060 They raise thy holy *t.*
564 Rise the city *towers*
921 The old grim *t.* of darkness
972 Princes...In spite of all your *t.*
1025 Lo! the heavenly spirit *t.*
1072 Its glittering *t.* the sun outshine

TOY, TOYS.

698 How vain a *t.* is glittering wealth
277 Fond of these earthly *toys*

TRA 168 TRE

826 And vainly strive with earthly t.
418 scorn to seek earth's golden t.
481 Dead to the world and all its t.
530 Why grasp at vain and fleeting t.
813 To gain earth's gilded t., or flee

TRAIN.
566 Soon you'll join that glorious t.
1068 There we'll join the heavenly t.

TRAMPLE, TRAMPLES, TRAMPLED.
329 T. on his precious blood
456 I t. on thy wealth and pride
599 Sin, death, and hell he *tramples*
380 *Trampled* on thy richest grace

TRANQUIL.
80 Season of rest! the t. soul
752 Blest is that t. hour of morn
1007 All is t. and serene

TRANSACTION.
447 'Tis done, the great t.'s done

TRANSFIGURED, TRANSFIGURING.
198 And lo! with the t. Lord
200 Gazing on that t. face
198 To prayer's *transfiguring* glow

TRANSGRESSED, TRANSGRESSION.
314 God's holy law t., Speaks
181 To take away *transgression* And
222 Mine, mine was the t.
1091 Let thy mercy veil t.

TRANSIENT.
49 How t. is our present pain
114 And end my t. days
168 They look beyond this t. world
665 The t. pain and strife
960 How t. every earthly bliss

TRANSITORY.
978 Earth's t. things decay
1068 Rise from t. things Toward

TRANSLATE, TRANSLATED.
502 And soon or later then t.
991 reign With our *translated* friend
1009 T. to that happier sphere

TRANSPORT, TRANSPORTED, TRANSPORTING.
801 fullness fill, And then t. away
987 Thy life I read...With t. all
60 With love divine *transported*
130 T. with the view I'm lost
216 And gaze, t. at the sight
966 T. from this vale, to live
701 heavy clay At t.at *transporting*
1038 O the t., rapturous scene

TRAVAIL.
529 See, Lord, the t. of thy soul
808 But to have shared the t. Which
911 Whom his soul in t. knew

TRAVEL, TRAVELING.
255 desert bloom...O'er which we t.
618 Guide Of all that t. to the sky
654 I t. calmly on, And sing in life
699 My feet shall t. all the length
801 Together t. on, And bear each
52 *Traveling* through...wilderness
720 We are t. home to God
960 If God be ours, we're t. home

TRAVELER, TRAVELERS.
354 Haste, t., haste! the night
737 Come, O thou T. unknown
935 T., o'er yon mountain's height
419 As *travelers* in thirsty lands
879 Let the little t. in

TREACHERY, TREACHEROUS.
723 T. lurked within thy soul
568 Heed not the *treacherous* voices

TREASURE.
29 And keep the precious t. there
228 And seek the t. there, that
265 Bringing down the richest t.
316 My never-failing t., filled
442 And have laid up their t. above
572 My wants are t.
612 My Saviour has my t.
984 Take this new t. to thy trust
1046 The heavenly t. now we have
1048 There we our t. place
1071 Our hearts and our t. already
1078 My t. and my heart are there

TREASURES.
103 New t. still of countless price
161 He t. up his bright designs
182 All our costliest t. bring
185 And, with the t. of his grace
647 Seek we, then, for heavenly t.
859 The t. of the earth and sea
897 And let love's t. still be spent
903 T. beyond the changing sky
962 He heaps up t. mixed with
962 Earth's fleeting t. I resign

TREE, TREES.
208 He bears our sins upon the t.
212 Extended on a cursed t.
250 Now let it view upon the t.
258 Once he prayed upon the t.
259 Here the fair t. of knowledge
310 On the bloody t. behold him
916 Bring forth the t. of life
974 leaf scarce whispers from the t.
1066 With the t. of life sustain
774 The blooming *trees* of life appear
953 Barren and withered t.
1076 And t. of life forever grow
1089 music...ring from all the t.

TREMBLE, TREMBLES, TREMBLER.
166 Prince of darkness...We t. not
667 a faith...That will not t. on
966 And t. on the brink of fate
1047 Christian, never t.

37 *Trembles* our hearts to find thee
412 And t. at the thought
840 Help each poor *trembler* to repeat

TREMBLING.
37 To thee our t. hearts aspire
54 Teach us to rejoice with t.
147 And worship thee with t. hope
234 A sudden t. shakes the ground
410 And t. at thy word
423 Where shall my t. soul be hid
536 I hold them with a t. hand
548 Confirm the t. will
562 And t. to its source return
625 Leave not my t. heart to fail
628 Thus t., to the things of time
665 The t. hand, the fainting
727 While our t. souls within
926 Speak to their t. hearts, and
996 And must my t. spirit fly
997 My t. soul shall stand
1028 T. they stand before the throne

TRESPASS, TRESPASSES.
433 My t. was grown up to heaven
308 I am dead in *trespasses* and sins

TRIAL, TRIALS.
614 Until life's t. time shall end
638 Keen was the t. once
727 Here in t., there in glory
568 His love foretells thy *trials*
632 Nor think our t. too severe
640 The t. that beset you The
643 Life with t. hard may press thee
671 And life, by t. furrowed, bears
679 For I will be with thee, thy t. to
679 When through fiery t. thy
715 Long as our fiery t. last
728 Have we t. and temptations
953 Who lengthens out our t. here
1066 Here they find their t. o'er

TRIBE, TRIBES.
79 People of many a t. and tongue
248 Let every kindred, every t.
910 Till every t. and every soul
89 Thither the *tribes* repair
184 Him shall the t. of earth obey
919 And savage t. attend his word
925 And wandering t.. in joyful
964 The busy t. of flesh and blood
1062 creation And all its t. were made

TRIBULATION.
680 The fire of t.
735 I fear no t.
777 Scores of heartfelt t.
1040 Through t. great they came

TRIBUTE.
12 Accept the t. which we bring
13 His t. of immortal praise
112 great Orig.nal The humble t. bring
294 To thee its grateful t. bring
459 When each glad heart its t. pays
592 The cheerful t. will I give

705 Their grateful t. pay
734 To his feet they t. bring
883 render The t. of our words
1087 The plains their t. bring

TRIFLES, TRIFLING.
516 Once I admired its t. too
758 The time for such t. with me now
83 O bid this *trifling* world retire

TRINITY.
118 Blest and holy T.
136 God in Three Persons, blessed T.
144 Chanting ..To the blessed T.
913 holy Three, Glorious T.
1108 O T. of love and power

TRIUMPH.
13 And count thy people's t. mine
19 And raise in death our t. higher
51 The great congregation his t. shall
91 Over death his t. won
93 I t. still. if thou abide with me
166 willed His truth to t. through us
175 I t. and adore
218 'Tis finished! let the t. rise
227 Lift your glad voices in t.
228 To-day we t. in thy life
228 enemy...his short-lived t. o'er
231 his sorrows ended, hail his t. now
233 In pomp of t. he has come
241 He makes me t. over death
350 To t. in your blest estate
452 I t. in the love divine
480 We raise our songs of t. higher
553 At the sign of t. Satan's host
569 This seeming t. o'er God's saints
585 O may I t. so, When
593 They see the t. from afar
626 Yet will I t. in the Lord
647 Bids us t. in his love
670 By thy blest feet in t. trod
812 to heaven he rose In splendid t.
917 That song of t. which records
921 We wait thy t., Saviour King
989 And now in t. sing
1011 And t. o'er sorrow and death
1013 Swell the t. of his train
1040 They sing the t. of his grace
1045 Ascribe...Their t. to his death
1061 The song of them that t.
1062 a thousand harps Bespeaks the t.
1065 But longing to t. with thee

TRIUMPHS.
1 The t. of his grace
190 Join the t. of the skies
219 The t. of the cross
226 Jesus t.! sing ye praises
260 Raise your joys and t. high
719 Never shall our t. end Till
821 He reigns and t. here
870 Here may thy truth fresh t. win
920 T. of mercy wrought by thee
923 To aid the t. of our King
928 The t. of thy conquering power
1004 Go, his t. to adorn
1025 T. in immortal powers

TRIUMPHANT.

10 And swell the loud t. song
20 Our t. voices raise
34 T. host! they never cease
65 Let Jesus here t. reign
75 we learn to be T. here below
77 T. from the tomb
245 gone up...With a t. noise
249 Hark, those loud t. chords
253 Join...host, T. in the sky
261 Their t. Lord and ours
657 ascend at last, T. with our Head
669 And join with the t. saints
681 And bear me t. away
713 eternity I'll spend, T. in his grace
932 T. reach their home
934 ringing, With one t. song
952 O may we all t. rise
1001 Reign with me t. now
1068 our Saviour will return T. in the
1076 T. o'er the world and sin

TRIUNE.

34 The T. God of holiness
48 And seraphs shout the T. God
72 To the great God T.
137 O God T., to thee we owe

TROOPS.

153 fire and storms, The t. of his
1104 Our t. shall lift their banners

TROPHIES.

248 Go, spread your t. at his feet
249 Rich the t. Jesus brings
908 powers of hell resign Their t. at

TROPIC.

939 Go to many a t. isle

TROUBLE.

33 In t.'s dark and stormy hour
115 They, unlinked with earthly t.
168 In t. our unfailing aid
402 To whom should I my t. show
643 Man may t. and distress me
659 And not a wave of t. roll
660 When storms of t. blow
667 That seas of t. cannot drown
728 Is there t. anywhere
1017 Well I know thy t., O my servant

TROUBLES, TROUBLED.

141 Though t. assail, and dangers
407 My sins and t. end
548 An end of all my t. make
621 Long as I live, when t. rise, I'll
650 What mighty t. hast thou shown
738 What t. have we seen
1071 The t. that come shall come to
161 Peace, troubled soul, thou need'st
316 And calms the t. breast
339 Thou seest my t. breast
491 A t. heart, that cannot rest

TRUE.

698 We will be t. to thee till death
942 All is t. that thou hast said

TRUMP.

211 The t. of God shall sound
850 Until the t. of God be heard
994 Soon shall the t. of God Give
1017 Swells the high t. that wakes
1019 The great archangel's t. shall
1022 Lord, ere the last dread t. be
1027 Whene'er the archangel's t. shall

TRUMPET.

72 The silver t. calls
326 The t. of the gospel sounds
331 Blow ye the t., blow
331 The gospel t. hear
332 O for a t. voice, On all the world
567 The t. call obey
582 Attend the t.'s sound
810 Sweetly the gospel t. sound
911 And, t.-tongued, proclaim
954 hear The t.'s welcome sound
970 Then let the last loud t. sound
989 When the last t.'s awful voice
990 Till the last t.'s joyful sound
996 Waked by the t.'s sound
1000 Hark! the judgment-t. sounds
1018 The seventh t. speaks him near
1023 shall the archangel's t. tone
1024 Attentive to the t.'s sound
1028 The t. sounds; the graves restore
1028 At the last t.'s sounding
1029 Hark! the t.'s awful sound
1033 shout...To hear his t. sound
1042 Till the last t.'s joyful sound

TRUMPETS.

229 Blow the full t., blow

TRUST.

43 we kneel, With t. and holy fear
140 In thee do we t., nor find thee
141 From them let us learn to t.
141 Our t. is all thrown on Jesus'
143 And t. him for all that's to come
157 O save...The souls that t. in thee
318 And those who put their t. in thee
391 May not a sinner t. in thee
432 I t. in thee, whose powerful word
453 I t. in his word; none plucks me
479 Himself hath caused to put your t.
493 In God we put our t.; If we our
510 n. place...Wherein to put my t.
541 In thee, O Lord, I put my t.
556 Give me to t. in thee; Be thou
595 His mine is all my t.
613 ne'er forsaken him Who puts his t.
614 But we can t. our all to thee
627 Nor let the good man's t. depart
633 Then is the time to t. our God
635 In thee I place my t. On thee
637 I'll always t. in thee
656 All my t. on thee is stayed
662 To his sure t. and tender care
671 Thou art my only t.
802 A t., O Lord, is in thee
865 We t., O Lord, In thee alone
984 Restore thy t.; a glorious form
1058 Father, perfect my t.
1059 But he whom now we t. in

1102 Whom shall we *t.* but thee, O Lord
1104 And let our *t.* be firm and strong
1105 Our fathers' God, in thee we'll *t.*

TRUSTS, TRUSTING.
69 Blest is the man that *t.* in thee
587 Who in the strength of Jesus *t.*
509 A *trusting* heart, a yearning eye

TRUTH.
8 Eternal *t.* attends thy word
9 Firm as a rock thy *t.* shalt stand
11 His *t.* at all times firmly stood
25 For his *t.* and mercy stand
55 Joyfully the *t.* receive
79 lands. Have heard thy *t.*, thy
81 And talk of all thy *t.* by night
135 Grant us thy *t.* to make us free
166 God hath willed His *t.* to triumph
166 God's *t.* abideth still
200 The eternal laws of *t.* and right
292 So when thy *t.* began its race
317 And while the *t.* of God remains
318 Thou art the *T.*:—thy word alone
318 Thou art the Way, the *T.*, the Life
377 But know the *t.* and live
456 all invite, This saving *t.* to prove
480 Thy goodness and thy *t.* we prove
510 My Saviour, on the word of *t.*
523 God of eternal *t.* and grace
526 O Jesus, full of *t.* and grace
527 I see thee full of *t.* and grace
528 That all mankind thy *t.* may see
529 Or doubt thy *t.*, which cannot
656 Thou art full of *t.* and grace
658 And formed my heart to love thy *t.*
672 Thy everlasting *t.*, Father, thy
691 Thy *t.* unchanged hath ever
701 Then *t.* begins to shine
740 His *t.* for ever stands secure
792 Our souls upon thy *t.* we stay
805 Full for all of *t.* and grace
814 If for thy *t.* they may be spent
819 To them thy sacred *t.* reveal
822 His saving *t.* proclaim
844 When... *T.* divine was never heard
865 listening throng Receive thy *t.* in
870 Here may thy *t.* fresh triumphs
876 Sing of the wonders of his *t.*
881 Source of *t.* whose beams alone
884 Love's written word of *t.*
913 Spirit of *t.* and love, Life-giving
1070 How sweet the *t.* those blessed
1112 Thine everlasting *t.* we prove

TRUTHS.
61 Let thy eternal *t.*, we pray
70 I'll spread thy sacred *t.* abroad
218 And *t.* are opened to our view
294 There, what delightful *t.* I read
296 Its *t.* upon the nations rise
373 thy soul apply To *t.* divinely given
829 Do thou the *t.* herein set forth

TRY, TRYING.
784 *T.* us, O God, and search the
254 grace In every *trying* hour
402 Thy *t.* power display

TUMULT.
109 Life's *t.* we must meet again
1108 And bid its angry *t.* cease

TUNE, TUNES.
4 And sweeter voices *t.* the song
19 And *t.* thy people's heart
21 *T.* our lips to sing thy praise
43 And *t.* our lips to sing
72 Thro' ages joined in *t.* Sing
81 O may my heart in *t.* be found
146 Wonder and joy shall *t* my heart
641 His praise shall *t.* my voice
726 *T.* my heart to sing thy grace
860 Or *t.* their hearts to grateful praise
38 Be short our *tunes*; our words be

TUNED, TUNEFUL, TUNELESS.
414 And angels *t.* their harps anew
232 Both *tuneful* heart and song
658 Yes; broken, *tuneless*, still, O Lord

TURMOIL.
973 There, when the *t.* is no more

TURN.
223 *T.* not from his griefs away
335 O *t.* ye, O turn ye, for why will ye
347 Sinners *t.*; why will ye die
348 *T.*, he cries, ye sinners, turn
368 And *t.* at once from every sin
368 And to the Saviour *t.*
373 *T.*, mortal, turn; thy danger
374 And bids you *t.* and live
438 He cannot *t.* away The presence
455 Keep me, lest I *t.* again Out of
487 *T.* again to God thy rest
487 Humbly to thy Jesus *t.*
555 When to the right or left I *t.*
561 Behold again we *t.* to thee
597 And scarcely can we *t.* aside
640 The love... To him alone will *t.*
723 *T.*.. O turn a favoring eye
872 We will early *t.* to thee
906 *T.* thee, brother; God can save
1094 O *t.* us not away; But hear

TURNS.
371 But he that *t.* to God shall live

TWILIGHT.
92 Softly fades the *t.* ray
579 But he shall come at *t.'s* close
644 Through the *t.*, soft and gray
905 Life's *t.* path, with pitfalls

TWO OR THREE.
40 Yet here, when *t.* or *t.* shall meet
850 Where *t.* or *t.* are met to raise

TYPE, TYPES.
73 The *t.* of heaven's eternal rest
199 O wondrous *t.*! O vision fair
210 The *types* and figures are fulfilled
305 No Jewish *t.* could cleanse us so

TYRANT.
677 Who braved a *t.'s* ire

U.

UNBELIEF.
151 Blind u. is sure to err
302 O help my u.
303 Pity my helpless u.
368 Convince us first of u.
377 Shut up in u., I groan
377 The bar of u. remove
416 Scatter all my u.
513 This u. remove

UNBELIEVING.
783 So may the u. world
1027 To still my u. fear

UNBLAMABLE.
543 U. in grace

UNCHANGED, UNCHANGING, UNCHANGEABLE.
176 goodness... U. from day to
299 The heart u. can never
552 Mine is an *unchanging* love
143 Our faithful, *unchangeable*
792 U., almighty Lord

UNCLEANNESS.
320 For sin and u., and every

UNCLOUDED.
87 worship... In heaven's u. light
661 U. beauty to the eye
663 hope of bliss U. yet remain

UNCONCERNED.
965 And yet how u. we go

UNCTION.
265 Come, with u. and with power
273 Thy blessed u. from above
276 Give power and u. from above
1060 mention of thy glory is u.

UNDISMAYED.
673 Hope and be u.
720 Bids us u. go on
813 Or, u. in deed and word
961 My spirit calm and u.

UNDISTURBED.
418 cheerful smiles sit u.
937 Joy and peace... U., shall

UNDIVIDED.
411 Eternal, u. Lord
793 One u. Christ proclaim

UNDO.
166 Should threaten to u. us

UNDONE.
358 For evermore u.
1022 good we knew and left u.

UNEMPLOYED.
744 No moment lingers u.

UNFAITHFUL.
196 Thy friends u. prove
300 Though I have most u. been
767 Have thy friends u. proved

UNFATHOMED, UNFATHOMABLE.
477 Whose depths u., no man
161 Deep in *unfathomable* mines
1112 U. depths of love

UNFEELING.
396 But this u. heart of mine

UNFEIGNED.
889 Both with lips and hearts u.

UNFETTERED.
982 Which his u. soul enjoys

UNFILLED.
691 We turn u. to thee again

UNFOLD, UNFOLDING.
61 thy word... U. its hidden store
161 His purposes... *Unfolding* every
933 The love of Christ u.

UNFULFILLED.
800 holy prayer... No longer u.

UNGENTLE.
196 Yet no u., murmuring word

UNGUARDED.
587 Leave no u. place

UNGRUDGING.
904 Teach us, with glad, u.

UNIMPROVED.
744 moment... U. below

UNION.
53 Thus may we abide in u.
196 grace that springs from u.
561 That marked our u. with the
780 And u. sweet and dear esteem
788 Lord, may our u. form a part
1009 There is no u. here of hearts

UNISON.
602 In u. with God's great thought
914 In u. with all our hearts

UNITE.
56 Thus u. we to adore him
74 Let all her sons u.
101 U. our hearts in love to thee
783 With bonds of love our hearts u.
793 U. and perfect us in one
795 U. and perfect them in one
800 U. thy people in their Head
829 God, our hearts doth still u.
801 Each to each u., endear
867 May we all there u., Happy
885 U., to swell the song To Christ
1054 Sweet bonds that u. all the
1098 U. us in the sacred love

UNITED, UNITING, UNITY.
785 Jesus, *u.* by thy grace
780 *U.* all, through Jesus' name
1106 God bless these hands *u.*
782 Blest be the dear *uniting* love
793 Giver of peace and *unity*

UNIVERSE.
75 This *u.* was made
121 displayed Throughout the *u.*
317 Throughout the *u.* it reigns
788 The glorious *u.* around
866 The *u.* obeys his nod
909 Thus through the *u.* shall
918 Make thou the *u.* thine own
1025 Sees the *u.* renewed

UNKNOWN.
130 Confess the Infinite *U.*
377 And blindly serve a God *U.*
415 When I rise to worlds *u.*
439 Thou great mysterious God *u.*
714 Unseen, but not *u.*
1024 That awful hour *u.*
1112 'Tis here thine *u.* paths we

UNMOVED.
293 *U.* amid the wreck of spheres
506 *U.* by threatening or reward
1019 Shall stand *u.* amidst them

UNPREPARED.
1028 All *u.* to meet him

UNRIGHTEOUSNESS.
420 Covered is my *u.*
493 From all *u.* To cleanse
656 I am all *u.*, False

UNRULY.
107 Curb thou for us the *u.* tongue

UNSEARCHABLE.
216 Will the *U.* be found

UNSEEN.
303 Thyself *u.*, unknown
714 *U.*, but not unknown
733 Though *u.*, I love the Saviour
756 story Of *u.* things above

UNSHAKEN.
250 But stand *u.* as thy love
763 *U.* as eternal hills

UNSINNING.
514 Restored to our *u.* state
786 And raised to our *u.* state

UNSPEAKABLE.
126 Greatness *u.* is thine
337 Peace, *u.*, unknown
435 And cry with joy *u.*
789 A joy *u.*
[See *Gift.*]

UNSPOTTED.
825 *U.* from the world, and pure

UNTRUE.
643 Thou art not, like man, *u.*

UNUTTERABLE, UNUTTERABLY.
438 Thine *u.* love
437 And swells *unutterably* full Of

UNVARIED.
1034 With that *u.* day

UNVEIL, UNVEILED, UNVEILING.
708 *U.*, O Lord, and on us shine
864 And dwell in *unveiled* glory here
328 *Unveiling* an immortal day
910 *U.* what rich stores of grace

UNWAVERING.
429 *U.* I believe

UNWEARIED.
196 *U.* in forgiveness still
406 And here I will *u.* lie
476 *U.*, may I thus pursue

UNWORTHY.
20 Though *u.* of thine ear
319 prepared, *U.* though I be
414 *U.* to be called a son

UP.
98 *U.* to the hills where Christ
236 Thou art gone *u.* on high
245 God is gone *u.* on high
443 From thence to bring him *u.*
576 *U.*, then, with speed
807 *U.* to that world of light

UPHOLD, UPHOLDS, UPHOLDEST, UPHELD.
478 *U.* me in the doubtful race
749 *Upholds* thee with his truth
876 *U.* and keeps you hourly
139 Thou by thy word *upholdest* all
531 thy word My soul long *upheld*
679 *U.* by my gracious, omnipotent

UPRAISED.
665 *U.* by an immortal power

UPWARD.
309 And *u.* bid them rise
612 Sweet to look *u.*, to the place
724 *U.* I fly, Still all my song
875 heart...Is *u.* drawn to God
956 *U.*, Lord, our spirits raise
970 Are we not tending *u.* too
1068 *U.* tends to his abode, To rest
1088 Pass *u.* unto heaven, And chide

URGE, URGED.
570 I *u.* my way to heaven
583 *U.* on your rapid course, Ye
594 And onward *u.* thy way
648 We *u.* our way with strength
853 voice within... *Urged* thee to

URNS.
978 As, in the heavens, the *u.* Divine

USE, USES, USEFUL.
14 From earthly u. for heaven's
906 powers God for noble uses gave
124 We cannot speak one useful

USURPER.
805 And end the u.'s reign

UTTERANCE.
711 All u. faileth there

UTTERMOST.
798 Which saves us to the u.

V.

VAIN.
79 one hath sought thy face in v.
83 Nor let me feel one v. desire
84 Far from my thoughts, v. world
123 In v. my soul would try To shun
339 Wilt thou let him die in v.
347 Will ye let him die in v.
364 Nor suffer him to die in v.
367 And shall he bleed in v.
389 Alas! they all must flow in v.
523 faith... Which cannot ask in v.
616 Be my v. wishes stilled
662 How v. are all things here below
758 no more of this world's v. store
885 None calls on thee in v.
912 prayers and labors Must be in v.
960 How v. is all beneath the skies
960 And all beneath the skies is v.
962 How v. are all his hopes and
1021 answer... For every v. and idle

VALE.
15 Through this dark v. of tears
156 I walk through death's dark v.
287 And e'en the gloomy v. of death
297 cheers... In this dark v. of tears
258 Beyond this v. of tears There is a
434 He followed me o'er v. and hill
482 path of peace... Through this v.
620 We journey through a v. of tears
646 lead us Through this gloomy v.
648 But hasten through the v. of woe
657 And look beyond this v. of tears
761 He will the v.of death illume
807 In this dark v. of woes, Never
826 The v. shall rise, the mountain
930 Though passing through a v. of
963 Shall quit, like me, the v. of tears
975 The shadowy v. unknown
1009 Beyond this v. of death

VALES.
180 To fertile v. and dewy meads
934 The shady v. and fountains

VALLEY, VALLEYS.
179 Through the v. and shadow of
181 righteousness . From hill to v.
257 Jesus hath cheered the dark v.
731 With us in the lonely v.
759 Say, why in the v. of death

1085 The valleys laugh and sing
1087 The v. laugh and sing, Forests

VANITY, VANITES.
456 Other knowledge... 'Tis all but v.
781 but part From lies and v.
107 Of earth's absorbing vanities
492 sever From earth's tempting v.
530 Above the v. of time
664 And life's dull v. no more
701 Then earthly v. depart

VANQUISHED, VANQUISHER.
73 And v. all our foes
231 Hell to-day is v., heaven is
566 Met and v. earth and hell
567 Till every foe is v.
778 The oppressor is v. and Zion
989 And v., quits the field
86 O Vanquisher of death

VAULT, VAULTINGS.
249 While the v. of heaven rings
723 By the v., whose dark abode
868 temple... whose vaultings were

VEIL.
18 And v. their faces while they cry
18 The v. that hides thy glory rend
119 Angels with both wings v. their
141 Cherubim and seraphim V. their
153 Or v. in shades your thousand
210 The v. is rent; in him alone
215 The temple's v. in sunder breaks
252 And glories v. thy face
303 The v. is on my heart
377 unknown Till thou the v. remove
381 The v. of unbelief remove
402 corners shine, And take the v.
427 I shall possess within the v.
435 Unless thou take the v. away
530 Let faith now pierce the v. and
561 Till the v. be lifted, Till our faith
711 The v. of sense hangs dark
714 The rending v. shall thee reveal
819 Then death the v. removing
954 To see without a v. his face
1045 to rise Within the v., and see
1050 breath Shall rend the v. in twain

VEILS, VEILED.
174 Here the dark v. of sense
40 Veiled in serener majesty
148 Bright, though v. in darkness
209 But when Jehovah v. his face
240 Yet thou hast v. in flesh thy light
861 Didst shine in glories v. and dim
1106 V. in the softened splendor

VENGEANCE, VENGEFUL.
146 Where v. and compassion
366 end in v. or in grace
391 Should sudden v. seize
1023 V. for all earthly wrongs
1091 Long and loud for v. call
280 Justly might thy vengeful dart
735 Direct thy v. thunder's aim

VENTURE.
340 V. on him, venture freely
1004 V. all thy care on him

VERDANT, VERDURE.
761 I view the v. scene
575 And duly shall appear, In verdure
912 Wastes rise in v., and mingle

VERGE.
958 While we, as on life's utmost v.

VESSEL, VESSELS.
573 A v. fitted for thy use
780 The grace through every v. flows
775 Vessels of mercy, sons of grace
1030 Our earthen v. filled
1030 And let the v. break
1107 power divine The water v.

VESTURE.
191 On his v. and his thigh
198 Beheld his v. glow with light
250 Thy v. keeps its crimson hue
835 Before us in thy v. stand
835 Thy v. dipped in blood

VEXED.
390 And v., and urged thee to depart

VICE.
949 The growth of v. restrain

VICISSITUDE.
978 Survivors in the v.

VICTIM, VICTIMS.
250 O thou eternal V., slain
314 The spotless V. dies
425 Behold for me the V. bleeds
456 The sin-atoning V. died
847 Christ, the V., Christ, the Priest
847 mighty V., from the sky
868 No incense is lighted, no victims
900 The v. of that deadly thirst

VICTOR, VICTORS.
226 Praises to the V.'s name
228 Welcome, thou V. in the strife
229 V. o'er death and hell
230 May raise the v.-strain
249 Crowns become the V.'s brow
249 Spread abroad the V.'s fame
256 adorns the mighty V.'s brow
566 Jesus points the v.'s rod
566 Strive the v.'s palm to win
567 The next the v.'s song
1062 open...gates And let the victors in

VICTORIOUS.
51 The name all-v. of Jesus extol
57 God hath made his saints v.
249 From the fight returned v.
284 V. death accord, And, with
330 O'er death...will make us v.
407 liberty By thy v. love
413 Thou wilt v. prove
459 O'er all may we v. prove

498 Let us v. be in death
847 Praise to our v. King

VICTORY.
218 The battle fought; the v. won
234 Where's thy v...grave
251 earth abroad The v. of his cross
260 Where's thy v...grave
322 His name...'Tis life and v.
381 And get thyself the v.
566 The prize of v.
567 From v. unto victory His army
569 Our v. cannot fail
577 banner flies And v. is his
581 Ne'er think the v. won
582 and be led To certain v.
583 This is the v...Before our faith
584 Thy feet with v. shod
585 The v. by my Saviour got
594 And, crowned with v., at thy feet
622 When by grace...the v.'s won
767 V. is thine at last
911 And vain is Satan's boast of v.
971 They fought the fight, the v. won
985 Now to the God of v. Immortal
1045 I ask them whence their v. came

VIGIL, VIGILS.
952 And all a solemn v. keep
1047 Always fast and v.
1060 Mine eyes their vigils keep

VIGOR, VIGOROUS.
605 When youthful v. is no more
749 like the eagle he renews The v.
1074 With v. arise And press to our
105 Sleep, which...more vigorous
547 With v. soul to rise

VILE, VILEST.
305 Lord, we are v., conceived in sin
319 And there may I, though v.
323 Millions of sinners, v. as you
561 O cast us not away, though v.
803 Every v. affection kill
930 prospect pleases...only man is v.
380 Vilest of the sons of men
1027 Though v. of them all

VINDICATE.
586 And v. thy gracious will
761 My heart shall v. my God

VINE, VINEYARD.
441 As the branch is to the v.
626 Although the v. its fruit deny
641 Though v. nor fig-tree wither
808 As laborers in thy vineyard, Lord
816 The v. of the Lord Before

VIOLENT.
589 'T is seized by v. hands

VIRGIN.
376 Nay, alas! thou foolish v., Hast
702 Jesus...The V.'s holy Son
954 Ye v. souls, arise, With all
977 And sweeter than the v. rose

VIRTUE.
154 When r. lies distressed Beneath
249 And every r. we possess
280 And every r. won
284 Give r.'s rich reward
289 gospel...Its utmost r. show
385 Let the world their r. boast
398 Or lost the r. of thy name
522 reveal the r. of thy love
587 Take every r., every grace
817 The r. of thy grace A large
832 May r., piety, and truth
875 Whose years, with changeless r.

VIRTUES, VIRTUOUS.
774 To him who all thy r. gave
978 The good man's r. light the
608 By kindly words and virtuous
1093 Here beneath a r. sway

VISION, VISIONS.
199 By this great r.'s mystery
695 Sweet is the r. of thy face
1058 The beatific r. Shall glad
1058 True r. of true beauty
189 Brighter visions beam afar
291 And r. of eternal day
864 All glorious though the r. were
1011 In r. of enraptured thought

VISIT, VISITED, VISITEST.
84 I wait a r., Lord, from thee
416 V., then, this soul of mine
893 In them thou mayest be visited
701 When once thou visitest the heart

VOICE.
3 To-day attend his r.
19 For whom we now lift up our r.
98 shalt hear My r. ascending high
123 There seems a r. in every gale
138 And utter forth a glorious r.
151 His r. sublime is heard afar
280 And his that gentle r. we hear
287 Turn us with gentle r.
353 Say, sinner, hath a r. within
371 Sinners, the r. of God regard
447 Charmed to confess the r. divine
537 And always hear thy r.
555 Thy r. still let me hear
591 'Tis God's all-animating r.
631 This r. shall make the pious
658 This r., transported, shall record
686 His r. behind me may I hear
697 O let me ever hear thy r.
711 But sweeter...still small r.
710 And when my r. is lost in death
717 And sweeter than music his r.
759 I know the...sound of thy r.
760 No tender r. like thine can
763 We hear within the solemn r.
794 We hear thy r., and open now
878 Wilt thou hear the r. of praise
921 V. echoes voice, and onward
980 'Tis but the r. that Jesus sends
975 One will be with me whose r.
1010 Our Father's r. demands him
1012 I hear a r. answer and say
1020 How could I bear to hear thy r.

1029 nature shaken By his r...prepare
1070 The r. of Jesus sounds o'er land
1087 raise Hand, heart, and r.
1093 Hark! the r. of nature sings

VOICES.
8 In cheerful sounds all r. raise
9 high as the heavens our r. raise
16 raise Your tuneful r. high
17 Let all on earth their r. raise
66 Your r. in his praise employ
188 Hark! what mean those holy r.
227 Lift your glad r. in triumph
227 Lift, then, your r. in triumph
232 Where love's sweet r. sing
315 With them let us our r. raise
563 Blend with ours your r. In
680 We lift our hearts and r.
911 Thousand r. Call us, o'er the
918 Awake...And raise your r. high
1105 To thee our grateful r. raise

VOID.
303 But O how dark and r. to me
458 Fill with thyself the mighty v.
515 Fill all this mighty r.
549 But they have left an aching r.
711 Left but a dismal r.; Jesus
741 With us no melancholy r.
1025 views With smiles the flaming r.

VOLUME.
292 But the blest r. thou hast writ

VOW.
43 Here we present the solemn r.
294 My tongue perform its solemn r.
417 That r. renewed shall daily
460 The r. is past beyond repeal
466 To him we make our solemn r.
466 A r. we dare not break
826 turn from you; God hears my r.
832 And would renew its solemn r.
945 Who hears our solemn r.

VOWS.
67 Accept our prayers...bless our v.
79 V. with their lips to thee
83 While thus my early r. I pay
96 As rising, now I send my r.
106 Lord, I my r. to thee renew
181 And daily r. ascend
314 Nor r...can e'er for sin atone
466 we turn our r. to prayers
467 My r. I will to his great name
759 songs of praise, their mingled r.
1084 Grateful r. and solemn praise

VOYAGE.
1011 The r. of life's at an end

W.

WAGE.
677 Earth and hell their wars may w.

WAGES.
808 We ask no other w., when

WAILING.
376 W. for thy sin
1013 Deeply w., Shall the true Messiah

WAIT.
30 We w., according to thy word
286 We w. the promise of our Lord
355 Lord, even so! we w. thine hour
403 Humbly on thee I w.
494 I w. thy coming from above
497 Humbly and confidently w.
505 Give me on thee to w., Till I
514 O Jesus, at thy feet we w.
524 Jesus, for this we calmly w.
668 And lo! I w. on thee, my Lord
673 W. thou his time, so shall this
675 do For the Lord on whom I w.
791 We w. thy coming from above
818 On thee we humbly w.
850 in patience w. Until he come
928 To w. for thine appointed hour
943 Still we w. for thine appearing
954 Then let us w. to hear...trumpet's
956 We a little longer w., But how
1088 Why w., they say, and wither
1090 On him we w.

WAITS, WAITED, WAITEST, WAITETH.
357 O Sinner, come, the Saviour w.
432 Obedient faith that w. on thee
1015 W. my anxious soul for thee
376 Jesus waited long to know thee
317 Thou waitest to be gracious still
376 Jesus waiteth, waiteth, waiteth

WAITING.
18 And let each w. spirit feel
29 And bid our w. minds attend
44 Here, to our w. hearts, proclaim
88 W. in his courts to-day
352 He still is w. to receive
293 Just as I am, and w. not
1003 W. to receive thy Spirit

WAKE.
4 W. every heart and every tongue
86 And w. dead souls to love
102 Come...bless us when we w.
106 Lord, when I from death shall w.
232 In Christ we w. and rise
263 W. my spirit, clear my sight
560 And w. me that I sleep no more
630 This voice shall w. the pious dead
899 They w. to life again
980 Then w. to perfect happiness
1042 When shall I w. and find

WAKES, WAKEFUL, WAKENING, WAKING.
372 Speak with that voice...w....dead
952 We will not close our wakeful
103 Our wakening and uprising
96 Let him have all my waking
100 My w. hours attend
724 Then, with my w. thoughts
745 Kept by...ever-w. love
979 Whose w. is supremely blest

WALK.
156 And me to w. doth make
291 And w. and talk himself with me
510 But chiefly long to w. with thee
655 Come back and w. therein
606 And closely w. with thee
609 W. in all the works prepared
642 And I will w. with him
642 And he will w. with me
655 So shall I w. aright
782 O may we ever w. in him
803 While we w. with God in light

WALL, WALLS.
210 The middle w. is broken down
40 Is Christ within these walls
89 Within these w. may peace
507 Yet these are not the only w.
770 Her w. before thee stand
776 With salvation's w. surrounded
856 benediction Shed within these w.
867 These w. we to thy honor raise
868 More simple and lowly the w.
869 Accept the w. that human hands
869 While round these hallowed w.
909 Rebuild thy w., thy bounds
1044 these eyes thy heaven-built w.
1060 Thine ageless w. are bounded

WANDER, WANDERED.
337 Weary souls, that w. wide
409 And w. while I pray
559 Left me long to w. wide
726 Prone to w., Lord, I feel it
755 If while on earth I w.
761 my soul Shall w. now no more
1032 And gladly w. up and down
554 wretched heart Has wandered
906 Brother, hast thou w. far
1085 To Christ, who, when we w.

WANDERER, WANDERERS.
370 Return, O w., return
553 See...A wretched w. mourn
554 O take the w. home
623 Jesus, the weary w.'s rest
724 Though like the w., The sun
1041 The w. there a home may find
1052 O w., come away
1111 The w.'s prayer thou bend'st
328 Come, wanderers, to my Father's
359 The Saviour calls his w. home
1039 rest, To mourning w. given

WANDERING, WANDERINGS.
9 And when, like w. sheep
102 If some poor w. child
298 Jesus...Restores our w. feet
388 O cease, my w. soul
400 what avails...My w. to and fro
434 I was a w. sheep
434 He saved the w. one
434 That found the w. sheep
511 To catch the w. of my will
552 Sought thee w., set thee
558 Call back a w. sheep
726 W. from the fold of God
726 Bind my w. heart to thee

12

753 Gather my *w.* spirit home
814 To seek the *w.* souls of men
622 Recall the *w.* spirits home
1074 Of heavenly birth, though *w.*
408 O let our weary *wanderings* end
411 prodigal...Reviews his *w.*

WANT.

175 Christ is rich... What can I *w.*
179 The Lord is my Shepherd, no *w.*
407 Nothing I ask or *w.* beside
494 I *w.* my God, my all
527 And come for all I *w.* to thee
589 To God your every *w.*
685 That all I *w.* I find in thee
717 In our *w.* or in our wealth
723 By thy life of *w.* and tears
732 relief Here for my every *w.*
776 And all fear of *w.* remove
889 From all *w.* and danger free

WANTS.

60 When we disclose our *w.*
134 Come, make your *w.*
282 Their children's *w.* supply
295 And all our *w.* supplied
323 Come, then, with all your *w.*
326 And drive our *w.* away
441 All my *w.* to him are known
465 All our *w.* by thee supplied
466 That with returning *w.*
617 eye Alone our real *w.* can see
672 Sees all thy children's *w.*
688 Make all my *w.* and wishes
689 Make all thy *w.* and wishes
706 cannot fail to have...*w.* supplied
715 Shepherd Divine, our *w.* relieve
754 I lay my *w.* on Jesus
818 Answer...And all our *w.* supply
818 Our *w.* are in thy view
1083 Maker, doth provide For our *w.*

WANTING.

567 Where duty calls...never *w.*
1010 He has what we are *w.*

WAR, WARS.

194 And man, at *w.* with man
577 Till...We hear of *w.* no more
582 Go forth to glorious *w.*
583 hand Which arms us for the *w.*
593 Thy saints in all this glorious *w.*
677 Earth and hell their *w.* may wage
713 Satan wages . most successful *w.*
777 Hear the voice of *w.* again
606 With thyself and God at *w.*
1101 And *w.* resounds its dire alarms
1101 And noise and *w.* are heard no
394 And from a land of *wars* and
677 Earth and hell their *w.* may
937 Then shall *w.* and tumults cease
1102 Make *w.* throughout the world to

WARFARE.

585 When all my *w.*'s past
767 All thy *w.* now is past
861 Thy glorious *w.*'s past
1114 sin in our hearts its wild *w.*

WARBLE.

78 songs Which *w.* from immortal
145 Let us, therefore, *w.* forth His
692 And *w.* to the silent night

WARM, WARMTH.

84 O *w.* my heart with holy fire
197 But *w.* sweet, tender, even yet
135 light is truth, whose *warmth* is
547 Give us with active *w.* to move

WARN, WARNS, WARNING.

555 O do thou always *w.* My soul
373 The earth...*warns* thee by her
353 Regard in time the *warning*
373 Is equal *w.* given; Beneath
543 And feel thy *w.* eye

WARRIOR, WARRIORS.

599 Behold the Christian *w.* stand
566 *Warriors* of the King of light

WASH, WASHED.

111 *W.* all the stains away
263 *W.* me in his precious blood
302 Here let me *w.* my guilty soul
319 may I, though vile as he, *W.* all
320 blood Can *w.* away the blot
336 To *w.* and be cleansed in his
350 And *w.* and seal the sons of God
389 Can these *w.* out my guilty stain
391 O *w.* my soul from every sin
425 Unless I *w.* my soul from sin
430 I *w.* my garments in the blood
461 I thirst...To *w.* me in thy
503 I cannot *w.* my heart But by
553 *W.* me, and make me thus thine
523 *W.* me, and mine thou art
434 'T was he that *washed* me in his
817 Who hath *w.* us in the tide
880 place...For all who are *w.* and
1066 *W.* their robes by faith below

WASTE, WASTES, WASTED, WASTING.

108 Much of my time has run to *w.*
912 *Wastes* rise in verdure, and
929 Then all these *w.* a dreary scene
906 Hast thou *wasted* all thy powers
965 Our *wasting* lives grow shorter

WATCH.

158 The angels *w.* him on his way
167 They come to *w.* around us here
223 *W.* with him one bitter hour
308 And *w.* the rising day
555 Always to *w.* and pray
568 Cease not to *w.* and pray
574 Help me to *w.* and pray
576 Up, *w.* and work, and pray
606 And every moment *w.* and pray
715 give The power to *w.* and pray
750 With thee to *w.* and pray
823 And *w.* thou daily o'er their
823 That they may *w.* for thee
899 To *w.* in silence o'er the land
952 Can we not *w.* one night for God
968 To *w.* and tremble, and prepare

WAT   179   WAY

1024 And *w.* a moment to secure
1047 *W.*, and pray, and fast
1047 Always *w.* and pray

WATCHES, WATCHED, WATCHEST.

135 Cheers the long *w.* of the night
376 In the silent midnight *w.*
693 Thee, in the *w.* of the night
1070 Angels, your faithful *w.*
658 Thy goodness *watched* my
116 *Watchest* where thy people be
881 Kindly *w.* all mankind

WATCH-FIRES.

921 On mountain tops the *w.-f.*

WATCHFUL, WATCHFULNESS.

108 angels keep Their *w.* stations
155 With *w.* care their charge
176 Beneath his *w.* eye His
266 Ever *w.*, ever kind, Thy
356 And in their *w.* hands bear
615 God's *w.* eye surveys
617 Thine ever *w.* eye Alone
949 O Father, let thy *w.* eye
1021 The *w.* power bestow
1024 And fill us now with *w.* care
543 The sacred *watchfulness* impart
928 Teach us, in *w.* and prayer

WATCHING.

189 *W.* long in hope and fear
568 Far more are o'er thee *w.*
675 Through constant *w.* wise
753 The *w.* power impart
954 May we be *w.* found
1015 *W.* for thee, till I stand
1015 *W.* for thy glad returning
1092 *W.* invisible, judging unheard

WATCHMAN.

745 Thy *W.* never sleeps
935 *W.*, tell us of the night
935 *W.*, does the beauteous ray
935 *W.*, will its beams alone
935 *W.*, let thy wandering cease

WATCHMEN.

582 Hark, how the *w.* cry
821 The *w.* join their voice
823 Let Zion's *w.* all awake
921 Where scattered wide the *w.*

WATCHWORD.

710 Prayer...Christian's...*w.* at the
800 One only *w.*, love

WATER.

72 And living *w.* flowing With soul
219 The *w.* and the blood
399 The living *w.* of thy grace
415 Let the *w.* and the blood
426 Behold, I freely give The living *w.*
625 When the great *w.*-floods prevail
678 Welcome at the *w.*-spring
881 And witness with the *w.* now
849 O *W.*, life bestowing

WATERS.

156 he leadeth me The quiet *w.* by
179 leadeth my soul where the still *w.*
336 The *w.* of life are now flowing
354 The *w.* swell, and death, and fear
362 Come to the living *w.*, come
388 Noah's dove...The cheerless *w.*
403 The *w.* soon will cease
622 By *w.* still, o'er troubled sea
656 While the nearer *w.* roll
679 When through the deep *w.* I call
683 see *w.* flowing Forth from the
761 Where limpid *w.* gently glide
776 See the streams of living *w.*
911 martyrs' ashes...on the *w.* cast
930 And you, ye *w.*, roll, Till, like
1012 The *w.* may fail from the sea
1055 celestial streams, Where living *w.*
1108 O Christ! whose voice the *w.*
1110 The *w.* are held in thy hand

WATERED, WATEREST, WATERING, WATERY.

817 word... *W.* by thy almighty
1086 seed...is fed and *w.* By God's
774 Thou *waterest* all the worlds
773 stream... *Watering* our divine
3 The *watery* worlds are all his
1076 The *w.* deep I pass With Jesus
1115 Guide us through the *w.* way

WAVE.

153 Let *w.* to wave resound his praise
774 And bear us on thy gentle *w.*
847 Israel...Through the *w.* that
982 So dies a *w.* along the shore
1004 Safe is the expanded *w.*
1108 arm, bound, the restless *w.*
1113 borne High on the broken *w.*
1114 When o'er the dark *w.* the red

WAVES.

130 Thy voice. Bade the *w.* roar
151 Rebel, ye *w.*, and o'er the land
165 At his command the *w.* rolled by
203 When the *w.* of sorrow roll
286 rushing wind Upon the *w.*
634 Even the *w.* a path afford
619 Though *w.* and storms go o'er my
651 The *w.* an awful distance keep
673 Through *w.*, and clouds, and
674 On thee, when *w.* of sorrow roll
676 a charge No *w.* can take away
721 Back the closing *w.* shall roll
933 Go where the *w.* are breaking
1033 Come, Lord of hosts, the *w.*
1112 While through the mighty *w.* we

WAVER.

826 And never let me *w.* more

WAXING.

1058 The times are *w.* late

WAY.

88 God has brought us on our *w.*
210 The living *w.* to heaven is seen
313 Thou art the only *w.* Ordained

WAY 180 WEE

318 Thou art the W.:—to thee alone
318 Thou art the W., the Truth, the
356 That lonely, unfrequented w.
450 Come hither, soul, I am the w.
450 And say, Behold the w. to God
511 And make an open w.
555 Come back! this is the w.
618 While held in life's uneven w.
675 Thy w., not mine, O Lord
655 let the w. That leads to it be
721 There let the w. appear, Steps
792 And give, O give us all one w.
801 We seek thy perfect w., Ready
839 here Be taught the better w.
897 Lord, lead the w., the Saviour
950 we pursue The true and living w.
970 And showed our feet the w.
996 Show me the w. to shun

WAYS.
232 And let thy life, through all its w.
672 Commit thou . . . w. into His hands

WAYWARD.
434 I was a w. child
434 No more a w. child
459 Our w., erring hearts incline
485 O'er this w. heart to reign

WEAK.
141 Satan . . . tells us we're w., our
171 I am w., but thou art mighty
181 And bid the w. be strong
252 Teach my w. heart, O Lord
340 Come . . . W., and wounded, sick
601 cross, let not . . . Fill thy w. spirit
712 But, Lord, the flesh is w.; Thy
764 And w., and powerless every arm
886 I am both w. and sinful
989 Perchance thy w. spirit in fear
1099 w. and strong may praise thee

WEAKNESS.
269 The w. of our flesh supply
280 Our w. pitying see
476 In w. be thy love my power
587 no unguarded place, No w.
686 Still let him with my w. stay
728 Jesus knows our every w.
994 the dust . . . 'T was sown in w.

WEALTH.
301 deceitful cares, Nor worldly w.
452 The wisdom, w., and strength of
478 So shall you share the w.
597 Thine . . . The w. of land and sea
698 To thee I owe my w. and friends
698 How vain a toy is glitt'ring w.
902 That precious w. shall be
958 And w. and honor gone

WEARY.
72 To-day on w. nations The
78 Fain would we leave this w. road
116 Thou art he who, never w.
176 Why . . . Press down your w.
316 And to the w. rest
328 Come, all ye w. ones, and rest

321 Ye w. spirits, rest
337 W. souls, that wander wide
340 Come, ye w., heavy-laden
358 where . . . Rest for the w. soul
350 Come, w. sinners, come
363 O to the w., faint, oppressed
392 W. of earth, myself, and sin
402 He calls the w., sinner home
406 I lift my w., longing eyes
426 Lay down, thou w. one, lay down
421 Lord, us w. sinners take
572 day's work . . . O yes, a w. day
627 And w. hours of woe and pain
629 Though long the w. way we tread
652 When the sad heart is w. and
689 complaints And w., sinful days
754 rest on Jesus This w. soul of
808 burden Of w. days for thee
815 When the w. ones we love enter
876 Give to the w. rest
913 Every w., wandering spirit
993 To leave the w. road
994 Rest for the w., way-sore feet
1022 This w. . . . dangerous night
1017 Thou art very w.
1047 I was w. too
1055 a rest For w. souls designed
1070 Come, w. souls, for Jesus bids
1071 'Tis w. waiting here; I long to

WEARIED, WEARINESS.
110 And w. nature seeks repose
592 toil And weariness to know
613 When from w. I climb
744 Our w. of life is gone
1019 above Work never can bring w.

WEEDS.
62 The w. of worldly care

WEEP.
21 Comfort those who w. and mourn
68 He heard . . . those who sit and w.
206 W. and gaze my soul away
379 W., believe, and sin no more
405 Did Christ o'er sinners w.
405 He wept that we might w.
455 thy feet . . . And there forever w.
511 And let me w. my life away
611 Must w. those tears alone
627 A blessing for the eyes that w.
654 If I must w. with thee, My Lord
759 In the valley of death should I w.
891 And w. with them that weep
894 And w. for others' woe
957 And we shall w. no more
1067 Never, never w. again

WEEPS, WEEPING.
371 Sinners, thy Saviour w. for thee
379 Jesus w., and loves me still
393 Weeping One of Bethany
405 In heaven no w. there
487 Lift to him thy w. eye
553 wipes tears From sorrow's w.
579 His seed with w. leaves
723 Scarce we lift our w. eyes
921 Bid her long night of w. cease

1010 'Tis only we are w....He
1035 wipe tears From every w. eye
1052 Where all the sounds of w. cease
1067 But these days of w. o'er
1070 morning's joy, and night of w.

WEIGH, WEIGHED, WEIGHT.
584 My soul, w. not thy life
222 grief and shame *weighed* down
196 on heart...A *weight* of sorrow
450 I felt its w. and guilt the more
673 Cast off the w., let fear depart
897 Who bore the world's sad w.
966 Give me to feel their solemn w.

WELCOME.
149 There is w. for the sinner
185 hosannahs...Thy w. shall
225 There on high our w. waits
234 And shout him w. to the skies
323 souls Are freely w. here
335 'Tis you he bids w.; he bids
338 Come and w., sinner, come
340 Now, ye needy, come and w.
346 W., pilgrim, to thy rest
357 Saviour waits This hour to w.
364 In Christ a hearty w. find
393 Wilt w., pardon, cleanse, relieve
414 arms of love To w. his return
647 Longing for the w. sound
741 W. eternity, Jesus is mine
781 We w. thee with warm accord
791 W. from earth; lo, the right
879 There to w., Jesus waits
961 I may the w. word receive
1000 W. from a world of woe
1000 W. to a land of rest
1018 How w. to the faithful soul
1035 And bring the w. day
1070 Singing to w. the pilgrims of
1107 How w. was the call, And sweet

WELL.
654 as thou wilt: All shall be w. for
935 W. and faithfully done
1001 Jesus smiles and says, W. done

WELL, (noun.)
36 Sat weary by the patriarch's w.
270 Life's ever-springing w.
431 The w. of life to us thou art
732 W. of life! from thee we draw

WEPT.
203 Jesus w.! those tears are over
654 Since thou on earth hast w.
738 In vain I have not w. and strove
796 And wonder why we w. at all

WESTERN.
918 In w. wilds and eastern plains
919 While w. empires own their Lord
933 Through all the w. vale

WHATE'ER.
430 W. in me seems wise or good
472 W. I have, whate'er I am
484 W. I say or do Thy

528 W. thou wilt, be done
622 W. I do, where'er I be
667 And then w. may come
946 W. we have and are
965 W. we do, where'er we be

WHEAT.
1083 W. and tares together sown

WHEELS.
918 Ye w. of nature, speed your
1035 Fly swifter round, ye w. of time

WHIRLWIND.
151 He yokes the w. to his car
1114 And O when the w. of passion

WHISPER, WHISPERS, WHISPERED.
425 W. within, thou Love divine
738 I hear thy w. in my heart
197 The last low *whispers* of our
280 And w. us of heaven
612 The w. of his love
701 And w. I am his
353 voice within Oft *whispered* to

WHITE.
253 In shining w. they stand
719 Let us walk with him in w.
727 W.-robed saints, who there
754 W. in his blood most precious
1066 Who are these arrayed in w.

WHOEVER.
323 W. will...O gracious word

WHOLE.
197 touch...And we are w. again
392 'Tis thou alone canst make me w.
397 wait the word that speaks me w.
434 'Twas he that made me w.
457 As Lord and Master of the w.
511 Which makes the wounded w.
532 Forgive and make my nature w.
538 Descend to make me w.
555 And Christ shall make thee w.
557 Thy faith hath made the w.
749 Whose grace hath made thee w.
788 a part Of that thrice happy w.
906 Turn thee; God will make thee w.
1099 That w. and sick, and weak and

WHOSOEVER.
355 Yea, w. will, O let him freely

WICKED, WICKEDNESS.
98 The w. shall not stand
735 wrath May rise the w. to consume
311 Unloose the bands of *wickedness*

WIDOW, WIDOWS.
178 And dries the w.'s tears
740 The w. and the fatherless
891 God of the w., hear
1002 Nor *widows* desolate

WIFE.
901 The w. regains a husband freed

WILDERNESS.
180 The barren *w*. shall smile
393 To me!—'Tis one great *w*.
542 A howling *w*.
646 Traveling through this *w*.
657 My comrades through the *w*.
723 In the savage *w*.
759 Or alone in this *w*. rove
926 Hark! in the *w*. a cry
1076 And through the howling *w*.

WILES.
722 Save...From his unsuspected *w*.

WILL.
23 Make us perfect in his *w*.
33 We seek to do thy *w*.
39 Teach us to know and do thy *w*.
47 Still hear and do thy sovereign *w*.
371 And learn his *w*. divine
394 But in thy *w*. may mine be lost
459 To have no other *w*. but thine
463 May thy *w*., not mine, be done
464 All thy *w*. by me be done
472 I wait thy *w*. to do, As angels do
481 Thy *w*. by all be done
502 According to thy *w*. and word
512 What can withstand his *w*.
514 Be it according to thy *w*.
517 Thy *w*. by me on earth be done
517 I ask...That I may do thy *w*.
529 To all my Saviour's righteous *w*.
529 And waits to prove thine utmost *w*.
537 Thy holy, just, and perfect *w*.
537 Thy only *w*. be done, not mine
562 Ready for all thy perfect *w*.
573 Work in me both to *w*. and do
590 Father, thy *w*. be done
614 Must do thy *w*. and praise thy
615 To his unerring, gracious *w*. Be
616 My soul shall meet thy *w*.
618 Father, thy *w*. be done
623 all things serve thy sovereign *w*.
628 Thy *w*. be done! I will not fear
635 Thy *w*. they all perform; Safe in
636 Teach us...To make thy *w*. our
651 O may thy *w*. be mine
654 My Lord, thy *w*. be done
800 Then shall thy perfect *w*. be done
801 And sweetly lose our *w*. in thine
809 And fit us for thy *w*.
814 Thy *w*. be done, thy name adored
872 Early let us do thy *w*.
901 Delighting in thy perfect *w*.
971 Still say, Thy *w*. be done
1002 Calmly say, Thy *w*. be done
1006 Happy in his *w*. I rest

WILLS, WILLED, WILLING.
173 And what he *w*. is best
1006 Surely what he *w*. is best
602 And whatsoe'er is *willed*, is done
85 My *willing* soul would stay
340 He is *w*.; doubt no more
510 When shall I find my *w*. heart

WILLOWS.
633 harps Down from the *w*. take

WIN.
166 And he must *w*. the battle
333 Content to die, that he might *w*.
509 yearning eye, Can *w*. their way
588 Be sure to *w*. the field
589 And *w*. the well-fought day
603 Be wise the erring soul to *w*.

WIND.
275 Come as a mighty rushing *w*.
278 Come as the *w*., with rushing
280 All-powerful as the *w*. he came
283 Thou who like the *w*. dost come
286 Like mighty rushing *w*. Upon
1041 There sweeps no desolating *w*.
1090 Ruler of *w*. and wave
1112 Whose power the *w*., the sea

WINDS.
151 The *w*. obey his will
151 Ye *w*. of night, your force combine
165 He beckoned, and the *w*. were still
268 Like mighty *w*., or torrents fierce
792 The *w*. shall cease, the waves
911 Flung to the heedless *w*.
1038 No chilling *w*., or poisonous
1086 The *w*. and waves obey him
1088 The hollow *w*. are calling, Come
1109 Whom *w*. and seas obey

WINE.
326 Like floods of milk and *w*.
362 Buy *w*., and milk, and gospel
631 Alone thou hast the *w*.-press trod
841 Remember this...in drinking *w*.
843 Ours is the *w*. of heaven
845 Drink the *w*. and break the bread
847 Gives his sacred blood for *w*.
850 The *w*. shall tell the mystery
890 Mourn for the *w*.-cup's fearful
1076 And oil and *w*. abound
1107 And plenteous was the mystic *w*.

WING.
83 My soul shall rise on joyful *w*.
250 On mightier *w*., in loftier flight
611 Did not thy *w*. of love Come
661 And rise on faith's expanded *w*.
685 And safe beneath thy spreading *w*.
724 Or if, on joyful *w*. Cleaving
913 On thy redeeming *w*., Healing

WINGS.
61 How should our souls on *w*. of love
97 Under the shadow of thy *w*.
116 And on the *w*. of every hour
152 And on the *w*. of mighty winds
158 safe...Beneath the *w*. divine
159 If on the *w*. of morn we speed
169 And safe beneath thy *w*. to rest
191 With peaceful *w*. unfurled
530 Arise, my soul, on *w*. sublime
628 And bid my soul, on angel *w*.
701 The *w*. of love and arms of faith
813 Thy shadowing *w*. around my
887 Spread thy *w*. of blessing o'er
969 Lend, lend your *w*.! I mount
978 My soul would stretch her *w*.

990 Their ransomed spirits soar, On *w.*
1025 And claps his *w.* of fire
1045 Give me the *w.* of faith to rise
1068 Rise, my soul, and stretch thy *w.*
1111 If on the morning's *w.* they fly

WINTER, WINTERS, WINTRY.
611 friends...When *w.* comes, are
744 The *w.'s* night, the summer's day
747 Where *w.* and clouds are no more
994 Sharp has your frost of *w.* been
1083 Ere the *w.* storms begin
1086 He sends the snow in *w.*
747 And why are my *winters* so long
1082 And *w.*, softened by thy care
875 soon, too soon, the *wintry* hour
928 And *w.* clouds o'ercast the sky

WIPE, WIPES, WIPED.
659 farewell...And *w.* my weeping
675 And *w.* the weeping eyes
810 *w.* the tears from weeping eyes
1032 And *w.* away his servant's tears
1035 His...hand shall *w.* the tears From
232 tears...He *wipes* from all our eyes
752 the penitential tear is *wiped* away

WISDOM.
51 All glory and power, all *w.* and
121 In *w.* infinite thou art
127 Thine, Lord, is *w.*, thine alone
132 To us, O Lord, the *w.* give
139 *W.*, and might, and love are thine
142 Through...works...*w.* shines
145 the God, Who by *w.* did create
147 Thine endless *w.*, boundless
150 God is *w.*, God is love
169 But thou, O Christ, my *w.* art
173 Whose *w.*, love, and truth, and
207 O loving *w.* of our God
286 inspire With *w.* from above
315 How great the *w.*, power, and
318 thy word alone True *w.* can impart
326 Eternal *W.* hath prepared A
329 The *w.* coming from above
329 *W.* divine! who tells the price
329 *W.* to silver we prefer
329 Happy the man who *w.* gains
329 *W.*, and Christ, and heaven are
345 *W.* if you still despise, Harder
356 And hate the *w.* from above
452 Let not the wise their *w.* boast
483 My *W.* and my Guide
485 *W.*, humbly casting down At thy
571 Be it my only *w.* here
655 My *w.* and my all
664 And learn that *w.* from above
671 Yes, heavenly *w.*, love divine
746 Filled with *w.*, love, and power
873 Be our *w.* and our guide
878 Let us each in *w.* grow
881 before whose face *W.* had her
913 Glorious Trinity, *W.*., Love, Might
930 Shall we...With *w.* from on high
951 *W.* ascribe, and might, and praise
1058 Where *w.* has no bound
1075 I all on earth forsake, Its *w.*, fame
1113 Eternal *w.* is their guide

His WISDOM.
134 O when *his w.* can mistake
452 And where is all *his w.* gone
642 *His w.* ever waketh, His sight is
866 *His w.* and his power display

Of WISDOM.
243 glorious names Of *w.*, love, and
643 God *of w.*, love, and might
873 They shall find the path *of w.*

Thy WISDOM.
125 *Thy w.*, with its deep on deep
136 *Thy w.*, equal to thy might
120 None but *thy w.* knows thy might
480 confess *Thy w.*, truth, and power
1112 *Thy w.* here we learn to adore

WISDOM'S.
329 price Of *w.* costly merchandise
564 Pour upon the nations *w.* loving
877 Be ours the bliss, in *w.* way To

WISE, WISEST.
345 Hasten, sinner, to be *w.*
350 Be *w.* to know your gracious day
430 Whate'er in me seems *w.* or good
571 A *w.* and understanding heart
603 Be *w.* the erring soul to win
673 How *w.*, how strong his hand
207 O *wisest* love! that flesh and

WISH.
101 When one their *w.*, and one their
173 If what I *w.* is good, And suits
239 If thou the secret *w.* convey
573 Lord, if thou didst the *w.* infuse
617 Not what we *w.*, but what we
637 thy hand: My God, I *w.* them there
661 presence...All that I *w.* contains
747 Have nothing to *w.* or to fear
823 Our every *w.* is stilled

WISHES, WISHFUL.
31 In thee their *w.* meet
154 And their best *w.* to fulfill
178 Jesus...Doth all my *w.* fill
205 Our ardent *w.* meet
661 My *w.* terminate in this
780 Our *w.* all above
814 Doth aught on earth my *w.* raise
1033 With *wishful* looks we stand
1038 I stand, And cast a *w.* eye

WITH.
669 And I shall be *w.* him
714 Yet art thou oft *w.* me
931 Still let them be *w.* thee

WITHDRAW, WITHDRAWN.
406 If thou *w.* thyself from me
559 Thou hast *withdrawn* thy grace

WITHER, WITHERS, WITHERED.
641 Though all the fields should *w.*
172 field It *withers* in an hour
739 *Withered* my nature's strength

WITHHOLD, WITHHOLDS.
428 What else can he w.
69 and withholds No real good from

WITHOUT.
102 For w. thee I cannot live
102 For w. thee I dare not die
667 When tempests rage w.

WITHSTOOD.
173 By earth and hell in vain w.

WITNESS.
6 Comforter, Thy sacred w. bear
221 And w. thou hast died for me
271 Thine inward w. bear, unknown
281 Then with our spirits w. bear
350 To apply and w. with the blood
356 Can w. better things
424 And bear thy w. with my heart
429 Cheered by that w. from on high
435 And w. with the blood
439 not... Without the inward w. live
439 If now the w. were to me
440 Now thine inward w. bear
466 W., ye men and angels, now
483 Let me thy w. live, When sin is
502 I want the w., Lord, That all I do
813 Be a true w. of my Lord
814 Thy faithful w. will I be
854 Come, thou W. of his dying
942 Mighty Spirit! W. to the Saviour's
1054 The Spirit's sure w., and smiles

WITNESSER, WITNESSES.
384 W. of Jesus' merit, Speak
594 A cloud of witnesses around Hold
650 His friends and w. to own
795 Stand forth thy chosen w.
805 We are Jesus' w.
911 spring a... seed Of w. for God
1045 While the long cloud of w. Show

WOE.
196 Thy life and death of w.
313 name... Can save from endless w.
320 heart... Can feel the sinner's w.
371 In pain... To reach eternal w.
412 with... tears, Eternal w. prevent
456 Me to save from endless w.
629 On thee we fling our burdening w.
667 on the brink Of any earthly w.
839 And save from endless w.
965 Infinite Joy, or endless w., Attends
971 And bids them leave a world of w.
971 But let our hearts in every w.
1051 For sin, the source of mortal w.
1057 plains they range, Incapable of w.

WOES.
194 But with the w. of sin and strife
204 When the w. of life o'ertake me
267 Bid my many w. depart
684 From every swelling tide of w.
721 So by my w. to be Nearer, my
797 We share our mutual w.
998 Are enough for life's w., full
1062 O joy, for all its former w.

WOLF.
790 For O, the w. is nigh
790 The w. can never harm

WONDER.
160 I'm lost In w., love, and praise
171 spend the everlasting day In w.
226 Come, ye saints, look here and w.
332 proclaim, And w. at his love
491 Lost in w., love, and praise
981 And heaven with praise and w.

WONDERS.
17 His w. to the nations show
27 Tell his w., sing his worth
83 The w. of thy love declare
146 How high thy w. rise
148 For the w. of creation, Works
161 mysterious way His w. to perform
174 we see The w. of thy love
225 Life eternal! O what w.
275 raise our song To reach the w.
282 Thy noblest w. here we view
291 I trace Diviner w. of thy grace
820 By all the w. ye shall do
838 We sing The w. of his love
876 Sing of the w. of his love
921 Come, Spirit, make thy w. known
946 show The w. of thy love
1076 And tell the w. he hath done
1097 fathers told... Thy w. in their days

WONDERFUL.
51 And publish abroad his w.
147 My God, how w. thou art
191 W. in council he, Christ
207 In all his words most w.
216 love explain Thy w. design
756 story More w. it seems

WONDERING.
63 And tell the w. nations round
673 So shalt thou, w., own his

WONDROUS, WONDROUSLY
118 Who can sing that w. song
202 O w. Lord, my soul would
211 When I survey the w. cross
441 Love that found me,—w. thought
766 Thy work... And w. to our eyes
871 We think upon his w. grace
987 All his w. love proclaim
1094 Yet wondrously from age to age

WORD.
40 Saviour, give them thy faithful w.
75 displayed By the eternal W.
119 We should take him at his w.
166 That w., above all earthly powers
263 W. of God, and inward Light
201 Till every heartfelt w. be mine
204 And let thy precious w. of grace
283 So brightly as thy written w.
294 But in thy blessed w. I trace
423 Though not a w. he spoke
453 I trust In his w.; none plucks me
475 To hear and keep thy every w.
525 Be mindful of thy gracious w.

WOR 185 WOR

526 sin...flee At Jesus' everlasting w.
528 Whose w., when heaven and earth
585 This blessed w. be mine, Just
585 They could not speak a greater w.
598 Sounds forth...ancient w., More
608 Whene'er we hear that glorious w.
620 God's blessed w. can part each
620 And thou shalt own his w.
632 Aid us to trust thy sacred w.
634 Jesus, one w. from thee Fills
668 Lord, I believe thy every w.
679 foundation...in his excellent w.
699 I trust in thy eternal w.
775 Be like your Lord, his w. embrace
836 According to thy gracious w.
849 Thy faithful w. believing, We
885 The all-subduing W., Healer of
913 Thou, whose almighty w. Chaos
929 Send them thy mighty w. to speak
1021 answer for...every w. I say
1050 Life from the dead is in that w.
1050 How shall I love that w.
1102 Where rest but on thy faithful w.

Holy WORD.
293 The hopes that *holy* w. supplies
516 And when I read his *holy* w., I
756 message...From God's own *holy* w.
773 That sacred stream, tnine *holy* w.

Sacred WORD.
39 To us the *sacred* w. apply With
101 Where parents love the *sacred* w.
299 Teach us to love thy *sacred* w.
302 voice...Sounds from the *sacred* w.
371 He calls you by his *sacred* w.
541 Thy *sacred* w. is passed
632 Aid us to trust thy *sacred* w.

The WORD.
29 May we receive *the* w. we hear
111 *The* w. of his grace shall comfort
168 Built by *the* w. of his command
289 Jesus, *the* w. bestow, The true
301 Where'er *the* w. of life is sown
443 *The* w. is ever nigh
493 *The* w. of God is sure, And
936 He hath given *the* w. of grace
952 Speak but *the* w., our souls shall
977 If firm *the* w. of God remains
1033 O that *the* w. were given

Thy WORD.
6 And give *thy* w. success: Spirit
39 Prepare us to receive *thy* w.
130 None but *thy* w. can speak thy
283 *Thy* w., almighty Lord, Where'er
288 *Thy* w. is power and life
292 And make *thy* w. my guide to
293 *Thy* w. shall shine in cloudless
298 Jesus, *thy* w., with friendly aid
299 Father of mercies, in *thy* w.
301 Almighty God, *thy* w. is cast
307 according to *thy* w.; Accomplish
377 Be it according to *thy* w.; Now
443 Let *thy* w. richly in me dwell
451 *Thy* W., thy all-creating Word
499 Be it according to *thy* w., And
506 I rest upon *thy* w.

514 According to *thy* w.
528 *Thy* w. may to the utmost prove
534 The consolations of *thy* w.
539 according to *thy* w.; Redeem
541 And I, who dare *thy* w. believe
593 Supported by *thy* w.
858 With *thy* w., the heavenly bread
865 Here may *thy* w. melodious sound
888 There, we know, *thy* w.
892 And we believe *thy* w.. Though
908 Send forth *thy* w., and let it fly
956 Bless *thy* w. to young and old
1065 'Tis good at *thy* w. to be here

WORDS.
160 O how can w. with equal warmth
291 O may the gracious w. divine
323 O what amazing w. of grace
461 Our w. are lost, nor will we know
470 All my w. and thoughts receive
819 O clothe their w. with power
819 And let those w. be ever thine
928 Thy w. with pleasure we recall

WORK.
19 While in the heavenly w. we join
24 When Jehovah's w. begun
81 Sweet is the w., my God, my King
82 Another six days' w. is done
264 Carrying on his w. within
307 Accomplish now thy w. in me
315 confess The w. is all divine
321 Grace all the w. shall crown
347 Asks the w. of his own hands
377 I know the w. is only thine
392 Thine is the w., and only thine
451 Thou only, Lord, the w. hast done
475 Jesus, let all my w. be thine
534 I look...Till he his w. begin
547 Nothing hath half thy w. to do
562 confirm my heart's desire To w.
565 W., for the night is coming
570 Yet will I, Lord, the w. complete
572 One more day's w. for Jesus
572 How sweet the w. has been
573 W. in me both to will and do
576 Up, then, with speed and w.
592 receive This humble w. of mine
596 O, it is hard to w. for God, To
597 W. shall be prayer, if all be
597 prayer...Itself with w. be one
607 Who will go and w. to-day
607 Let his w. your pleasure be
609 Every w. I do below, I do it to
672 Fix on his w. thy steadfast eye
781 Then, when the mighty w. is
806 Let us all our w. fulfill
816 proceed In Jesus' w. below
891 O happiest w. below, Earnest
936 When be first the w. begun
936 He alone the w. hath wrought
955 I have finished the w. thou didst
1017 Christian...How they w. within
1019 In heaven...W. never...bring
1049 For w. itself is love

WORKS.
3 We are his w., and not our own
48 By all thy w. on earth adored

133 His w., through all this wondrous
136 All thy w. shall praise thy name
139 By all thy w., be paid to thee
142 Through all his mighty w.
231 their true Creator, all his w.
314 Nor w. which we have done
446 A faith that would by w. be
461 What are our w. but sin and
475 Joyful from my own w. to cease
521 And we from our own w.
573 And still in all my w. maintain
586 Let all my w. in thee be wrought
606 And offer all my w. to thee
609 Him in outward w. pursue
786 Our faith by w. to approve
809 But if our w. in thee be wrought
809 That all around our w. may see
820 By all the w. that I have done
866 His wondrous w., through ages
909 And God his w. destroy
910 And in thy w., by all beheld
1001 Followed by their w. they go
1102 Remember, Lord, thy w. of old

WORKERS, WORKING, WORKMAN.
818 As w. with their God
481 Thy mighty *working* may I feel
591 *Workman* of God! O lose not

WORLD.
61 sweet employ In that eternal w.
134 From w. to world the joy shall
292 Bless the dark w. with heavenly
313 Save through this w. of night
648 This weary w. we cast behind
807 Up to that w. of light Take
820 Bid the whole w. my grace
826 Away, vain w.! sin, leave me now
897 side by side In this wide w. of ill
914 To the bright w. above, Break
1023 When this w. shall pass away
1079 When this passing w. is done

The WORLD.
75 'Twas great to speak *the* w. from
91 Did *the* w. from darkness bring
102 Ere through *the* w. our way we
105 That with *the* w., myself, and
221 If all *the* w. through thee may
271 unknown To all *the* w. beside
282 Till through *the* w. thy truth has
327 Let all *the* w. fall down and
332 But Jesus came *the* w. to save
358 *The* w. can never give The bliss
395 And cast *the* w. and flesh behind
435 O that *the* w. might know The
451 That spake at first *the* w. from
509 And see how from *the* w. at once
516 Let worldly minds *the* w. pursue
549 void, *The* w. can never fill
561 Nor could *the* w. a joy afford
583 *The* w. cannot withstand its
613 *The* w. may call itself my foe
675 Wherever in *the* w. I am, In
722 Never let *the* w. break in
752 *The* w. I leave
768 Though *the* w. in arms combine
781 Leaving *the* w., thou dost but

793 So shall *the* w. believe and know
820 I'm with you till *the* w. shall end
822 O that *the* w. might taste and see
829 Death to *the* w. we here avow
867 May it before *the* w. appear
907 beams... To all *the* w. with light
913 O'er *the* w., far and wide
920 And let *the* w., adoring, see
921 And cause *the* w. to know thy
912 Round *the* w. diffuse thy rays
942 O'er *the* w. thine influence shed
969 *The* w. recedes... It disappears
1071 *The* w. is growing old
1101 almighty breath Can sink *the* w.

WORLDS.
15 Lord of the w. above, How
17 He made the shining w. on high
57 W. his mighty voice obeyed
133 Till listening w. shall join the
153 choirs Shall till the w. above
291 In w. below and worlds above
429 Sovereign of all the w. on high
611 As darkness shows us w. of
870 O God, through countless w. of
893 poverty... When all the w. are
1025 By w. on worlds destroyed

WORLDLY.
382 W. good I do not want
605 I would not sigh for w. joy
753 By w. thoughts oppressed
968 For w. hope, or worldly fear
1078 From w. hope and fear

WORM, WORMS.
214 devote... head For such a w. as I
302 A guilty, weak, and helpless w.
460 Do thou assist a feeble w.
470 If so poor a w. as I May to
668 If such a w. as I can spread
966 A w. of earth, I cry
1027 Shall such a worthless w. as I
1075 He calls a w. his friend
1117 Who shall a helpless w. redeem
38 And *worms* have learned to lisp
116 To save rebellious w.
216 Himself to w. impart
965 What dying w. are we
976 What timorous w. we mortals are

WORMWOOD.
223 O the w. and the gall
248 ne'er forget The w. and the gall

WORSHIP.
3 Come, w. at his throne
12 Let every act of w. be Like
33 To thee... belong all w., love, and
34 angels join To w. God aright
48 We w. thee, the common Lord
54 There, in w. purer, sweeter
66 W. and thanks to him belong
74 obey To w. at his throne
87 And purer w. may we pay
89 Oft as they meet for w. here
94 We... bless thee ere our w. cease
98 And w. in thy fear
140 O w. the King, all-glorious

152 Give w. to his majesty
180 W. Christ, the newborn King
191 Come and w. at his feet
246 W., honor, power, and blessing
272 I w. thee, O Holy Ghost
272 I love to w. thee
281 May w. only thee
360 And w. him with fear
549 thy throne, And w. only thee
660 And w. at thy feet
852 And humbly w. at thy feet
869 hands Have raised to w. thee
925 And in thy courts to w. thee
1032 appear, And w. at thy feet
1059 And w. face to face
1093 Ever own and w. God
1100 Let all the people w. thee
1105 Where they might freely w. thee

WORSHIPED, WORSHIPING.
79 Who in the spirit w. thee
38 thrones around Fall *worshiping*

WORSHIPER, WORSHIPERS.
36 Thy favored w. may dwell
92 Where the evening w. seeks
372 Thy real w.
1013 To his ransomed *worshipers*

WORTH, WORTHY.
27 Tell his wonders, sing his w.
243 All are too mean to speak his w.
2 *Worthy* the Lamb that died, they
2 W. the Lamb our hearts reply
2 Jesus is w. to receive Honor
13 O may I w. prove to see
246 Thou art w. to receive; Loudest
680 And if thou count us w., We
936 W. is the work of him

WOUND.
212 Who could thy sacred body w.
240 It flows from every streaming w.
306 To ease the pain and heal the w.
311 W., and pour in, my wounds to
327 Though sin and sorrow w. my
538 Deepen the w. Thy hands have
906 He can heal thy bitter w.
1057 Shall there our spirits w.

WOUNDS.
32 With all thy w. appear
32 And all thy w. to sinners cry
213 When we behold thy bleeding w.
257 Rich w., yet visible above
306 Deep are the w. which sin has
311 Wound, and pour in, my w. to
319 stream Thy flowing w. supply
337 Fly to those dear w. of his
339 Open all his w. again
374 And shows his w. and spreads
379 Saviour stands, Shows his w.
420 The w. of Jesus for my sin
425 His w. are open wide
438 Five bleeding w. he bears
454 And lo! in his w. I continue
456 His w. for me stand open
461 To dwell within thy w.; then

WOUNDED.
185 The w. soul to cure
267 Heal my w., bleeding heart
316 It makes the w. spirit whole
320 When w. sore, the stricken
341 W., impotent, and blind
415 the blood From thy w. side
611 If, when deceived and w. here
683 Here bring your w. hearts
1031 And still extends his w. hands

WRATH.
95 My sins might rouse his w. to
95 But yet his w. delays
127 Thy wakened w. doth slowly
142 His w. and justice stand To guard
165 Surround my steps in all their w.
258 From impending w. release us
308 Flee from the w. to come
310 The mountains, in their w., Their
379 Can my God his w. forbear
389 Can these avert the w. of God
389 On me I feel thy w. abide
415 Save from w. and make me pure
735 Let me alone, that all my w.
735 O turn thy threatening w. away
743 guilt Of sin, and w. divine
805 Saved with them from future w.
813 Whose w. or hate makes me
996 to shun Thy dreadful w. severe
1017 The day of w., that dreadful day
1023 Day of w., O dreadful day
1028 Behold his w. prevailing
1092 Let not thy w. in its terror

WREATHE, WREATHS.
807 When will peace w. her chain
807 Soon shall peace w. her chain
594 When victors' *wreaths* and

WRECK, WRECKS.
1025 And mount above the w.
204 cross...Towering o'er the *wrecks*

WRENCH.
993 not death to bear The w. that

WRETCH, WRETCHED, WRETCHEDNESS.
369 I'll tell him I'm a w. undone
385 I, a w. undone and lost
427 grace...That saved a w. like me
608 Without...thyself, I were a w.
299 Here may the *wretched* sons of
304 in gulf. . We w. sinners lay
460 A w. sinner, lost to God
554 How oft this w. heart Has
312 free From *wretchedness* and woe

WRESTLE, WRESTLES, WRESTLED, WRESTLING.
589 W., and fight, and pray
737 And w. till the break of day
217 The Saviour *wrestles* lone with
1045 They *wrestled* hard, as we do now
458 *Wrestling*. I will not let thee go
584 prolong the w. of the night
737 W., I will not let thee go, Till

WRITE, WRITING, WRITTEN.
142 And will he w. his name
377 And w. thy name upon my heart
482 Spirit's law...O w. it on my
1023 Then the *writing* shall be read
837 love Be *written* on our minds

WRONG, WRONGS.
191 Two thousand years of w.
591 the side that seems W. to man's
1023 Every w. shall be set right
196 The *wrongs* that we receive

Y.

YEAR.
579 The y. delays not long
878 While the circling y. has sped
905 With every passing y. we make
916 through Another various y.
948 Welcome each closing y.
949 The y. is gone, beyond recall
949 we may praise thee, y. by year
950 Lord, through another y.
951 Who spares us yet another y.
953 And spares us yet another y.
953 spare, Another and another y.
953 And, lo, we see another y.
955 Roll round with the y.
956 Hasted through the former y.
965 The y. rolls round, and steals
1080 The fresh and fading y.
1088 The y., its life resigning

YEARS.
9 truth...stand, When rol'ing y.
25 Like the y. of his right hand
73 Through endless y. to live
125 I see thee in the eternal y.
191 When with the ever-circling y.
229 Lord of the rolling y.
250 Thy y., O Lord, can never fail
257 Crown him the Lord of y.
907 And as the y., an endless host
918 Not many y. their rounds shall
919 And pray that future y. may
950 Our few revolving y.
952 So many y. on sin bestowed
957 A few more y. shall roll
963 Pass a few swiftly fleeting y.
964 art God, to endless y. the same

YEARN, YEARNS, YEARNING, YEARNINGS.
691 Our restless spirits y. for thee
488 my heart... *Yearns* with infinite
469 A trusting heart, a *yearning* eye
510 With *yearnings* unexpressed

YESTERDAY.
203 Y., to-day, to-morrow...the same
386 Now as y. the same
445 To-day as y. the same
572 Christ is dearer Than y.
805 Jesus' name, Now as y.

YIELD, YIELDS.
104 I y. my powers to thy command
240 When thou did-t there y. up
352 My heart I y. without delay
353 And y. thy heart to God's control
401 Nay, but I y.. I yield: I can
466 Ourselves to Christ we y.
566 Never y., nor lose by flight
738 Y. to me now, for I am weak

YOKE.
363 And cannot from its y. get free
495 Break off the y. of inbred sin
606 Give me to bear thy easy y.
623 Give me thy easy y. to bear
722 Tamely to thy y. submit
785 And bear thine easy y.
811 Beneath his easy y. they move
904 Help us, O Lord, thy y. to wear

YONDER.
755 Ah, what shall I be y.
1010 Till we shall meet him y.

YOUNG.
16 Y. men and maidens, raise
286 The y., the old, inspire
877 Delightful work! y. souls to win

YOUTH, YOUTHFUL.
832 Dawn even with its...y.
873 Those who seek me in their y.
876 The promise made to earliest y.
877 To guide untutored y.
884 To guide our steps in y.
885 Shepherd of tender y., Guiding
977 When y. its pride of beauty
1089 y. renewed and frenzy calmed
889 thousands slain, The y. and the

Z.

ZEAL.
74 To spread with holy z. around
415 Could my z. no languor know
485 Z. shall haste on eager wing
560 With holy, conquering z. inspire
560 For z. I sigh, for zeal I pant
560 But ah! my z. soon dies away
561 Where is the z. that led us then
586 And let my knowing z. be joined
586 With calm and tempered z.
762 My z. inspire
819 Suppress their fear, inflame...z.
883 Nor did their z. offend him
1045 His z. inspired their breast

ZION.
67 Praise waits in Z., Lord, for thee
69 Great God, attend, while Z. sings
89 Z., in all thy palaces, prosperity
330 When on Z. we stand, having
561 Z. beams with light
631 So, when on Z. thou shalt stand
644 With songs to Z. we return
766 stone Which God in Z. lays
767 Welcome news to Z. bearing

767 Z., long in hostile lands
767 Z. still is well beloved
768 Z. stands with hills surrounded
768 Z., kept by power divine
768 Happy Z., what a favored lot
770 To Z. shall be given, The
772 His Z. cannot move
773 Z. enjoys her monarch's love
775 Z., assert thy liberty
776 Z., city of our God
778 Daughter of Z., the power that
778 oppressor is vanquished, and Z.
821 Z., behold thy Saviour King
871 In Z. God is known, A refuge
883 To Z. Jesus came
912 Z. in triumph begins her mild
1043 Shouting, their heavenly Z. gain
1064 With him I on Z. shall stand
1065 Return to the Z. above

Of ZION.

759 Ye daughters of Z., declare,
778 Daughter of Z., awake from thy
778 Daughter of Z., the power that
909 Daughter of Z., from the dust
925 O light of Z., now arise
1061 They stand, those halls of Z.

ZION'S.

15 That love the way to Z. hill
36 Not now on Z. height alone

46 Regard our prayers for Z. peace
76 strength Of Z. heavenly dome
342 News from Z. King proclaim
346 Come the way to Z. gate
720 Z. city is in sight
764 Thus fair was Z. chosen seat
767 Great deliverance Z. King
769 at length In Z. courts appear
771 work revive, In Z. gloomy hour
774 spring...from Z. mount in
787 But we are come to Z. hill
821 feet Who stand on Z. hill
823 Let Z. watchmen all awake
856 Holy Z. help forever
883 reigneth On Z. heavenly hill
912 brightness of Z. glad morning
918 Be this thy Z. favored hour
922 From Z. mount send forth
925 On Z. holy towers to shine
928 And glory beam on Z. gates
932 Prepared for Z. war
1046 With him on Z. hill
1076 On Z. sacred height

ZIONWARD.

79 Their faces Z. were set
879 Little travelers Z.

ZONE.

779 Till her sons from z. to zone

DOXOLOGIES.

Index of Lines.

13 All praise to the Father, the Son
14 All glory be to thee
15 All praise be given
19 All glory and worship from earth
2 And shall be evermore
3 And new-creating breath
3 And Spirit all-divine
4 And Spirit, One in Three
4 And shall forever be
5 And equal adoration be
6 And all the saints in earth and
8 And saints on earth adore
13 And Spirit, thrice holy and blest
15 And Spirit, Three in One
16 And all thy hosts in heaven
17 And shout the joyful story
18 And spread his fame, till time shall
8 As now it is, and so shall last
10 As through countless ages past
16 As was from the beginning
19 As was, and is now, and shall ever

16 Ascribe we equal glory
5 Attend the almighty Father's name
12 Author of the new creation

2 Be glory, as it was, is now
4 Be glory, as it was, is now
8 Be glory as in ages past
6 By all the angels near the throne
16 By all who know thy name below

15 Crown him, in every song

17 Each ransomed spirit sings
11 Endless praises to Jehovah,
5 Eternal Comforter, to thee
6 Eternal praise and glory given
18 Eternal praise and worship be
10 Evermore his praise shall last

9 Father, Son, and Holy Ghost
10 Father, Son, and Holy Ghost! As

14 Father, Son, and Holy Ghost, Thy
18 From age to age, ye saints, his

7 Glory to God the Son
16 Glory to God be given
11 God the Father, God the Son
11 God the Spirit, joined in glory
11 Great Jehovah! we adore thee

12 Him by whom our spirits live
14 Holy, holy, holy Lord, All glory

5 Immortal honor, endless fame

14 Join we with the heavenly host

3 Let saints and angels join
15 Let all his praise prolong
16 Let all thy works adore thee
14 Live by earth and heaven adored

6 Now to the great and sacred Three

10 O Father Almighty, to thee be
17 Of thy redeeming love
11 On the same eternal throne
15 On earth, in heaven
16 One Deity, in Persons Three

1 Praise God, from whom all blessings
1 Praise him, all creatures here
1 Praise him above, ye heavenly host
1 Praise Father, Son, and Holy Ghost
9 Praise eternal as his love
9 Praise him, all ye heavenly host
10 Praise the name of God most high
10 Praise him, all below the sky
10 Praise him, all ye heavenly host
12 Praise the God of our salvation
12 Praise the Father's boundless love
12 Praise the Lamb, our expiation
12 Praise the Spirit from above.

9 Sing we to our God above

2 The God whom we adore
3 The God of mercy be adored
3 The One in Three, and Three in One
5 The Saviour Son be glorified
6 The Father, Son, and Spirit, be
8 The God whom heaven's triumphant
13 The eternal, supreme Three in One
14 The Three in one, the One in Three
17 Then glorious King of kings
6 Through all the worlds where God
7 Thy everlasting praise we sing
14 Thy Godhead we adore
17 Thy wondrous love and favor
2 To Father, Son, and Holy Ghost
3 To praise the Father and the Son
4 To God, the Father, Son,
7 To God the Father's throne
7 To God the Spirit, praise
8 To Father, Son, and Holy Ghost
11 To Jehovah, Three in One
12 To the one Jehovah give
14 To praise thee evermore
15 To God, the Father, Son, And
15 To him your hearts belong
16 To Father, Son, and Spirit
17 To thee be praise forever
18 To Father, Son, and Spirit, ever

12 Undivided adoration

13 Was, is, and shall still be confessed
17 We'll celebrate thy glory
8 When time shall be no more
3 Who calls our souls from death
3 Who saves by his redeeming word
5 Who for lost man's redemption died
7 With all our powers, eternal King
17 With all thy saints above
19 With Christ and the Spirit, one God

7 Your highest honors raise

CONSECUTIVE INDEX OF FIRST LINES OF HYMNS.

The figures on the left indicate the number of the Hymn in the Hymnal; on the right the number in the old Hymn Book; the meters are indicated at the end of each line.

1–55

#	First Line	Meter	Old #
1	O for a thousand tongues	C.	1
2	Come, let us join our	C.	4
3	Come, sound his praise	S.	12
4	Awake, and sing the song	S.	2
5	Stand up, and bless the	S.	14
6	Come, thou almighty	6,4.	25
7	Jesus, we look to thee	S.	35
8	From all that dwell below	L.	11
9	Before Jehovah's awful	L.	16
10	O holy, holy, holy Lord	L.	46
11	All people that on earth	L.	—
12	Jesus, thou everlasting	L.	10
13	O render thanks to God	L.	17
14	Lift up your heads, ye	L.	—
15	Lord of the worlds above	H.	24
16	Young men and maidens	H.	21
17	Let all on earth their	C.P.	19
18	Thou God of power, thou	C.P.	31
19	Jesus, thou soul of all our	C.P.	13
20	Heavenly Father, sovereign	7.	41
21	Lord, we come before thee	7.	57
22	Christians, brethren, ere we	7.1122	
23	Now may He who from the	7.1125	
24	Songs of praise the angels	7.	9
25	Thank and praise Jehovah's	7.	15
26	Glory be to God on high	7.	40
27	Praise the Lord, his glories	7.	—
28	Come, let us who in Christ	C.	3
29	Once more we come before	C.	38
30	See, Jesus, thy disciples see	C.	34
31	Infinite excellence is thine	C.	50
32	Jesus, thou all-redeeming	C.	51
33	O God, our strength, to thee	C.	54
34	A thousand oracles divine	C.	95
35	Father of heaven, whose	L.	62
36	O thou to whom, in ancient	L.	63
37	O thou, whom all thy saints	L.	30
38	Eternal Power, whose high	L.	27
39	Thy presence, gracious God	L.	28
40	Not here, as to the prophet's	L.	33
41	Come, ye that love the Lord	S.	909
42	Father, in whom we live	S.	904
43	With joy we lift our eyes	S.	47
44	Jesus, where'er thy people	L.	56
45	Blest hour, when mortal	L.	—
46	O thou, our Saviour, Brother		591
47	Lo! God is here! let us	L.6l.	36
48	Infinite God, to thee we	L.6l.	44
49	O Christ who hast prepared	L.	—
50	O God, to us show mercy	7,6.	—
51	Ye servants of God	10,11.	18
52	Lord, dismiss us with thy	8,7,4.1127	
53	May the grace of Christ	8,7.1129	
54	In thy name, O Lord	8,7,4.	49
55	Come, thou...Spirit	8,7,4.11;6	

56–110

#	First Line	Meter	Old #
56	Round the Lord, in glory	8,7.	—
57	Praise the Lord!	8,7.	—
58	Hark! the notes of angels	8,7.	8
59	Lord, dismiss us with	8,7.1123	
60	Lord, when we bend before	C.	61
61	Before thy mercy-seat	C.	60
62	O God, by whom the seed	C.1128	
63	Come, ye that love the	C.	6
64	Come, thou Desire of all	C.	48
65	Within thy house, O Lord	C.	29
66	Come, let us tune our	L.	5
67	Praise waits in Zion, Lord	L.	59
68	Servants of God, in joyful	L.	20
69	Great God, attend, while	L.	26
70	Eternal God, celestial King	L.	918
71	Hosanna to the living	L.	—
72	O day of rest and gladness	7,6.	—
73	Awake, ye saints, awake	H.	245
74	With joy we hail the	C.	39
75	The Lord of Sabbath	C.	149
76	This is the day the Lord	C.	244
77	Again the Lord of life	C.	—
78	Lord of the Sabbath	L.	251
79	Millions within thy courts	L.	619
80	Sweet is the light		—
81	Sweet is the work, my God	L.	241
82	Return my soul, enjoy	L.	247
83	My opening eyes with	L.	594
84	Far from my thoughts	L.	243
85	Welcome, sweet day	L.	242
86	This is the day of light	S.	—
87	Hail to the Sabbath day	S.	249
88	Safely through another	7,6l.	—
89	Glad was my heart to hear	S.	252
90	Day of God, thou blessed	7.	248
91	On this day, the first	7.	—
92	Softly fades the twilight	7.	—
93	Abide with me! Fast falls	10.	—
94	Saviour, again to thy dear	10.	—
95	Once more, my soul	C.	609
96	Awake, my soul, to meet	C.	593
97	All praise to Him who	C.	618
98	Lord, in the morning	C.	595
99	Now from the altar of our	C.	611
100	Lord of my life, O may	C.	604
101	Happy the home when	C.	—
102	Sun of my soul, thou	L.	—
103	New every morning	L.	—
104	My God, how endless	L.	606
105	Glory to thee, my God	L.	607
106	Awake, my soul, and with	L.	597
107	Now doth the sun ascend	L.	—
108	Thus far the Lord hath	L.	612
109	Again as evening's shadow	L.	—
110	When, streaming from	L.	—

111–178　　　192　　　179–246

No.	Title	Meter	Tune
111	We lift our hearts to thee	S.	603
112	See how the morning sun	S.	602
113	The day is past and gone	S.	—
114	In mercy, Lord, remember	C.	616
115	Silently the shades	8.7.	—
116	Saviour, breathe an	8.7.	609
117	Softly now the light	7.	608
118	We all believe in one	8.7.7.	—
119	O God, of good the	L.P.	87
120	O God, we praise thee	C.	72
121	Hail, Father, Son, and	C.	103
122	There seems a voice in	C.	66
123	Lord, all I am is known	C.	83
124	Father, to thee my soul	C.	99
125	O God, thy power is	C.	—
126	O God, thou bottomless	L.	168
127	Thine, Lord, is wisdom	L.	88
128	Eternal depth of love	L.	94
129	Blest Spirit, one with God	L.	—
130	God is the name my soul	L.	100
131	Holy as thou, O Lord	L.	160
132	Ere mountains reared	L.	82
133	Come, O my soul	L.	78
134	The Lord is King! lift up	L.	—
135	Lord of all being	L.	—
136	Holy, holy, holy	11,12,10.	—
137	O holy, holy, holy Lord	7.	—
138	The spacious firmament	L.	65
139	Father of all, whose	L.	73
140	O worship the King	10,11.	—
141	Though troubles assail	10,11.	744
142	The Lord Jehovah reigns	H.	77
143	This God is the God we	S.	85
144	Holy, holy, holy Lord	7,6/.	—
145	Let us with a gladsome	7.	—
146	Father, how wide thy	C.	91
147	My God, how wonderful	C.	—
148	Mighty God! while	8,7.	—
149	There's a wideness in	8,7.	—
150	God is love; his mercy	8,7.	—
151	The Lord our God is	C.	79
152	The Lord descended from	C.	74
153	Praise ye the Lord	C.	111
154	Let every tongue thy	C.	89
155	Which of the monarchs	C.	850
156	The Lord's my Shepherd	C.	—
157	O thou, who, when we	C.	893
158	There is a safe and secret	C.	—
159	Jehovah, God, thy gracious	C.	98
160	When all thy mercies	C.	845
161	God moves in a mysterious	C.	745
162	Kingdoms and thrones to	L.	—
163	When Israel, of the Lord	L.	751
164	Peace, troubled soul	L.	781
165	The tempter to my soul	L.	889
166	A mighty fortress is our	8,7,6.	—
167	They come, God's	L.	—
168	God is our refuge and	L.	847
169	God of my life, whose	L.	762
170	How do thy mercies close	L.	890
171	Guide me, O thou great	8,7,4.	832
172	My soul repeat his praise	S.	—
173	Away, my needless fears	L.	892
174	Thy way is in the sea	S.	841
175	Lord, I delight in thee	S.	913
176	How gentle God's	S.	—
177	How tender is thy hand	S.	895
178	Thou very-present Aid	S.	894
179	The Lord is my Shepherd	11.	849
180	The Lord my pasture	L.6/.	848
181	Hail to the Lord's	7,6.	126
182	As with gladness men of	7,6/.	—
183	Joy to the world! the Lord	C.	—
184	To us a Child of hope is	C.	121
185	Hark, the glad sound! the	C.	118
186	Brightest and best of	11,10.	117
187	When marshaled on the	L.	—
188	Hark! what mean those	8,7.	114
189	Angels, from the realms	8,7,4.	119
190	Hark! the herald-angels	7.	125
191	Bright and joyful is the	7.	120
192	While shepherds watched	C.	113
193	Mortals, awake, with angels	C.	116
194	It came upon the midnight	C.	—
195	Calm on the listening ear	C.	—
196	What grace, O Lord, and	C.	—
197	We may not climb the	C.	—
198	The chosen three, on	C.	—
199	O wondrous type! O vision	L.	—
200	O Master, it is good to be	L.	—
201	When the blind suppliant	L.	—
202	How beauteous were the	L.	—
203	Jesus wept! those tears	8,7,7.	—
204	In the cross of Christ I	8,7.	—
205	Never further than thy cross	7.	—
206	When on Sinai's top I see	7.	293
207	Praise to the Holiest in the	C.	—
208	We sing the praise of him	L.	—
209	From Calvary a cry was	L.	135
210	'Tis finished! the Messiah	L.	114
211	When I survey the	L.	145
212	Extended on a cursed tree	L.	137
213	Lord Jesus, when we stand	L.	—
214	Alas! and did my Saviour	C.	146
215	Behold the Saviour of	C.	134
216	With glorious clouds	C.	128
217	'Tis midnight; and on	L.	—
218	'Tis finished, so the Saviour	L.	143
219	The royal banner is	C.	—
220	O Love divine, what hast	L.6/.	133
221	Would Jesus have the	L.6/.	141
222	O sacred Head, now	7,6/.	—
223	Go to dark Gethsemane	7,6/.	—
224	Hark! the voice of love	8,7,4.	112
225	Sing with all the sons of	8,7.	—
226	Come, ye saints, look	8,7,4.	—
227	Lift your glad voices	10,11,12.	153
228	Welcome, thou Victor in	C.	—
229	Rise, glorious Conqueror	6,4.	—
230	The day of resurrection	7,6.	—
231	Welcome, happy morning	11.	—
232	Awake, glad soul! awake	C.	—
233	The morning kindles all the	L.	—
234	He dies! the Friend of	L.	148
235	The Lord is risen indeed	S.	151
236	Thou art gone up on high	S.	—
237	Our Lord is risen from the	L.	154
238	Jesus, thy blood and	L.	174
239	Jesus, my Advocate above	L.	165
240	O Christ, our King, Creator	L.	—
241	Majestic sweetness sits	C.	—
242	I know that my Redeemer	L.	179
243	Join all the glorious names	H.	177
244	Rejoice, the Lord is King	H.	899
245	God is gone up on high	H.	157
246	Hail, thou once despised	8,7.	178

No.	First Line	Meter	Tune
247	We shall see him in our	8,7.	—
248	All hail the power of Jesus'.	.	175
249	Look, ye saints, the sight.	8,7,4.	—
250	O thou eternal Victim	L.6l.	172
251	Jesus, the Conqueror	S.	739
252	Lord, how shall sinners	S.	166
253	Enthroned is Jesus now	S.	176
254	With joy we meditate the	C.	163
255	Jesus, the Lord of glory	C.	170
256	The head that once was	C.	158
257	Crown him with many	S.	—
258	Father, hear the blood of	8,7.	167
259	Christ, the Lord, is risen	7.	—
260	Christ, the Lord, is risen	7.	152
261	Hail the day that sees Him	7.	156
262	Gracious Spirit, Love divine.	7.	187
263	Holy Spirit, Truth divine	7.	—
264	Granted is the Saviour's	7.	—
265	Holy Ghost, dispel our	8,7.	197
266	Holy Spirit, Fount of	8,7.	199
267	Holy Ghost, with light	7.	—
268	On all the earth thy Spirit	L.	202
269	O come Creator Spirit blest.	L.	—
270	Enthroned on high	C.	193
271	Great Spirit, by whose	C.	185
272	I worship thee, O Holy	C.	—
273	Come, Holy Ghost, our	L.6l.	—
274	O for that flame of living	L.	859
275	Come, Holy Spirit, raise our	L.	—
276	O Spirit of the living God	L.	195
277	Come, Holy Spirit, heavenly	C.	191
278	Spirit Divine, attend our	C.	—
279	Come, Holy Ghost, our	C.	679
280	Our blest Redeemer, ere he	C.	—
281	Eternal Spirit, God of truth	C.	184
282	O thou that hearest prayer	H.	183
283	Thou who like the wind	7,5.	—
284	Come, Holy Ghost, in love.	6,4.	—
285	Come, Holy Spirit, come	S.	—
286	Lord God, the Holy Ghost	S.	194
287	Blest Comforter divine	S.	186
288	Thy word, almighty Lord	S.	686
289	Jesus, the word bestow	S.	689
290	Upon the Gospel's sacred	L.	—
291	When quiet in my house.	L.6l.	687
292	The heavens declare thy	L.	—
293	The starry firmament on	L.	—
294	Now let my soul, eternal	L.	688
295	The counsels of redeeming	C.	676
296	What glory gilds the sacred	C.	678
297	How precious is the book	C.	683
298	Hail, sacred truth! whose	C.	690
299	Father of mercies, in thy	C.	677
300	Bright was the guiding star	C.	684
301	Almighty God, thy word	C.	—
302	How sad our state by nature.	C.	323
303	God is in this and every	C.	313
304	Plunged in a gulf of dark	C.	181
305	Lord, we are vile, conceived.	L.	309
306	Deep are the wounds which.	L.	326
307	Jesus, a word, a look from.	L.	316
308	My former hopes are fled	S.	324
309	How helpless nature lies	S.	311
310	Ah, how shall fallen man	S.	312
311	O that I could repent! O	S.	318
312	Our sins on Christ were	S.	132
313	Jesus, thou Source divine	S.	109
314	God's holy law transgressed.	S.	205
315	How great the wisdom	C.	289
316	How sweet the name of	C.	296
317	Thy ceaseless, unexhausted.	C.	298
318	Thou art the Way:—to thee	C.	168
319	There is a fountain filled	C.	290
320	When wounded sore, the	C.	—
321	Grace! 'tis a charming	S.	248
322	What majesty and grace	S.	286
323	O what amazing words of	C.	294
324	Salvation! O the joyful	C.	291
325	The Saviour! O what	C.	285
326	Let every mortal ear	C.	301
327	Of Him who did salvation	L.	292
328	How sweetly flowed the	L.	287
329	Happy the man who finds	L.	297
330	The voice of free grace	12.	303
331	Blow ye the trumpet, blow	H.	300
332	Let earth and heaven agree.	H.	506
333	When time seems short	L.6l.	—
334	Come, thou long-expected .	8,7.	—
335	O turn ye, O turn ye, for	11.	—
336	Delay not, delay not, O	11.	—
337	Weary souls that wander	7.6l.	343
338	From the cross uplifted	7,6l.	351
339	Hearts of stone, relent	7,6l.	340
340	Come, ye sinners, poor	8,7,4.	341
341	Come to Calvary's holy	8,7,7.	345
342	Sinners, will you scorn	8,7,4.	—
343	Hear, O sinner, mercy	8,7,4.	—
344	Come, said Jesus' sacred	7.	—
345	Hasten, sinner, to be wise	7.	333
346	Pilgrim, burdened with thy	7.	—
347	Sinners, turn; why will ye	7.	355
348	What could your Redeemer.	7.	356
349	While life prolongs its	L.	329
350	Sinners, obey the gospel	L.	350
351	Come, O ye sinners, to the	L.	353
352	God calling yet! shall I not.	L.	—
353	Say, sinner, hath a voice	L.	—
354	Haste, traveler, haste! the	L.P.	—
355	The Spirit in our hearts	S.	—
356	Ye simple souls that stray	S.	851
357	All things are ready, come	S.	—
358	O where shall rest be found.	S.	335
359	Come, weary sinner, come	S.	358
360	My son, know thou the	S.	346
361	Now is the accepted time	S.	330
362	Ho! every one that thirsts	L.	352
363	With tearful eyes I look	L.	—
364	Come, sinners, to the gospel.	L.	348
365	Vain man, thy fond	C.	338
366	Why should we boast of	C.	332
367	Lovers of pleasure more	C.	347
368	Come, O thou all-victorious.	C.	328
369	Come, humble sinner, in	C.	359
370	Return, O wanderer, return.	C.	354
371	Sinners, the voice of God	C.	3.4
372	Thou Son of God, whose	C.	327
373	Beneath our feet, and o'er	C.	337
374	Jesus, Redeemer of	C.	343
375	Late, late, so late! and	10.	—
376	In the silent midnight	8,5.	—
377	Author of faith, to thee	C.P.	372
378	O Lamb of God, for	C.P.	412
379	Depth of mercy! can there	7.	403
380	Sovereign Ruler, Lord of all.	7.	402
381	O thou who hast our	C.P.	370
382	Lamb of God for sinners.	7,6,8.	—

13

No.	Title	Meter	Page	No.	Title	Meter	Page
383	Lamb of God, whose	7,6,8.	283	451	Glory to God, whose	L.	308
384	Lord, I hear of showers	8,7,3.	—	452	Let not the wise their	L.	453
385	Let the world their	7,6,8.	431	453	O what shall I do my	10,11.	457
386	God of my salvation	7,6,8.	405	454	All praise to the Lamb	10,11.	458
387	Lord of mercy and of	7,5.	632	455	Lord, and is thine anger	7,6,8.	883
388	Like Noah's weary dove	S.	—	456	Vain, delusive world	7,6,8.	880
389	Wherewith, O Lord, shall	L.	361	457	Come, Saviour, Jesus, from	L.	566
390	Stay, thou insulted Spirit	L.	420	458	God of my life, what just	L.	366
391	Show pity, Lord, O Lord	L.	398	459	O Thou, who hast at thy	L.	816
392	Jesus, the sinner's Friend	L.	408	460	Lord, I am thine, entirely	L.	801
393	Just as I am, without one	L.	—	461	I thirst, thou wounded	L.	529
394	My soul before thee		425	462	O Love, thy sovereign aid	L.	821
395	When, gracious Lord, when	L.	417	463	Prince of peace, control my	7.	516
396	O for a glance of heavenly	L.	374	464	Father of eternal grace	7.	519
397	Lord, I despair myself to	L.	364	465	Thine forever!—Lord of	7.	—
398	Jesus, thy far-extended	L.	321	466	Witness, ye men and angels	C.	—
399	And wilt Thou yet be	S.	865	467	What shall I render to my	C.	—
400	When shall Thy love	S.	421	468	My God, accept my heart	C.	—
401	And can I yet delay	S.	428	469	Let Him to whom we now	C.	527
402	Ah! whither should I go	S.	360	470	Father, Son, and Holy	7,6l.	525
403	Out of the depths of woe	S.	429	471	Abraham, when severely	L.	773
404	O that I could repent, With	S.	373	472	My soul and all its powers	H.	656
405	Did Christ o'er sinners	S.	378	473	Lord, in the strength of	S.	730
406	Father, I stretch my hands	C.	401	474	O God, what offering	L.6l.	533
407	O that I could my Lord	C.	416	475	Behold the servant of the	L.6l.	830
408	We sinners, Lord, with	C.	—	476	Jesus, thy boundless	L.6l.	833
409	I would be thine: O take	C.	368	477	Thou hidden love of God	L.6l.	829
410	O for that tenderness of	C.	384	478	I thank thee, uncreated	L.6l.	823
411	O sun of righteousness	C.	391	479	Prisoners of hope, lift up	L.6l.	489
412	When rising from the bed	C.	363	480	Father of everlasting	L.6l.	468
413	O that Thou wouldst the	C.	376	481	Come, Holy Ghost	L.P.	885
414	The prodigal, with	C.	430	482	The thing my God doth	S.	507
415	Rock of ages, cleft for me	7,6l.	409	483	Jesus, my Truth, my Way	S.	488
416	Christ, whose glory fills	7,6l.	423	484	God of almighty love	S.	567
417	By thy birth, and by thy	7,6l.	395	485	King of kings, and wilt		—
418	Lord, how secure and blest	L.	473	486	Saviour of the sin-sick	7.	530
419	Great God, indulge my	L.	475	487	Gracious soul, to whom	7,6l.	—
420	Now I have found the	L.6l.	437	488	Jesus, full of love divine	7.	—
421	My hope is built on	L.6l.	—	489	Light of life, seraphic fire	7.	557
422	And can it be that I	L.6l.	415	490	Holy Lamb, who thee	7.	534
423	In evil long I took delight	C.	—	491	Love divine, all love	8,7.	488
424	Why should the children of	C.	162	492	Well for him who all	S,7.	—
425	My God, my God, to thee I	C.	412	493	Ye ransomed sinners, hear	H.	495
426	I heard the voice of Jesus	C.	—	494	Ever fainting with	7,6,8.	543
427	Amazing grace! how sweet	C.	—	495	O that my Lord of sin	L.	510
428	Eternal Sun of		465	496	O thou, to whose call	L.	825
429	Sovereign of all the worlds	C.	472	497	Lord, fill me with a humble	L.	581
430	Jesus, to thee I now can fly	C.	110	498	Behold the throne of grace	S.	540
431	Fountain of life, to all	C.	503	499	And wilt the mighty God	S.	—
432	Father of Jesus	C.	438 & 439	500	Jesus, I live to thee	S.	—
433	What shall I do my God to	C.	307	501	Blest are the pure in	S.	417
434	I was a wandering sheep	S.	—	502	O come, and dwell in me	S.	—
435	Spirit of faith, come down	S.	477	503	Father, I dare believe	S.	418
436	Here I can firmly rest	S.	—	504	Had I the gift of tongues	S.	841
437	How can a sinner know His	S.	459	505	Jesus, my strength, my hope	S.	576
438	Arise, my soul, arise	H.	474	506	I want a heart to pray	S.	577
439	Thou great mysterious	C.P.	451	507	Walk in the light! so shalt	C.	812
440	Abba, Father, hear thy	7,6l.	467	508	Being of beings, God of	C.	42
441	Chief of sinners though I	7,6l.	—	509	O how the thought of God	C.	—
442	O how happy are they	12,9.	452	510	My Saviour, on the word	C.	—
443	Oft I in my heart have	7,6,7.	482	511	I want a principle within	C.	579
444	Trembling before thine	L.	—	512	I know that my Redeemer	C.	483
445	Author of faith, eternal	L.	445	513	Lord, I believe a rest	L.	484
446	We have no outward	L.	436	514	O Jesus, at thy feet we wait	C.	510
447	O happy day that fixed my	L.	454	515	O joyful sound of gospel	C.	172
448	Into thy gracious hands I	L.	446	516	Let worldly minds the	C.	805
449	My soul, with humble favor	L.	463	517	Jesus, the Life, the Truth	C.	566
450	Jesus, my all, to heaven is	L.	448	518	Jesus, thine all-victorious	C.	536

No.	Title		No.	Title	
519	Jesus, my Life, thyself	C. 522	587	Soldiers of Christ, arise	S. 725
520	Jesus hath died that I	C. 526	588	Soldiers of Christ, lay hold	S. 726
521	O for a heart to praise my	C. 520	589	Pray, without ceasing pray	S. 728
522	Come, O my God, the	C. 546	590	Lord, as to thy dear cross	C. —
523	God of eternal truth and	C. 515	591	Workman of God! O lose	C. —
524	Come, O Thou greater than	L. 493	592	Son of the carpenter	C. —
525	Holy, and true, and	L. 503	593	Am I a soldier of the cross	C. 734
526	O Jesus, full of truth and	L. 523	594	Awake, my soul, stretch	C. 834
527	Jesus, in whom the	L. 583	595	I'm not ashamed to own	C. 812
528	God of all power, and truth	L. 494	596	O it is hard to work for	C. —
529	He wills that I should holy	L. 481	597	Behold us, Lord, a little	C. —
530	Arise, my soul, on wings	L. 806	598	O still in accents sweet and	C. —
531	O God, most merciful and	L. 501	599	Behold the Christian	L. 721
532	What! never speak one evil	L. 505	600	Ye faithful souls who Jesus	L. 840
533	Forever here my rest shall	C. 524	601	Take up thy cross, the	L. —
534	Jesus, the sinner's rest	C. 486	602	It may not be our lot to	L. —
535	I ask the gift of	C. 537	603	Go, labor on; spend and be	L. —
536	My God, I know, I feel thee	C. 831	604	Jesus, and shall it ever be	L. 813
537	Thy presence, Lord, the	C. 505	605	My gracious Lord, I own	L. 817
538	Deepen the wound Thy	C. 517	606	Forth in thy name, O Lord	L. 628
539	What is our calling's	C. 480	607	Hark, the voice of Jesus	8.7. —
540	O Love divine, how sweet	C.P. 528	608	Faith of our fathers	L.6/. —
541	But can it be that I should	C.P. 511	609	Lo! I come with joy to	7,6,8. —
542	O glorious hope of perfect	C.P. 491	610	Father, whate'er of earthly	C. —
543	Help, Lord, to whom for	C.P. 575	611	O thou who driest the	C. 748
544	O God, thy faithfulness I	C.P. 768	612	When languor and disease	C. 662
545	Saviour, on me the grace	C.P. 499	613	O Friend of souls! how	C. —
546	Sweet was the time when	C. 870	614	Father of love, our Guide	C. —
547	My drowsy powers, why	C. 853	615	Since all the varying scenes	C. 749
548	My head is low, my heart	C. —	616	While thee I seek	C. 624
549	O for a closer walk with God	C. 809	617	Author of good, we rest on	C. 683
550	As pants the hart for	C. 863	618	O Thou, who in the olive	C. 638
551	Come, let us to the Lord our	C. —	619	O Thou from whom all	C. 752
552	Hark, my soul! it is the	7. 454	620	We journey through a vale	C. 747
553	O Thou, whose mercy hears	S. 874	621	I love the Lord; he heard	C. 885
554	How oft this wretched	S. 880	622	He leadeth me! O blessed	L. —
555	Gracious Redeemer, shake	S. 861	623	Eternal Beam of light divine	L. 757
556	Thou seest my feebleness	S. 614	624	My hope, my all, my Saviour	L. 578
557	O Jesus, full of grace	S. 872	625	God of my life, to thee I call	L. 755
558	Jesus, let thy pitying eye	7,6,8. 879	626	Away, my unbelieving fear	L. 784
559	Jesus, Friend of sinners	7,6,8. 875	627	Deem not that they are	L. 746
560	O Thou who all things	L. 854	628	Thy will be done! I will	L. —
561	O where is now that	L. 858	629	O Love divine, that stooped	L. —
562	O Thou who camest from	L. 572	630	When Power divine, in	L. 794
563	Onward, Christian soldiers	6,5. —	631	Thou Lamb of God, thou	L. 756
564	Forward! be our	6,5. —	632	O God, to thee we raise our	L. 700
565	Work, for the night is	6,6,5. —	633	Your harps, ye trembling	S. —
566	Soldiers of the cross	7,7,7,6. —	634	Jesus, one word from thee	S. —
567	Stand up, stand up for	7,6. —	635	My spirit, on thy care	S. —
568	Go forward, Christian	7,6. —	636	If, on a quiet sea	S. 783
569	Fear not, O little flock	C.P. —	637	My times are in thy hand	S. —
570	Are there not in the	C.P. 818	638	O what, if we are Christ's	S. —
571	Be it my only wisdom	C.P. 846	639	God is my strong salvation	7,6. 727
572	One more day's work	7,6,5,4. —	640	O happy band of pilgrims	7,6. —
573	I and my house will serve	C.P. 626	641	Sometimes a light	7,6. —
574	A charge to keep I have	S. 570	642	In heavenly love abiding	7,6. —
575	Sow in the morn thy seed	S. 212	643	Jesus, I my cross have	8,7. —
576	Make haste, O man, to live	S. —	644	Only waiting, till the	8,7. —
577	Arise, ye saints, arise	S. 740	645	Full of trembling	8,7,7. 659
578	Laborers of Christ, arise	S. —	646	Gently, Lord, O gently	8,7,4. —
579	The harvest dawn is near	S. —	647	Vain are all terrestrial	8,7. 798
580	Let us keep steadfast	S. —	648	Leader of faithful souls	L.6/. 837
581	My soul, be on thy guard	S. 731	649	Though waves and	L.6/. 789
582	Hark, how the watchmen	S. 723	650	Jesus, to thee our hearts	L.6/. 888
583	Urge on your rapid course	S. 727	651	Peace, doubting heart	L.6/. 790
584	My soul, weigh not thy life	S. —	652	Come unto me, when	11,10. —
585	I the good fight have fought	S. 738	653	Take the name of Jesus	8,7. —
586	Equip me for the war	S. 732	654	My Jesus, as thou wilt	6. —

#	Title	Meter	No.
655	Thy way, not mine, O Lord	6,	—
656	Jesus, lover of my soul	7,	288
657	Come on, my partners in	C.P.	925
658	Thy mercy heard my	C.P.	672
659	When I can read my title	C.	736
660	Grant me within thy courts	C.	839
661	Thy gracious presence, O	C.	778
662	How vain are all things	C.	797
663	O who, in such a world as	C.	750
664	My span of life will soon be	C.	782
665	Out of the depths to thee	C.	—
666	Must Jesus bear the cross	C.	—
667	O for a faith that will not	C.	568
668	Lord, I believe thy every	C.	828
669	Lord, it belongs not to my	C.	—
670	O thou, whose filmed and	C.	—
671	From lips divine, like	C.	—
672	Commit thou all thy griefs	S.	779
673	Give to the winds thy fears	S.	780
674	Thou Refuge of my soul	S.	764
675	Father, I know that all my	8,6.	—
676	Go not far from me, O my	8,6.	—
677	God of Israel's faithful	7,6,7.	787
678	To the haven of thy	7,6,8.	—
679	How firm a foundation	11.	—
680	Head of the Church	7,8,7.	886
681	Still out of the deepest	8.	—
682	Lead, kindly Light	10,4,10.	—
683	Come, ye disconsolate	11,10.	304
684	From every stormy wind	L.	554
685	O Lord, thy heavenly grace	L.	624
686	Jesus, my Saviour, Brother	L.	573
687	O thou pure Light of souls	L.	—
688	Sweet hour of prayer	L.	—
689	Prayer is appointed to	L.	549
690	What various hindrances	L.	558
691	Jesus, thou joy of loving	L.	—
692	God of my life, through all	L.	924
693	O God, thou art my Good	L.	795
694	Lord Jesus Christ, my Life	L.	—
695	Though all the world my	L.	—
696	My Lord, how full of sweet	L.	—
697	Thou dear Redeemer	C.	—
698	My God, my Portion and	C.	908
699	My Saviour, my almighty	C.	906
700	Jesus, the very thought	C.	—
701	O Jesus, King most	C.	—
702	O Jesus, thou the beauty	C.	—
703	O 'tis delight without alloy	C.	910
704	My God, the spring of all	C.	503
705	Yes, I will bless thee, O my	C.	921
706	Prayer is the breath of God	C.	—
707	There is an eye that never	C.	—
708	Unveil, O Lord, and on us	C.	—
709	I love to steal awhile away	C.	647
710	Prayer is the soul's sincere	C.	550
711	Sweet is the prayer whose	C.	658
712	Talk with us, Lord, thyself	C.	902
713	Far from the world, O Lord	C.	644
714	Jesus, those eyes have	C.	—
715	Shepherd Divine, our wants	C.	553
716	Our Father, God, who art	C.	551
717	They who seek the throne	7.	—
718	Come, my soul, thy suit	7.	557
719	Jesus is our common Lord	7.	934
720	Children of the heavenly	7.	838
721	Christ, of all my hopes the	7.	—
722	God of love, who hearest	7.	582
723	Saviour, when, in dust, to	7.	564
724	Nearer, my God, to thee	6,4,6.	—
725	More love to thee, O	6,4,6.	—
726	Come, thou Fount of	8,7.	901
727	Here on earth, where foes	8,7.	—
728	What a friend we have in	8,7.	—
729	O my God, how thy	8,7.	—
730	Sweet the moments	8,7.	—
731	Always with us, always	8,7.	—
732	Laboring and heavy	8,7.	—
733	O thou God of my	8,7.	914
734	Praise, my soul, the King	8,7.	—
735	O wondrous power	L.6l.	560
736	Thou hidden Source	L.6l.	917
737	Come, O thou Traveler	L.6l.	649
738	Yield to me now	L.6l.	651
739	The Sun of righteousness	L.6l.	652
740	I'll praise my Maker	L.P.	923
741	Fade, fade, each	6,4,6.	—
742	Saviour, who died for	6,4,6.	—
743	O could I speak	C.P.	—
744	How happy, gracious	C.P.	911
745	To the hills I lift mine	7,6,7.	562
746	See the Lord, thy	7,6,7.	563
747	How tedious and tasteless	S.	907
748	Thou Shepherd of Israel	S.	916
749	O bless the Lord, my soul	S.	884
750	Come at the morning	S.	—
751	My God, my Life, my Love	S.	909
752	My God, is any hour	S,8,8,4.	—
753	The praying spirit	S.	556
754	I lay my sins on Jesus	7,6.	—
755	I know no life divided	7,6.	—
756	I love to tell the story	7,6.	—
757	My God, I am thine	11,12.	922
758	O tell me no more	10,11.	—
759	O Thou, in whose	11,8.	—
760	I need thee every hour	6,4,7.	—
761	My Shepherd's mighty	6,4,7.	915
762	My faith looks up to thee	6,4.	581
763	O where are kings and	C.	—
764	With stately towers	C.	223
765	Happy the souls to Jesus	C.	929
766	Behold the sure	C.	959
767	On the mountain's top	8,7,4.	—
768	Zion stands with hills	8,7,4.	236
769	How lovely are thy	C.	—
770	I love thy kingdom	S.	237
771	O Lord, thy work revive	S.	588
772	Who in the Lord confide	S.	231
773	God is the refuge of his	L.	—
774	Great source of being	L.	227
775	Awake, Jerusalem, awake	L.	234
776	Glorious things of thee	8,7.	243
777	Hear what God the Lord	8,7.	238
778	Daughter of Zion, awake	11.	—
779	On thy Church, O	7,6.	224
780	How sweet, how heavenly	C.	—
781	Come in, thou blessed	C.	—
782	Blest be the dear uniting	C.	1121
783	Our God is love	C.	683
784	Try us, O God, and	C.	700
785	Jesus, united by thy grace	C.	704
786	Lift up your hearts to	C.	916
787	Not to the terrors of the	C.	—
788	The glorious universe	C.	691
789	All praise to our redeeming	C.	711
790	Jesus, great shepherd	C.	701

#	Title		#	#	Title		#
791	Brethren in Christ........L.	709		859	O Lord of hosts............L.	—
792	Unchangeable, almighty...L.	702		860	Not heaven's wide range..L.	968
793	Giver of peace and unity..L.	698		861	This stone to thee........L.	962
794	Saviour of all, to thee.....L.	710		862	Enter thy temple glorious.L.	—
795	Jesus, from whom all.....L.	225		863	The perfect world.........L.	970
796	Still one in life and one...L.	—		864	When to the exiled seer...L.	961
797	Blest be the tie that binds..S.	712		865	Great King of glory........H.	964
798	And are we yet alive......S.	707		866	The Lord our God alone...L.	—
799	Blest are the sons.........S.	694		867	And will the great eternal.L.	969
800	One sole baptismal sign...H.	—		868	We rear not a temple.....H.	—
801	Thou God of truth.........H.	699		869	O Thou, whose own........C.	—
802	Glory be to God above....7.	696		870	O God, through countless..C.	967
803	While we walk with God..7.	720		871	Great is the Lord our God..S.	965
804	Jesus, Lord, we look to...7.	705		872	Saviour, like a shepherd.8,7,4.	—
805	Come, and let us sweetly..7.	718		873	God has said, Forever..8,7,4.	—
806	Christ from whom all.....7.	706		874	Children,loud hosannas.8,7,4.	—
807	When shall we meet.....6,5.	—		875	By cool Siloam's shady....C.	1010
808	Lord of the living.........7,6.	—		876	Come, Christian children..C.	—
809	Except the Lord conduct.C.P.	218		877	Delightful work! young...C.	1007
810	Go forth, ye heralds.......L.	—		878	Wilt thou hear the voice .7.8.	—
811	High on his everlasting...L.	217		879	Little travelers Zionward..7.	—
812	The Saviour, when........L.	203		880	I think, when I read.11,8,12,9.	—
813	Shall I, for fear of feeble..L.	655		881	Mighty One, before whose..7.	1008
814	Saviour of men, thy.......L.	653		882	Hosanna! he the children's.C.	1012
815	Draw near, O Son of God..L.	213		883	When, his salvation.....7,6.	—
816	And let our bodies part....S.	221		884	We bring no glittering..7,6.	1014
817	Lord, if at thy command...S.	230		885	Shepherd of tender......6,4.	—
818	Lord of the harvest, hear...S.	207		886	I love to hear the story...7,6.	—
819	Father of mercies, bow....L.	215		887	Holy Father, send thy....8,7.	—
820	Go, preach my gospel.....L.	204		888	Saviour, who thy flock...8,7.	—
821	How beauteous are their...S.	215		889	Gracious Saviour, gentle..8,7.	—
822	Jesus! the name high.....C.	219		890	Mourn for the thousands..S.	—
823	Let Zion's watchmen all...C.	206		891	O praise our God to-day....S.	—
824	Jesus, the word of mercy..C.	210		892	We give thee but thine.....S.	—
825	Captain of our salvation..C.	629		893	Jesus, my Lord, how rich..C.	—
826	I am baptized into thy.....L.	—		894	Father of mercies, send....C.	1032
827	See, Israel's gentle........C.	256		895	'Tis thine alone, almighty.C.	—
828	Behold what condescend'g.C.	261		896	She loved her Saviour.....C.	—
829	O Lord, while we confess..C.	—		897	Lord, lead the way........C.	—
830	Rites cannot change the ..S.	—		898	Who is thy neighbor.......C.	—
831	Come, Father, Son........S.	255		899	Life from the dead........C.	—
832	This child we dedicate....L.	—		900	When, doomed to death...L.	—
833	In that sad memorable...L.6l.	263		901	Bondage and death........L.	—
834	The King of heaven his....C.	266		902	How blest the children....C.	1033
835	Jesus, at whose supreme..C.	265		903	Rich are the joys which...C.	—
836	According to thy gracious.C.	268		904	Help us, O Lord, thy yoke..L.	1035
837	O Love divine.............C.	—		905	Dear ties of mutual.......L.	—
838	In memory of the Saviour's.C.	—		906	Brother, hast thou.........7.	—
839	If human kindness meets. C.	270		907	As shadows, cast by cloud..C.	—
840	That doleful night before..C.	264		908	Jesus, immortal King......C.	998
841	Glory to God on high.....S.	280		909	Daughter of Zion, from...C.	229
842	O what delight is this....S.	277		910	Great God, the nations...C.	—
843	No gospel like this feast...S.	—		911	Flung to the heedless.....6.	1000
844	Many centuries have fled.7,6l.	—		912	Hail to the brightness..11,10.	—
845	Till He come; O let.....7,6l.	—		913	Thou, whose almighty..6,4.	988
846	Let all who truly bear.....S.	267		914	Light of the lonely.......C.	—
847	At the Lamb's high feast...7.	—		915	The Lord will come........C.	—
848	Jesus, all-redeeming Lord..7.	272		916	Almighty Spirit, now......C.	986
849	O bread to pilgrims given.7,6.	—		917	Soon may the last glad....L.	1005
850	By Christ redeemed...8,8,8,4.	—		918	Sovereign of worlds.......L.	997
851	Author of our salvation...L.	271		919	Jesus shall reign...........L.	999
852	To Jesus, our exalted Lord.L.	278		920	Arm of the Lord, awake...L.	995
853	Jesus spreads his banner..8,7.	281		921	Eternal Father, thou hast..L.	—
854	Come, thou everlasting...8,7.	279		922	Assembled at thy great...L.	990
855	Now in parting, Father..8,7,4.	—		923	Behold, the heathen.......L.	976
856	Christ is made the sure..8,7.	—		924	Head of the Church, whose.L.	982
857	On this stone now laid....7.	963		925	Though now the nations...L.	992
858	Lord of hosts! to thee....7.	966		926	Comfort, ye ministers.....L.	209

No.	Title	Meter	Tune
927	Shepherd of souls	L.	972
928	Jesus, thy Church	L.	987
929	Look from thy sphere	L.	—
930	From Greenland's icy	7,6.	973
931	Roll on, thou mighty	7,6.	977
932	The morning of light	7,6.	—
933	Our country's voice is	7,6.	—
934	When shall the voice	7,6.	1001
935	Watchman, tell us	7.	1003
936	See how great a flame	7.	1002
937	Hasten, Lord, the glorious	7.	996
938	Hark! the song of jubilee	7.	1004
939	Go, ye messengers of God	7.	984
940	O'er the gloomy hills	8,7,4.	—
941	Souls in heathen	8,7,4.	—
942	Who but thou, almighty	8,7,4.	—
943	Light of those whose	8,7.	367
944	Saviour, sprinkle many	8,7.	—
945	Come, let us use the grace	C.	1054
946	Sing to the great	C.	1055
947	Join, all ye ransomed sons	C.	1049
948	Awake, ye saints	C.	—
949	The year is gone	C.	—
950	Our few revolving years	S.	1057
951	Wisdom ascribe	L.6f.	1048
952	How many pass the	L.6f.	1047
953	The Lord of earth	H.	1056
954	Ye virgin souls, arise	H.	1050
955	Come, let us anew	10,5,11.	1053
956	While, with ceaseless	7.	1052
957	A few more years shall	S.	—
958	How swift the torrent	S.	1053
959	Lord, let me know mine	S.	1061
960	How vain is all beneath	L.	1060
961	Shrinking from the cold	L.	1066
962	Almighty maker of my	L.	1062
963	Pass a few swiftly fleeting	L.	1067
964	O God, our help in ages	C.	1059
965	Thee we adore, eternal	C.	1058
966	Thou God of glorious	C.P.	1064
967	If death my friend and	C.P.	640
968	And am I only born	C.P.	1072
969	Vital spark of heavenly	P.	675
970	Why do we mourn	C.	1034
971	Why should our tears	C.	1082
972	Hark! from the tombs	C.	1069
973	Through sorrow's night	C.	1095
974	Behold the western	C.	—
975	That solemn hour	C.	—
976	Why should we start	L.	1070
977	The morning flowers	L.	1097
978	Earth's transitory things	L.	—
979	Asleep in Jesus! blessed	L.	—
980	How sweet the hour	L.	1076
981	Shall man, O God of life	L.	1093
982	How blest the righteous	L.	1088
983	The saints who die	L.	1075
984	I yield thy bosom, faithful	L.	1091
985	O for an overcoming faith	C.	1074
986	Who shall forbid our	C.	—
987	Thy life I read, my	C.	1071
988	Calm on the bosom	C.	—
989	When the last trumpet's	C.	1100
990	O for the death of those	S.	1081
991	Servant of God, well done	S.	1086
992	Rest from thy labor, rest	S.	—
993	It is not death to die	S.	—
994	Rest for the toiling hand	S.	—
995	And must this body die	S.	1096
996	And am I born to die	S.	1068
997	When on the brink	S.	669
998	I would not live alway	11.	949
999	Thou art gone to	13,11,12	—
1000	Spirit, leave thy house	7.	1101
1001	Hark! a voice divides	7.	1078
1002	Jesus, while our hearts	8,7.	642
1003	Happy soul, thy days	8,7.	1090
1004	Deathless spirit, now	7.	671
1005	Lowly and solemn	6,5.	—
1006	Wherefore should I	7,6f.	637
1007	Tender Shepherd	7,8,7.	—
1008	Go to thy rest, fair child	6.	—
1009	Friend after friend	6,8,8.	1071
1010	The precious seed	7,6.	—
1011	Weep not for a brother	8.	1089
1012	Man dieth and wasteth	8.	1073
1013	Lo! He comes, with	8,7,4.	1111
1014	Lift your heads, ye	8,7,4.	1103
1015	O'er the distant	8,7,4.	—
1016	Christ is coming	8,7,4.	—
1017	The day of wrath	L.	1109
1018	He comes! he comes	L.	1105
1019	The great archangel's	L.	1115
1020	That awful day will	C.	1114
1021	And must I be to	C.	1109
1022	O Son of God, in glory	L.	—
1023	Day of wrath, O dreadful	7.	—
1024	Thou Judge of quick	S.	1198
1025	Stand the omnipotent	7,6,8.	1118
1026	Lo, the day, the day of	S.	—
1027	When thou, my	C.P.	—
1028	Great God! what do I	8,7.	1117
1029	Day of judgment, day	8,7,4.	—
1030	How happy every child	C.	926
1031	A stranger in the world	C.	927
1032	And let this feeble body	C.	954
1033	Come, let us join our	C.	955
1034	Ye golden lamps of	C.	—
1035	Lo, what a glorious sight	C.	—
1036	Forth to the land of	C.	—
1037	There is a land of pure	C.	930
1038	On Jordan's stormy	C.	931
1039	There is an hour of	8,6.	937
1040	Lo! round the throne	L.	947
1041	There is a land mine eye	L.	—
1042	What sinners value	L.	—
1043	Arm of the Lord, awake	L.	235
1044	Jerusalem, my happy	C.	942
1045	Give me the wings	C.	953
1046	The heavenly treasure	C.	708
1047	Christian, dost thou see	0,5.	—
1048	While through this world	S.	932
1049	There is no night in	S.	—
1050	Forever with the Lord	S.	934
1051	Far from these scenes	S.	928
1052	Come to the land	S.	—
1053	One sweetly (Irregular)	6.	—
1054	'Mid scenes of confusion	11.	—
1055	And is there, Lord	S.	—
1056	We know, by faith	S.	952
1057	O what a mighty change	S.	955
1058	The world is very evil	7,6.	—
1059	Brief life is here our	7,6.	—
1060	For thee, O dear, dear	7,6.	—
1061	Jerusalem the golden	7,6.	—
1062	Ten thousand times	7,6,8,6.	—

#	Hymn	
1063	Away with our sorrow....8.	939
1064	I long to behold Him.....8.	950
1065	O when shall we sweetly..8.	951
1066	Who are these arrayed....7.	948
1067	High in yonder realms....7.	—
1068	Rise, my soul, and ....7,6,7.	935
1069	Lift your eyes of faith.....7.	936
1070	Hark, hark, my soul...11,10.	—
1071	O paradise! O paradise.8,6,6.	—
1072	My heavenly home is.....L.	—
1073	Come, let us ascend ....12,9.	938
1074	Come, let us anew...10,5,11.	953
1075	The God of Abrah'm....6,8,4.	944
1076	Though nature's.......6,8,4.	945
1077	The God who reigns... 6,8,4	946
1078	How happy is the........C.P.	941
1079	When this passing......7,6.	—
1080	Lord, in thy name thy ....C.	—
1081	Fountain of mercy, God ..C.	1025
1082	Eternal source of every...L.	1023
1083	Come, ye thankful people .7.	—
1084	Praise to God, immortal ..7.	—
1085	Sing to the Lord of......7,6.	—
1086	We plow the fields and ..7,6.	—
1087	The God of harvest......6,4.	1026
1088	The leaves, around me..7,6.	—
1089	My country, 'tis of the...6,4.	—
1090	God bless our native ....6,4.	—

#	Hymn	
1091	Dread Jehovah! God....8,7.	1019
1092	God, the All-Terrible.11,10,9.	—
1093	Swell the anthem... ....7.	—
1094	Great King of nations ....C.	—
1095	In grief and fear to thee...C.	—
1096	Come, let our souls adore..C.	1020
1097	O Lord, our fathers oft ...C.	1029
1098	Lord, while for all ....C.	1031
1099	Thine arm, O Lord ....C.	—
1100	Great God of nations .....L.	1024
1101	Great ruler of the earth ..L.	1027
1102	O God of love, O King ... L.	—
1103	Great God! beneath.......L.	1030
1104	Now may the God ....L.	—
1105	To thee, O God, whose...L.	—
1106	O Love, divine and..... 7,6.	—
1107	How welcome was the....8.	—
1108	Eternal Father! strong .L.C.	—
1109	Lord of earth, and.....7,6,8.	1039
1110	O Thou, who hast....... 8.	1012
1111	While o'er the deep ......L.	—
1112	Lord of the wide ....L.	1041
1113	How are thy servants.....C.	1038
1114	When through the torn..12.	1045
1115	Lord, whom winds.....7.	1037
1116	I too, forewarned........L.	673
1117	In age and feebleness..L.C.	671

INDEX OF HYMNS

ADOPTED FROM THE OLD HYMN BOOK WITHOUT CHANGE; AND OF HYMNS ADOPTED WITH CHANGE.

I.—HYMNS ADOPTED WITHOUT CHANGE.

NOTE.—The changing of a word or two, without a change of meaning, is not noticed. For example "prodigal" for "long-lost son" in hymn 414.

A

#	First line	Author
574	A charge to keep I....	C. Wesley.
1031	A stranger in the.....	C. Wesley.
84	A thousand oracles....	C. Wesley.
440	Abba, Father, hear....	C. Wesley.
471	Abraham, when	C. Wesley.
836	According to thy.	J. Montgomery.
310	Ah, how shall fallen...	I. Watts.
214	Alas! and did my.....	I. Watts.
97	All praise to him who..C.	Wesley.
789	All praise to our ......C.	Wesley.
454	All praise to the ......C.	Wesley.
962	Almighty Maker...	Anne Steele.
916	Almighty Spirit.	J. Montgomery.
593	Am I a soldier of the ...I.	Watts.
968	And am I only born..C.	Wesley.
798	And are we yet alive..C.	Wesley.
401	And can I yet delay....C.	Wesley.
422	And can it be that ....C.	Wesley.
1032	And let this feeble.....C.	Wesley.
1021	And must I be to......C.	Wesley.
807	And will the great.	P. Doddridge.

A–B

#	First line	Author
809	And wilt Thou yet....	C. Wesley.
189	Angels, from....	J. Montgomery.
570	Are there not in the...	C. Wesley.
438	Arise, my soul, arise..	C. Wesley.
580	Arise, my soul, on...	T. Gibbons.
577	Arise, ye saints, arise...	T. Kelly.
920	Arm of the....	W. Shrubsole, Jr.
550	As pants the hart.	Tate & Brady.
922	Assembled at thy.	W. B. Collyer.
445	Author of faith	C. Wesley.
377	Author of faith, to....	C. Wesley.
617	Author of good, we..	J. Merrick.
851	Author of our.........	C. Wesley.
775	Awake, Jerusalem....	C. Wesley.
106	Awake, my soul, and...	T. Ken.
96	Awake, my soul ..	P. Doddridge.
72	Awake, ye saints.	Elizabeth Scott.
173	Away, my needless...	C. Wesley.
571	Be it my only wisdom.	C. Wesley.
9	Before Jehovah's......	I. Watts.

No.	Hymn	Author
61	Before thy	W. H. Bathurst.
529	Behold the	J. Montgomery.
923	Behold the heathen	Mrs. Voke.
215	Behold the Saviour	S. Wesley.
766	Behold the sure	I. Watts.
828	Behold what	J. Peacock.
508	Being of beings	C. Wesley.
373	Beneath our feet	R. Heber.
799	Blest are the sons of	I. Watts.
782	Blest be the dear	C. Wesley.
797	Blest be the tie	J. Fawcett.
931	Blow ye the trumpet	C. Wesley.
791	Brethren in Christ	C. Wesley.
191	Bright and	J. Montgomery.
186	Brightest and best	R. Heber.
511	But can it be	C. Wesley.
417	By the birth	Sir R. Grant.
806	Christ, from whom	C. Wesley.
250	Christ, the Lord, is	C. Wesley.
22	Christians, brethren	H. K. White.
405	Come, and let us	C. Wesley.
831	Come, Father, Son	C. Wesley.
279	Come, Holy Ghost	C. Wesley.
277	Come, Holy Spirit	I. Watts.
369	Come, humble sinner	E. Jones.
1096	Come, let our souls	Anne Steele.
955	Come, let us anew	C. Wesley.
1074	Come, let us anew	C. Wesley.
1073	Come, let us a-ccnd	C. Wesley.
2	Come, let us join our	I. Watts.
66	Come, let us tune	R. A. West.
915	Come, let us use the	C. Wesley.
28	Come, let us who	C. Wesley.
718	Come, my soul, thy	J. Newton.
133	Come, O my soul	T. Blacklock.
368	Come, O thou	C. Wesley.
521	Come, O Thou	C. Wesley.
351	Come, O ye sinners	C. Wesley.
657	Come on, my partners	C. Wesley.
457	Come, Saviour	J. Bourignon.
364	Come, sinners, to the	C. Wesley.
3	Come, sound his	I. Watts.
61	Come, thou Desire	Anne Steele.
851	Come, thou	C. Wesley.
726	Come, thou Fount	R. Robinson.
55	Come, thou soul	J. Evans.
259	Come, weary sinners	C. Wesley.
683	Come, ye disconsolate	T. Moore.
310	Come, ye sinners	J. Hart.
41	Come, ye that I ye	I. Watts.
63	Come, ye that	Anne Steele.
926	Comfort, ye ministers	C. Wesley.
909	Daughter of	J. Montgomery.
90	Day of God	Hannah F. Gould.
627	Deem not that	W. C. Bryant.
538	Deepen the wound	C. Wesley.
306	Deep are the	Anne Steele.
877	Delightful work	J. Strapham.
379	Depth of mercy	C. Wesley.
405	Did Christ o'er	B. Beddome.
815	Draw near, O Son	C. Wesley.
1094	Dread Jehovah	Unknown.
251	Enthroned is Jesus	T. J. Judkin.
270	Enthroned on high	T. Haweis.
586	Equip me for the	C. Wesley.
132	Ere mountains	Harriet Auber.
623	Eternal Beam	C. Wesley.
128	Eternal depth	Zinzendorf.
38	Eternal Power	I. Watts.
284	Eternal Spirit, God	T. Cotterill.
212	Extended on a cursed	Gerhardt.
81	Far from my thoughts	I. Watts.
713	Far from the world	Cowper.
1051	Far from these	Anne Steele.
258	Father, hear the	C. Wesley.
146	Father, how wide	I. Watts.
593	Father, I dare	C. Wesley.
406	Father, I stretch my	C. Wesley.
42	Father, in whom	C. Wesley.
464	Father of	J. Montgomery.
480	Father of everlasting	C. Wesley.
35	Father of heaven	J. Cowper.
819	Father of mercies	B. Beddome.
299	Father of mercies	Anne Steele.
894	Father of mercies	P. Doddridge.
911	Fling to the idle	M. Luther.
533	Forever here my	C. Wesley.
1020	Forever with	J. Montgomery.
606	Forth in thy name	C. Wesley.
431	Fountain of life	C. Wesley.
1081	Fountain of	A. Flowerdew.
1009	Friend after	J. Montgomery.
8	From all that dwell	I. Watts.
209	From Calvary	J. W. Cunningham.
684	From every stormy	H. Stowell.
930	From Greenland's	R. Heber.
328	From the cross	T. Haweis.
645	Full of trembling	C. Wesley.
1045	Give me the wings	I. Watts.
673	Give to the winds	Gerhardt.
793	Giver of peace	C. Wesley.
89	Glad was my	J. Montgomery.
776	Glorious things	J. Newton.
841	Glory to God on high	J. Hart.
451	Glory to God, whose	C. Wesley.
105	Glory to thee, my God	T. Ken.
820	Go, preach my gospel	I. Watts.
245	God is gone up	C. Wesley.
343	God is in this and	C. Wesley.
649	God is my strong	J. Montgomery.
168	God is our	J. Montgomery.
130	God is the name	I. Watts.
161	God moves in a	Cowper.
558	God of all power	C. Wesley.
484	God of almighty love	C. Wesley.
722	God of love, who	C. Wesley.
692	God of my life	P. Doddridge.
625	God of my life	Cowper.
169	God of my life	C. Wesley.
386	God of my Salvation	C. Wesley.
321	Grace! 'tis a	P. Doddridge.
555	Gracious Redeemer	C. Wesley.
262	Gracious Spirit	J. Stocker.
669	Grant me within	Montgomery.
69	Great God, attend	I. Watts.
1103	Great God! beneath	Roscoe.
1100	Great God of nations	Unknown.
871	Great is the Lord	I. Watts.
1101	Great Ruler	Anne Steele.
774	Great Source	Doddridge.

271	Great Spirit, by whose...*Hawels.*
173	Guide me, O thou.*W. Williams.*
504	Had I the gift.........*Stennett.*
121	Hail, Father, Son.....*C. Wesley.*
298	Hail, sacred truth......*Buttress.*
246	Hail, thou once......*Bakewell.*
181	Hail, to the Lord's..*Montgomery.*
87	Hail to the Sabbath....*Bulfinch.*
1003	Happy soul, thy days..*C. Wesley.*
765	Happy the souls......*C. Wesley.*
972	Hark! from the tombs..*I. Watts.*
582	Hark, how the.......*C. Wesley.*
185	Hark, the glad......*Doddridge.*
938	Hark! the song....*Montgomery.*
224	Hark! the voice......*J. Evans.*
188	Hark! what mean.....*Cawood.*
937	Hasten, Lord, the.....*H. Auber.*
345	Hasten, sinner, to be....*T. Scott.*
1018	He comes! He comes.*C. Wesley.*
234	He dies! the Friend...*I. Watts.*
529	He wills that I should.*C. Wesley.*
680	Head of the Church...*C. Wesley.*
924	Head of the Church..*C. Wesley.*
20	Heavenly Father.....*Unknown.*
543	Help, Lord to whom..*C. Wesley.*
811	High on his.......*Spangenberg.*
362	Ho! every one.......*J. Wesley.*
525	Holy, and true.......*C. Wesley.*
131	Holy as thou, O Lord..*C. Wesley.*
490	Holy Lamb, who....*A. S. Dober.*
266	Holy Spirit, Fount of.....*Judkin.*
1113	How are thy.........*J. Addison.*
821	How beauteous are.....*I. Watts.*
902	How blest the.........*H. Auber.*
982	How blest the...*Mrs. Barbauld.*
437	How can a sinner.....*C. Wesley.*
315	How great the........*Beddome.*
1030	How happy every.....*C. Wesley.*
744	How happy, gracious..*C. Wesley.*
1078	How happy is the.....*J. Wesley.*
309	How helpless nature.*Anne Steele.*
952	How many pass......*C. Wesley.*
554	How oft this......*Anne Steele.*
207	How precious is the......*Fawcett.*
302	How sad our state......*I. Watts.*
980	How sweet the hour...*Bathurst.*
316	How sweet the name...*Newton.*
328	How sweetly flowed...*Bowring.*
958	How swift the torrent.*Doddridge.*
747	How tedious and.......*Newton.*
177	How tender is........*Hastings.*
602	How vain are all things.*I. Watts.*
960	How vain is all......*D. E. Ford.*
573	I and my house.......*C. Wesley.*
525	I ask the gift.........*C. Wesley.*
512	I know that my.......*C. Wesley.*
242	I know that my......*S. Medley.*
1064	I long to behold.......*C. Wesley.*
621	I love the Lord.........*I. Watts.*
770	I love thy kingdom...*T. Dwight.*
709	I love to steal......*P. H. Brown.*
478	I thank thee............*Scheffler.*
585	I the good fight.......*C. Wesley.*
461	I thirst, thou.......*Zinzendorf.*
506	I want a heart to pray.*C. Wesley.*
511	I want a principle.....*C. Wesley.*

409	I would be thine........*A. Reed.*
998	I would not live....*Muhlenberg.*
967	If death my friend....*C. Wesley.*
839	If human kindnesss...*G. T. Noel.*
636	If, on a quiet sea.......*Toplady.*
710	I'll praise my Maker...*I. Watts.*
595	I'm not ashamed......*I. Watts.*
1117	In age and feebleness.*C. Wesley.*
114	In mercy, Lord........*Herzog.*
833	In that sad............*C. Wesley.*
54	In thy name, O Lord....*T. Kelly.*
32	Infinite excellence......*Fawcett.*
48	Infinite God, to thee..*C. Wesley.*
159	Jehovah, God........*J. Johnson.*
307	Jesus, a word.........*C. Wesley.*
848	Jesus, all-redeeming..*C. Wesley.*
559	Jesus, Friend........*C. Wesley.*
710	Jesus, great Shepherd.*C. Wesley.*
520	Jesus hath died.......*C. Wesley.*
908	Jesus, immortal King..*Seymour.*
527	Jesus, in whom.......*C. Wesley.*
719	Jesus is our common..*C. Wesley.*
804	Jesus, Lord, we look...*C. Wesley.*
656	Jesus, Lover of my....*C. Wesley.*
450	Jesus, my all..........*Cennick.*
519	Jesus, my Life.......*C. Wesley.*
686	Jesus, my Saviour.....*C. Wesley.*
505	Jesus, my strength....*C. Wesley.*
483	Jesus, my Truth......*C. Wesley.*
374	Jesus, Redeemer.......*C. Wesley.*
919	Jesus shall reign.......*I. Watts.*
853	Jesus spreads his........*R. Park.*
251	Jesus, the Conqueror..*C. Wesley.*
517	Jesus the Life.........*C. Wesley.*
255	Jesus, the Lord.....*B. W. Noel.*
822	Jesus! the name......*C. Wesley.*
392	Jesus, the sinner's....*C. Wesley.*
280	Jesus, the word......*C. Wesley.*
518	Jesus, thine all........*C. Wesley.*
12	Jesus, thou everlasting.*I. Watts.*
19	Jesus, thou soul......*C. Wesley.*
313	Jesus, thou Source...*Anne Steele.*
228	Jesus, thy blood.....*Zinzendorf.*
476	Jesus, thy boundless...*Gerhardt.*
928	Jesus, thy Church.....*Bathurst.*
430	Jesus, to thee........*C. Wesley.*
650	Jesus, to thee our.....*C. Wesley.*
7	Jesus, we look to thee.*C. Wesley.*
1002	Jesus, while our....*T. Hastings.*
243	Join all the glorious...*I. Watts.*
947	Join all ye ransomed..*C. Wesley.*
383	Lamb of God, whose..*C. Wesley.*
648	Leader of faithful......*C. Wesley.*
17	Let all on earth........*I. Watts.*
846	Let all who truly bear.*C. Wesley.*
332	Let earth and heaven.*C. Wesley.*
326	Let every mortal........*I. Watts.*
154	Let every tongue......*I. Watts.*
469	Let him to whom.....*C. Wesley.*
452	Let not the wise......*C. Wesley.*
385	Let the world.........*C. Wesley.*
516	Let worldly minds..*J. Newton.*
823	Let Zion's........*P. Doddridge.*
786	Lift up your hearts.....*C. Wesley.*
1069	Lift your eyes of......*C. Wesley.*
227	Lift your glad......*H. Ware, Jr.*

L–O   202   O

1014	Lift your heads...... *C. Wesley.*	1	O for a thousand...... *C. Wesley.*
489	Light of life........ *C. Wesley.*	985	O for an overcoming... *I. Watts.*
47	Lo! God is here... *Tersteegen.*	271	O for a flame of living. *Lathurst.*
1013	Lo! He comes...... *C. Wesley.*	440	O for that tenderness.. *C. Wesley.*
1040	Lo! round the.... *M. L. Duncan.*	990	O for the death..... *Montgomery.*
123	Lord, all I am is........ *I. Watts.*	542	O glorious hope........ *C. Wesley.*
59	Lord, dismiss us...... *E. Smythe.*	62	O God, by whom the... *R. Heber.*
52	Lord, dismiss us..... *W. Shirley.*	521	O God, most merciful. *C. Wesley.*
497	Lord, fill me with...... *C. Wesley.*	119	O God, of good....... *Scheffler.*
418	Lord, how secure........ *I. Watts.*	961	O God, our help...... *I. Watts.*
252	Lord, how shall..... *Anne Steele.*	23	O God, our strength... *H. Arbor.*
460	Lord, I am thine...... *S. Davies.*	683	O God, thou art..... *Montgomery.*
513	Lord, I believe...... *C. Wesley.*	126	O God, thou bottomless... *Lange.*
668	Lord, I believe a rest.. *C. Wesley.*	870	O God, though........ *Knowles.*
175	Lord, I delight in..... *J. Ryland.*	632	O God, to thee .... *C. Richardson.*
397	Lord, I despair myself *C. Wesley.*	120	O God, we praise thee... *N. Tate.*
817	Lord, if at thy........ *C. Wesley.*	447	O happy day that..... *Doddridge.*
98	Lord, in the morning... *I. Watts.*	10	O holy, holy, Loly..... *J. Conder.*
473	Lord, in the strength.. *C. Wesley.*	412	O how happy are they. *C. Wesley.*
959	Lord, let me..... *J. Montgomery.*	514	O Jesus, at thy feet.... *C. Wesley.*
1109	Lord of earth......... *C. Wesley.*	557	O Jesus, full of grace.. *C. Wesley.*
858	Lord of hosts... *J. Montgomery.*	526	O Jesus, full of truth... *C. Wesley.*
387	Lord of mercy....... *R. Heber.*	378	O Lamb of God, for... *C. Wesley.*
818	Lord of the harvest.. *C. Wesley.*	1097	O Lord, our.... *Tate and Brady.*
78	Lord of the Sabbath.. *Doddridge.*	685	O Lord, thy heavenly.... *Oberlin.*
1112	Lord of the wide...... *C. Wesley.*	771	O Lord, thy work.. *P. H. Brown.*
505	Lord, we are vile....... *I. Watts.*	540	O Love divine, how.... *C. Wesley.*
60	Lord, when we..... *J. D. Carlyle.*	229	O Love divine, what.. *C. Wesley.*
1098	Lord, while for all..... *Wreford.*	462	O Love, thy sovereign.. *C. Wesley.*
1115	Lord, whom the..... *C. Wesley.*	13	O render thanks. *Tate and Brady.*
491	Love divine, all love.. *C. Wesley.*	276	O Spirit of the... *J. Montgomery.*
367	Lovers of pleasure... *C. Wesley.*	411	O Sun of righteousness. *J. Montgomery.*
		311	O that I could repent... *C. Wesley.*
1012	Man clieth and .... *G. P. Morris.*	404	O that I could repent... *C. Wesley.*
53	May the grace of..... *J. Newton.*	495	O that my land of sin.. *C. Wesley.*
681	Mighty One...... *W. C. Bryant.*	250	O thou eternal Victim. *C. Wesley.*
193	Mortal, awake........ *S. Medley.*	619	O thou from whom... *T. Harris.*
547	My drowsy powers.... *I. Watts.*	733	O thou God of my.... *T. Olivers.*
762	My faith looks up to. *R. Palmer.*	46	O thou, our Saviour... *C. Wesley.*
101	My God, how endless... *I. Watts.*	282	O Thou that hearest... *J. Burton.*
757	My God, I am thine... *C. Wesley.*	36	O Thou to whom..... *J. Pierpont.*
425	My God, my God...... *C. Wesley.*	496	O Thou, to whose..... *Tersteegen.*
608	My God, my Portion.... *I. Watts.*	5	O Thou who all... *From German.*
704	My God, the spring..... *I. Watts.*	562	O Thou who camest.... *C. Wesley.*
695	My gracious Lord..... *Doddridge.*	611	O Thou who driest.... *T. Moore.*
624	My hope, my all........ *T. Coke.*	459	O Thou, who hast. *Mrs. Cotterill.*
83	My opening eyes..... *J. Hutton.*	381	O Thou who hast our.. *C. Wesley.*
630	My Saviour, my...... *I. Watts.*	1110	O Thou, who hast.. *H. F. Gould.*
761	My Shepherd's....... *T. Roberts.*	618	O Thou, who in... *Mrs. Hemans.*
360	My son, know..... *Brackenbury.*	157	O Thou, who, when... *C. Wesley.*
584	My soul, be on thy...... *G. Heath.*	37	O Thou, whom all thy. *C. Wesley.*
391	My soul before Thee..... *Richter.*	553	O Thou whose..... *Anne Steele.*
449	My soul, with...... *Livingstone.*	703	O 'tis delight without... *I. Watts.*
664	My span of life... *F. M. Carper.*	323	O what amazing... *S. Medley.*
		842	O what delight is this. *C. Wesley.*
860	Not heaven's wide.... *Unknown.*	453	O what shall I do my... *C. Wesley.*
90	Now from the altar..... *Mason.*	1035	O when shall we...... *C. Wesley.*
420	Now I have found...... *Rothe.*	561	O where is now that.... *T. Kelly.*
364	Now is the accepted.... *Doball.*	378	O where shall... *J. Montgomery.*
291	Now let my soul. *Higinbotham.*	663	O who, in such. *J. Montgomery.*
23	Now may He who... *J. Newton.*	735	O wondrous power.... *C. Wesley.*
		327	Of Him who did... *Bernard of C.*
749	O bless the Lord........ *I. Watts.*	443	Oft in my heart........ *C. Wesley.*
502	O come, and dwell.... *C. Wesley.*	268	On all the earth........ *H. More.*
549	O for a closer walk...... *Cowper.*	857	On this stone......... *Pierpont.*
667	O for a faith that....... *Bathurst.*	95	Once more, my......... *I. Watts.*
396	O for a glance of heavenly. *Hart.*	29	Once more we come.... *J. Hart.*
521	O for a heart to praise. *C. Wesley.*	716	Our father God..... *A. Judson.*

No.	Title	Author
950	Our few revolving	B. Beddome.
237	Our Lord is risen	C. Wesley.
312	Our sins on Christ	J. Fawcett.
403	Out of the	J. Montgomery.
963	Pass a few swiftly	C. Wesley.
164	Peace, troubled soul	Eccking.
304	Plunged in a gulf	I. Watts.
153	Praise ye the Lord	I. Watts.
589	Pray, without ceasing	C. Wesley.
689	Prayer is appointed	J. Hart.
710	Prayer is the	J. Montgomery.
463	Prince of peace	M. A. S. Barber.
479	Prisoners of hope	C. Wesley.
244	Rejoice, the Lord	C. Wesley.
82	Return, my soul	J. Stennett.
370	Return, O	W. B. Collyer.
1068	Rise, my soul	Seagrave.
415	Rock of ages	A. M. Toplady.
931	Roll on, thou	J. Edmeston.
324	Salvation! O the	I. Watts.
116	Saviour breathe	J. Edmeston.
791	Saviour of all	C. Wesley.
814	Saviour of men	J. J. Winkler.
486	Saviour of the sin-sick	C. Wesley.
545	Saviour, on me the	C. Wesley.
936	See how great a flame	C. Wesley.
112	See how the	Elizabeth Scott.
827	See Israel's gentle	P. Doddridge.
716	See the Lord, thy	C. Wesley.
991	Servant of God, well	C. Wesley.
68	Servants of God	J. Montgomery.
813	Shall I, for fear of	J. J. Winkler.
715	Shepherd divine	C. Wesley.
927	Shepherd of souls	C. Wesley.
391	Show pity, Lord	I. Watts.
961	Shrinking from the	C. Wesley.
615	Since all the varying	J. Hervey.
946	Sing to the great	C. Wesley.
350	Sinners, obey the	C. Wesley.
371	Sinners, the voice of	J. Fawcett.
587	Soldiers of Christ	C. Wesley.
588	Soldiers of Christ	C. Wesley.
24	Songs of praise	J. Montgomery.
917	Soon may the last	Mrs. Voke.
429	Sovereign of all	P. Doddridge.
918	Sovereign of worlds	Mrs. Voke.
380	Sovereign Ruler	T. Raffles.
1000	Spirit, leave thy	J. Montgomery.
435	Spirit of faith, come	C. Wesley.
390	Stay, thou insulted	C. Wesley.
711	Sweet is the prayer	Unknown.
81	Sweet is the work	I. Watts.
54	Sweet was the time	J. Newton.
712	Talk with us, Lord	C. Wesley.
25	Thank and	J. Montgomery.
1020	That awful day	I. Watts.
840	That doleful night	J. Hart.
205	The counsels of	Stennett.
1017	The day of wrath	Sir W. Scott.
1075	The God of Abrah'm	T. Olivers.
1087	The God of	J. Montgomery.
1077	The God who reigns	T. Olivers.
1019	The great archangel's	C. Wesley.
256	The head that once was	T. Kelly.
1016	The heavenly treasure	C. Wesley.
834	The King of	P. Doddridge.
179	The Lord is my	J. Montgomery.
235	The Lord is risen	T. Kelly.
142	The Lord Jehovah	I. Watts.
180	The Lord my	J. Addison.
953	The Lord of earth	C. Wesley.
75	The Lord of	S. Wesley, Jr.
151	The Lord our God	H. K. White.
977	The morning	S. Wesley, Jr.
755	The praying spirit	C. Wesley.
414	The prodigal	Mrs. Sigourney.
983	The saints who die	C. Wesley.
325	The Saviour! O	Anne Steele.
812	The Saviour	P. Doddridge.
138	The spacious	J. Addison.
739	The sun of	C. Wesley.
165	The tempter	J. Montgomery.
482	The thing my God	C. Wesley.
330	The voice of free	Burdsall.
955	Thee we adore	I. Watts.
1037	There is a land	I. Watts.
1039	There is an hour of	Tappan.
122	There seems a voice	Mrs. Opie.
127	Thine, Lord, is wisdom	Lange.
143	This God is the God	J. Hart.
76	This is the day	Harriet Auber.
318	Thou art the Way	Doane.
18	Thou God of power	J. Walker.
801	Thou God of truth	C. Wesley.
439	Thou great	C. Wesley.
477	Thou hidden love	Tersteegen.
736	Thou hidden Source	C. Wesley.
674	Thou refuge of my	Anne Steele.
556	Thou seest my	C. Wesley.
748	Thou Shepherd of	C. Wesley.
372	Thou Son of God	C. Wesley.
178	Thou very present	C. Wesley.
1076	Though nature's	T. Olivers.
925	Though now the	L. Bacon.
141	Though troubles	J. Newton.
649	Though waves	J. A. Rothe.
973	Through sorrow's	H. K. White.
108	Thus far the Lord	I. Watts.
317	Thy ceaseless	C. Wesley.
661	Thy gracious	Anne Steele.
658	Thy mercy heard	Sir R. Grant.
39	Thy presence	J. Fawcett.
537	Thy presence, Lord	C. Wesley.
174	Thy way is in the	J. Fawcett.
288	Thy word	J. Montgomery.
210	'Tis finished! the	C. Wesley.
852	To Jesus, our	Anne Steele.
745	To the hills I lift	C. Wesley.
184	To us a Child of	J. Morison.
784	Try us, O God	C. Wesley.
792	Unchangeable	C. Wesley.
984	Unveil thy bosom	I. Watts.
583	Urge on your rapid	C. Wesley.
647	Vain are all terrestrial	D. E. Ford.
456	Vain, delusive world	C. Wesley.
365	Vain man, thy fond	J. Hart.
969	Vital spark of heavenly	A. Pope.
507	Walk in the light! so	B. Barton.
935	Watchman, tell	Sir J. Bowring.

884 We bring no... *Harriet Phillips.*	349 While life prolongs... *T. Dwight.*
446 We have no... *C. Wesley.*	192 While shepherds *Tate & Brady.*
620 We journey through.. *B. Barton.*	616 While thee I seek.*H. M. Williams.*
1056 We know, by faith... *C. Wesley.*	1018 While through.. *J. Montgomery.*
111 We lift our hearts to... *C. Wesley.*	803 While we walk with... *C. Wesley.*
837 Weary souls, that... *C. Wesley.*	956 While, with ceaseless. *J. Newton.*
1011 Weep not for a brother. *C. Wesley.*	772 Who in the Lord... *C. Wesley.*
85 Welcome, sweet day... *I. Watts.*	970 Why do we mourn for.. *I. Watts.*
296 What glory gilds the... *Cowper.*	971 Why should our tears.. *Bathurst.*
822 What majesty and... *Stennett.*	424 Why should the... *I. Watts.*
433 What shall I do my... *C. Wesley.*	976 Why should we start... *I. Watts.*
190 When all thy mercies.*J. Addison.*	951 Wisdom ascribe, and... *C. Wesley.*
305 When, gracious Lord.. *C. Wesley.*	216 With glorious clouds... *C. Wesley.*
659 When I can read my... *I. Watts.*	74 With joy we hail.*Harriet Auber.*
211 When I survey the... *I. Watts.*	43 With joy we lift... *J. Jervis.*
163 When Israel, of the.*Sir W. Scott.*	254 With joy we meditate... *I. Watts.*
612 When languor and... *Toplady.*	764 With stately... *Harriet Auber.*
205 When on Sinai's.*J. Montgomery.*	65 Within thy house, O.. *Unknown.*
997 When on the brink... *Collyer.*	221 Would Jesus have the.*C. Wesley.*
630 When Power... *Sir J. E. Smith.*	
291 When quiet in my... *C. Wesley.*	600 Ye faithful souls who.*C. Wesley.*
412 When rising from... *J. Addison.*	51 Ye servants of God... *C. Wesley.*
934 When shall the... *J. Edmeston.*	356 Ye simple souls that... *J. Wesley.*
400 When shall Thy love.. *C. Wesley.*	954 Ye virgin souls... *C. Wesley.*
989 When the last... *W. Cameron.*	705 Yes, I will bless... *Heginbotham.*
1114 When through the... *R. Heber.*	738 Yield to me now, for.. *C. Wesley.*
864 When to the exiled.*G. Robinson.*	16 Young men and... *C. Wesley.*
1006 Wherefore should I... *C. Wesley.*	
389 Wherewith, O Lord... *C. Wesley.*	768 Zion stands with hills... *T. Kelly.*
155 Which of the... *C. Wesley.*	

II.—HYMNS ADOPTED WITH CHANGE.

NOTE.—To the right of the number A. stands for *altered*, L. *lengthened*, and S. *shortened*.

A–C	C–G
402 s. Ah! whither should. *C. Wesley.*	311 a. Come to... *J. Montgomery.*
248 l. All hail the power. *E. Perronet.*	672 l. Commit thou all.. *P. Gerhardt.*
996 a. And am I born to... *C. Wesley.*	
816 l. And let our bodies... *C. Wesley.*	1001 a. Deathless spirit, now.*Toplady.*
995 s. And must this body.. *I. Watts.*	
1043 a. Arm of the Lord... *C. Wesley.*	70 a. Eternal God... *Wrangham.*
4 a. Awake, and... *W. Hammond.*	1082 a. Eternal Source.. *P. Doddridge.*
591 l. Awake, my soul.*P. Doddridge.*	128 s. Eternal Sun of... *C. Wesley.*
626 s. Away, my... *C. Wesley.*	194 s. Ever fainting with.. *C. Wesley.*
1063 a. Away with our... *C. Wesley.*	809 s. Except the Lord... *C. Wesley.*
475 s. Behold the servant.. *C. Wesley.*	139 l. Father of all, whose.*J. Wesley.*
498 a. Behold the throne. *J. Newton.*	132 a. Father of Jesus... *C. Wesley.*
701 l. Blest are the pure... *J. Keble.*	470 a. Father, Son, and... *C. Wesley.*
287 a. Blest Comf'r...*Mrs. Sigourney.*	121 s. Father, to thee my.. *C. Wesley.*
510 a. Bright was... *Harriet Auber.*	
875 l. By cool Siloam's... *R. Heber.*	802 s. Glory be to God... *C. Wesley.*
	26 s., a. Glory be to God.. *C. Wesley.*
825 s. Captain of our. *H. J. Gauntlett.*	939 l. Go, ye messengers.*J. Marsden.*
720 l. Children of the... *J. Conник.*	523 l. God of eternal... *C. Wesley.*
416 a. Christ, whose... *C. Wesley.*	677 a. God of Israel's... *C. Wesley.*
481 a. Come, Holy Ghost... *C. Wesley.*	458 s. God of my life... *C. Wesley.*
1023 l. Come, let us join.. *C. Wesley.*	311 a. God's holy law... *Beddome.*
522 s. Come, O my God... *C. Wesley.*	419 l. Great God, indulge.. *I. Watts.*
737 l. Come, O thou... *C. Wesley.*	1028 l. Great God! what *Kingsmill.*
6 s. Come, thou almighty.*C. Wesley.*	865 a. Great King of glory *Francis.*

261 *l*. Hail the day that....*C. Wesley*.	544 *s*. O God, thy.........*C. Wesley*.
329 *a., s*. Happy the man ..*C. Wesley*.	474 *s*. O God, what offering.*J. Lange*.
1001 *l*. Hark! a voice......*C. Wesley*.	515 *s*. O joyful sound of...*C. Wesley*.
552 *l*. Hark, my soul! it is...*Cowper*.	407 *l*. O that I could my...*C. Wesley*.
190 *s*. Hark! the herald....*C. Wesley*.	413 *a*. O that Thou........*C. Wesley*.
58 *l*. Hark! the notes of ...*T. Kelly*.	1057 *s*. O what a mighty....*C. Wesley*.
777 *l*. Hear what God ......*Cowper*.	1038 *s*. On Jordan's stormy..*Stennett*.
339 *a*. Hearts of stone .....*C. Wesley*.	779 *a*. On thy Church, O...*H. Auber*.
904 *s*. Help us, O Lord, thy..*Cotterill*.	280 *a., l*. Our blest........*H. Auber*.
265 *a*. Holy Ghost, dispel .*Gerhardt*.	783 *a*. Our God is love....*J. Cotterill*.
882 *s*. Hosanna! be the.*Montgomery*.	
170 *l*. How do Thy........*C. Wesley*.	651 *l*. Peace, doubting....*C. Wesley*.
	67 *l*. Praise waits in.*Sir J.E.Smith*.
1116 *a*. I too, forewarned...*C. Wesley*.	
448 *l*. Into thy gracious......*Dessler*.	723 *a., l*. Saviour, when.*Sir R.Grant*.
	30 *s*. See, Jesus, thy......*C. Wesley*.
1044 *a., l*. Jerusalem, my...*Unknown*.	981 *s*. Shall man, O God...*T. Dwight*.
604 *l*. Jesus, and shall it...*J. Grigg*.	347 *l*. Sinners, turn; why.*C. Wesley*.
835 *s*. Jesus, at whose.....*C. Wesley*.	117 *l*. Softly now the....*G. W. Doane*.
795 *s*. Jesus, from whom ..*C. Wesley*.	575 *l*. Sow in the.....*J. Montgomery*.
558 *a., l*. Jesus, let thy.....*C. Wesley*.	1025 *s*. Stand the ....*C. Wesley*.
239 *a*. Jesus, my Advocate.*C. Wesley*.	5 *a*. Stand up and.*J. Montgomery*.
531 *s*. Jesus, the sinner's....*Toplady*.	
824 *s*. Jesus, the word of ..*C. Wesley*.	788 *s*. The glorious...*J. Montgomery*.
32 *s*. Jesus, thou all......*C. Wesley*.	152 *l*. The Lord descended.*Sternhold*.
308 *l*. Jesus, thy far......*C. Wesley*.	863 *a*. The perfect.......*N. P. Willis*.
785 *s*. Jesus, united by.....*C. Wesley*.	319 *l*. There is a fountain...*Cowper*.
44 *l*. Jesus, where'er thy...*Cowper*.	861 *a., l*. This stone..*J. Montgomery*.
	966 *l*. Thou God of.........*C. Wesley*.
943 *a., l*. Light of those....*C. Wesley*.	1024 *s*. Thou Judge of......*C. Wesley*.
455 *s*. Lord, and is thine ..*C. Wesley*.	631 *s*. Thou Lamb of God....*Richter*.
286 *s*. Lord God, the...*Montgomery*.	913 *l*. Thou whose.........*Marriott*.
100 *s*. Lord of my life ...*Anne Steele*.	987 *s*. Thy life I read, my..*Stennett*.
15 *s*. Lord of the worlds...*I. Watts*.	218 *a., l*. 'Tis finished! so...*Stennett*.
21 *l*. Lord, we come..*W. Hammond*.	
	348 *a*. What could your....*C. Wesley*.
79 *s*. Millions within..*Montgomery*.	539 *s*. What is our........*C. Wesley*.
308 *s*. My former hopes are..*Cowper*.	532 *l*. What I never speak.*C. Wesley*.
536 *l*. My God, I know, I..*C. Wesley*.	690 *l*. What various.,....*Cowper*.
751 *s*. My God, my Life, my.*I. Watts*.	1093 *l*. Who are these......*C. Wesley*.
472 *s*. My soul and all its..*C. Wesley*.	366 *s*. Why should we ....*M. Wilkes*.
40 *l*. Not here, as to..*Montgomery*.	493 *s*. Ye ransomed ....*C. Wesley*.

SUMMARY.

No. of Hymns adopted from the old book *without* change................ 621
No. of Hymns adopted from the old book *with* change 122
Hymns *added* 374

    No. of Hymns in Hymnal*... 1117
    No. of Hymns dropped.. 386

*This does not include the Doxologies, which number 19 in the Hymnal, and the same in the old book.

THE END.

www.ingramcontent.com/pod-product-compliance
Lightning Source LLC
Chambersburg PA
CBHW021730220426
43662CB00008B/790